12/6

NEW LETTERS
of
Robert Browning

NEW LETTERS
of
Robert Browning

Edited with Introduction and Notes

by

William Clyde DeVane
Yale University

and

Kenneth Leslie Knickerbocker
University of Tennessee

LONDON
JOHN MURRAY
1951

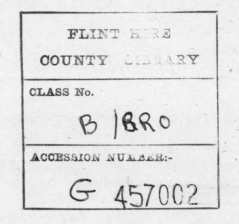

PREFACE OF ACKNOWLEDGMENTS

THE DEBTS we have incurred in collecting and editing the letters of Browning which appear in this volume are almost without number. Our debts to owners of the letters, individuals, and institutions, who have allowed us to publish them are recorded in brackets at the foot of each letter. Our warmest thanks go with these notations. The reader will immediately see the great extent of our indebtedness to the Yale University Library, the New York Public Library, the Huntington Library, the J. P. Morgan Library, the Victoria and Albert Museum, the Library of Congress, the Baylor University Library, the Boston Browning Society, and the collections of Mr. John M. Schiff and Lord Crewe. For single letters we wish to thank Mr. Chauncey B. Tinker, Mrs. Margaret Tuckerman Clark, Mr. Kenneth Curry, the late Mr. Arthur E. Case, Mr. Earl Leslie Griggs, Mr. Frederick W. Hilles, Mrs. Olive M. Furnivall, and Mr. Richard L. Purdy; also Ohio Wesleyan University and the Boston Athenaeum.

But merely to list our benefactors is surely not enough, for invariably the giver gave of himself with the gift. At Yale the Keeper of Rare Books, Mr. Chauncey B. Tinker, has been indefatigable in his search for new letters, and his able assistants, Miss Emily Hall and Miss Marjorie Wynne, have been unfailingly helpful and patient. We remember with gratitude the early kindness of the late Mr. William T. H. Howe for his hospitality and permission to use the letters in his possession, and also the later helpfulness of Mr. John Gordan of the New York Public Library when the same letters became a part of the magnificent Berg Collection. To Miss Belle da Costa Greene of the Morgan Library we owe special thanks, and also to Mr. Frederick B. Adams, Jr., the curator. Dr. A. J. Armstrong of Baylor University has likewise been an unfailing source of help. The officials of the Huntington Library have given us constant assistance. We wish also to thank Sir John Murray for permitting us to publish these letters, and Mr.

John Grey Murray for supplying us with valuable information.

Our colleagues in the various places where we have worked likewise deserve our heartiest thanks. At Yale we wish to thank in particular Professors Gordon S. Haight, Frederick W. Hilles, and Richard L. Purdy. At the University of Tennessee our special debt is to Professor John C. Hodges, Mr. William Jesse, Miss Ruth Ringo, Miss Eleanor Goehring, and Miss Dorothy Ryan. At Cornell University we received the graciously given assistance of Professor Leslie N. Broughton and Clark S. Northup. We are also most grateful to Mr. Francis P. Allen of the Rhode Island State College. Mr. Knickerbocker wishes also to have recorded his gratitude to the American Council of Learned Societies for a grant-in-aid, and especially to his brother, the late Mr. H. R. Knickerbocker, for financial assistance as a supplement to the grant-in-aid mentioned above.

In one of his letters to Chapman, the publisher, in the Fifties when there were few purchasers of his books and many of his wife's, Browning provides us with an apt phrase: "us," he says, referring to Mrs. Browning and himself, *"Us*—I am the church organ-bellows' blower that talked about *our* playing." Like Browning, we speak of "our playing," but we are entirely aware that there would be no music without the inestimable assistance of Dorothy Knickerbocker and Mabel Phillips DeVane. All that is good in this book is good because they have made it so. We may also apply to them another sentence which Browning wrote to Miss Hickey about her annotated edition of his *Strafford:* "You best know—but I seem to guess at—the infinite obligations I am under to you."

KENNETH LESLIE KNICKERBOCKER
WILLIAM CLYDE DEVANE

April 24, 1950

CONTENTS

BIBLIOGRAPHICAL NOTE

A few works, those most frequently used in the notes, have after the first full citation been referred to by an abbreviated title. Beside such customary abbreviations as *D.N.B.* for the *Dictionary of National Biography* and *D.A.B.* for the *Dictionary of American Biography,* the key to abbreviated titles is here appended for the convenience of the reader.

LETTERS

The Letters of Robert Browning and Elizabeth Barrett Barrett, 1845–1846, 2 vols., London, 1899. Referred to as *Letters of R.B. and E.B.B.*

Letters of Robert Browning to Miss Isa Blagden, arranged for publication by A. J. Armstrong, Waco, Texas, 1923. Referred to as *Letters to Isa Blagden.*

Letters of Robert Browning collected by Thomas J. Wise, edited with an Introduction and Notes by Thurman L. Hood, New Haven, 1933. Referred to as *Letters,* ed. Hood.

Robert Browning and Alfred Domett, edited by Frederic G. Kenyon, London, 1906. Referred to as *Browning and Domett.*

Letters of Elizabeth Barrett Browning Addressed to Richard Hengist Horne, edited by S. R. Townshend Mayer, London, 1877. Referred to as *Letters of E.B.B. to R. H. Horne.*

Letters of Elizabeth Barrett Browning, edited with Biographical Additions by Frederic G. Kenyon, 2 vols., London, 1897. Referred to as *Letters of E.B.B.*

Elizabeth Barrett Browning: Letters to Her Sister, 1846–1859, edited by Leonard Huxley, LL.D., London, 1929. Referred to as *E.B.B.: Letters to Her Sister.*

BIOGRAPHIES

Mrs. Sutherland Orr, *Life and Letters of Robert Browning*, revised and in part rewritten by Frederic G. Kenyon, London, 1908. All references are to this revised edition. Referred to as Orr, *Life.*

W. Hall Griffin and Harry Christopher Minchin, *The Life of Robert Browning*, London, 1910. Referred to as Griffin and Minchin, *Life.*

Henry James, *William Wetmore Story and his Friends*, 2 vols., London, 1903. Referred to as James, *W. W. Story.*

T. Wemyss Reid, *Life, Letters, and Friendships of Richard Monckton Milnes, First Lord Houghton*, 2 vols., London, 1890. Referred to as Reid, *Life of R. M. Milnes.*

DIARIES AND WORKS OF REFERENCE

The Diaries of William Charles Macready, 1833–1851, edited by William Toynbee, 2 vols., London, 1912. Referred to as *Macready Diaries*, ed. Toynbee.

The Browning Collections: The catalogue of Sotheby, Wilkinson and Hodge, the auctioneers who dispersed the Browning library, works of art, household goods, etc. in London in 1913. Referred to as Sotheby, *Browning Collections.*

William C. DeVane, *A Browning Handbook*, New York, 1935. Referred to as DeVane, *Browning Handbook.*

The Browning Society's Papers, 1881–1891. This is a series of reports, papers, and proceedings which were published in several parts throughout these years by the London Society. Referred to as *Browning Society's Papers* with the appropriate reference to dates and parts.

Intimate Glimpses from Browning's Letter File, assembled by A. Joseph Armstrong, Ph.D., Litt. D., Baylor University's Browning Interests, Series Eight, Nos. 3 and 4. Waco, Texas, 1934. Referred to as *Browning's Letter File*, ed. Armstrong.

Grace E. Wilson, *Robert Browning's Portraits*, Waco, Texas, 1943. Referred to as Wilson, *Browning's Portraits.*

INTRODUCTION

I

THE GREAT English tradition of personal letter writing which rose so delightfully with Dorothy Osborne in the seventeenth century reached its apex no doubt, in the polished, witty, and often malicious letters of Thomas Gray and Horace Walpole in the next century. In their hands letter writing became an art and the writers became artists willing to devote an infinite amount of leisure to it. From relative retirement at Cambridge or Strawberry Hill they watched their little worlds as spectators and poured out to their favorite friends their observations, their fancies, and their wit. For the time being, at least, no one existed save the writer and his correspondent, and the world was well lost for the *mot juste,* the exquisite turn, and the intimate warmth of a mutual sympathy. Even so, they were keenly aware that posterity would listen to what they said. But the Industrial Revolution changed the tone of that leisurely aristocratic world. The few great writers of letters in the nineteenth century were different. Somehow Charles Lamb and Edward FitzGerald found the necessary leisure to write excellent letters, but for the wit of the earlier century they substituted humor; they were less stately and formal, and more personal and intimate. Oddly enough, they are not so sure as their predecessors that posterity is looking over their shoulders as they write, and, except for Byron, they do not seem to expect an audience beyond the recipient of the letter.

As a writer of letters Browning was not often in the great tradition. Letter writing was not a major occupation for him. Usually he wrote his letters to accomplish a particular purpose, and most of them, like some of his poetry, were dashed down on paper as fast as his busy mind could work. His letters are, in the main, matters of business, the prose side of his life. Occasionally in the present collection he will try very hard to be playful and allusive, which is his tone with Fanny Haworth, or to be literary and sophisticated, which is sometimes his tone with Macready, or to be gracious, as he always is in his later years when some advantage is to be gained for

B

his son. As often happened in his poetry, his powers of expression often achieve astonishing success. Only in writing to Elizabeth Barrett in 1845–46 did he steadily put himself out to be entertaining or to heap all the riches of his nature at the feet of his correspondent. Though a self-conscious awareness of posterity is occasionally evident, it is worth noting that Browning was willing to have his letters to E.B.B., and apparently only these, survive. That he winced at any personal revelations about himself or his wife during his lifetime cannot be doubted. He asked Isa Blagden never to show his letters to her. Yet one cannot be sure that he consistently objected to posthumous publication of whatever survived him. It is doubtful that he could have felt any more keenly about his own letters than he did about those of Mrs. Browning; yet he thought he hardly had the right to burn anything she had written, and when he had the opportunity to possess and, if he wished, destroy her letters to Mrs. Eckley, he preferred to have them pass on to his son.

Though the letters here assembled are not in the literary tradition of letter writing, they are nonetheless a true revelation of Robert Browning's personality. He did not fit the conception of the poet as a bard, as Tennyson did so admirably. He was, as Lockhart noticed, not one of your "damned literary men." Through these letters we see him successively as an eager young man on the edges of the theatrical and literary world of London, a devoted son and husband, a careful man of business, a warm friend, a discriminating critic, a fierce controversialist against his critics, a strong partisan in favor of his son, and at last a social lion of London with an engagement book filled a month ahead each year from December until August. As he recognized, he had the good fortune to attach to himself the affections of many admirable and generous women, and they did a great deal to make his life happy and comfortable. Through all the years we see a consistent character: honest, forthright, friendly, passionate at times, realistically minded, learned in unexpected rather than orthodox ways, of middle-class origin and not quite a gentleman in the older snobbish and elegant sense of that title, but altogether honorable in all dealings with his fellows.

A considerable number of his contemporaries thought him insensitive and unaware of the impression he made upon others. We may cite as examples of this the opinions of Benjamin Disraeli, Charles Kingsley, and Mary Gladstone. But they were thinking of the social and public man, not of the poet. For the greater part Browning's letters are those of the healthy man of the world, and we need in most instances to resort to the poetry to see his deeper nature and his more private thoughts. His letters generally, and always excepting many of those he wrote to Miss Barrett before their marriage, are notable for their reticences. We know now that Browning, though his life was mainly a fortunate and happy one, had a fair share of suffering—the misunderstanding of the critics, the long delay of recognition, the heartsick sense of failure, financial anxieties, the precarious health of his wife and her early death, the loneliness of the following years, the gradually deepening disappointment in the character and the career of his much-loved son. The letters in this volume give only glimpses, now and again, of these private griefs. We see instead the healthy self-confidence, energy, and courage which are a part of his poetic as well as of his personal character.

II

Since Browning's death in 1889 three major collections of his letters have been published, and three smaller ones. Among these are not included the letters printed in whole or in part in several of his biographies, such as Mrs. Sutherland Orr's authorized *Life and Letters of Robert Browning*, first published in 1891 and revised by F. G. Kenyon in 1908, or Griffin and Minchin's *The Life of Robert Browning*, 1910, or Miss Lilian Whiting's *The Brownings; Their Life and Art*, 1911. The major collections are these: (1) *The Letters of Robert Browning and Elizabeth Barrett Barrett, 1845–46*, 2 volumes, 1899; (2) *Letters of Robert Browning to Miss Isa Blagden*, arranged for publication by A. J. Armstrong, 1923; and (3) *Letters of Robert Browning, Collected by Thomas J. Wise*, edited with an Introduction, Notes, and Appendix by Thurman L. Hood, 1933. The minor collections are as follows: (1) *Robert Browning and Alfred Domett*, edited by F. G. Kenyon, 1906; *Twenty-Two Unpublished Letters of Elizabeth Barrett Browning and Robert Browning Addressed to Henrietta and Arabella Moulton-Barrett*, 1935; and (3) *Robert Browning and Julia Wedgwood*, edited by Richard Curle, 1937. Each of these large and small collections requires a brief comment.

The Letters of Robert Browning and Elizabeth Barrett Barrett,

1845–46, contain by far the most intimate letters Browning ever wrote. They were published in 1899 in London with scant editorial attention. This was done under the direction of Robert Wiedemann Barrett Browning, the poet's son, with a minimum of editorial assistance from F. G. Kenyon and Roger Ingpen. (These letters have recently been republished in one volume, edited by F. G. Kenyon, and called *The Browning Love-Letters.*) Vitally useful for biographical purposes as these letters are, the scholar has to find his own way through the two volumes without sufficient aids. The letters are chronologically arranged, and their ordering is in all probability correct, since the poet himself numbered and arranged them. But there is no annotation worthy of the name, and the introductory remarks and index are inadequate. The transcription of the text we may presume to be reasonably accurate, though frequent doubts arise. The holograph letters are now in the Wellesley College Library, and the correspondence should be well edited and republished. Chesterton's comment that even if they are published a hundred times they will still be private is characteristically extravagant. Because of the intimate and allusive nature of the letters the task of editing will be difficult as well as huge.

The *Letters of Robert Browning to Miss Isa Blagden,* arranged for publication by Professor A. J. Armstrong of Baylor University, cover the ten years immediately following the death of Mrs. Browning in 1861. Miss Blagden had been a close friend of the Brownings in Florence and was of immense help to the poet in the early days of his bereavement. By agreement, they were to write to each other regularly, she on the 12th and he on the 19th of each month. While she lived Miss Blagden kept him in touch with the Italian world which he had abandoned. For us, the letters are important for the light they cast upon the poet's moods and progress in the years when he made the difficult readjustment to English life. There is clear evidence that the dating in Professor Armstrong's edition is inaccurate; and it is also evident that the text needs to be transcribed afresh. There is no editorial apparatus, such as annotation and index, and the usefulness of the volume is accordingly impaired. The holograph letters are in the Browning collections of Baylor University, and Browning scholarship will be materially advanced when they are re-edited and republished as they will be in the near future.

Professor Thurman L. Hood of Trinity College, Hartford, Connecticut, edited the *Letters of Robert Browning, Collected by Thomas J. Wise,* gathering under one cover the several small volumes which Wise had printed privately in 1896–97, 1907–08, and 1912 under the title *Letters of Robert Browning to Various Correspondents.* Professor Hood was also able to add a number of new letters. His volume is especially important for Browning's later years, and a great deal of light is shed upon the poetry. The most notable feature of the work, however, is that for the first time an editor of Browning's correspondence undertook to supply the necessary editorial aids for a volume of letters and provided an introduction, relatively full annotation, and a useful index. The editorial work was not perfectly done, and the reader wishes occasionally for a fuller annotation and a more complete index. Nevertheless, one must be grateful to Professor Hood for his services to Browning scholarship in this volume.

Besides these three major collections, there are the three smaller volumes of correspondence. *Robert Browning and Alfred Domett,* edited by Frederic G. Kenyon, is an account of the friendship between the poet and a young neighbor of his in Camberwell who left England for New Zealand in 1842. Domett is, of course, the friend referred to directly in Browning's poems—in "Waring" (1842) and "The Guardian Angel" (1855), and possibly in "Time's Revenges" (1845). Setting them in a generous running commentary, Kenyon edited the letters, 23 in number, which Browning wrote to Domett between 1840 and 1846—years from which few of the poet's letters have survived save those to Miss Barrett in 1845–46. This collection is especially important for the light it sheds upon the temper of Browning at the time when he was possibly at the nadir of his literary career, when he had failed as a playwright for the stage and had blighted his poetic reputation by the publication of *Sordello.*

The small volume, *Twenty-Two Unpublished Letters of Elizabeth Barrett Browning and Robert Browning Addressed to Henrietta and Arabella Moulton-Barrett,* was issued as a book by the United Feature Syndicate of New York in 1935. Earlier in the year the letters had been published serially in a popular magazine. This correspondence covers the period of Browning's marriage, and the letters were written between 1846 and 1859, two years before Mrs

Browning's death. The published volume confesses to no editor, and indeed it is clear that no editing has been done save of the most elementary and often misguided kind. The ten letters written by Browning show him in his intimate relationship as a devoted husband and an affectionate relative by marriage. They do not add appreciably to what was already known about his personality. As a whole, the volume may be regarded as a supplement to Mr. Leonard Huxley's *Elizabeth Barrett Browning, Letters to Her Sister, 1846–59.*

A far more careful treatment is accorded to a group of 28 letters from Browning to Julia Wedgwood, edited by Richard Curle and published in New York in 1937. There are, in addition, two letters from the poet to Miss Wedgwood's mother. The volume is a record of the friendship between Browning and a Victorian bluestocking considerably younger than he in the lonely years after Mrs. Browning's death and his return to London in 1861. Miss Wedgwood, a member of the distinguished family, suffered from deafness and even more seriously from several kinds of Victorian inhibitions. To describe the affair between them as an intellectual flirtation is to miss the suffering of Miss Wedgwood, through no fault of Browning's; but the affair may be regarded as a precursor of Browning's proposal to Louisa Lady Ashburton in 1871. Besides the biographical disclosures, the letters provide some interesting literary comment from Browning, especially his sketch of the way he would have written the story of Enoch Arden. While adequate, the editorial efforts of Mr. Curle are not strenuous: the text is clear enough, but there is little annotation, and more could have been done to provide a better setting for the letters.

In addition to the formal collections, there are single letters and small groups of letters printed, most of them with little or no editing, in all sorts of books and magazines. The most considerable group is made up of those addressed to the Storys and used by Henry James in his two volumes, *William Wetmore Story and His Friends.* The original manuscripts, we have been informed, have recently gone to the Keats-Shelley Museum in London, and will perhaps soon be edited. James, of course, provided no formal editorial apparatus for the portions of the letters which he printed. From one to several letters to different persons—to Milsand, Mrs. Bronson, Madame Belloc, Gunsaulus, Kingsland, Ruskin, Carlyle,

Allingham, Rossetti, and many others—appear in a great variety of places. Perhaps the next step toward making accessible Browning's complete correspondence is the collecting and editing of all his letters printed separately in books and magazines.

From the comments above it may be inferred that in general the editing of Browning's correspondence has not been on a consistently high level of scholarship. It is obvious that the time is approaching, though it has not yet arrived, when a complete and thoroughly edited collection of the poet's letters can be made. This is to perform for him the service which has in recent years been performed for Wordsworth and Thackeray. It is the hope of the editors of the present volume that we may have provided a beginning and a standard which will advance Browning scholarship toward that goal. It is also our hope to bring nearer another desideratum of Browning scholarship: a full and proportioned biography of the poet. Until the correspondence is fairly complete this latter task cannot be undertaken with assurance.

III

The present collection has the virtue of adding materially to the total record of Browning's life and poetry, but its special distinction is that it contains a relatively large proportion of letters from the poet's early and middle years, periods which have not been well represented in other large collections of Browning's correspondence. The letters to his London friends of the late Thirties and early Forties—Macready the tragedian, Forster the critic, Moxon the publisher, and Fanny Haworth, for example—show the overanxious striving of the young man to make his place in the literary and social world of the metropolis. The letters to Chapman, the Brownings' publisher, in the Fifties and Sixties, as well as those to Reuben Browning, the poet's uncle, show the financial anxieties which underlay the smooth surface of his life in Italy and later in London.

We have followed the practice of placing the source and ownership of each letter in the lower left-hand corner, partly in grateful acknowledgment of our debt to the individuals and the institutions who have so generously assisted us in assembling the letters, and partly as an aid to Browning scholars. It will be seen at once that the great bulk of the letters fall into a number of large groups, and that each group represents roughly a phase and a period of the poet's life. The letters in the Yale University Library, for example, are spread over his whole career, but a considerable number of them were written between 1835 and 1843 when Browning was strenuously attempting to become a successful playwright. A number of letters of this period, from which few written by Browning have survived, also come from the Huntington Library.

Three groups of letters in this volume cover the period of Browning's married life. These are the ones in the Morgan Library, which show in detail the relations of Browning to his publisher, Chapman; those in Lord Crewe's collection, which portray his relations with Richard Monckton Milnes, later Lord Houghton; and those from the Victoria and Albert Museum, which show the close friendship between Browning and John Forster, the critic and biographer.

For the later years letters have mainly come to us from the New York Public Library, the Boston Browning Society, and the collection of Mr. John M. Schiff. These exhibit Browning as a successful man of letters and a social lion. But this is a very rough division. The letters are arranged chronologically, and a large collection such as the Yale one or the Berg Collection of the New York Public Library provides letters from all parts of the poet's career.

While we have attempted to include every hitherto unpublished letter of Browning's that we could obtain, we know that the present collection is not complete. There are single letters and small groups of letters in England, America, Italy, and France that we have not been able to secure. Sometime in the future these may be collected into another volume. Still another volume may be made of Browning letters which have been published in magazines and periodicals, or partially published in various biographies and studies of the poet. With a very few exceptions the letters included in the present volume are published now for the first time. These exceptions are recorded in the notes to the particular letter. To deal with Browning's total correspondence is a long task, and we have thought it best to bring out the present volume at once as an aid and a spur to the larger enterprise. Meanwhile, a census of Browning letters is being compiled by Professors Leslie N. Broughton and Clark S. Northup of Cornell University which will show the full dimensions of the task.

IV

A few words need to be said here in explanation of our editorial procedure. Browning wrote in so impatient and dashing a style that nothing short of a facsimile would reproduce the appearance of his script. Since abbreviations, hyphens, capitals, colons, equal signs, parentheses sometimes within parentheses, commas and dashes, often double punctuation, and sometimes no punctuation at all, are characteristic of Browning's habits as a letter writer, we have interfered as editors only at those points where guidance is needed for the sake of clarity. We have substituted colons for equal signs and provided a full stop when it seemed necessary. We have written out the ampersands, and filled out some abbreviated words, always indicating by square brackets our additions. In a few cases we have corrected Browning's spelling, but usually in proper names or place names we have allowed his spelling to stand. In his mention of books and periodicals we have provided a consistency that he lacked, by substituting italics for his quotes, and have put poems in quotes where he underscored. Actually the changes have been relatively few.

Generally Browning's text is very clear, but there is occasionally some hasty handwriting which is difficult to decipher, and now and again a manuscript has been torn or damaged. Our conjectures and interpolations are in brackets, and where the conjecture seems dubious to us we have added a mark of interrogation within the brackets. It was Browning's usual practice to place the date and address from which he was writing at the head of the letter. Occasionally, however, they were written at the foot. For the convenience of the reader we have normalized the punctuation of date and address and have consistently put them in the upper right-hand corner of the printed letter.

In any correspondence so much depends upon the precise and correct dating of the letters that we have taken extraordinary pains to obtain the facts and to give our reasons for arriving at a decision. To some, such care may seem pedantic, but our experience in Browning scholarship has made us thoroughly conscious of the necessity for careful work in this regard as in others. The correct dating of a letter seems to us a matter of primary importance if the

B*

correspondence is to be used as the basis for serious literary or biographical study.

The reader will see at once the third goal which, as editors, we set for ourselves. This was to annotate as fully as possible the references which Browning makes in his letters to people, places, and events. We have tried to make each letter as clear to a reader today as it was to the original recipient. At times, for some readers, we have doubtless explained the obvious. At times we have deliberately repeated information in order that a browsing reader will have before him facts apposite to the letter he is reading. For cross references the index will be the best guide, but we have pointed up within the notes themselves certain significant relationships. In brief, it has seemed to us that if a letter of Browning—or of anyone else—is worth printing, it is worth every effort to make even its minutest details intelligible.

The effort has cost us days and weeks and years, and in a number of cases we have been baffled and cannot now recover the identity of some obscure person or some trivial event after the lapse of possibly a century. As we have not shirked the problem in any case, whatever our success, so we have not tried to bury our failures silently. It may often prove more useful in such cases to confess our defeat. The total result is, we hope, that we have provided for the scholar of nineteenth-century literature a running commentary upon the career, associations and friendships, thoughts and passions, of one of the great and original poets of that time.

New Letters of Robert Browning

To William Charles Macready [1]

Camberwell,
Dec. 20, 1835.

Dear Sir,

Many thanks for your kind invitation; I shall be delighted to visit you on the day appointed.[2] Only, I must remark on the manifest unfairness of taunting me with the "distance to be defied," when you so effectually provide against my showing a particle of gallantry in encountering it.[3] If the *offer of a bed* be equivalent to the chasing-away of all Quixote's Giants,—surely the *direction to the Stage-coach* amounts to the not leaving him a solitary windmill to shake a spear at. Believe me, Dear Sir,

Your most obedient, faithful Svt

W. C. Macready, Esq.   Robt Browning, Junr.

[Yale]

To William Charles Macready [1]

Camberwell, May 28, 1836.

Dear Sir,

The admiration I have for your genius is too assured and "thorough-shine" to admit certain misgivings which commonly

1. William Charles Macready (1793–1873), the eminent actor and stage manager, had met Browning at the home of W. J. Fox on November 27, 1835, and had "requested to be allowed to improve [his] acquaintance with him." (*The Diaries of William Charles Macready, 1833–1851*, ed. William Toynbee [2 vols., London, 1912], I, 264.) This letter from Browning responds to Macready's first invitation to visit him. The exuberance and literary allusiveness of the letter are characteristic of the youthful Browning.

2. The appointed day was probably December 31, and the occasion a New Year's Eve party attended by a half-dozen guests including John Forster, a mutual friend. (See *Macready Diaries*, ed. Toynbee, I, 267.)

3. Camberwell in Surrey and Elm Cottage at Elstree, Macready's country home in Hertford, were separated by about 15 miles, but London lay between.

1. *Paracelsus*, published in August, 1835, had extended greatly Browning's circle of literary and theatrical friends. The lowliest of the arts in England at that time was the "neo-Elizabethan" theater, which was at once imitative and melodramatic. Night after night with a varying group of fellow enthusiasts Browning attended Macready's performances of Shakespeare until he was sure that he had caught the secret of the stage. On May 26, 1836, at a dinner given

attend a less absolute conviction. My mind is made up to believe that you comprehend me as you comprehend Macbeth or Ion,—that while you understand how intensely I feel, you see a reason for the wretched little I say,[2] and are satisfied with that little. I shall be at no pains, therefore, to set advantageously forth the proposition I am about to make,—in perfect faith that you know why "nice affection" should "scorn meaner hands"[3] and be far removed from presumption while it aspires most earnestly.

I am now engaged in a work which is nearly done:[4] I allow myself a month to complete it: from the first of July I shall be free: if, before then, any subject shall suggest itself to you—I will give you my whole heart and soul to the writing a Tragedy on it to be ready by the first of November next:[5] should I be unequal to the task, the excitement and extreme effort will have been their own reward:—should I succeed, my way of life will be very certain, and my name pronounced along with yours.[6]

in celebration of Talfourd's play, *Ion*, Macready asked Browning to write him a tragedy. This letter two days later solemnly takes up Macready's offer.

2. Compare Browning's lines in "Waring":

> True, but there were sundry jottings,
> Stray-leaves, fragments, blurs and blottings,
> Certain first steps were achieved . . .

3. Browning is here paraphrasing a line from Spenser's *Faerie Queene*, Bk. I, Canto VIII, st. 40: "Entire affection hateth nicer hands." It is one of the few references that Browning ever made to the poetry of Spenser.

4. The work was *Sordello* which was probably completed in May, 1839, three years after the date of this letter. (See William C. DeVane, *A Browning Handbook* [New York, 1935], pp. 71, 77.) Apparently Browning set aside *Sordello* for *Strafford*, for on August 3, 1836, Macready mentions the play for the first time: "Forster told me that Browning had fixed on Strafford for the subject of a tragedy; he could not have hit upon one that I could have more readily concurred in." (*Macready Diaries*, ed. Toynbee, I, 340.)

5. That Browning regarded this promise as virtually contractual appears clear from the fact that on October 31 he reported to Macready that *Strafford* was finished. (*Macready Diaries*, ed. Toynbee, I, 354.) Actually the play was still incomplete on November 19; finishing and altering it required another five months.

6. Mrs. Orr, referring to *Macready's Reminiscences* (ed. Sir F. Pollock, London, 1875), says that an "entry of May 30 [1836], the occasion of which is only implied, shows with how high an estimate of Mr. Browning's intellectual importance Macready's professional relations to him began." (Mrs. Sutherland Orr, *Life and Letters of Robert Browning*, revised . . . by Frederic G. Kenyon [London, 1908], p. 33.) The occasion was, of course, the present letter of May 28, and Macready met Browning's fulsomeness in kind. He wrote in his diary: "Arriving at chambers, I found a note from Browning. What can I say

I wish you, from my soul, all health and happiness, and am ever, Dear Sir,

Most faithfully yours,

[New York Public Library]   Robert Browning

To William Charles Macready

Camberwell.
Thursday Mor[nin]g.
[Probably October 12, 1837] [1]

My dear Macready,

I availed myself last night of your kind pass-port, for which I am sure Mrs. Macready has thanked you, "mending my weakest phrase," as she obligingly promised. The getting-up of the new piece is *most* admirable:—do not you think the last scene would be improved by the *withdrawal of Clotilde and Herman* during the matrimonial arrangement of the Baron and Aunt,—the fun of which would come out better were not the real lovers in the way? [2] Just as I pondered this, Cattermole,[3] who was next me, made the same remark. I should like Miss Faucit [4] to incline her head merely,

upon it? It was a tribute which remunerated me from the annoyances and cares of years: it was one of the very highest, may I not say the highest, honor I have through life received." (*Macready Diaries*, ed. Toynbee, I, 321.)

1. The play referred to in this letter is *The Novice*, by William Dimond, first presented by Macready on the night of October 11, 1837, at the Haymarket Theatre. (See Allardyce Nicoll, *A History of Early Nineteenth Century Drama, 1800–1850* [Cambridge, 1930], II, 297.) October 11 was a Wednesday in 1837; consequently this letter written on Thursday, the day after the play opened, should be dated October 12.

2. *The Novice* was cut, then put back into rehearsal on October 12 and 13 and presented for the second and last time the night of October 13. (See *Macready Diaries*, ed. Toynbee, I, 416–417.)

3. George Cattermole (1800–68), the water-color artist. Like Browning at this time he moved in the theatrical set of which Macready was the center. He illustrated the Waverley Novels and Dickens' *Barnaby Rudge;* pictures by Cattermole may be seen at the South Kensington Museum, "Lady Macbeth" and "Macbeth and the Murderers" among them; and at the Edinburgh National Gallery.

4. Miss Faucit, Warde, and Anderson were, of course, members of the cast. Helen Faucit became a distinguished actress and supported Macready in feminine leads for several years. She became a life-long friend to Browning. She married Sir Theodore Martin, official biographer of the Prince Consort, and became the Lady Martin of the poet's later years. As Helen Faucit she took the heroine's parts in Browning's *Strafford, A Blot in the 'Scutcheon,* and *Colombe's Birthday.*

instead of "praying" downright, in the scene with Mr. Warde; and are not Mr. Anderson's hessians un-artistlike, a little, and unfavourable to the expression of "amourousness," as Godwin would say? [5] —You must excuse my selfishness in this matter—for wishing you a splendid success is nothing better. As for the charming piece, impleat *orbem* (the dress-circle) and all that's *orbum*,[6] and may it gratify you as much as,

My dear Macready,
Yours ever faithfully

[Huntington]   Robert Browning.

To Edward Moxon

Monday, 4. p.m.
[January, 1839?] [1]

My dear Moxon,

Here is Shelley—I wish there were time to go thro' the book carefully. You will see at a glance which are the real corrections of errors, and which mere attempts to clear the text by tracing the

5. William Godwin (1756–1836), novelist, philosopher, and writer on political theory. His book, *An Enquiry Concerning Political Justice* (1793), made him the philosophical leader of English radicalism. Shelley became Godwin's disciple, intimate friend, and son-in-law, a fact which would have appealed to the youthful Browning. The poet's reference here is to Godwin's notorious opinions on human affections.

6. Impleat . . . : may it satisfy the circle, and all that pertains to the circles.

1. The date of this letter is highly conjectural, since Browning only wrote "Monday, 4. p.m." The most likely date is early in 1839, for in the spring of that year Moxon published the *Poetical Works of Shelley*, edited by Mary Wollstonecraft Shelley, in 4 volumes, and may well have sought textual advice upon the poems from Browning, who was known to have a great interest in Shelley. There may be some reason for placing the letter in 1851, when Browning is known to have been talking with Moxon about writing the preface to 25 letters which purported to have been written by Shelley. (See *Letters of Robert Browning, Collected by Thomas J. Wise*, ed. with an Introduction and Notes by Thurman L. Hood [New Haven, 1933], pp. 36, 345.) Moxon published the letters with Browning's preface but withdrew the volume when the letters were proved to be forgeries. Browning had known Moxon since 1835. When Moxon was prosecuted for publishing *Queen Mab* complete in the second edition of the *Poetical Works*, he was defended by Thomas Noon Talfourd, a friend to Browning as well as Moxon. (See the *Examiner* for June 26, 1841, p. 412, and also *The Letters of Mary W. Shelley*, ed. Frederick L. Jones [Norman, Oklahoma, 1944], II, 149.)

construction,—as in the lines on the "Medusa," "Song for Tasso" [2] etc. Don't be in any haste to get done with the book which I am in no want of.

[Huntington]

Ever yours
R Browning

To Miss Euphrasia Fanny Haworth [1]

Thursday Night
[April, 1839] [2]

Dear Miss Haworth,

You once said "letters were vile things"—they will be admirable things with me ere long, for the virtue and knack have gone out of me; I talk better, rather, than I used,—certainly better; and as one swings over briar and puddle best with one pole only, so do "come over into Macedonia and help us"—[3] besloughed in a comparison.

It must be this warm-chilly April weather, sweet-sour like violet punch, that undoes me. Soberly—eh? Oh! Those rhymes are rare— everybody knows *I* beat the world that way—can tie and untie English as a Roman girl a tame serpent's tail—but rare are those rhymes all the same. Do you know I was, and am, an Improvisatore of the *head*—not of the *hort* (vide Cheveley) [4]—not you! (Know anything about me.)

2. Both of Shelley's poems here mentioned by Browning appear in the famous pirated Benbow edition of 1826 called *Miscellaneous Poems*. We know that Browning had this volume in his possession and first became acquainted with Shelley's poetry through it. (See Frederick A. Pottle, *Shelley and Browning, A Myth and Some Facts* [Chicago, 1923]. For Browning's notes "On the Medusa of Leonardo da Vinci" see p. 84.) It would be pleasant to believe that Browning is here lending his own copy of the Benbow edition to Moxon for the publisher's use in preparing another edition of Shelley's poems.

1. Fanny Haworth lived in Barham Cottage, Elstree, near the Macreadys, who were responsible for introducing Browning to her. She was the first of many female correspondents who received similar inconsequential, chatty letters from Browning.

2. Below Browning's words, "Thursday Night," the date "Apl. 1839" is written in pencil by another hand. The reference in the letter to Macready's difficulty with the Covent Garden Renters serves to substantiate April, 1839, as the correct date. For conclusive evidence on date see nn. 4, 5, and 8 below.

3. "And a vision appeared to Paul in the night; there was a man of Macedonia standing, beseeching him, and saying, Come over into Macedonia and help us." (Acts 16:9.)

4. Doubtless a reference to Lady Lytton Bulwer's *Cheveley; or, the Man of Honour* (London, 1839), an easily recognizable satire on prominent Londoners

You read Balzac's *Scènes* etc—he is publishing one, *Béatrix*, in the feuilleton of the *Siècle*, day by day—[5] I receive it from Paris two days old and usually post it off to a friend of mine, as soon as skimmed. But the four or five first chapters were so delightful that I hate myself for not having sent them to Barham—and console myself only by knowing that you are spared a sad disappointment as well—for the going on of it all is naught—a story of Guérande in Bretagne.[6] He makes it out a sort of Venice. I told somebody on the point of going to Bordeaux, to get there if he loved me (he does, I think). "Why" quoth he "I pass within five or six miles of it"—i.e., overland, by Nantes;—yet all my wisest charming went to the deaf adder—I don't believe the man will take the trouble to leave his route.[7]

---

and man's heartless treatment of women. The book caused a minor sensation and was satirized in the anonymous *Lady Cheveley; or, the Woman of Honour,* which, in turn, was satirized by another anonymous piece, *Cheveley's Donkey, or the Man in the Ass's Hide,* both 1839.

5. "*Béatrix.* . . . Les deux premières parties actuelles de cet ouvrage, *les personnages* et *le drame,* datées de janvier 1839 . . . ont paru d'abord dans *Le Siècle,* du 13 au 26 avril et du 10 au 19 mai 1839, sous le titre de *Béatrix ou les amours forcés.*" (C. V. M. A. Spoerlberch de Lovenjoul, *Histoire des œuvres de H. de Balzac* [Paris, 1879], p. 22.)

6. The first chapters of *Béatrix,* admired by Browning, are purely descriptive, so much so that an anonymous critic complains as follows: "Enfin, dans sa dernière manière, il [Balzac] arrive à des exagérations inouïes de prolixité; dans *Béatrix,* par exemple, plus de cent pages sont consacrées à la description de la ville Guérande, de la maison Guenic et aux portraits du baron, de sa femme, de leurs domestiques, de leurs amis, de leurs aïeux, etc." (Quoted in the *Grand dictionnaire universel du XIXe Siècle.*)

7. The word "unless" has been scratched through at this point in the letter. Perhaps Browning's enthusiasm was kindled by such a passage in *Béatrix* as the following: "Every artist, nay, and every one who is not an artist, who passes through Guérande, feels a desire—soon forgotten—to end his days in its peace and stillness, walking out in fine months on the Mall that runs round the town from one gate to the other on the seaward side. Now and again a vision of this town comes to knock at the gates of memory; it comes in crowned with towers, belted with walls; it displays the robe strewn with lovely flowers, shakes its mantle of sand-hills, wafts the intoxicating perfumes of its pretty thorn-hedged lanes, decked with posies lightly flung together; it fills your mind, and invites you like some divine woman whom you have once seen in a foreign land, and who has made herself a home in your heart." (*Béatrix,* trans. James Waring [Definitive Library Edition], XIII, 7.) Twenty-seven years after reading *Béatrix* Browning visited Le Croisic, near Guérande and wrote to Miss Isabella Blagden: ". . . opposite is Guérande, the old capital of Bretagne, —you have read about it in Balzac's *Béatrix.*" The following year he was at Le Croisic again and wrote: "I dearly like this wild place: Guérande, where I

Did Miss Macready tell you of the outrageous rascality of the Covent G. Renters, or their representatives? [8]

Don't let me leave out the praises of your nonsense.

My eye is caught by an old proof of an article by Fox, my Chiron in a small way: [9] I wonder whether this is not the style you like? Tell me—it is a good sample of his ware.

Do you know Milnes' Poems? or himself peradventure? [10]

I shall put in a funny thing disinterred along with Fox's lucubration—very funny I thought it at the time—the print too!

Write very soon, pray.

R B.

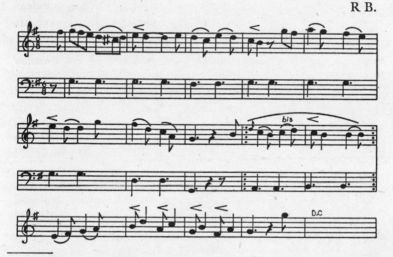

was two days ago, is delightful . . . Depend on it, the imaginative men are no exclusively poets and painters, as Balzac knew well enough." (*Letters,* ed. Hood pp. 100, 121.)

8. Macready had been actor-manager at Covent Garden Theatre from 1837 to 1839, holding his position only on a gentleman's agreement. He summarized his difficulty at this time in the following words: "It appears these wretched scoundrels have kept me on for two years in the delusion that I have been the lessee of the theatre upon a mutual pledge of honour which they have utterly disregarded and held as nothing." (*Macready Diaries,* ed. Toynbee, I, 508–511.) He later estimated that he had been cheated out of £350.

9. In an earlier letter to Fanny Haworth, Browning had called William Johnson Fox, well-known Unitarian preacher and social reformer, his "literary father." (See Orr, *Life,* p. 96.) For the aid which Fox gave to the young poet see W. Hall Griffin and Harry Christopher Minchin, *The Life of Robert Browning* (London, 1910), pp. 42–44, 57–58, 72, 74–75, 89, 109, 136.

10. Richard Monckton Milnes, later Lord Houghton (1809–85), was first acquainted with Browning through *Strafford* which Milnes read as soon as it

What the children were singing last year in Venice, arm over neck.

[Huntington]

To Miss Euphrasia Fanny Haworth

Thursday Night
[May, 1840] [1]

My dear Miss Haworth,

Yours received some five minutes since—fancy! But the truth is I am glad to find you have not been indisposed—as I feared. As to *Sordello* [2]—enfoncé! You say roses and lilies and lilac-bunches and lemon-flowers about it while everybody else pelts cabbage stump after potato-paring—nay, not everybody—for Carlyle [3] . . but I won't tell you what Milnes told me Carlyle told him the other day: (thus I make you believe it was something singular in the way of praise—connu!) All I need remark on in your note is the passage you want cleared up: "What are you to be glad of?" Why that as I stopped my task awhile, left off my versewriting one sunny June day with a notion of not taking to it again in a hurry, the sad disheveled form I had just been talking of, that plucked and pointed, wherein I put, comprize, typify and figure to myself Mankind, the whole poor-devildom one sees cuffed and huffed from morn to midnight, that, so typified, she may come at times and keep my pact in mind, prick up my republicanism and remind me of certain engagements I have entered into with myself about that same, renewed me, gave me fresh spirit, made me after finishing Book 3d commence Book 4th; what is involved here? [4] Only one does not

was published. (See T. Wemyss Reid, *Life, Letters, and Friendships of Richard Monckton Milnes, First Lord Houghton* [London, 1890], I, 196.) Milnes had published two volumes of verse in 1838: *The Memorials of a Residence on the Continent, and Historical Poems* and *Poems of Many Years.* He belonged to the group of Tennyson's Cambridge friends.

1. Written in pencil below "Thursday Night" are the words "Circa 1840." The references to Carlyle's lectures and Macready's attending them point to May, 1840, as the date of this letter. (See *Macready Diaries,* ed. Toynbee, II, 59–60.)

2. *Sordello* was published in early March, 1840. Miss Haworth is memorialized in the poem as "Eyebright," a fact which may help to explain the flowers of appreciation here mentioned by Browning.

3. In the original letter Carlyle is spelled Carlile, here and twice below. The letter "y" has been traced over the "i's," but the original spelling is clearly legible.

4. Miss Haworth might well wish that Browning would explain his explana-

like serving oneself as a certain "Watson" served Horace in a translation I have: e.g. Book 1. Ode 1. Lines 1 and 2: "O Mæcenas, descended from Kings (*Tuscan, that is Etrurian*) your Ancestors, (*O you who have proved yourself to be*) both my patron (*since you kindly reconciled me with Augustus*) and a sweet honor to me (*by your Quality and politeness to poor me whose father was nothing but a Freedman*) etc. etc. etc.[5]

You don't know, it seems, that I have announced Three Dramas? —I see—the fly-leaf was left out of your copy. I am in treaty with Macready about one of these—which I am going [6] to send him, I should say rather—which I think clever and he will think stupid.[7] Don't fear, however, any more unintelligible writing— —

Carlyle is lecturing with éclat—the Macreadys go, and the Bishop of Salisbury, and the three Miss Styles that began German last week.[8] I have still your Tieck,[9] remember.

Ever yours faithfully

[Huntington]   R Browning

---

tion. The passage from *Sordello* here in question is in Bk. III, ll. 967 ff. The first lines of this passage may be quoted for comparison with Browning's prose paraphrase:

> My English Eyebright, if you are not glad
> That, as I stopped my task awhile, the sad
> Dishevelled form, wherein I put mankind
> To come at times and keep my pact in mind,
> Renewed me,—hear no crickets in the hedge.

5. The reference is probably to the *Odes, Epodes,* and *Carmen Seculare of Horace, translated into English Prose, with notes,* etc., [by David Watson] (1741). There is a copy of this book in the British Museum, but we have not been able to see it.

6. The word "going" is written over the word "about."

7. On the flyleaf of *Sordello, Pippa Passes* was announced as nearly ready for publication along with *King Victor and King Charles* and *Mansoor the Hierophant,* later called *The Return of the Druses.* The treaty with Macready concerned the last of these three. Browning accurately prophesied Macready's judgment upon the play, for the actor called it "mystical, strange and heavy" and eventually returned it unproduced to the poet. (See *Macready Diaries,* ed. Toynbee, II, 80; also the letter of August 23, 1840, below, from Browning to Macready.)

8. Macready attended Carlyle's lectures on *Heroes and Hero-Worship* on May 5, 8, 12, and 19, and mentions seeing Browning on the first three of these occasions. The lecture on May 12 was upon the Hero as Poet (Dante and Shakespeare), and in it Carlyle spoke of playhouse managers as "the most insignificant of human beings."

9. Browning wrote to his friend Alfred Domett on March 5, 1843: "How do you get on with German? I read tolerably—and find the best help in Schlegel

To William Charles Macready

Camb[erwe]ll, Monday M[ornin]g.
[June, 1840] [1]

Dear Macready,

Since I saw you I have considerably altered and, I hope, improved my play; the three acts are now five, as you advised, and *go* the better for it—such as they are I will send them as soon as I can—but I am not in the best health, and my copyist [2] is from home—this I mention lest you should think me sleepy or sulky this wondrous June-weather . . while I am, with best regards to Mrs. and Miss Macreadys,

Ever yours

[Yale]   RBrowning.

To William Charles Macready

Camberwell
Sunday Night
[August 23, 1840] [1]

So once again, dear Macready, I have failed to please you! The Druzes *return*, in another sense than I had hoped: for though, to

and Tieck's translation of Shakespeare." (*Robert Browning and Alfred Domett*, edited by Frederic G. Kenyon [London, 1906], p. 52.)

1. The notation "1838?" in a hand other than Browning's appears under Browning's signature and again on the fourth page of the folded notepaper. This date, however, cannot be correct, for Browning was in Italy from April until July, 1838. The play referred to in the text of this letter can only be *The Return of the Druses*, and we know that Macready read this play sometime during the summer of 1840. (See DeVane, *Browning Handbook*, p. 120.) Since June is mentioned in the letter, we may conclude that June, 1840 is the correct date. The Brownings moved from Camberwell in December, 1840.

2. Browning's sister, Sarianna, was often his amanuensis in these years.

1. Browning's promise at the end of this letter to call for the manuscript of *The Return of the Druses* "some morning this week" was apparently fulfilled on August 27, when Macready made this entry in his diary: "Browning came before I had finished my bath, and really *wearied* me . . . with his self-opinionated persuasions upon his *Return of the Druses*. I fear he is for ever gone. . . . Browning accompanied me to the theatre, at last consenting to leave the MS. with me for a second perusal." (*Macready Diaries*, ed. Toynbee, II, 76.) It is apparent that Browning had called to retrieve his manuscript but that once again Macready had been unable to relinquish it gracefully. The Sunday night preceding August 27 was August 23, a date for this letter which seems to fit the facts. The one alternative date would be September 13, the Sunday before the Thursday on which Browning actually did get back his manu-

confess a truth, I have worked from the beginning somewhat in the spirit of the cucumber-dresser in the old story (the doctor, you remember, bids such an one "slice a platefull—salt it, pepper it, add oil, vinegar etc etc and then . . throw all behind the fire") —spite of this, I *did* rather fancy that you would have "sympathized" with Djabert in the main scenes of my play: and your failing to do so is the more decisive against it, that I really had you *here,* in this little room of mine, while I wrote bravely away—*here* were you, propping the weak, pushing the strong parts (such I thought there might be!)—now majestically motionless, and now "laying about as busily, as the Amazonian dame Penthesilé" [2]— and *here,* please the fates, shall you again and again give breath and blood to some thin creation of mine yet unevoked—but *else-where—enfoncé!* [3] Your other objections I think less material— that the auditory, for instance, know nothing of the Druzes and their doings *until I tell them* (which is the very office I take on myself) that they are men and women oppressed and outraged in such and such ways and desirous of being rid of their oppressor and outrager: if the auditory thus far instructed (and I considered that point sufficiently made out) call for a previous acquaintance with the Druzes before they will go along with such a desire . . are they not worthy compatriots of the Hyde-park gentleman who "could not think of pulling a man out of the Serpentine to whom he had not been previously introduced"?

I intend to be with you in a day or two under the greenwood at Arden [4]—but, ask me whence the "banished Duke" comes, why they banish him and how,—and you confound me . . who yet

script. But Macready's entry in his diary for September 15 seems to rule out this possibility: "Again read what I could of Browning's . . . *Return of the Druzes.* . . . Wrote to him, and, offering to do all in my power, gave him my reconsidered opinion" (II, 80). September 15 was a Tuesday. Browning's letter, therefore, headed *Sunday* could not be a reply to Macready's note; nor could this *Sunday* be September 20, for on Thursday, September 17, Browning procured his manuscript and would hardly, therefore, promise to call for it "some morning this week."

2. Possibly a reference to Spenser's lines in the *Faerie Queene*, Bk. V, Canto VII, st. 31:

Full fiercely layde the Amazon about,
And dealt her blowes unmercifully sore.

3. Browning had used this same emphatic word of dismissal for *Sordello.* See above, letter of May, 1840 to Fanny Haworth.

4. That is, Macready's home, Elm Cottage, at Elstree.

shall rejoice from my heart when Duke Frederick makes restitution
at the end . . so much can "that one word, banished" (as Juliet
says) effect! [5] Surely such matters are the *"donnés,"* the given quan-
tities, the logical "be it conceded"'s, without which there is no working problem of deducing an *ergo,*—and so it has been from the
very dawn and cock-crow-time of the drama (for it is edifying to
observe how in some primitive Mystery (Johan à Tadcastre's or
Robert Leicestensis' essay in King John's reign) the courtship of
the Sultan of Mesopotamia's daughter by the "King of Port's"
nephew [6] shall have rivetted the attention of all London or St.
Albans for six hours together.)—And so I could remark on your
other "misgivings"—the sole and simple point, let me say, on which
I find you, to my judging, attackable: this note (written "on a spurt"
at midnight and with a sad headache) is from me to you, and for
no third overlooker: to the devil all flattery! with the exception of
Miss Horton [7] there is not an actor or actress on the stage I can
look at without loathing (that's the word) beside yourself: they
vulgarize, and bestialize,[8]—no matter, you will not comprehend
me: Charles Kean I never saw (he talks about "these *hangmen's*
hands"—"with a fine burst" (says a paper of yesterday)—and sees
"gouts of *blood*" "with even a finer"—(I never saw him) [9]—why
don't you force the whole herd to run violently down a steep place
into the sea? [10] Kean wants to be Macbeth three times a week . .
people go to see if he can manage it; *you are* and have been this—
how many years?—Macbeth—as everybody knows: why not be
something else? Were *I you* (save the mark!)—it should be my first
condition with a playwright that his piece should be new, essentially
new for better or for worse: if it failed . . who that has seen you
perform in some forty or fifty parts I could name, would impute the

5. Browning's argument, based on *As You Like It,* was apropos of having
seen Macready play Jaques on the night of August 12, a few hours after the two
had talked of *The Return of the Druses.* (See *Macready Diaries,* ed. Toynbee,
II, 73.) For the reference to Juliet see *Romeo and Juliet,* III, ii, 113–114.

6. Browning illustrates his point by imaginary authors and plays, but cites
a kind of play that hardly existed in King John's reign. "Courtship" is written
above a word that has been scratched out.

7. Miss Priscilla Horton was a versatile young actress of the time, capable
of such diverse roles as the Fool in *King Lear* and Juliet.

8. A word has been heavily stricken through at this point.

9. Charles Kean (1811–68) was Macready's most dangerous and despised
rival; the inner circle of Macready's friends seemed also to be scornful of Kean
as a sign of loyalty to Macready.

10. Matt. 8:32.

failure to you who were Iago on Thursday and Virginius [11] on
Saturday? If it did not fail . . were it even some poor *Return of
the Druzes*, it would be something yet unseen, in however poor a
degree—something, therefore, to go and see. Laugh at all this—
I write, indeed, that you may . . for is it not the characteristic of
those who withdraw from "the scene" to "take on us the mystery of
things, as if [we] were God's spies"?—"And we'll wear out, in a
walled prison" (my room here) "sects and packs of great ones that
ebb and flow by the moon"! [12] for tomorrow will I betimes break
new ground with So and So—an epic in so many books . . . let it
but do me half the good "Sordello" has done—be praised by the
units, cursed by the tens, and unmeddled with by the hundreds!
God bless you, dear Macready, and send you the man and the
Trag[edy] and *how* [13] both of you will be hailed from the back of
the boxes, by,

> Yours ever
>
> RBrowning

I have left out the essential amid this chatt[er]—and have not
thanked you for your offer to forward my play to Webster. [14] He
knows by this [time,?] I should say, another mode in which performances he ought to approve of, reach him! "I will rather sue
to be despised!" [15]—or send it to Madame Vestr[is] [16] leaving your
name out by a pure oversight! Keep it safe, please, till I call on you
some morning this week.

[Yale]

11. Chief character in the play *Virginius* by James Sheridan Knowles (1784–
1862). This play was first produced in 1820 and was a favorite of Macready
throughout his career.

12. *King Lear*, V, iii, 16–19. A favorite passage with Browning.

13. A word has been scratched out after "how."

14. Benjamin Nottingham Webster (1797–1882) was manager of the Haymarket Theatre where Macready was playing at the time of this letter. On
August 12 Macready had explained orally to Browning that Webster would
not produce *The Return of the Druses* for nothing. (*Macready Diaries*, ed.
Toynbee, II, 73.)

15. *Othello*, II, iii, 276.

16. Madame Vestris, born Lucia Elizabeth Bartollozi (1797–1856), became in
1831 "the first female lessee the stage had known" (*D.N.B.*). The theater which
she leased was the Olympic where during the Thirties such extravaganzas as
Olympic Revels, Olympic Devils, and *Venus and Adonis* were triumphantly
produced. In 1840 she was acting the part of Princess Is-a-belle in Planché's
burlesque *The Sleeping Beauty in the Wood*. Toynbee describes her as an
actress of "numerous conquests, not always with credit to her reputation."
(*Macready Diaries*, ed. Toynbee, I, 38.)

To Dr. John Anster [1]

Hatcham, New Cross, Surrey [2]
April 28, 1841.

My dear Sir,

Some years ago I received a very beautiful and melodious volume of Poetry—*Xeniola* [3]—you had been good enough to send me: it arrived by a very circuitous route and considerably after the date of the kind letter that was enclosed in it, and I very unfortunately allowed myself to imagine that a little longer delay in acknowledging your courtesy would not much matter, while it would allow me to accompany my thanks with a Poem on which I was engaged. [4] That Poem, however, took a longer time to complete than I had anticipated—I was forced to travel—I have not a single acquaintance in Dublin . . in short the thanks I should have delivered then, I only deliver now—they have kept warm all the same. The facility of the Post enables me to beg your acceptance of the trifle you receive, [5] and your leave to forward its successors in due course. If you will further signify to me any way a packet would easily reach you—(I am so unacquainted with these matters)—I will also send the work I published last year—*Sordello*.

Begging once more that you will accept my true thanks and forgive the tardiness of their expression,

I am, Dear Sir,
Yours obliged
R Browning.

Dr. Anster
[Yale]

1. John Anster (1793–1867), Regius Professor of Civil Law at the University of Dublin, was a poet, and translator of Goethe's *Faust*. His name appears in Browning's early pocket address book with the address, 96 L. Baggot St., Dublin.
2. In December, 1840 the Browning family moved from Camberwell to a larger house with larger grounds at Hatcham in Surrey. To reach it, Browning wrote to Laman Blanchard, one had to "conquer the interminable Kent Road, pass the turnpike at New Cross, and take the first lane with a quickset hedge to the right." (See Griffin and Minchin, *Life*, pp. 122–123.)
3. *Xeniola* (Dublin, 1837) consists of translations from Schiller and Fouqué in addition to a few original poems.
4. Probably *Sordello*. (See DeVane, *Browning Handbook*, pp. 71–75.)
5. *Pippa Passes*, which was published in April, 1841.

To William Charles Macready

Forster's Rooms.
Tuesday M[ornin]g
[April 26, 1842][1]

My dear Macready,

I have forborne troubling you about my Play[2] from a conviction that you would do the very best possible for us both in that matter: but as the Season is drawing (I suppose) to an end,[3] and no piece is at present announced in the Bills, it has struck me that in all likelihood the failure of *Plighted Troth*[4] may render it inexpedient in your opinion to venture on a fresh Trial this Campaign; and I stand, if I remember rightly, next in succession on your List.[5] I need not say that I would not for the world be the cause of any considerable anxiety to you . . much less of loss in any shape—and that I shall therefore most entirely acquiesce in whatever you consider expedient to be done, or left undone.—But, here is my case— that quiet, generally-intelligible, and (for me!) popular sort of thing, was to have been my *Second Number* of Plays[6]—on your being gracious to it, I delayed issuing any farther attempts for nearly a year—and now have published a very indifferent substitute,[7] whose success will be problematical enough. I have nothing by me

1. The evidence for the suggested date of this letter is as follows: *Plighted Troth* was withdrawn after the performance on April 20, 1842; from implications in the letter itself one gathers that Browning wrote it soon after that date; in 1842 the first Tuesday after April 20 occurred on April 26, the date suggested for this letter.

2. *A Blot in the 'Scutcheon,* placed in Macready's hands early in 1841. (See DeVane, *Browning Handbook,* p. 124.)

3. Macready's theater, Drury Lane, closed on May 23.

4. *Plighted Troth,* by the Reverend C. F. Darley, was given its one and only performance on the night of April 20, 1842. Forster, from whose rooms Browning is writing, was one of an impromptu committee which decided after the curtain fell what was to be done with the play.

5. Darley's *Plighted Troth* was first read by Macready on August 6, 1841. Browning's *Blot in the 'Scutcheon* was not read until September 26, 1841, and then only upon the insistence of Forster. The precedence of *Plighted Troth* over the *Blot* was more apparent than real, for Macready had had the *Blot* in his possession since early 1841 and had simply chosen to place *Plighted Troth,* as well as another play, *The Patrician's Daughter,* ahead of the *Blot* on his list.

6. *Pippa Passes,* published in April, 1841, was the first in the series of "Bells and Pomegranates."

7. *King Victor and King Charles,* published on March 12, 1842.

at all fit to be substituted for the work in your hands.[8] Will you have the kindness to say if I am mistaken in my conjecture as to your intentions?—And if you will at all object to my withdrawing it, in that case, and printing it at once—the booksellers' season being no[w] in the prime? [9] I write th[is] in haste, and without muc[h] consideration, but you wil[l] interpret for the best.

Ever yours faithfully,

[Yale]   R Browning.

To [Miss Euphrasia Fanny Haworth] [1]

New Cross, Hatcham, Surrey
Sat[urda]y M[ornin]g
[May, 1842] [2]

Now, was *ever* such a strong-head such a wrong head? My dear friend, as I am to be believed, I read your note twice before I found out its drift—having clean forgotten all about the reading-proceeding, and supposing you had misunderstood some part of the Moxon-disquisition. All I meant, as I thought I had said, was that my recitation of my own verses is too bad for any deliberate purpose, and that, if you were expecting even a little, you would be sadly disappointed: what I meant to try, would have done tolerably well "next morning"—do you see? *Do* you see? And do you *not*

8. Browning had the manuscript of *The Return of the Druses* in hand, but doubtless was deliberately seeking a means, through a threat of publication, of stirring Macready into acting the *Blot*.

9. Macready's reply to Browning's letter, written during the first week of May, is summarized in a letter, dated May 22, 1842, from the poet to his friend Domett: ". . . a couple of days after you left [about May 2 or 3], I got a note from Macready—the disastrous issue of the play [*Plighted Troth*] you saw of Darley's brother, had frightened him into shutting the house earlier than he had meant. Nothing new this season, therefore, but next, etc., etc." (See *Browning and Domett*, p. 36.

1. This letter was printed by Professor William Lyon Phelps in "Landor and Browning," *Journal of English Literary History*, I (December, 1934), 231–234. It is reprinted here with corrections in the transcription and with annotations. The style is the chief reason for conjecturing that Miss Haworth was the recipient. (Compare letters of April, 1839 and May, 1840 to Miss Haworth.) Attached to this letter is Landor's famous tribute to Browning, a clipping from the London *Morning Chronicle* dated November 23, 1845. There is no apparent connection between the clipping and the letter.

2. Domett departed from England during the last week in April, 1842, and if, as Browning recalls, the departure took place on a Saturday the full date would be April 30, 1842. It may be assumed that this letter was written soon after.

see, that if you seriously so please, I will run over now, then, how-soever, whensoever, and give you enough and over that! Do you but get a pretty girl (mind!)—and a low reading table—but the girl's prettiness matters most.

When I wrote, (it is but just to say) I was in real sorrow of heart, —for my dear friend Alfred Domett, God bless him, left that night (was it not Saturday?)—for New Zealand. Now, he, to my knowl-edge, presented himself to Moxon with the poem I send you,— and not even his earnest handsome face (the proffered Amount-in-full-of Expenses, I knew would not avail—but—) not his sincere voice and gentlemanly bearing—could tempt Moxon to look at a line of it. So, he printed it where you see ³—they would print Mont-gomery's execrabilities.⁴ And the poem fell dead from the press— that poor creature Wilson, who had paralleled Domett with Mil-ton in his customary bleating-speech, an[d] praised away at a mad rate so long as his poems were contributions to *Blackwood* ⁵—never said a little sneaking Scotch word about *this!*—I told D. how Moxon would act—and as simple telling succeeded so indifferently with him, I wanted really to spare you, (by telling it you a little more explicitly,)—a mortification—as there is no doubt it would be. I shall now tell you (*au secret*) ⁶ that the *most* bepraised Poetess of that time, met with the same rebuff just after—thro' a real friend's mediation too!

Write and say your favour rests again on

Yours ever,

RB.

The copy is a proof sheet—pray keep it safely.
[Yale]

3. Domett's *Venice* was published by Saunders and Otley, the same firm that had charged £30 for publishing Browning's *Pauline*.

4. The pronoun "they" is ambiguous but possibly refers to Saunders and Otley, who would print whatever an author was willing to pay for, even, Browning surmises, Robert Montgomery's "execrabilities." For an extension of this opinion of Montgomery see below, letter to R. H. Horne, Autumn, 1843.

5. The leading article in *Blackwood's Magazine* for April, 1837 is called "Our Two Vases." The writer, probably John Wilson (Christopher North), welcomes "the offerings of the young sons of song" and quotes, among many other selections, two poems of Domett: "The Portrait" and "A Christmas Hymn." At the conclusion of the latter the critic exclaims to the reader: "You are remembering Milton's Hymn on the Morning of Christ's Nativity!" (*Black-wood's Magazine*, LXI, 445.)

6. This parenthesis has been inserted above the line, with a caret after "you."

To An Unidentified Correspondent

New Cross, Hatcham,[1]
Sept[embe]r 3 [1842?]

My dear Friend,

I should take shame to myself for having so long allowed your kind note to lie in my desk unacknowledged—did not my conscience reassure me: I have been in a ferment of bother, and sure about nothing. To-morrow morning I leave for the country—not, I fear, to see Leicester—mais ça viendra avec le bon temps. I have not been able to call on M. Desplace [2]—et pour cause: my sister has been in the country till the end of last week, and I want to ask him to dinner: the moment I return I shall do myself that pleasure. Unluckily the train from Euston Square starts at 6 a.m.—so that to call on him, while in the neighbourhood, would be impossible. I shall not be gone long, however.

I had meant to say earlier that, by some unaccountable *lápsus memoriæ*, you have no recollection of my having sent back that clever article of M. Desplace, in the long letter I wrote to you about him— *I* particularly remember the circumstance. So will you, I hope, on a little consideration. I have more letters to write to less pleasant people: you and all your ménage are quite well, I trust— as are all of us, here.

Ever yours,

[Yale]   R B.

To William Charles Macready

New Cross, Hatcham, Surrey.
Thursday, Oct[obe]r 13. [1842] [1]

My dear Macready,

I managed to get to the Theatre this evening for the first time: and how impressed I was by your admirable Faliero [2] I wished to

1. Browning lived at New Cross, Hatcham from December, 1840 to September, 1846. This letter was written sometime between those dates.

2. Possibly J. B. Desplace who with Capo de Feuillide edited *Le Garde national* (Paris, 1848). There is a Desplace listed in Browning's early address book at 38 George Street, Hampstead Road. A line has been drawn through this address.

1. The date of the letter is set by the annotation in heavy pencil upon the back of the page, "Browning, October 13, 1842."

2. The many entries upon Byron's *Marino Faliero* in the *Macready Diaries* show that the part of Faliero was a favorite with the actor.

take up some couple of minutes in telling you, with perhaps another thing or two, at the play's end— [3] on presenting my card at the Stage-door for that purpose, I was first of all informed (as civilly as could be) that "you never admitted anybody till you were dressed" [4]—but as, in reply to my enquiry, they also said, "no new regulation on the subject had taken place since last season," I still begged that my card might be sent up: this being done, I waited some time longer, and at length got my card again with the assurance that your dresser "dared not" present it. Now, either I have unwittingly been singularly intrusive at times for some years past— in which case, I am sorry,—or some novel order has been issued by you, and if so, it is precisely because I am sure it must be a most proper one, that I write at once with a real friend's anxiousness that some better mode of enforcing it may be hit on. For I cannot imagine how somebody with something to say (instead of myself with next to nothing at all) could have helped himself or you under such circumstances: and since there must be plenty of such people, I think it my duty to write, and at once.

I trust Mrs. Macready and your Sister are well— I could not see them anywhere. *You must* be well.

Ever, my dear Macready,
Yours most truly,
Robt. Browning.

[Yale]

To Edward Moxon

New Cross, Surrey. Thursday.
[Probably November 17, 1842] [1]

My dear Moxon,

Forster, whom I have just seen, strongly recommends that the Lyrics should not appear before the beginning of next week—as he

---

3. A word has been scratched out at this point.

4. Browning must have been excluded purposely. It was Macready's custom to receive his friends after the play, and at the first performance of *Marino Faliero* on October 5 he had recorded that "Forster, Maclise, and all my people came into my room." (*Macready Diaries,* ed. Toynbee, II, 185.)

1. The reference to "Lyrics" points to the *Dramatic Lyrics* of 1842 or possibly to the *Dramatic Romances and Lyrics* of 1845. The reference to Forster's review of "Annual poetry," however, decides the case for 1842. *The Keepsake* for 1843 was reviewed in the *Examiner* on Saturday, November 19, 1842. The pamphlet *Dramatic Lyrics* was published in the latter part of November, 1842 as the third number in the "Bells and Pomegranates" series. Browning's let-

wants to get the start of such Squintowls as the *Spectator* etc., and
yet thinks his notice had better be delayed till the Saturday [2] after
next,—as he is forced to cumber *this* number with Annual poetry
and the praise of it. He gave me my choice of *now* or *then*, however
—and I had him do as he thought best for us both.[3]

Yours ever faithfully,

[Huntington]   R Browning.

To Richard Hengist Horne [1]

New Cross, Hatcham, Wednesday
[Autumn, 1843] [2]

Dear Horne,

Let's to work at once—and talk after, if post-time serve.

Hood and Hook [3] / "Act freely, carelessly, and capriciously; as if
our veins ran with quicksilver; and not utter a phrase but what shall

---

ter, therefore, was probably written on the Thursday before Forster's review
of *The Keepsake* appeared.

2. In the letter the word "week" has been struck through and "Saturday"
written above it.

3. When the *Dramatic Lyrics* appeared the "Squintowls" remained silent,
and but for Forster's review which was published as prearranged in the *Examiner* for November 26 the pamphlet would have gone almost completely
unnoticed.

1. Richard Henry (later Hengist) Horne (1803–84) began a correspondence
with Miss Elizabeth Barrett Barrett in 1838 which led to close association in
several literary enterprises, chief of which were *Poems of Geoffrey Chaucer
Modernized* (London, 1841) and *A New Spirit of the Age* (London, 1844). On
the latter of these works Robert Browning, as the present letter shows, lent a
hand; indeed, there is evidence in the letter that Horne used it as he worked.
Most of the passages he used have been canceled with a single stroke; and the
names of Miss Martineau and Mrs. Jameson have been bracketed, as well as
those of Miss Barrett and Mrs. Norton. Horne records that "the mottoes, which
are singularly happy and appropriate, were for the most part supplied by Miss
Barrett and Robert Browning, then unknown to each other." (*Letters of Elizabeth Barrett Browning Addressed to Richard Hengist Horne*, ed. S. R.
Townshend Mayer [London, 1877], I, 136.)

2. Smith and Elder announced in the *Athenaeum* for February 24, 1844 that
A New Spirit of the Age would be published March 5. This letter was written
sometime, therefore, well before March 5, 1844. According to Griffin and
Minchin it was in the autumn of 1843 that Miss Barrett and Browning were
helping Horne choose mottoes for his book. (*Life*, p. 147.)

3. This quotation appears as one of four which introduce the chapter on
"Thomas Hood and the Late Theodore Hook." (R. H. Horne, *A New Spirit
of the Age* [London, 1844], p. 52.) Thomas Hood (1799–1845), poet and editor

come forth steeped in the very brine of conceit, and sparkle like
salt in fire."

Ben Jonson: Cynthia's Revels.

*Henry Taylor.*⁴/ (to exemplify what you contrast—"sound-sense
poetry with the passionate and the imaginative." [?Loye]!)—

> Then put on all thy gorgeous arms—thy helmet
> And brigandine of brass; thy broad habergeon,
> Vant-bras and greaves, and gauntlet, and thy spear
> A weaver's beam, and seven-times-folded shield!—
> I only with an oaken staff will meet thee,
> And raise such outcries on thy clattered Iron,
> Which long shall not withold [sic] me from thy head,
> That in a little time while breath remains thee
> Thou oft shalt wish thyself at Gath!

Milton: Samson Ags.

The Dramatists and the Stage ⁵

1. Too popular is Tragic Poesy
   Straining his tip-toes for a farthing fee.

---

of *Hood's Magazine,* did "sparkle like salt in fire" in his whimsical poems, but
is best known for "The Song of the Shirt" and "The Bridge of Sighs," "genuine
Volkslieder of the nineteenth century." (*D.N.B.*) Theodore Edward Hook
(1788–1841), novelist, miscellaneous writer, "and the most brilliant improvisatore, whether with pen or at the piano, that his country has seen." (*D.N.B.*)
Browning in one quotation caught accurately the characteristics of these two
writers.

4. Horne used four quotations to introduce the chapter on "Henry Taylor
and the Author of 'Festus' " but did not include the lines which Browning
quoted—inaccurately—from *Samson Agonistes.* Sir Henry Taylor (1800–86)
was the author of *Philip van Artevelde,* which, published in 1834, ran into
seven editions by 1872. The dignity and refinement of Taylor is perhaps represented by the "oaken staff" and the "passionate imagination"—an analogy too
tenuous for Horne's use. Philip James Bailey (1816–1902) was and is known
likewise for a single work. *Festus* appeared first in 1839 and reached an eleventh
edition in 1889, by which time it had grown to more than 40,000 lines. He sent
the edition of 1845 to Elizabeth Barrett, who found that "the fine things were
worth looking for." (*Letters of Robert Browning and Elizabeth Barrett Barrett 1845–1846* [London, 1899], I, 375, 384.)

5. The motto here is the only one used to introduce the chapter on Sheridan
Knowles and William Macready. (Horne, *A New Spirit of the Age,* p. 84.) James
Sheridan Knowles (1784–1862), dramatist, wrote more than 15 plays, none of
which has any literary distinction, a fact which sharpens the point of the quotation selected by Browning. Along with Knowles, William Macready was chosen
to represent the drama in *A New Spirit of the Age.*

> Painters and Poets, hold your ancient right!
> Write what you *will*—and write not,—what you *might!*
> Their limits be their list,—their reason, will!
>> Bishop Hall, 4th Satire.

—But the thing of things to say—is out of the Prologue to Goethe's *Faust,* which I have spent much time this morning in a hunt after —and with no success. The "Poet," there, answers the solicitations or requirements of the "Messenger"—that he should popularize and degrade his style and matter *ad captand. vulg.*[6]—and answers famously: I would get the book had I time—cannot you refer to some *Translation*—Hayward's *Prose,* or Anster's *verse?* [7]—it is well worth while.

Bob Montgomery [8] (while *quoting* from Hall)

> Parnassus is transformed to Zion-Hill,
> And Jewry-palms her steep ascents do fill.
> Now good St. Peter weeps pure Helicon
> And both the Maries make a music-moan—
> Yea, and the prophet of the heavenly lyre,
> Great Solomon, sings in the English quire.
> And is become a new-found Sonnetist,
> Singing his love, the holy Spouse of Christ,
> Like as she were some light-skirts.
>> *Bp. Hall, Satire 8.*

Miss Martineau [9]

> —She walks thro' the great city, veiled
> In virtue's adamantine eloquence,

6. *Ad captandum vulgus:* for the sake of pleasing the crowd.

7. Abraham Hayward (1801–84) translated Goethe's *Faust* "with Remarks on former Translations" (London, 1834). John Anster translated *Faust,* Pt. I and published it as *Faustus, A Dramatic Mystery* (London, 1835). For Dr. Anster's relations with Browning see letter of April 28, 1841.

8. The first seven lines of this quotation, along with one other quotation, introduce the chapter on Robert Montgomery. Poetaster and preacher, Montgomery (1807–55) wrote what Macaulay describes as "detestable verses on religious subjects." (See *Selection from Correspondence of Macvey Napier, Esq.,* ed. Macvey Napier [London, 1879], pp. 79–80.) Browning writes of "Montgomery's execrabilities." (See above, letter of May, 1842.) Browning's motto fitted perfectly, especially the last two lines which Horne did not use. In the fifth line "quire" has been stricken out and "lyre" substituted for it.

9. The first five lines of this quotation, along with two other quotations,

"Gainst scorn, and death, and pain thus trebly mailed;
And blending in the smiles of that defence,
The serpent and the dove—wisdom and innocence—
Thus she doth equal laws and justice teach
To woman, outraged and polluted long,
Gathering the sweetest fruit in human reach
For those fair hands, when free—while armed wrong
Trembles before her look!

Shelley, Revolt of Islam.

Mrs. Jameson.[10]

yet shouldst thou silent be,
The rose and lily which thou strowest
All the cheerful way thou goest
Would direct to follow thee!

Middleton (I *think*)

"Mrs. Shelley and the very few Imaginative Romancists." [11]

Sweet whispers are heard by the Traveller,
Which make Night——Day:
And a silver shape like his early love doth pass,
Upborne by her wild and glittering hair,
And when he awakes in the fragrant grass,

---

serve to introduce the chapter on "Harriet Martineau and Mrs. Jameson." Harriet Martineau (1802–76) published a long series of devotional books, many of them with social significance. She described herself as gaining power "from earnestness and intellectual clearness"—two qualities which Browning's motto may suggest. In the first line of the quotation "unassailed" has been stricken out and "veiled" substituted for it. Mrs. Anna Brownell Jameson (1794–1860) was best known for her *Characteristics of Shakespeare's Women* (London, 1832). Browning's motto for her is a prescient tribute to the kindness she was destined to bestow on the Brownings after their flight from England in 1846. Victim of an unhappy marriage, she took delight in strewing "rose and lily . . . all the cheerful way" of the Brownings. The motto for Mrs. Jameson was not used, probably because it more accurately described her personality than her literary work.

11. Three quotations were used to introduce the chapter on "Mrs. Shelley and Imaginative Romance," but Browning's selection is not among them. Mrs. Mary Wollstonecraft Shelley (1797–1851) produced several imaginative tales; the best known of these in her time as in ours is *Frankenstein*. It is probable that Browning did not know Mrs. Shelley personally, and judging from the suggested motto one may doubt that he was well acquainted with her characteristic literary work.

He finds night—day!

(Too good?)   Shelley: The Two Spirits.

Bulwer [12] (*general ambition* in literature)

Pitch thy project high!
Sink not in spirit! who aimeth at the sky
Shoots higher much than he that means a tree.[13]
Let thy mind still be bent, still plotting where,
And when, and how, the business may be done—
Slackness breeds worms; but the sure traveller
Though he alights sometimes still goeth on.
Active and stirring spirit live alone:
Write on the others— "Here lies such an one"!

(Not good enough?)   Geo: Herbert. The Temple

Croker or his *Kindred* [14]

"When men strike at genius, they strike at the face of God,
in the only way wherein he ever manifests it to them."

Landor.

Miss Barret [*sic*] [15]

I'll sail on the flood of the tempest dark,
With the calm within, and the light around!

12. The first five lines of this quotation, along with a quotation from Mallet, serve to introduce the chapter on "Sir Edward Bulwer Lytton." (Horne, *A New Spirit of the Age*, p. 188.) Sir Edward Bulwer-Lytton (1803–73), novelist and politician, was the father of Robert Lytton (Owen Meredith) with whom the Brownings became intimate in Florence. Bulwer-Lytton demonstrated his ambition clearly enough by writing more than a dozen novels between 1827 and 1843; how high he pitched his project is another matter.

13. Browning wrote and then struck through "if" after "than." The correct reading is "Shoots higher much than if he meant a tree." Browning started the clause correctly and then changed his mind.

14. Horne did not include a chapter on Croker and therefore did not use Browning's devastating suggestion. John Wilson Croker (1780–1857), a leading contributor to the *Quarterly Review*, struck most viciously at genius in his article on Keats.

15. It was not long after this that Browning learned to spell Miss Elizabeth Barrett's name. The chapter on "Miss E. B. Barrett and Mrs. Norton" is introduced by three quotations, among which Browning's suggestion for Miss Barrett is not included. Miss E. B. Barrett wrote some of the chapters for *A New Spirit of the Age* and had an active part in deciding who should be included and who excluded from the project. Her part is set forth in *Letters of E.B.B. to R. H. Horne*, I, 131–272; II, 3–57.

—And thou, when the gloom is deep and stark,
Look from thy dull earth, slumber-bound,—
My moon-like flight thou then may'st mark!

                                        Shelley

Mrs. Norton [16]

As one who drinks from a charmed cup
Of foaming and sparkling and murmuring wine—
Whom a mighty Enchantress, filling up,
Invites to love with her kiss divine.

                                        Shelley

(The Clock!—I got yours late on Monday (being out) and was out yesterday perforce. I will try again at Macaulay and Banim [17]—but do *you* do.

                                        Yours ever,

[Yale]   R.B.

To F. O. Ward [1]

New Cross, Hatcham, Surrey
Feb. 18. 1845.

My dear Ward,

I send you *one* poem [2] as long as the two I promised—(about 4 pages, I think) and I pick it out as being a pet of mine, and just the

16. This quotation is one of three used as mottoes for the chapter on "Miss E. B. Barrett and Mrs. Norton." (Horne, *A New Spirit of the Age*, p. 130.) Mrs. Caroline Elizabeth Sarah Norton (1808–77) was the author of *The Dream and Other Poems* (London, 1840). She was one of three handsome granddaughters of Richard Brinsley Sheridan and the subject of much gossip, including some in Elizabeth Barrett's letters to Browning. (*Letters of R.B. and E.B.B.*, II, 309–310.)

17. Thomas Babington Macaulay (1800–59), historian, poet, essayist, and politician, moved outside the orbit of the Brownings. Macaulay is given a chapter to himself in *A New Spirit of the Age*, and the motto from Shelley may have been suggested by Browning. A chapter is devoted to "Banim and the Irish novelists." John Banim (1798–1842), Irish novelist, along with his brother Michael (1796–1874) projected a series of tales which would be to Ireland what the Waverley Novels were to Scotland. The result was the *O'Hara Tales*, which accurately portray Irish peasant character.

1. F. O. Ward was subeditor of *Hood's Magazine* and took over the editorship during Hood's illness. In a letter to John Kenyon dated July 29, 1850, Browning mentions Ward as a "capital fellow, full of talent and congeniality." (See *Letters*, ed. Hood, p. 30.)

2. The poem which Browning sent was evidently "The Tomb at St. Praxed's

thing for the time—what with the Oxford business,[3] and Camden society [4] and other embroilments.

I am very anxious to hear how Mr. H.[5] is. Have you heard from Mr. Procter? [6] And did you re-consider the luckless *Eothen* matter? [7]

Ever yours

R Browning

I shall be glad of proof and copy as soon as may be.

[Morgan]

(Rome, 15—)," which was published in the issue of *Hood's Magazine* for March, 1845.

3. The "Oxford business" is the so-called "Tractarian Movement," whose center was at Oxford, though interest in the question was national. The movement was begun by Keble's sermon on "National Apostasy" in 1833 and was continued under the leadership of John Henry Newman in *Tracts for the Times.* In 1841 the famous *Tract 90,* the last of the series, appeared, but the religious controversy continued unabated. In 1843 Newman issued a formal retraction of all the hard things he had said against Rome, and it is clear that through these years Newman was, as he himself later described it, "on his deathbed as regards membership with the Anglican Church." He was received into the Roman Catholic Church on October 9, 1845. The timeliness of Browning's poem, later called "The Bishop Orders His Tomb," is apparent. So is Browning's position in the controversy.

4. The Camden Society was founded in 1838 in honor of William Camden (1551–1623) the famous antiquarian. It was devoted to historical studies and the publication of early English documents. Its researches during its first seven years were much used in the Tractarian controversy. John Kenyon was a member of the society and gave its publications to Elizabeth Barrett.

5. Thomas Hood, poet and editor, died of tuberculosis on May 3, 1845.

6. Bryan Waller Procter (1787–1874)—who used the pen name Barry Cornwall—was a friend of both Hood and Browning. Browning dedicated *Colombe's Birthday* to him. He was probably called upon as was Browning for a free contribution to *Hood's Magazine* when Hood became ill.

7. *Eothen, or Traces of Travel Brought Home from the East* was written by Alexander William Kinglake (1809–91) and published in 1844. An explanation of Browning's reference is contained in a letter written by Kinglake to R. M. Milnes. Milnes, along with Browning, Procter, Ward, and others, undertook to help Hood during his illness by securing contributions to *Hood's Magazine.* He applied to Kinglake who answered that he had already jeopardized his standing as a barrister by publishing *Eothen,* that he could not further risk his reputation by publishing in a magazine, and that he would prefer to offer £10 "to buy an article from some competent litterateur." He proposed that the article, if bought, should be presented to Hood as a gift from its author. It is hardly possible that Kinglake's suggestion should be other than "luckless." His letter is dated February 21, 1845. (See Reid, *Life of R. M. Milnes,* pp. 347–348.)

To Edward Moxon

Wednesday night.
[Probably November 19, 1845] [1]

Dear Moxon,

I'll be bound, now, people are always "snubbing" me, like friend Harness [2] t'other day, just because they fancy I have nobody to take my part—whereas, look here,—what has come to me this very morning! But I keep such matters to myself and so nobody is the wiser . . or rather the nobodies are not the wiser!

In earnest,—very kind and gracious this of Landor, is it not? And I am, I hope, properly proud of it, and so, knowing your own friendly sympathy, I have got a copy made for you for which you shall thank me [3]—(you who love Chaucer, and can appreciate the felicity of the epithet "hale" as applied to him)—when I see you in a day or two. Forster's notice . . is that not most generous, too? [4] Mr. Harness forsooth! If he goes and does the "quizzing article" he

1. The evidence indicates that this letter was written after November 15, 1845, the date of Forster's review of *Dramatic Romances and Lyrics* in the *Examiner,* and that it was written near November 21, the day upon which Elizabeth Barrett received her copy of Landor's famous lines in praise of Browning. The manuscript of Landor's verses is dated November 19, 1845. Since November 19 was the Wednesday preceding November 21 in 1845 and since Browning mentions Forster's review of November 15 as if it were still fresh enough for comment, we conclude that this letter was written on Wednesday night, November 19, 1845. Browning's excitement over Landor's praise is evident; it was natural enough that he should share it with Moxon, his publisher and friend.

2. The Reverend William James Harness (1790–1869), author of the *Life of William Shakespeare* (1825), wrote reviews for the *Quarterly Review.* Nothing in that magazine for 1845, however, contains any mention of Browning. How Harness snubbed Browning is not known.

3. Browning's sister Sarianna apparently made the copies which were sent to Elizabeth Barrett, John Kenyon, Moxon, and perhaps others. On November 21 Elizabeth Barrett wrote: "And must not these verses of Landor's be printed somewhere—in the *Examiner?* and again in the *Athenaeum?*" (*Letters of R.B. and E.B.B.,* I, 288.) They were printed in the *Morning Chronicle* on November 22. Browning's father had Landor's lines printed for circulation among his friends. (Griffin and Minchin, *Life,* p. 134.)

4. In his review of *Dramatic Romances and Lyrics* in the *Examiner* for November 15, 1845, Forster predicted confidently that some of the poems in the volume would survive for posterity.

hints at, I'll be hanged if I don't rhyme him to death like an Irish Rat! [5]

Ever yours faithfully,

[New York Public Library]   R. Browning.

TO ELIOT WARBURTON [1]

New Cross, Hatcham, Surrey.
July 29, '46.

My dear Warburton,

I seem not to care for the misfortune of being unable to see Ireland with you as you propose, in the extreme gratification at your having proposed it, and so! I daresay my company would have given you pleasure after a fashion—for I conjecture that your pleasure usually reaches you reflected by those on whom you have first bestowed it. I go to Italy, in all probability at the end of September,[2] and have an engagement (conditional on my accepting any) to spend a week elsewhere—but such little business as I can boast, will keep me here most likely.

Take the best thanks and best wishes, my dear Warburton, of

Yours ever faithfully,

[Mr. Chauncey B. Tinker]   Robert Browning.

5. Harness apparently never wrote the "quizzing article." Browning breathed fire against his critics for many years, but it was not until 1876 in the *Pacchiarotto* volume that he actually tried to rhyme a critic to death. The critic he assaulted in 1876 was Alfred Austin who was later to succeed Tennyson as poet laureate. Browning lived long enough and was earnest enough in his purposes to carry out every project he had proposed for himself during his early years.

1. Bartholomew Elliott George Warburton (1810–52), usually known as Eliot Warburton, was a generous, venturesome Irishman. He was a friend of Milnes, Kinglake, and the Procters. After leaving Cambridge he attempted to study law but gave it up for travel and writing. In 1843 he journeyed to Syria, Palestine, and Egypt, and published in 1844 (dated 1845) his work in two volumes called *The Crescent and the Cross*, or *Romance and Realities of Eastern Travel*. This work was published in at least 17 editions.

2. Browning had in mind, of course, his hope of being married to Miss Barrett and taking her to Italy. The marriage took place on September 12, 1846, and on September 19 Mrs. Browning left her father's house and joined Browning for the journey to Southampton, Paris, and finally to Italy.

To Miss Euphrasia Fanny Haworth

Saturday, M[ornin]g 8½ [1846?] [1]

My dear Miss Haworth,

I write one minute, or less, after the receipt of yours . . for I am too disposed to seize the first slight (yet, *not* so slight neither) chance of doing you service . . too glad am I in doing this to let our next post go by: *by no means have to do with Pickering,* whom I know, by the experience of an uncle, and bookmaking man, to be *the worst person in* the world for your purpose.[2] This is the main service—but I think I render you another by mentioning that "Smith and Elder" of Cornhill, I *know* (in the person of the principal acter in the Firm, Mr. Geo. Smith Jr.) [3]—to be liberal and honest—*very* liberal. They get up illustrated works like yours, have good connexion[s], and bestir themselves about what is trusted to them,— besides which, I fancy they have just now an ambition of getting hold of the higher sort of authors—they printed the *Spirits of the Age,* Leigh Hunt's capital *Fancy and Imagination,* and were, I *know,* most handsome in their treatment of the writers.[4] Beside, de-

1. *A New Spirit of the Age,* mentioned in the text of this letter, was published March 5, 1844. The Brownings left London in September, 1846. This letter falls somewhere between these two dates. Since Miss Haworth's book, *St. Sylvester's Day and Other Poems,* did not appear until 1847, a date near the terminal possibility seems a valid assumption.

2. William Pickering (1796–1854), whatever may have been his reputation for dealing with authors, had established a publishing business "solely devoted to the highest branches of literature." (*D.N.B.*) Through his knowledge of books "united to the most perfect integrity" he had gained "through life the friendship and esteem of book-loving people." (*Gentleman's Magazine* [July, 1854], Pt. II, p. 88.) The experience of Browning's uncle, William Shergold Browning, occurred in connection with Pickering's publication of his *History of the Huguenots during the Sixteenth Century* (London, 1829), 2 vols. Ten years later W. S. Browning wrote a third volume in response to "the very favourable reception" accorded the first two volumes. Pickering published this addition and bound it in the same mottled boards used for the original two volumes.

3. George Smith was later to become Browning's publisher; see below, letter of March 8, 1873, n. 1.

4. For *A New Spirit of the Age* see letter to R. H. Horne, Autumn, 1843. Leigh Hunt's *Imagination and Fancy* (London, 1844) is an illustrated anthology. George Smith's generosity to Hunt consisted of paying off a debt of £40 to Thomas Powell (who had accepted Hunt's manuscript of *Imagination and Fancy* as collateral) and then giving Hunt an additional £60 for the rights to the manuscript. (See Leonard Huxley, *The House of Smith-Elder* [printed for private circulation, London, 1923], p. 35.)

pend on it, the *City* contains the bookbuyers such as are to be found in these days. Should you wish to treat with them—(I shall not be at the pains of saying what you must know, that I shall be all the better pleased if you, or your friend, should know of another such House, or a better if possible) . . but, if you *should* like to try them, I will write a note to go with you, if you please.

Good, best luck go to you any way! No time—tonight, I fill Stall J, wherever that may be,—and will look out for you

Ever yours

[Yale]   RB

To Arabella and Henrietta Barrett [1]

Pisa, Feb. 8, '47

I have to thank you, my dearest sisters, for two of the kindest notes in the world. It is an unspeakable delight to me to find that I can sympathize with Ba in everything, and love most dearly the two whom she loves most dearly. I know, and nobody so well, what you have lost in her—that is, lost for a time—yet your generosity pardons me that loss, while your *woman's* tact and quickness of feeling does justice to the conduct which occasioned it—for both of which, I am, and always shall be most truly and gratefully your debtor. You tell me that the way to pay such debts is to love Ba—but I cannot obey you there—she takes all my love for her own sake—just as you,—whom I was prepared and eager to love for her sake,—you make me love you on your own account. You wish to know how Ba is—from me, as well as from her. I assure you that thro' God's goodness she appears quite well; *weak* certainly, as compared to persons in ordinary health, but with no other ailment perceptible. A few days ago, she seemed to have caught a slight cold—(thro' her kind

---

1. Arabella, or Arabel as she was called, was the youngest of the Barrett girls, seven years Elizabeth's junior, and a favorite of both elder sisters. Henrietta was three years younger than Elizabeth. During the stay of six months in Pisa (October, 1846 to April, 1847) the Brownings spent much of their time acquainting each other with the minutest characteristics of members of their respective families. What one loved, the other was to learn to love. "I will answer for it that he loves you," wrote Mrs. Browning, "and we talk of you so much that almost he has learnt his lesson of everything about you, and all the reasons for love." (*Elizabeth Barrett Browning, Letters to Her Sister, 1846–1859,* ed. Leonard Huxley, LL.D. [London, 1929], p. 4.)

care of Wilson,[2] who has been ill, as I am sure Ba will have told you) —but yesterday and to-day the few symptoms of ailing etc. have disappeared. Dr. Cook, the physician [3] we called in to Wilson, who had seen Ba just on his arrival, expressed his surprize and delight at the manifold improvement in her appearance—and he observed to Wilson, "this comes of a visit to Pisa *in time*"—(he is learned in pulmonary disease and has written a book about it)—he has just returned, moreover, from England—"where the cold was intense" he said. Here, also, the cold has been considerable, and we are too indebted to the good already produced by the climate to peril it by going out rashly at this (as we hope) the winter's end: but I t[rus]t and believe that, with the stock of strength *preserved* thro' the winter we shall [so profit?] by the coming fine weather, as to need fear no relapse. Ba sleeps admirably—and is steadily diminishing the doses of morphine, quite as much as is prudent.[4] I daresay she explained to you the cause of the Apothecary's mistake about the prescription, at the beginning—he really believed his morphine to be so superior to what we could get in England that he felt himself bound to diminish the quantity— Ever since, his performances have been unexceptionable—indeed, he is said to be one of the best Chymists in Italy. What, I think, you would be most struck with in Ba, is the strengthened voice—Wilson hears it, she says, thro' her door and ours. I cannot tell you of other qualities that are "strengthened," however—no words can convey the native sweetness, unselfishness of that dear nature! Yet I have been used to

2. Wilson had been Elizabeth Barrett's maid for several years and had now thrown in her lot with the Brownings.

3. Mrs. Browning wrote to Miss Mitford, possibly at the same moment Browning was writing this letter, "For myself, the brightness round me has had a cloud on it lately by an illness of poor Wilson's. . . . She would not go to Dr. Cook till I was terrified one night, while she was undressing me, by her sinking down on the sofa in a shivering fit. Oh, so frightened I was, and Robert ran out for a physician; and I could have shivered too, with the fright. But she is convalescent now, thank God!" (*Letters of Elizabeth Barrett Browning*, ed. with Biographical Additions by Frederic G. Kenyon [London, 1897], I, 319.)

4. Mrs. Browning had begun taking laudanum under physician's orders as early as 1837. She later shifted to morphine as a treatment for her pulmonary trouble. The best and most circumstantial account of Mrs. Browning's drug addiction may be found in Jeanette Marks, *The Family of the Barrett* (New York, 1938), index, "Elizabeth Barrett Browning, dependence on opium."

the kindest of natures, and am by no means likely to err from excess of indulgence to any one.

You found fault, I am told, with our midnight attendance at Mass on Christmas Eve, but we took great precautions and the Cathedral is but a few paces from our house. When the weather permits (and not before) we hope to make an excursion to Siena, Colle, and Volterra, fine old Etruscan cities, one and all. In the meantime, we are in Carnival season, and I saw full half a dozen masqueraders yesterday,—a more effective sermon on the vanity of human pleasure you would not wish to hear! It may grow better by and bye. There is to be a grand affair in August, a service to a particular picture of the Virgin "Sotto gli Organi" which they say, saved the city from the earthquakes last year—but we shall be away.[5] I believe I have filled my envelope without telling you very much, but another time I shall succeed better. Know me for your most affectionate

[New York Public Library]   RB.

To Miss Euphrasia Fanny Haworth

Florence, June 29, 1847.

Dear Miss Haworth,

I have let a long time go by since your letter reached me at Pisa —one reason was, that the parcel containing your book [1] ought to have arrived directly, but did not—and the gap of time once grown big, widens so insensibly! I wonder if you are in London,—at all events, I will thank you, and very sincerely, for both book and letter. I don't know how the former may have "succeeded," [2] as people say—but the striking things ought to strike most where they are least expected,—which means, that I, who have known you long

5. The Brownings left Pisa for Florence in April, 1847, long before this "grand affair."

1. Miss Haworth's book, *St. Sylvester's Day and Other Poems* . . . with illustrative designs by the author (London, 1847) had been projected some months before Browning left England. In the advertisement of the book (see next note) the publisher, Jeremiah How, states that the volume is "elegantly bound" and will sell for 10s. 6d.

2. Miss Haworth's book was advertised in the *Spectator* for January 2, 1847 as "This day published," but no review of the book appeared in either the *Spectator* or the *Athenaeum*. There is little evidence to show that the book was successful at all.

and prophesied about you loudly,—am prepared for a good deal whenever you seriously address yourself to write or draw. But is it in you to take the trouble?—there my prophesyings dwindle into a mutter! Or perhaps it is only said to bore you—for words are no use, you will do as you please.[3]—And I—(if you care to have such an illustration)—I should not altogether wonder if I do something notable one of these days, all through a desperate virtue which determines out of gratitude—(not to man and the reading public, by any means!)—to do what I *do not* please: I could, with an unutterably easy heart, never write another line while I have my being—which would surely be very wrong considering how the lines fall to poets in the places of this world generally. So I mean to do my best whatever comes of it—meantime, (not a stone's cast from the housetop under which I write) sleep, watch, and muse those surpassing statues of Michael Angelo,—about the merits of which there are very various opinions, as you know.[4]

What can I tell you about myself? I have been here some ten weeks—gone like a day! The weather which threatened excessive heat, in May, has become quite cool and propitious, so that I hope to be able to stay even till the middle of July. My wife, who had an illness at Pisa, is quite well. We go about, sit on the bridge and see people pass, or take an ice inside Doney's after the vulgarest fashion— We know next to nobody,— Powers the Sculptor,[5] we see every now and then, and have made a pleasant acquaintance

3. Professor Griffin surmised that Browning was impatient with Miss Haworth because she printed in *St. Sylvester's Day and Other Poems* a poem called "To Miss Barrett, on Hearing of Her Secluded Life from Illness" *after* Miss Barrett had become Mrs. Browning. (Griffin and Minchin, *Life*, p. 139.) This letter, however, indicates that Browning thought Miss Haworth lazy in pursuing her artistic and literary ambitions.

4. The statues of the Medici monument are housed in the sacristy in San Lorenzo, a stone's throw from Casa Guidi. Michelangelo (1475–1564) worked on this project, with interruptions, from 1522 to 1534. The resulting statues take rank as among his finest works in sculpture, but the monument as planned remains unfinished. Browning's reference implies that whatever variety of opinion there may be about his works, he cannot refuse the compulsion laid upon him, as it was upon Michelangelo, to do his best. The mood of "Old Pictures in Florence" is suggested by this passage.

5. Hiram Powers (1805–73), an American sculptor, arrived in Florence in 1837 and remained there for the rest of his life. Mrs. Browning wrote a sonnet to his sensationally popular sculpture "The Greek Slave," which he had completed in 1843.

with the Hoppners, the old friends of Byron.[6] But what do you think we are setting our hearts upon?—A permission to go and stay at Vallombrosa—a real month or two months' stay—but the Abbot-general is said to be savage on the subject, just now, and everything is to be feared—"Whether, if we wrote him a mollifying latin letter?" says my Wife. "Rather a Greek one," say I, "and so *stifle* the old fellow at once." We do not despair, but that is all.

Today, being St. Peter's feast, ends the time of feasts; we saw by a pure accident, on turning the edge of our street, the horse race,— but we took quite trouble enough to see the notable "Cocchi" or chariots, last Wednesday—and I can warrant you that a better spectacle waits you every day that a man calls a cab and four leave the stand to dispute his custom—but the fireworks in the evening, with the illumination of the Arno, were magnificent.

July 4. We have got a kind of recommendation tantamount to a permission to go and stay at Vallombrosa,[7] and there we hope to pass a few cool weeks accordingly at this month's end: the weather is very bearable and we can easily stay till then.—Whom do you know that I know in London? If you see Mrs. Gibson you shall re-member me to her.[8] How I thank you for the portrait of my sister

6. Richard Belgrave Hoppner (1786–1872), English consul at Venice, was, said Byron, "A thoroughly good man." (*Conversations of Lord Byron with the Countess of Blessington* [London, 1834], p. 135.) The Hoppners knew Shelley, too, who described Mrs. Hoppner as "a most agreeable and amiable lady" (*Shelley's Prose Works*, ed. H. Buxton Forman [1880], IV, 33, letter of August 23, 1818), and the Hoppners as "the most amiable people" he ever knew. (Edward Dowden, *Life of Shelley* [London, 1886], II, 227.)

7. Vallombrosa is a summer resort 10 miles southeast of Florence in the Apennines, where several religious orders established monasteries. Mrs. Browning in a letter to Mrs. Jameson dated August 7, 1847, describes the journey to Vallombrosa and the disappointingly brief stay: "The worst was that, there being a new abbot at the monastery—an austere man, jealous of his sanctity and the approach of women—our letter, and Robert's eloquence to boot, did nothing for us, and we were ingloriously and ignominiously expelled at the end of five days. For three days we were welcome; for two more we kept our ground; but after *that*, out we were thrust. . . . Nothing could be more provoking." (See *Letters of E.B.B.*, I, 333.)

8. Perhaps this is Mrs. Thomas Milner Gibson (1844–85), mentioned by Mrs. Browning as doing a disservice to spiritualism through the absurdity of "sending out cards for 'spiritual séances,' just as she would for *matinées dansantes!*" (E.B.B.: *Letters to Her Sister*, p. 312.) She had married Gibson (1806–84) in 1832 and had become an early advocate of mesmerism and spiritualism. Her literary salon attracted Dickens, Hugo, Louis Blanc, Browning, and others. (See Edmund Yates, *Recollections* [London, 1884], I, 252–253.)

—which may be more like the person you see in her, than my particular fancies—and yet it is not unlike even those—the features, understand, are clearly hers—only the expression strikes me as not the accustomed one— I have put it here, opposite me.

Goodbye, dear Miss Haworth—I cannot write, out of the very fullness of matter—one day perhaps I sha[ll] see you and talk it all over—as you propose—but in any case I shall always keep your kindness and sympathy in my mind and heart. Meantime, I am glad you know the Arnoulds—my very dear friends too.[9] Also you are good to like Sarianna—who would be angry if I simply said that she *"liked"* you! What good people there are in the world, and at London, when one is away at Florence! Will you write to me not in return for this notable piece of penmanship but for your own friendship's sake?—which is always of the old value to yours ever faithfully

                                                                    RB

My wife sends her true regards. She continues very well.
[Yale]

To Mrs. Anna Maria Hall [1]

Florence, Dec. 5, '48.

Dear Mrs. Hall,

Certainly I do not "forget you"—knowing better the value of pleasant memories, such evenings as this, when our olive-wood fire

9. Born in Camberwell, Joseph Arnould (1814–86) was one of Browning's oldest friends, and had shared chambers with Alfred Domett in 1841 during the months of the trio's greatest intimacy. Arnould married Maria Ridgway in 1841. He wrote verses for Jerrold's *Weekly Newspaper* and leaders for the *Daily News,* all the while carrying on his legal activities. In 1848 he published *Law of Marine Insurance and Average.* In 1859 he was appointed to the Supreme Court of Bombay and was knighted. (See Griffin and Minchin, *Life,* pp. 80, 82, 83.)

1. Anna Maria Hall, nee Fielding (1800–81), was the wife of Samuel Carter Hall (1800–89) with whom she collaborated in the editing of the *Art Union Journal* and in other artistic and literary enterprises. Mrs. Browning and Mrs. Hall had for many years admired each other's work. In a letter to Haydon in April, 1843 Mrs. Browning names Haydon and Mrs. S. C. Hall as the "two people in the world [who] understand 'every word' of me!!" (*Letters from Elizabeth Barrett to R. B. Haydon,* ed. Martha Hale Shackford [New York, 1939], p. 31.) In 1844 Elizabeth Barrett recommended to R. H. Horne that Mrs. Hall be included in his *New Spirit of the Age* because of her "characteristic sketches illustrative of her native Ireland." (*Letters of E.B.B. to R. H. Horne,* I, 266–267.)

burns capitally, and the roast chestnuts and mulled Montepulciano
help its comfort. I should be very happy to associate myself with
your undertaking,[2] and so would my wife, who for her part, too,
"forgets" none of Mrs. Hall's bygone kindnesses;[3] but what can
we do? Here are we beginning our third year of Tuscan life,—in
the palace, to be sure, of the Guidi, patrons of Masaccio, and over
the way-acquaintances of the *Madonna della Seggiola*, but at a woeful distance from Mr. Vernon's gallery, which neither of us ever
saw! If he had but laid in a stock of Paolo Uccellos,—the Beato,
Memmi, Gaddi and the like,[4]—we were your man and woman! As
it is,—how get the second-sight (as I see proofs of it, in the criticisms
of people on the above, certainly never gifted with a first sight)
without a visit to London—which may, or may not be for us next
year.[5] One thing is certain,—that we, both of us, thank you very

2. "In 1848 Robert Vernon, before presenting his pictures to the National
Gallery, gave permission to Hall to engrave and publish the whole of them in
the *Art Union Journal*." (*D.N.B.*, "S. C. Hall.") The request made of the
Brownings was apparently that they write descriptive verses to accompany
some of the pictures from the Vernon Collection. Hall doubtless remembered
the verses which Browning had written in 1841 for Maclise's picture, "Sere-
nade," verses which he afterward expanded into the poem, "In a Gondola."
(See *Letters*, ed. Hood, p. 199.)

3. Mrs. Browning wrote to Haydon in April, 1843 acknowledging that she
was one of Mrs. Hall's "many readers" and added: "From her husband I had
one or two kind notes once, when he had the editorship of Colburn's [*New
Monthly*] *Magazine*, and I was a contributor to the same." (*Letters from Elizabeth Barrett to R. B. Haydon*, p. 32.) The publication of "The Romaunt
of Margaret" in the *New Monthly Magazine* in July, 1836 made Miss Barrett
known to the reading public. Moreover, Forster's laudatory review of Browning's *Paracelsus* had appeared in the same magazine three months earlier.
Then in the September issue for 1836 Fanny Haworth's two "Sonnets to the
Author of Paracelsus" were published in the same periodical. Both Mr. and
Mrs. Browning, therefore, had cause to remember the Halls with gratitude.

4. Masaccio (1401–28), Paolo Uccello (1397–1475), Fra Angelico (1387–1455),
called "il Beato," Memmi (?–1357?), and Gaddi (*ca.* 1300–66) were all painters
of old pictures in Florence. "Uccellos," however, would have been very difficult to obtain, for his works have all perished. The "Madonna della Seggiola" is Raphael's famous painting hanging in the Pitti Palace, not far from
Casa Guidi where the Brownings were living at this time.

5. It was not till July, 1851, that the Brownings returned to London for a
visit. By that time about one third of the work on the Vernon Collection had
been completed by Hall and Mrs. Hall, with the help of such recruits as Leigh
Hunt, Mary Howitt, and Charles Mackay. (*The Vernon Gallery of British
Art*, ed. S. C. Hall [London, 1854], 4 vols.)

heartily for your sympathy and kind words—and, with best remembrances to Mr. Hall, pray believe me ever,

Yours very faithfully,

[Huntington]   Robt Browning.

To Reuben Browning [1]

Venice, June 12, 1850.

My dear Reuben,

I wrote a little note, inside a large letter, to you last week—Thursday the 5th and hope you received it duly:—in case of an accident, I may as well tell you it contained an expression of my very unaffected regret at having caused you so much trouble—partly thro' a misunderstanding on my part of your exact meaning and wishes (though they seem simple enough on reconsideration) and partly thro' the press of circumstances, which make it impossible to know as precisely at a distance as I should at London, what monies of mine have been paid in to my account, or not paid. I also told you that the Bill I had drawn at Florence, payable at the beginning of June, would be met by a payment of Mr. Kenyon's of [£]50 "in June"—as he wrote [2]—and that if the second Bill—due at the end

1. Reuben Browning was the poet's uncle, nine years his senior. A gifted student of the classics, Reuben had encouraged the studies of the young Browning. It was through his good offices that the young poet began his friendship with Comte Amédée de Ripert-Monclar in 1834. The Browning family was closely connected with banking—Browning's father served for many years in the Bank of England—and as a young man Reuben Browning entered the banking firm of the Rothschilds. In 1850 he was in their London office. As may be seen from this letter he was of great service to the poet in the management of financial affairs. Robert and Elizabeth Barrett Browning began their married life on what they regarded as a modest but secure financial basis. Mrs. Browning had £8,000 in the funds, mainly invested in shipping funds, and this brought in an income of £300 a year. She also received some income from the sale of her books. Browning's income from his books at this time was negligible, and it is not clear that he had any other resources. In spite of the relative cheapness of living in Florence, where for example they paid only 25 guineas for their handsome apartment in Casa Guidi, the Brownings were frequently in financial straits. This was especially true in 1850, when the expenses following Mrs. Browning's illnesses and the birth of their son on March 9, 1849, came home to them. This was somewhat eased by Kenyon's gift of £100 a year at the birth of their son (see n. 2, below). At the date of the present letter Browning is arranging funds to take his family to England after an absence of five years.

2. John Kenyon, called "Kenyon, the magnificent" by Mrs. Browning, was a

of the same month, drawn on you and Rothschild thro' Schielin here,—were not previously met by the Ship-Div[iden]ds (which have never yet been so late in payment)—I had instructed Mr. K.— by a note in the same packet,—to pay you the amount from a reserve we have, of £200 in the Bank,—set apart for the very purpose of meeting such emergencies. I further explained the necessity of using Rothschilds' credit—not being known at Venice—and begged you to apologize to him if it was necessary. On calling this m[ornin]g on Schielin he showed me a letter he had received from R[othschilds'] in your hand—kindly accepting my bill, and merely mentioning generally the informality of using an expired credit. I write now, first to say that if, by any accident, my former letter should have been lost,—you will of course immediately act upon this recapitulation of its contents,—by applying to my father for the money advanced—as I will give Sarianna ³ a similar recapitulation of the letter to herself,—which would be missing too. And next,— to beg that you will send me at *Lucerne*,⁴ whither I am going— either an official permission to use the remainder of the credit (£50)—or a fresh one for that sum,—or some equivalent authorisation to get the money when I shall arrive there—as otherwise I shall be in the greatest difficulty,—not knowing anybody there. I

wealthy and cultivated gentleman in London society. He was her second cousin and took great interest in her literary career. Like the Barretts and the Brownings he was connected with the West Indies plantations. He had been a schoolfellow of the poet's father and first met Robert Browning at a literary gathering in 1836. He was instrumental in getting Browning to write to Miss Barrett in 1845 and watched the courtship of the next year and two thirds with insight and sympathy. When the son of Mr. and Mrs. Browning was born on March 9, 1849, Kenyon settled £100 annually upon the parents, and the £50 mentioned in the letter is probably his semiannual payment. When *Aurora Leigh* appeared in 1856 it was dedicated to Kenyon. When Kenyon died in December of the same year he left the Brownings £11,000.

3. Sarianna Browning, christened Sarah Anna after her mother, was born on January 7, 1814. She had much of the ability and spirit of her brother. She never married but made a home for her father after the death of her mother in 1849, and after 1866 made a home for the poet. Before Browning's marriage Sarianna was often his amanuensis, and in later years she was his constant companion. She survived her brother by several years.

4. In the summer of 1851 the Brownings sublet their apartment in Casa Guidi and proceeded to Venice, where they spent almost a month. From Venice they went to Padua, Brescia, Milan, and to Como and Lucerne, which particularly delighted them. They traveled by way of Paris and arrived in London late in July. They had not been in England since their flight in September, 1846.

hope to be able to get as [fa]r as Lucerne,—thro' Como,—on my present stock—and if on my arrival, or as soon as possible after, I find a letter from you telling me exactly how matters stand between us,—if you have been duly reimbursed—and what sum of mine you may have in hand—I will, according to the information received, draw on you either at three, two or one month's date, as you shall desire. Besides the Ship-money,—averaging £120,—there will be a Bank Div[idend] in July for £44 odd. Will you have the kindness to forgive all this trouble I am forced to put you to?—And pray lose no time in writing, as I shall wait for your letter before I try to do anything. (N.B. Schielin charges 1 percent *commission* (double the highest Florentine charge)—and *much more* for bills at three months' date—in addition to the clever "dodge" of having no *napoléons d'or* ready, two days ago, when I went for my money— and then telling me this morning when I returned for them—that the value having risen *since then*, I must pay more for them—as indeed I did. Note, yesterday being a Festa was *no day* at his Bank.) I have barely time to add that I had meant to stay at Recoaro,[5]— near here,—but find it will be better to go on to Lucerne,—and there wait till I see what I can do. I don't know whether I shall visit Milan—the heat is considerable just now,—and my boy's cheeks seem paler than I like. Otherwise we are very well. My wife repeats her kindest thanks and regards. Ever yours most affectionately,

R Browning.

Perhaps, it will be the most expeditious plan (as this is my last day here—I start early to-morrow for Padua, etc.) to send *this*, with what I shall write and enclose, as the explanation of the *business part* of my letter,—to Sarianna thro' my Father.

I beg pardon—but you see how I have spoiled my letter in a hurry —please send all inside to Sarianna.

[Huntington]

5. A small town in the mountains north of Venice, notable for its medicinal iron waters.

To Sir Thomas Noon Talfourd [1]

26 Devonshire St.[2]

Sept. 23, '51.

My dear Talfourd—(as I know your kindheartedness will suffer me to call you)—I can hardly be sorry at the mistake, tho' abundantly painful to me, which has drawn from you such a letter as puts an end to all such pain once and forever. But you must understand me, and not be very angry that the fear (however groundless) of having dropped from whatever cause from that place in your esteem, which I prized so much, discomposed the ordinarily clearer sight I seem to have of persons and things. Had I but obliged you *once*, for your thousand goodnesses to me, I should have been *sure* of your old feeling—but I have not even that "once" to refer to,—and why should

1. Thomas Noon Talfourd (1795–1854), often known as Serjeant Talfourd because of his position at the Bar, had been friendly to Browning since 1836. Besides being a lawyer and judge of eminence and M.P. for Reading, Talfourd was a poet and essayist and the friend and biographer of Lamb. On Talfourd's birthday on May 26, 1836, he gave a party at his house after Macready's performance of his play *Ion*. Browning was present and was toasted by Talfourd as among the "Poets of England." (See Griffin and Minchin, *Life*, pp. 76–77.) Dickens dedicated *Pickwick* to Talfourd. In 1841 Talfourd eloquently defended Moxon in the Shelley case (see above, letter of January, 1839, n. 1); in the same year Browning dedicated *Pippa Passes* to Talfourd. In 1849 Talfourd, Forster, and Procter helped Browning prepare his poems for the first collected edition of his works, which was published in that year. The cause of the misunderstanding mentioned in the letter above is not known. It may possibly be explained by the following excerpt from a letter of Mrs. Browning to Miss Mitford (November 12, 1851): "I saw no Mr. Harness; and no Talfourd of any kind. The latter was a kind of misadventure, as Lady Talfourd was on the point of calling on me when Robert would not let her. We were going away just then." (*Letters of E.B.B.*, II, 31.) Talfourd died of apoplexy on March 13, 1854. By some, especially his friend Miss Mitford, perhaps an unreliable witness, he was thought to be vain and jealous of rival dramatists, but the reasons for Browning's gratitude to him are clear. Talfourd responded to the friendliness in the present letter by writing a sonnet to Browning. (See below, letter to Moxon dated December 17, 1851.)

2. The address on this letter, 26 Devonshire St., was the lodging near the home of John Kenyon which the Brownings took during their visit to London. From this house several letters were written as Browning prepared to return to Paris. On this same day he wrote to Dr. W. C. Bennett, Thomas Carlyle, and William Allingham. (For the first two of these letters see *Letters*, ed. Hood, pp. 34, 35; for the third see *Letters to William Allingham*, ed. H. Allingham and E. B. Williams [London, 1911], pp. 94–95.) The Brownings left London on September 25 and resided in Paris until the end of June, 1852, when they returned once more to London.

you not have simply discontinued to care about me? That such is not the case,—however rationally one might have apprehended it, —*this*, do believe me, will send me comparatively rejoicing across the channel to-morrow—which else I should cross with unmixed regret. My wife sympathizes in all this,—and is besides, gratified and grateful at your special notice of herself. I have said something of this, for us both, to Lady Talfourd—but I could not go without this one word to your old friendship.

> Ever yours faithfully and thankfully,

[Huntington]   Robert Browning.

To Edward Chapman [1]

> 26 Devonshire St.
> Sept. 23, '51.

Dear Mr. Chapman,

I am much obliged to you for your prompt attention to my request—and only regret that you have supposed that I should be troubled by details which would be of the greatest interest to me.

1. This letter is the first in a series of 46 addressed to Edward Chapman of the publishing firm of Chapman and Hall, Ltd., who succeeded Moxon as Browning's publisher in 1848 and in 1849 published the first collected edition of his works. This series of letters to Chapman, preserved in the J. P. Morgan Library, illuminates a hitherto neglected relationship in the biographies of Browning. (For a treatment of these letters as a group and of their significance in Browning's career as a poet see K. L. Knickerbocker, "Browning and His Critics," *Sewanee Review* [July, 1935].) The key to the increasing fretfulness of Browning in this relationship—a fretfulness which finally led to a break with Chapman—is found in Chapman's daughter's comment on her father, that she doubted "whether he could ever have been a very good business man." (See Arthur Waugh, *A Hundred Years of Publishing, Being the Story of Chapman and Hall, Ltd.* [London, 1930], p. 4.) There is ample evidence that Browning, though a poet, was a good manager of his financial affairs, and Chapman's carelessness increasingly irritated him. Although Chapman and Hall were Browning's publishers for more than a decade, little is said of the poet in the history of the publishing house referred to above. The explanation is that Browning left Chapman and Hall in the middle Sixties, just as his work was becoming popular enough to be profitable. Mr. Waugh puts it thus: "Browning stayed with Chapman and Hall for many years . . . But in those years at any rate [he] never really conquered the literary tastes of his native land" (p. 78). Browning came to Chapman in the first instance probably because the firm was Mrs. Browning's publisher. He left Chapman and Hall for Smith, Elder and Co. when he felt that Chapman was careless to the point of dishonesty in not paying promptly the royalties due to his friend, Miss Isa Blagden, for her novels. See Appendix C.

This acc[oun]t would seem to be only the usual half-yearly one: I should be very glad to have it *with exact details;* indeed, a *separate account* of my books and my wife's, for the last, and every following half year—next Christmas and so following. On the whole, everything seems tolerably satisfactory in the sale of the different books —even of mine, which will, I doubt not, succeed in the long run— but I am vexed at the ill luck of *Christmas-Eve* etc.[2] Was the price too high? Could anything be done by judicious advertizing at the seasons the book treats of? Could one put in some illustrations, even now? I might get you a few good ones. I refer all to your better knowledge and practice, and meantime reciprocating your cordiality and good wishes, on my wife's part as well as my own, I remain, my dear Mr. Chapman,

Yours very faithfully,

[Morgan]   Robert Browning.

To Edward Moxon

Paris, Avenue des Champs Elysées, 138
[December 17, 1851.][1]

My dear Moxon,

No sooner had I sent off my letter to my sister, than I got, by next day's post, your kind note. I am very sorry to have been frightened for nothing, like most frightened people in this world. I was right, however, in counting upon *your* promptitude,—for, you see, you *did* write to me immediately on the receipt of my packet. Since then, I have duly been put into possession of your very liberal remittance.[2] I do hope that you will be no loser by your very hand-

2. *Christmas-Eve and Easter-Day,* published at Easter in 1850, was the first new work of Browning issued by Chapman and Hall. The price was 6s., the average for a new volume of poetry. The sale of the volume was disappointing, only 200 copies having been sold. Possibly Browning thought the price too high because of his experience with the pamphlets of the "Bells and Pomegranates" series, published by Moxon at prices ranging from 6d. to 1s. 6d. *Christmas-Eve and Easter-Day* was advertised in the *Athenaeum* and perhaps elsewhere at Christmas, 1850, and was listed among Chapman and Hall books at irregular intervals. No illustrations were added.

1. On December 17, 1851, Browning wrote to Thomas Noon Talfourd, thanking him for a sonnet he had written about Browning. (See *Letters,* ed. Hood, p. 37.) Browning's note to Talfourd is "the accompanying little note of acknowledgement" which Browning here asks Moxon to deliver for him. Since, therefore, the note to Talfourd is dated December 17, 1851, the letter to Moxon should bear the same date.

2. Possibly this remittance had to be returned to Moxon, for it was in pay-

some behavior. You gain my best thanks, at all events, for it—whatever they may be worth. I will spare no pains with the proofs, or anything else I can do in connection with the matter.

I also have to thank you for the communication of Talfourd's sonnet [3]—an evidence of his old kind feeling which has much gratified me. I will trouble you to forward to him (since, I suppose, —he transmitted the paper by you) the accompanying little note of acknowledgement. (No—I won't trouble you, on second thoughts.) [4]

The bitter cold weather cannot but affect my wife's chest—but not so as to disquiet me. Do you ever run over to Paris? Our little bandbox apartment has not even the *hole in the wall*, that I had hoped never to be without, when the question was where to stow a friend for a night: but accommodations abound, and we would have a merry evening, at all hazards. Meantime, believe me,

With many thanks, My dear Moxon,
Yours ever faithfully,

[Huntington]   Robt. Browning.

To Edward Chapman

Paris, Avenue des Champs Elysées, 138
Jan. 16, '52.

My dear Sir,

Will you allow me to remind you of your promise to furnish us at Christmas with the regular account of the sale of our books? My wife and I are anxious to know what has been the exact success, so far, of cash sale—both hers and mine. I shall be much obliged by a prompt attention to this request [1] of, my dear Sir,

Yours very faithfully,
Robert Browning.

I don't know whether you see, by any chance, the *Revue des deux Mondes;* the number of yesterday (Jan. 15) has an article on my

---

ment for the "Essay on Shelley," written by Browning late in 1851 and intended as a preface to letters of Shelley which, before distribution in published form, were discovered to be spurious. Browning's fright obviously might have taken a different turn!

3. Published under the title "Sonnet to Robert Browning; Suggested by a Sunset of Unusual Beauty," *Household Words,* IV (November 2, 1851), 213.

4. The parenthesis was crowded in after the next paragraph had been begun.

1. Scribbled below the date of this letter is the date February 20, 1852, presumably a record of reply—prompt attention indeed from Chapman.

wife, as that of Aug. 15, last year, contained one on my own things.[2]
I noticed the other day that you prefix to an advertisement of
Christmas Eve, an opinion from a journal—if that is the best course
(of which I have doubts)—why not take your extract from some real
authority in the matter—such as the admirable critic in question? [3]
[Morgan]

To Edward Chapman

58 Welbeck St.
Tuesday Sept. 14. [1852] [1]

My dear Sir,

I should really be glad to have the account at once, if you can so
far oblige me, for I shall leave London very shortly now. Will you
be good enough to attend to this?

Ever yours truly

[Morgan]   R. Browning.

2. The articles on the Brownings had appeared under the general title
La Poésie anglaise depuis Byron. The critic, Joseph Milsand, had devoted his
first article to Tennyson and his second to Browning—a review running to
28 pages, on Browning's poetry in general, with special attention to his latest
work *Christmas-Eve and Easter-Day.* The third article of the series dealt with
three poets, John Edmund Reade, Henry Taylor, and Mrs. Browning. Milsand's evaluation is interesting, for most critics of the time would have ranked
Mrs. Browning second only to Tennyson, and Browning among the minor
poets. Milsand later became one of Browning's most intimate friends.

3. Browning's objection to the quotation of an opinion from an English
journal was based partly on his reluctance to owe anything to the critics and
partly upon his knowledge that only by selection and deletion could such a
quotation be twisted into a favorable advertisement of his works. For example,
an advertisement of *Christmas-Eve and Easter-Day* in the *Athenaeum* for
April 13, 1850 quoted an opinion as follows: "The book before us is the work
of a poet . . . From its perusal intelligent minds may rise enriched with new
images of beauty and new stimulants to thought." The original review began:
"The book before us is the work of a poet; though if this fact should gain but
a limited recognition, the writer will have only himself to blame."

1. The Brownings were at 58 Welbeck Street, near the Barrett home in Wimpole Street, from June to November of 1852, when they returned to Florence.
Since they were never again at 58 Welbeck Street, this note may safely be dated
1852.

To William Charles Macready [1]

58 Welbeck St. Cavendish Sq.
Sept. 23. '52.

My dear Macready,

Pray forgive me for writing if it pains or troubles you, as it may, perhaps. How can I help telling you—tho' in but a poor word or two—that I dare think I can sympathise with you—even in my infinitely removed degree—dare think I comprehend your loss, having been taught by a loss of my own. Those were happy days when I lived in such affectionate intimacy with your family: and if some few of the idler hopes of that time came to nothing, at least all the best and dearest memories of a friendship I prized so much remain fresh in my heart as ever—else it would be too sad *now*. May God comfort you in this calamity. I will only say that I am, dear Macready,

Most affectionately yours
Robert Browning

May I beg to be remembered to Miss Macready,—and any with you who may not have forgotten me.

[Yale]

To Richard Monckton Milnes [1]

Florence, Dec. 27, '52.

My dear Milnes,

Your know you bade me let you know something about myself from time to time. A curious thing turns up here, which may in-

1. Macready, apparently, has written "Browning" across the top of this letter and, below the date, "October 6," possibly his date of reply. After the quarrel between Browning and Macready over the production of *A Blot in the 'Scutcheon* in 1843, the two men had not been on speaking terms. This letter, the occasion of which was the death of Mrs. Macready, is Browning's attempt to renew an old friendship and to forget old disagreements. It seems to have been successful. The loss of his own which Browning refers to in the letter was probably the death of his mother in March, 1849.

1. Richard Monckton Milnes (1809–85), poet, prose writer, and politician, laid his greatest claim to fame on the variety, the quality, and the quantity of his friends in literary, political, and aristocratic circles. The peerage refused by his father, Pemberton Milnes, was accepted by him in 1863, when he became Baron Houghton of Great Houghton. To know Milnes was to have an almost certain approach to any distinguished person in England. (See T. Wemyss Reid, *Life, Letters, and Friendships of Richard Monckton Milnes, First Lord Houghton* [London, 1890], 2 vols., *passim*.)

terest you—I will get rid of it in fewer words than it deserves, for the friend who procures me the opportunity of carriage for the parcel sits here waiting for it.

Cardinal Gualterio was Papal Nuncio at Paris from 1700 to 1706. He returned there in 1712, in a private capacity. He was instituted "Cardinal Protector of England" subsequently, and acted in Rome as the confidential agent of the "King of Engd";—the Pretender. He died in 1728. His descendant, the Marchese Gualterio, possesses the whole mass of his official and private correspondence—he talks broadly of "about 500 quarto volumes"—these include all the original despatches from the Papal Court to the Nuncio, an unbroken series, together with copies of all papers transmitted thither by the Cardinal. The collection also includes a body of correspondence of the Nuncio's nephew, Cardinal Luigi Gualterio, himself Nuncio at Paris and Naples. Out of all this, the documents relating to the Stuarts exclusively would make, it is stated, six quartos—"a parlous contribution." The rest is the affair of the leading agents of the Pope in different parts of Europe. I suppose one rarely meets with such an occasion of inclining a curious eye upon these darknesses. I never saw the actual Gualterio, but the friend who has had the rummaging of his inheritance is divided between admiration of such a Godsend, and fears lest any but ourselves profit by it; so he has told me all this and more, and brought me a sample of the same —there it cumbers the edge of my table (of marble, luckily)—letters about the "blessed majesty of England," fresh as if the ink had dried last week. Of course, Gualterio wants to sell his ware—and I believe he has offered it to the British Museum: if it ought to be secured to us, it ought—that's all. And that one of those able to judge whether it ought, may have an inkling of the matter, I write this preliminary to the pamphlet which it accompanies—a sort of "saggio" or Taste of the Contents which Gualterio has had privately printed ('ware this paternal government and its white-coated friends!)—just a few copies, of which my friend brings me three— one for yourself, another quite naturally to the Italians' everything in *issimo* Lord Palmerston, and a third for Mr. Hallam, if you will please to commend it to him.[2] Letter 1. is surely interesting just

---

2. Browning's appeal, probably along with pressure from others, brought results, for the *Catalogue of Additions to the Manuscripts in the British Museum in the years MDCCCLIV–MDCCCLX* (printed by order of the Trus-

now—and do note the characteristic impudence of the third one on the institution of the King of Prussia.

I hope, and my wife, from our hearts that all your house prospers—will you remember us both to Mrs. Milnes? [3] We have carried those pleasant sights of you a long way off, but we often refer to them and find them fresh and good as ever. We go on to Rome when we are well wearied from Florence (style of us family people!) What do you say of your Soulouque now? Does he stick his knees into the real animal of France, or remain aloft, as you thought, bestriding after Sancho's fashion, an imaginary dapple—the empty saddle, to wit—some Gines de Passamonte having stolen the tame beast from under him while he slept? [4] No, they're *his*—as I'm yours, dear Milnes, and quite as affectionately,

Robert Browning

Mr. Macaulay has general and special accounts and catalogues of the whole business. [5]

[Lord Crewe]

---

tees, 1875) describes Add. MSS. 20,241–20,686, acquired in 1854, as follows: "The voluminous correspondence and official and partly private papers of Cardinal Filippo Antonio Gualterio, Papal Vice-legate of Avignon in 1696, Nuncio in France in 1700–1706, Cardinal-Protector of Scotland in 1706, and of England in 1717, containing much relating to the affairs of James II and the elder Pretender; and of his nephew Cardinal Luigi Gualterio, Vice-legate of Ferrara in 1730–1735, Inquisitor of Malta in 1739–1743, Nuncio in Naples in 1744–1753, and in France in 1754–1759" (*Notice*, p. vi). Browning knew that Milnes was exactly the right person to undertake these negotiations, for Milnes like his father enjoyed the lifelong intimacy and friendship of Lord Palmerston, in 1853–55 approaching the zenith of his political career. Palmerston was *issimo* to Italians because of his foreign policy opposing all European tyrannies, especially the Austrian. Milnes had been one of Arthur Hallam's most intimate friends at Cambridge and had easy access, therefore, to the father, Henry Hallam, the distinguished historian and trustee of the British Museum.

3. Milnes had married the Honourable Annabel Crewe in 1851. The Brownings had met her on their visit to England in that year.

4. Faustin Soulouque (1782–1867) in 1847 became President of the Republic of Haiti, then in 1849 crowned himself Emperor. "Il débouta par le massacre les principaux bourgeois de Port-au-Prince, refusa de payer l'indemnitie à la France. . . . Ce tyran, Faustin-Soulouque-Napoleon-Robespierre, est demeuré célèbre par sa vanité ridicule." (*La Grande encyclopédie*, "Haiti.") Browning's figure from Cervantes' *Don Quixote* is most characteristic.

5. Milnes also knew intimately Thomas Babington Macaulay, whose *History of England* published in 1849 had established a record for popularity and had thereby made him the obvious historian to whom the Marchese Gualterio would send accounts and catalogues.

To Edward Chapman

Florence, March 5, '53.

My dear Sir,

Many thanks for your note duly delivered by Mr. Lever.[1] The account can't be otherwise than right, and I shall draw on you for the balance whenever we want anything rather pleasant. With this, you receive one vol. of the *Poems*—the second—and the First shall follow as soon as possible.[2] You can begin at once, I suppose,—indeed it would be a pity to keep such judicious book-buyers waiting a minute more than must needs be. There are very few and trifling alterations, you will see—changes of punctuation for the most part—and these are so obvious to a careful printer, that we won't put you to the trouble of sending proofs—throwing ourselves wholly on your peoples' kindness and intelligence;—only let them stick scrupulously to what is done. I condole with you about my own bad job—I'll be bound you haven't sold a copy of *Christmas Eve;* [3] yet I heard only last week about its success in America. Things may mend, however. Have you heard from Mrs. Martin? (Helen Faucit) She is going to bring out one of my things, *Colombe's Birth-*

1. Charles Lever (1806–72) the novelist was added to the list of Chapman and Hall authors in 1852. The Brownings at this time did not know him well. Mrs. Browning in a letter to Miss Mitford in November, 1850 mentions a visit from Lever but adds that "he only wanted to see that we had the right number of eyes and no odd fingers. Robert in return for his visit, called on him three times, I think, and I left my card on Mrs. Lever; but he never came again." (*Letters of E.B.B.* I, 465.) As early as 1844, while R. H. Horne and Miss Barrett were preparing *A New Spirit of the Age,* Miss Barrett wrote: "I *cannot* read Lever—honestly and without affectation, I *cannot,*" and went on to give her reasons. (*Letters of E.B.B. to R. H. Horne,* pp. 268–271.) Lever's biographer, Edmund Downey, explains that Lever "did not feel at ease in the presence of the author of *Aurora Leigh*"—a premonitory restlessness surely, for *Aurora Leigh* was not published until 1856. (*Charles Lever, His Life in His Letters* [Edinburgh, 1906], I, 306–307.)

2. Mrs. Browning's *Poems* had already been through two editions, the first in 1844 with Moxon as publisher and the second in 1850, a reprint by Chapman and Hall. She was now at work on a complete revision; the few and trifling alterations in volume two were followed by "alterations and corrections . . . so considerable" in volume one that a postscript indicating the extent of the revisions was added to the advertisement. See letter to Chapman on April 15, 1853.

3. Browning doubtless means that no copies have been sold since the last semiannual accounting. Mrs. Browning mentions the sale of 200 copies soon after the publication of the poem in 1850. (*Letters of E.B.B.,* I, 447.)

day, at the Haymarket next month. I told her to get a copy of it (in the *Poems*) from you, if she wanted one. Theatrical matters chop and change, and this may come to nothing sooner than something—but if there were to be any sort of success, it would help the poems to fetch up their lee-way, I suppose.[4] Hadn't you better advertise, in that case?—You know best, of course. Meantime, I shall give you something saleable, one of these days—see if I don't.

Poor Forster is indeed attacked, I hear, as you feared he might be.[5] I shall try to get news to him directly. We have cold weather, snow on the mountains, rain in the streets, and the Arno all but over his bounds every now and then. There is a warm sun out today however. "The same to *you!*"—from my wife as well as, my dear Sir,

> Yours ever faithfully,
> Robert Browning.

After all, we think that as there *are* some alterations in the poems, unless you have some person in your eye on whom you and we may *altogether depend*, it will be safer to send the proofs to Miss Barrett, 50 Wimpole St. She will overlook them carefully and you must not mind any unscientific "ℳ, sm. caps. run on" and the like! But if you can safely save yourself the trouble and us the danger, do so.

[Morgan]

4. Helen Faucit (see above, letter of October 12, 1837, n. 4), at this time Mrs. and later Lady Martin, had acted in *Strafford* and *A Blot in the 'Scutcheon.* In reply to her letter of January 22, 1853 (published in *Baylor University Browning Interests*, ed. A. J. Armstrong, 2d ser. [Waco, Texas, 1931], p. 9), Browning had written to her on January 31, 1853, giving her his "delighted" permission to "do anything for 'Colombe,'" including a condensation into three acts. (Orr, *Life*, p. 185.) She was simply requested to "follow the corrections in the last edition," which she was to obtain from Chapman and Hall. This was the revision of the play which had appeared in the collected poems published by them in 1849. It had been originally published by Moxon as Pt. VI of the "Bells and Pomegranates" series. Helen Faucit's production of the play at the Haymarket in April, 1853 ran for seven performances. Mrs. Browning correctly called this a "succès d'estime," recognizing that the play was somewhat "subtle and refined for pits and galleries." (Orr, *Life*, p. 186.) The reviewer in the *Athenaeum* for April 30, 1853, called attention to the dangers of these qualities: "The involuntary tear was often felt upon the cheek. . . . Whether the taste of the public for so refined a creation on the stage is yet formed, remains to be seen."

5. Forster became seriously ill in 1853. (Richard Renton, *John Forster and His Friendships* [London, 1912], p. 27. See also below, next letter.)

To John Forster [1]

Florence, Ap[ri]l 12, '53.

I was very glad to see the outside of your note, even—for it shewed, dear Forster, that your right hand had not been affected, as last year. Still it is very sad to think of you shut up for eight weeks. I won't begin on this, however, only believe I wish you your old health with all my heart—so do all your friends, as I see, or hear, at this distance. If I were in London, to go and sit with you as of old, would be the pleasantest thing I could do. Take the wish for the deed. I wish I could write a word you would like to hear, even now —but we have relapsed into the old sleepy life and depend on your papers for news. I was vexed to leave England without seeing you, but we had been delayed far too long [2]—my wife's cough was getting worse—we feared some fine seasonable frosty weather would land-lock us and end all. I don't know how it happened that you got my note so late—it should have been delivered at once, to prevent such trouble as you took—but we went in a hurry and all touching us partook of it.

Yes, we hear of the American Copy-right Bill—without much belief in its bringing good to us.[3] You suggest that my wife should append some new poems to this next edition [4] so as to save it—but *would* they save it? You remember the last "dodge." They would

1. John Forster (1812–76), journalist, critic, and biographer of Swift, Landor, and others, became acquainted with Browning in 1835. As chief literary and dramatic critic of the *Examiner* he reviewed *Paracelsus* on September 6 of that year. He and Browning were soon friends, and in 1836 we find Browning helping Forster with his *Life of Strafford*. Forster was intimate with Macready and for several years aided Browning's dramatic aspirations at every opportunity. The poet owed a great deal to Forster. But Forster was dictatorial and proprietary, and the friendship was not smooth. Upon Browning's rise to public notice, Forster patronized him a good deal, and the friendship ended in the Sixties when the two men quarreled so bitterly that Browning threatened to throw a decanter at Forster's head. (See *Memories of Half a Century*, compiled and ed. by R. C. Lehmann [London, 1908], chap. 8. See also *John Forster: by One of his Friends* [London, 1903], p. 38; and Renton, *Forster and His Friendships*.)

2. Though the Brownings had planned to leave England in September, 1852 they actually left in early November.

3. At least 11 international copyright bills were drafted between 1843 and 1846 and were one after another killed in committee.

4. The third edition of Mrs. Browning's *Poems;* see above, letter to Chapman on March 5, 1853.

go on reprinting the old two volumes—reserving the new things for some separate publication—saying nothing about them meanwhile. The books are of their full bulk as it is—the expense of printing etc. would increase very unnecessarily. And besides the corrected copy is sent home and in hand by this time.[5] We see a good number of Americans—(had five with us last evening)—they are kind and well-wishing—we shall get nothing better than visits of that sort—and a letter now and then, such as I had the other day—no, my wife had it, speaking of the success of that poor *Christmas Eve* which hasn't paid printing yet. Who cares, after all! One of last night's visitors brought an Indian ornament for our child—to his great delight—"for this, with all the rest, were books ordained." You speak of *Colombe—that* is altogether "the house's" venture, mind. Somebody wrote to me the other day using a phrase that looked like a quotation from some bill or newspaper paragraph, to the effect that the play was "adapted to the stage by the author"— a mistake: all I heard of proposed adapting was that the theatres want the five to be made *three* acts. I bade them do so, by all means.[6] In fact, one may as well suppose oneself dead and quiet and let the bustling care for you now as they will have to do soon enough —if they *do* care at all. I told Miss Faucit to do just what she liked, and dare say she will do neither more nor less, one whit, on that account. I always liked her. How odd the remembrance of play- going seems now—seven years since I was away—and for three or four years previous I had become strange to the benches, or boards, should one say? I knew that new misery of poor Macready when I wrote, and would not bring it in, on purpose, not knowing how you might be. I believe I was present at the poor boy's baptism (with you?) and acted as proxy for Talfourd who was sponsor, but ab- sent. Am I wrong? How does dear Macready bear up—I have no heart to send a word to him—God bless and comfort him, I can

5. Sent on April 6. See below, letter to Chapman on April 15, 1853.
6. On April 12, 1853, before the production of *Colombe's Birthday* Mrs. Browning, in anticipation of a possible failure, wrote that her husband had "prepared nothing at all, suggested nothing, modified nothing," that he had "referred them to his new edition, and that was the whole." (*Letters of E.B.B.*, II, 112–113.) For what occasion Browning marked for stage presentation the copy of *Colombe* which came into the possession of Edmund Gosse remains a mystery; Browning, trying in 1881 to recall the circumstances, supposed that he had marked it for Helen Faucit. (DeVane, *Browning Handbook*, p. 133.)

say to you at least.[7] I would travel, were I he—get out of that miserable house—but who can advise another?

We see something every now and then, and always to our great pleasure, of Mr. Lytton—an older friend of yours, very likely than myself even.[8] One can hardly imagine a more interesting and attracting young man, and there is plenty of stuff in him, you will see —or probably, have seen. You inveterate Forster—*marry*, will you? [9] How else will you get a son whom people shall look to, for your sake, and then like for his own—witness this father's-son of him who wrote *My Novel*, which I am reading even now.[10] And let my son be friends with yours ("as Shafalus to Procrus, I to you") [11] as you, dearest old friend, with your ever affectionate

R. B.

My wife's kindest regards.

What think you—Barnum has made a serious proposal to the *Madiai*,[12] to exhibit them in the U. S. Fact!!!

[Victoria and Albert Museum]

To Edward Chapman

Florence, April 15, '53.

Dear Mr. Chapman,

Thanks for the note just received. The First volume was duly dispatched hence on the day you wrote it—the 6th—and, I wish, may only just have reached you; for, see, I enclose a new beginning

7. Walter Francis Sheil Macready, aged 13, died on February 3, 1853, less than five months after the death of Mrs. Macready.

8. Robert Lytton (1831–91), son of Sir Edward Bulwer-Lytton, met the Brownings in Florence in November, 1852, and immediately became a great favorite with them. Forster had known Lytton since 1832, three years before he met Browning.

9. Late in 1856, at the age of 44 Forster married Mrs. Eliza Ann Colburn. Dickens' comment on the approaching marriage was: "I have the most prodigious, overwhelming, crushing, astounding, blinding, deafening, pulverizing, scarifying secret of which Forster is the hero, imaginable." (Renton, *Forster and His Friendships*, p. 95.)

10. *"My Novel"* or *Varieties in English Life* by Pesistratus Caxton [Edward Bulwer-Lytton] (1853), 4 vols.

11. *Pyramus:* Not Shafalus to Procrus was so true.
    Thisbe: As Shafalus to Procrus, I to you.
             (*A Midsummer Night's Dream*, V, i, 201–202.)

12. We have been unable to find a reference to this incident among P. T. Barnum's many operations. Perhaps the Madiai are the Madi, a Negro race of the Nile Valley, notable for their generous treatment of women and for their interesting sepulchral monuments.

to the first poem in it, the "Drama of Exile," which my wife is very anxious should be substituted for the present one—or, rather, it is an insertion, not a substitution. Will you have the goodness to see that the Printers don't stumble in such a ticklish place? They have simply to print this page of copy as the beginning of the poem —title and all—and when they get to the end of the copy, to go on to [the] corresponding line in the printed book.

I also enclose a word of *postscript* to follow the *advertisement* —for the alterations and corrections were so considerable that some notice of them is no more than proper.[1] Both our thanks for all the trouble you will take, and believe me, my dear Sir,

Yours very faithfully,

R. Browning.

I shall ruin you in *postage*—but they say the unpaid letters go the safelier.

[Morgan]

To Reuben Browning

Bagni di Lucca

July 18th '53

Dear Reuben,

I have left your kind letter, written just after the appearance of "Colombe,"[1] far too long unanswered. As before, you were the first to give me news of its success [2]—for such, on the whole, it may be called. I have heard nothing more since the beginning of June, when Miss Faucit was playing it at Manchester, with much the same result: everybody praised her highly, which really delights me; the other actors seem poor creatures, and I won't admit that the play, with its Hero left out, is a play at all. It was very good of you to go and see and report as promptly as you did.

Ever

RB [3]

[Huntington]

1. Because of the extensive revisions this edition of Mrs. Browning's *Poems*, the third, is of considerable importance. Some details of the revision are given in Thomas J. Wise, *A Bibliography of the Writings in Prose and Verse of Elizabeth Barrett Browning* (printed for private circulation, London, 1918), p. 67.

1. *Colombe* was produced in London seven times in April, 1853.

2. Mrs. Browning in a letter to Miss Haworth in June, 1853 said of the performance of *Colombe*: "Most of our friends took for granted that we had supernatural communications on the subject, and did not send us a word." (*Letters of E.B.B.*, II, 118–119.)

To Edward Chapman

Bagni di Lucca, Toscana, Italia
Aug. 24, '53 [1]

My dear Sir,

I should be glad to have the account, and to know how you get on with the new Edition. There seems to be a strange delay in bringing it [out;] people write to us about it, and so forth.[2] When it does appear, may I trouble you to send two copies to Wimpole St.— (to "Geo. Barrett, Esq." and to "Miss Barrett.") Also a copy, together with *Casa Guidi,* my poems, and *Christmas Eve* to Reuben Browning, Esq.—Messrs. Rothschilds', New Court, St. Swithin's Lane—for Mrs. Hedley, Rue d'Astry 12, Faubourg St. Honoré, Paris." [3] Will you finally have the goodness to put the enclosed letter into the post-box. I shall hope to hear from you before I leave this place.

We are quite well, and enjoy the fine weather more than you do, I fear. I was happy to hear of Forster's return to health, but must write myself to him. Lever is at La Spezzia.

Ever yours faithfully,

[Morgan]   R. Browning.

To Edward Chapman

Bagni di Lucca, Toscana. Aug. 29. [1853][1]

My dear Mr. Chapman,

You will have received a letter a few days ago concerning the new Edition, and such copies as we wished for certain relatives. We have

3. The complimentary close and the initials of the signature are taken for granted in this letter, for they are represented by a wavy line and no decipherable letters. Below is written the address: "Reuben Browning, Esq., care of Messrs N. M. Rothschild and Sons, New Court, St. Swithin's Lane, London."

1. The Brownings arrived at Bagni di Lucca on July 18 and settled into a "lazy life" in the "beautiful and joyous little place" tucked away in the mountains of Tuscany. See letter to Mrs. Kinney in *Letters,* ed. Hood, p. 40. The peace and idleness of this retreat made the Brownings impatient to see something come from the preceding months of literary labor.

2. Characteristically, Chapman bided his time, and it was not until October 15 that the third edition of Mrs. Browning's *Poems* was announced in the *Athenaeum* as published "This Day."

3. Mrs. Hedley, nee Jane Graham-Clarke, Mrs. Browning's aunt on her mother's side, left Paris on her way to London at this time. See letter to Chapman dated August 29, 1853.

1. For date see letter of August 24, 1853.

since heard that Mrs. Hedley [2] will soon be in London. Will you therefore have the kindness to make up the parcel (of *all* our books) and put it by until she sends for it:—two copies of the new edition to Wimpole St. for Geo. Barrett Esq. and Miss Barrett:—and a copy (*at once*) to John Kenyon Esq.[3] 39 Devonshire Place, Reg[ent's] P[ark].

Yours very sincerely,

[Morgan]   Robt. Browning.

To John Forster

Florence, Nov. 13, '53.

My dear Forster,

I was grieved indeed, a few days ago, by Lytton's communicating to me so much of a note from you as related to a recent calamity. It is sad to think of such a loss as that, coming when you are least prepared for it—out of your old health and spirits. I daresay you remember I was with you one morning when you were oppressed with *Strafford* for the Cyclopedia and you had to endure a similar misfortune [1]—Now *I* remember it! I can write, now, even less than I could say, then; but I do wish you comfort with all my heart—believe it, my dear Forster! Poor Macready, too, will have to bear more sorrow, I fear—if I don't misunderstand what your friend Black [2] tells me. Very sad all of it, and not least so that one can only say "very sad."

For the rest, you must be regaining health, by the last news I had from Mr. K.[3] It was a good thing that there seemed one smile

2. See letter of August 24, 1853, n. 3.

3. A distant relative of Elizabeth Barrett and as important in the lives of the poets as any other single person. It was he who introduced the two, and it was through his generosity that, on his death in 1856, the Brownings were made comparatively independent of book royalties for a livelihood. See letter to Reuben Browning dated June 12, 1850, n. 2.

1. Forster's sister Jane died in 1853; his father, John Forster, had died in 1836. In April, 1836, Browning had come to Forster's aid in completing the *Life of Strafford*, which was part of Lardner's *Cyclopedia*.

2. This is possibly John Black (1783–1855), for over a quarter of a century editor of the *Morning Chronicle* and one of the early friends of Macready. (See *Macready Diaries*, ed. Toynbee, I, 314.) The serious illness of some member of Macready's family is indicated.

3. John Kenyon (1784–1856), kinsman of Elizabeth Barrett Browning and benefactor of the Brownings. See above, letter of June 12, 1850, n. 2.

D

possible at an expression of your letter—where you spoke of ills incidental to "middle-age." Not yet, I assure you, as I remember you so long ago as last year. Do you but take the care of yourself that "middle age" is bound to bethink himself of, and another spirit will appropriate it all, and deal more efficaciously with it. I shall need you to keep me and mine company for long days yet, and are *we* old, I wonder? [4] I hope to see you in early summer—to enjoy rest and much more as I could not last year. Meanwhile I set out for Rome tomorrow (by Perugia)—shall arrive in a week, I trust —and stay the winter.[5] So one is blown about, till there's a quiet for the Landorian "old leaf." [6] I am in stress and strain, with a great day's work before me, but these two or three words I would write— and do you read them with your old good fellowship, and few as they are they will serve the end.

My wife would have you understand her sympathy and every good wish for you. God bless you, my dear Forster—

Yours affectionately ever

[Victoria and Albert Museum]   R. Browning

To Richard Monckton Milnes

Florence, Nov. 14, '53.

My dear Milnes,

The Bearer of this, Mr. Wood, a young sculptor of great promise, would needs make medallions of my wife and myself, here at Florence.[1] He loves poets and poetry very heartily, and would particularly like to show you what he has done. I assure him and myself

---

4. Forster was born on April 2, 1812, just 33 days earlier than Browning.

5. The Brownings were in Rome from November, 1853 to May, 1854, and in Florence from May, 1854 to May, 1855 when they set out for London. They arrived in June.

6. Landor was admired and cared for by both Browning and Forster. See John Forster, *Walter Savage Landor: a Biography* (London, 1868), *passim;* and Kate Field, "Last Days of Walter Savage Landor," *Atlantic Monthly* (April, 1866). In 1853 Landor had published a volume of conversations and essays entitled *The Last Fruit off an Old Tree;* the "old leaf" refers to his habit of commenting, poetically and otherwise, upon his longevity.

1. Marshall Wood (*ca.* 1830–82), whose medallion of Browning done in Florence was his first exhibit for the Royal Academy in 1854. Between 1854 and 1875 he exhibited 23 other works, busts, statues, and medallions. (Algernon Graves, *The Royal Academy of Arts: A Complete Dictionary of Contributors and Their Work . . . 1769–1904* [London, 1905–06], VIII, 339.)

that you will let me be the intermediary in this, and that you will
"look to like, if looking liking move." [2] I am in the trouble of departure for Rome tomorrow—and it is night now, so commending
my wife and myself to the remembrance, pray do *you* remember me
for

Yours ever faithfully,

[Lord Crewe]   Robert Browning.

To Sarianna Browning [1]

Rome, Via di Bocca di Leone 43.
Dec[embe]r 19.' '53.

Dearest,

Yours came safely a day or two ago: we are all well, thank God,
and hope the worst is past in all matters. The little girl was moved
two days ago to her own house, and barring unforeseen relapses, is
out of danger. The governess in much the same state, or not quite
so well perhaps: the father and mother going about their old life
much in the old way, but effectually *struck,* of course. We have done
nothing all this while, nor desired to do much—but shall begin to
go out.[2] We know Fanny Kemble [3] and others. Thackeray and

---

2. *Romeo and Juliet,* I, iii, 98.

1. Sarah Anna Browning (1814–1903), named after her mother, changed the
spelling of her name perhaps to make the distinction at least orthographically
obvious. After the death of the poet's father, Robert Browning, Sr., in 1866
Sarianna became her brother's constant companion, so close to him, indeed,
that as Elizabeth Barrett never received a letter from Robert after her marriage
to him, so Sarianna rarely received letters from him after they settled in London in 1866. The present letter was probably addressed to Paris where Miss
Browning was living with her father.

2. The Brownings left Florence November 15 and arrived in Rome November 23, where lodgings had been procured for them by their American friends,
the Storys. The morning of the 24th Edith Story (Edie in Browning's letters of
later years) brought news that her little brother Joseph (a child about two years
older than Pen) was stricken with convulsions. Both the Brownings watched by
the child's bed until he died that evening at eight o'clock. During the day
Edith became suddenly ill and at first was confined by order of the physicians
to the Brownings' apartment. Late in the day she was moved to a bed in the
apartment below the Brownings occupied by William Page, the American
painter. The children's English governess contracted the same malady, described by Mrs. Browning as "gastric fever, with a tendency to the brain." The
agitation of the Brownings is shown best in *Letters of E.B.B.,* II, 146–155.

3. Frances Anne Kemble (1809–93), described as a "gifted but unequal
actress," also wrote plays and poems, and with her sister Adelaide Kemble (Mrs.

daughters arrived, called on us, were very genial and kind, took tea next night or so, and are lodging close by. He became very ill suddenly—of obstruction in the stomach, and was smartly treated, but is now well again (*don't say a word to his mother,*—who is apt, the girls say, to frighten herself to death). I go to take them out (the girls at least) to walk this morning.[4] We find things very much dearer than at Florence, with the exception of *game* which is very cheap,—*much* more so than common meat; this suits us exactly, and it is a fact that we have lived for the last three weeks on nothing else—woodcocks and snipes being cheapest—two woodcocks cost 14*d.*—a hare 18 *d.* etc. We like least, paying for lodging, instead of getting it for next to nothing—never mind, however. So many thanks for the "Album"—too good by far for Pennini, but he won't give it up. I was glad to see your drawings in it. He is quite well, quite good. Ba is very well, goes out—the weather being very mild. I hear this m[ornin]g it is cold at Florence—and *what* in London, I wonder, to say nothing of the "fogs" reported in *Galignani*.[5] I got a long letter from Mr. K. the other day. He has not thrown up Wimbledon, as I feared,—only taken a small house in the I[sle] of Wight, one in a row of seven building[s] by his friend Sir C. Fellowes,[6] and has thoughts of letting Wimbledon—finding I hardly understand what faults with it, or the neighbourhood neither. I see Murray is going to reprint an American book of travels in Italy by Mr. Hillard we knew a few years ago, it having had a great success in the U[nited] States—so much the worse for them, for it is really a very commonplace affair, far beneath what I should have judged the author capable of producing,—see it, however, if you can, for the sake of the pleasing account of "the Brownings"—very kindly meant of course.[7] We don't hear that our house is let in

---

Sartoris) was popular in the intellectual society of Rome and London. Mrs. Browning was "much impressed by her" and exclaimed, "What a voice, what eyes, what eyelids full of utterance!" (*Letters of E.B.B.*, II, 147. See also Margaret N. Armstrong, *Fanny Kemble* [New York, 1938].)

4. The girls were Anna Isabella Thackeray (later Mrs. Ritchie), aged 15, and Harriet Marion Thackeray (later Mrs. Leslie Stephen), aged 13.

5. *Galignani's Messenger* (1814–1904) was the chief source of English news for Englishmen traveling on the continent.

6. The Brownings were to visit Mr. Kenyon's place on the Isle of Wight in October, 1856. Sir Charles Fellows (1799–1860), archaeologist and traveler, spent "the latter part of his life . . . in the Isle of Wight." (*D.N.B.*)

7. George Stillman Hillard (1808–79) published his book *Six Months in*

Florence, which is provoking. I am most happy that Papa has got thro' his cold—and that you have done the same. This will reach you about the day after Christmas day, I suppose. I would have written yesterday but no post leaves this place on Sundays. We shall be obliged to see some of the Christmas sights, I suppose,— midnight mass, etc. All the city will be illuminated with gas for the first time,—I don't care a straw about such things. The Thackeray girls find everything delightful—"better than in Paris." My own indifference will go off no doubt, but if you knew what a deal of sad business there was, you would wonder I stay at all—indeed, I do think that if I had been able to afford such a step, I should have gone back again to Florence. We found Mrs. Brotherton (Mrs. Carm[ichae]l Smith's friend) not the miserable woman she supposes but quite happy and content with her great bearded husband; perhaps, however, you know nothing about the matter: it was supposed she was attached to Mr. Morton—if so, she has got over, remarkably well, what Mrs. S. declared would "kill her"— and so much the wiser she.[8] I am glad Jane is going to marry, as I

Italy in 1853. The twenty-first edition appeared in 1881, a great success, indeed. The passage on the Brownings amounts to an encomium of two pages, ending with the comment that "a union so complete as theirs—in which the mind has nothing to crave nor the heart to sigh for—is cordial to behold and something to remember" (I, 178–179).

8. The gossip referred to here by Browning may be clarified by the following facts. Mrs. Carmichael-Smythe (1792–1864), Thackeray's mother with whom he regularly corresponded, lived in Paris from 1838 to 1861 and was, as Thackeray's letters indicate, in close and fairly constant touch with Saville Morton, Paris correspondent of the London *Daily News* and intimate friend of Thackeray's. On March 15, 1852, Thackeray wrote to his mother: "I am very much pained indeed to hear of Morton, and you may say that I say so. He is shocking about women. Directly I hear of his being fond of one, I feel sorry for her. He lusts after her and leaves her. You may read this to him if you like." (*Letters and Private Papers of William Makepeace Thackeray*, ed. Gordon N. Ray [Cambridge, Massachusetts, 1945–6], III, 24. Professor Ray provides an excellent short sketch of Morton, I, cl–clii.) It is not clear when Mary Brotherton became involved with Mr. Morton, if indeed she became involved at all. In any event what Mrs. Carmichael-Smythe "declared would 'kill her' " must have been the death of Mr. Morton, who was murdered with a butcher knife wielded by Elliot Bower, a jealous husband, on October 1, 1852. Mrs. Brotherton's "great bearded husband" was A. H. Brotherton, a minor landscape painter who had in 1846 exhibited at the Royal Academy a picture called "A Sea-shore Reverie." (See Graves, *The Royal Academy of Arts; A Complete Dictionary . . . 1769–1904*, I, 304); Brotherton's addresses are listed as "Rome and 215 Regent Street." See also Ulrich Thieme, *Allgemeines Lexikon der bil-*

was sure she would— I conjecture by Aunt's leaving the place that
it is sold or what is equivalent,—poor old place! What do you lose
by being out of all the sad work! [9] I don't write more, wishing you
to get the letter at once. Love to dearest Papa—best regards to the
dear Corkrans.[10] I will write to Milsand when I can. The table turning at Florence, writing, etc. was wholly unsatisfactory to *me*, to
Story, and to Lytton—to all almost. The names were spelt imper-
fectly and (foolishly) repeated rightly to see if they *were* the names
. . which *then*, of course, they proved to be.[11] God bless you,

[New York Public Library]   · RB

To Edward Chapman

Rome, Via Bocca del Leone 43.[1]
March 30, '54.

Dear Mr. Chapman,

Many thanks for the account—my books will creep on, perhaps,
and my wife's run on, no doubt. But I have only time to say a word

---

denden Künstler, [Leipzig, 1907–] V, 71.) Thackeray, who had known Brotherton for more than ten years, wrote of him on December 31, 1853, as "so crazy that
I can scarce let the girls go to him," and again in January, 1854, he wrote that
"he is mad and tipsy and foolish, and we can't get on." (See *Letters of Thackeray,* ed. Ray, III, 333, 337.) Mrs. Brotherton wrote three books, one of them
a novel called *Respectable Sinners* (London, 1863), which went into a second
edition in 1865. Browning mentions this novel to Miss Blagden in a letter of
July 19, 1863; see below.

9. It is probable that the aunt referred to is Mrs. Christiana Silverthorne,
Browning's mother's sister. It was she who gave him £30 for the publica-
tion of *Pauline* in 1833. The place referred to as possibly sold might be the
Silverthorne house in Portland Place, Peckham Road, Camberwell, near Brown-
ing's childhood home. James Silverthorne, the poet's favorite cousin, died in
May, 1853 (see the poem "May and Death"), and perhaps this was the cause
of Mrs. Silverthorne's action. Jane may have been a younger member of the
Silverthorne family. Sarianna Browning was keeping house for her father in
Paris at this time.

10. Mr. and Mrs. Fraser Corkran. Mr. Corkran was Paris correspondent
for the *Morning Chronicle,* and both were intimate friends of Joseph Milsand.

11. Mrs. Browning wrote on May 16, 1853: "We tried the table experiment
in this room [Casa Guidi] a few days since . . . and failed; but we were impatient, and Robert was playing Mephistopheles, as Mr. Lytton said, and there
was little chance of success under the circumstances. . . . Robert . . . won't
believe, he says, till he sees and hears with his own senses." (*Letters of E.B.B.,*
II, 117.) Sarianna was a skeptic along with her brother.

1. The Brownings arrived in Rome late in November, 1853 and remained
there until late May, 1854.

about what presses more immediately. We want you to do us a bit of a favour. My wife's sister is much interested in the Ragged Schools.[2] She wants us to help, by contributing a poem a-piece which she would print and sell, at a bazaar that will take place on the 19th. of April. Now we should like to give her the paper and the printing into the bargain. Here are the poems. Will you kindly get two or three hundred copies struck off, in the simplest fashion, with as much taste as is consistent with cheapness—so that they may be sold, say, at sixpence a copy? No covers, you know, or anything but the plain sheetful simply doubled into shape—making the best show you can for [the] little we want to spend. Will you have the goodness to get this done *at once* (otherwise all our labor will be thrown away) and charge the same, together with the postage of this heavy letter *to our account*—not on any consideration allowing Miss Barrett to interfere—except to correct the proof which you can send her with the copy. Please also to keep the said copy clean —as she will sell the M.S. as an autograph, with other ware of a like character. You must consider, at once, us and the charity and the benevolent public who want as much for their pence as possible.[3]

I write fast for the post—but should you see Forster,[4] tell him I

2. Between this sentence and the next the following words have been scratched through: "Were formed a few years ago and are now flourishing."

3. Miss Arabella Barrett had been interested in the so-called Ragged Schools —homes for destitute girls—for several years. She suggested the means of raising money outlined in this letter. On March 4 Mrs. Browning had written to her that she and her husband would send verses for the bazaar. Probably one or both of the poets delayed writing the poems until late in March when haste became necessary if the poems were to be ready for the bazaar to be held on April 19. Mrs. Browning's contribution was called, frankly enough, "A Plea for the Ragged Schools of London." Browning's offering consisted of a versification of a tale from Luther's *Table-Talk*, which Browning called "The Twins" and republished the following year in *Men and Women*. (For discussion of this poem see DeVane, *Browning Handbook*, pp. 235–236.) The "plain sheetful simply doubled into shape" was turned into a pamphlet of 16 pages issued in light buff-colored paper wrappers with trimmed edges. A copy of the first edition, along with a manuscript of the poems, is in the Morgan Library. Exactly how many copies of the original edition were struck off is not known. In 1887 a bundle of copies turned up in London and each copy sold for 2s. Since that time the pamphlet has once more become scarce and difficult to find. Browning's next letter to Chapman, on July 1, 1854, indicates that the venture was hardly a successful one.

4. See below, Browning's letter to Forster dated April 2, 1854.

have just ascertained by a letter from Mr. Kenyon that a letter of his, directed to me a month ago, has been lost—to my sorrow.

Ever yours faithfully,
Robert Browning.

[Note added by E.B.B.]

Dear Sir, *My* idea is that two or three hundred copies would be inadequate to the purpose, and that the expense attending double the number would be very slight. The female side of a house however, is inapt at calculations. Will you judge between us and decide on what seems to you best. The sale is to take place at the Baker Street Bazaar. Be so good as to let my sister have the proof[?] [5]

[Morgan]

To John Forster

Rome, Via Bocca di Leone 43.
April 2, '54.

My dear Forster,

So, meaning me the great pleasure of a letter's receipt, you have missed it; and I, the comfort of getting it—Mr. Kenyon's letter and all its enclosures having miscarried. I have tried the wretched post here with the usual no-effect. The Postmaster is one Priesa Massiano, the oldest Roman here, being just descended from Fabius the Delayer—and his, or their, motto very happily surmounts the office-door, and tells you that "cunctando" the old Rome was saved, and the new one ought to be saved—tho' the power celestial will have a word to say to that. It seems much longer than usual since I heard from you—six or seven months ago for certain. The winter is over now, and you must get well in time for my summer transit, for come I will if I can—and do all I would have done last time. A note from Chapman gave no bad account of you, however. How shocked I was,—how utterly sad and strange it must have been to you,—to receive the news of poor Talfourd's death.[1] I thought him hale and lively when I saw him last. I shall try and write a word to his wife. Those old days, Forster—at your rooms—then the play;

5. The note at this point runs off the page, and a few remaining words are undecipherable. Chapman perhaps compromised the estimates of the poets. Browning, of course, was uncomfortably right—at least not so far wrong as his wife.

1. Sir Thomas Noon Talfourd died suddenly of apoplexy while addressing a grand jury at Stafford on March 13, 1854.

then the projects! What happened to me, think you, some six weeks ago? I was talking on the Pincian to an acquaintance, when a stranger touched my arm and said in French, "Is that *you*, Robert?" It was my old friend Monclar,[2] who, after an absence of seventeen years, had recognized *my voice* (my back being turned). He seemed not much changed, after a time. I don't think you ever saw him. Well, this has been a less fructuous visit to Rome for us than we had anticipated. We arrived one night, and the next morning were called in to the Storys', who had meant to make Rome twice Rome to us,—to see their only boy of six years and a half die in convulsions. Their other child was in great danger for a while—then rallied, relapsed and gave them sadness enough till they were forced to break up their establishment here and go to Naples—but at Velletri, the first night's stage thither, the worst symptoms occurred and they were detained for a week—when I received a despairing letter saying all hope was over and I *must* go and be with them at the end. I set off in a few minutes, effected the journey in a few hours, and found things had taken a favourable turn. I sate up a night, and left them much lighter of heart next morning; since then the child's state has improved steadily,—tho' all is not safe yet, by any means. You know them, I remember, and may be interested in hearing all this.[3] This sorrow of theirs took us into its shadow also—and then the weather was unfavourable to my wife's power of enjoyment. Last, I have let myself be too much entangled with people's calls, cardleavings, and kindnesses of all sorts, having not been without social engagements for each evening for many a week now. I don't know whom, of new people, you would be interested in, however new to *me*, that is, but, perhaps, Lockhart [4]

2. Comte Amédée de Ripert-Monclar (1807–71) had met Browning in the summer of 1834 through Reuben Browning. Browning, according to Mrs. Orr (*Life*, p. 72), credited Monclar with providing the original inspiration to write *Paracelsus*. In appreciation Browning dedicated the poem to his friend. The meeting in Rome is told by Mrs. Orr, though the interval of 17 years has increased to 20 in her account. For the best short account of Monclar and Browning see Griffin and Minchin, *Life*, pp. 64–65.

3. For more details of the death of Joseph and the dangerous illness of Edith Story see *Letters of E.B.B.*, I, 147–154.

4. John Gibson Lockhart (1794–1854), biographer and son-in-law of Sir Walter Scott, critic for *Blackwood's Magazine* and editor of the *Quarterly Review* from 1825 to 1853, had become prematurely old as a result of what his doctors called "excessive abstinence." After his retirement in 1853 he wintered

—of whom I saw a good deal lately: what think you of his choosing to like me very much—being so unlike, as he said, "a damned literary man!" He, Mrs. Sartoris,[5] F. Kemble,[6] and I had a picnic at Frascati [7] last week—at Ostia [8] the week before and at Valderano [9] the week before. He's gone in woeful case, to England, with some friends, one of whom was seriously taking counsel as to what he should do if Lockhart died in the passage: "Would there be any indelicacy in asking him, do you think?" I suggested that a similar question to Hobhouse,[10] about the relative advantages of being pickled and sent home, or consigned to the snug lying of the Abbey, had not been duly appreciated. Talking of "damned literary men," Chapman's account has come in,—I daresay you know the result,— this half year we have sold 70 copies of the *Poems,* and I have at last a balance in his hands—or better say, on his little finger tip— of seven pence! [11] Chronicle that. I shall see if I can do any better with my new book,[12] which I have hopes in on these grounds (by

---

in Rome but returned to Abbotsford to sink slowly to his death on November 25, 1854.

5. Mrs. Edward John Sartoris, nee Adelaide Kemble (1814?–79), vocalist and author, maintained "one of the pleasantest houses in Rome," near the Trinità dei Monti. The Brownings saw much of her on this and subsequent visits to Rome.

6. Frances Anne Kemble (1809–93), the actress, better known as Fanny, was the divorced wife of an American planter, Pierce Butler. She was at this time making her home in America but had returned to Rome for a visit with her sister, Adelaide Kemble Sartoris. See *Letters of E.B.B.,* II, 154, 158, 159, 167.

7. Southeast of Rome 15 miles, the papal village of Frascati with its elaborate fountains and gardens commands a striking view of Rome and the Campagna that lies between. Browning's poem, "Two in the Campagna," may have been a result of this excursion.

8. Southwest of Rome 14 miles, at the mouth of the Tiber River, Ostia is, next to Pompeii, the best example of an ancient Roman town.

9. The word here seems to be Valderano but such a place name is not discoverable in Rome or in its environs.

10. John Cam Hobhouse, Lord Broughton (1786–1869), Byron's stanchest and most intimate friend, visited Byron many times at Newstead Abbey and traveled with him abroad. It may be that Browning's anecdote refers to one of Hobhouse's visits at Newstead. Hobhouse records this sequence of events in his diary for 1812: "June 9—at Newstead . . . June 13—arrived in London after a week of delirium." (See Lord Broughton, *Recollections of a Long Life* [London, 1909], I, 40.) Perhaps on some such occasion, either in England or abroad, Byron may have offered Hobhouse the choice Browning mentions.

11. See opening of letter to Edward Chapman dated March 30, 1854. The *Poems* are those of the collected edition of 1849.

12. *Men and Women,* published on November 17, 1855.

"book" I mean a set of poems, of various show and substance, not one poem). I have not seen many notices of what passes in England, but I did see, and was glad, that another edition of your *Goldsmith* [13] was announced. Won't you write me the letter you ought to have given me and tell me all about yourself and a little about others? I heard of your writing to Lytton sometime ago. Do you know,—you *must*,—Miss Cushman? [14] She will receive soon her admirable pictures—portraits of herself, a friend, and the artist,—by William Page. [15] They are *so* admirable, that I would have you see them,—about which there can be no difficulty; I never saw such modern art, certainly. I know the painter,—as noble a fellow as his works show him. Do see them the moment they arrive. Our painters will say their little say against them, you may be sure, but he can bear it. And now you must take more thanks for having written to

13. Forster's *Life of Goldsmith*, published early in 1854, quickly reached a second edition.

14. Charlotte Saunders Cushman (1816–76), American actress, made her debut on the operatic stage at the age of 19 in the part of the Countess Almaviva in *The Marriage of Figaro*. She seems to have met Browning as early as 1838 at the residence of Henry Chorley, music critic for the *Athenaeum;* she acted first on the English stage on February 14, 1845, after learning much from Macready. Walter Pritchard Eaton, who wrote the account of Miss Cushman for the *D.A.B.*, says, "there can be little doubt that Charlotte Cushman was the most powerful actress America has produced." She was "tall, strong-framed, deep-voiced, almost masculine in some respects, without feminine beauty certainly, and totally unable to conquer audiences by 'sex-appeal.' " See Rudolf Lehmann's picture, #18 in H. C. Marillier, *Men and Women of the Century* (London, 1896), for a portrait of Miss Cushman. At her death she left more than half a million dollars. Her favorite roles were Queen Katherine, Lady Macbeth, and Meg Merrilies. She met the Brownings frequently in Paris and Italy. See Emma Stebbins, *Charlotte Cushman: Her Letters and Memories of Her Life* (New York, 1878).

15. William Page (1811–85), portrait painter, was born in Albany, New York. He began preparing for the Presbyterian ministry at 17, but at 19 he decided to become a painter. He moved to Boston in 1844 and painted portraits of John Q. Adams, Josiah Quincy, Charles Sumner, James Russell Lowell, Wendell Phillips, and others. In 1849 he went to Italy for a sojourn of 11 years. He became a Swedenborgian, a fact which appealed to Mrs. Browning. Page worked on the theory that the lapse of years did not tone a picture, and he undertoned his portraits. In Rome he painted one of Browning that was much admired, but within a couple of years the portrait became almost black, and the likeness can hardly be discerned now. In October, 1855, Browning sent the portrait to Rossetti with the words: "So fares it with Page's pictures for the most part; but they are like Flatman the Poet's famous 'Kings' in a great line he wrote—'Kings do not die—they only disappear!' " (See *Letters*, ed. Hood, p. 41.)

me, more hopes that you will write again—a word at least ere I leave Rome, so that I may feel something of you before I see you, if that may be. (April 5) This was delayed, thro' interruptions of various sorts, and now you will get it by the long overland post. Goodbye, dear Forster. My wife's truest regard accompanies mine. She is well, I think I have said, and the boy also.

Ever yours most affectionately,

[Victoria and Albert Museum]   Robert Browning.

To John Forster

Florence, June 5, '54

My dear Forster,

Lytton sent me your last note some weeks ago.[1] The letter that was lost has never come to hand, alas![2] I was very glad to hear of you,—the lecture, talk of travelling and other proofs of what the old doctors call "a return to a laudable habit of body"—and now I see a little more of the mind of you by an *Examiner* or two, sent by Lytton also. I am truly happy that the "large composition" I have been used to admire has done itself justice—the Pym-like build[3] of you, which made chairs creak and floors groan when we turned over books together in the *Strafford* crisis.[4] Do you really think of going westward or do you joke? At this distance, it seems as good a business[5] as anybody's, now rising, standing, or lying down in England. But you are there, and I here—so to tell you of what I do here, I would not answer your note at once that I might get to know a little what we are likely to do. We left Rome last week, after no very prosperous sojourn—the good we found being

1. The note, sent to Lytton in Florence, was sent on to Browning in Rome.
2. See opening sentence of letter to Forster dated April 2, 1854.
3. John Pym (1584–1643) was more truly the hero of Browning's play *Strafford* than either the title character or his master Charles II. Pym was a very large man, commanding in appearance.
4. During Forster's illness in 1836 Browning had helped him prepare the *Life of Strafford* for Lardner's *Cyclopedia*. This letter supports the view that the two men worked together. F. J. Furnivall, who republished the biography as Browning's in 1892, asserted that on three occasions Browning had laid claim to a large share of the work—had "put the Strafford papers under his arm, walkt off, workt hard, [and] finisht the *Life* by himself." See "Forewords," in *Robert Browning's Prose Life of Strafford*, pp. v–vi; and below, letter of December 17, 1887, n. 3.
5. Lecturing in America? With Dickens, Forster's friend, as a model?

just what we had least expected, in an afflux of friends old and new.
The place is ill-starred, under a curse seemingly, and I would not
live there for the Vatican with the Pope out of it. This old Florence
takes us to its breast like a friend after one defection—but I fear
we can't stay in Italy and rest, as I am fain to do. Our child is grown,
and not much otherwise than well, but his looks do not content us,
and tho' he is fast regaining his ripe cheeks, northern air would be
precious just now. We shall go, I suppose—tho' not for a few weeks.
I must be in London, or Paris at farthest, to print my poems. You
enquire about these, and, I think, are anticipating another press
matter than I shall have to show. Did you mean a joint work of my
wife and myself, you once wanted us to write? This is what I have
written—only a number of poems of all sorts and sizes and styles
and subjects—not written before last year, but the beginning of
an expressing the spirit of all the fruits of the years since I last
turned the winch of the wine press.[6] The manner will be newer
than the matter. I hope to be listened to, this time, and I am glad I
have been made to wait this not very long while. My wife's poem is
a long one, a novel in verse. I know not one word of it.[7] I shall be
ready by the Autumn—she in the Spring,—we count on it, at least.[8]
Can one do anything with the American Booksellers, do you know?
They tell us it is possible. But the talking usually blows a great
round shiny bubble which a touch of the Yankee finger breaks
promptly enough. You must know,—more, infinitely, than sanguine
American friends,—whether one *can* get a trifle for proofs in advance, etc.[9]

I have missed newspapers in travelling and thro' press of occupation, and know little of what is doing. I must go and see you, that
is clear. Will you be glad of it, as I shall? If I don't go, I shall send a
picture painted by that wonderful Page, I wrote of![10] 'Tis myself,

6. Browning is speaking, of course, of *Men and Women*. He last "turned
the winch of the wine press" in writing *Christmas-Eve and Easter-Day*, which
appeared on April 1, 1850. From this date, then, until early in 1853, Browning
says he had written no poetry. In view of other circumstantial evidence it is
difficult to take this statement literally. See, for example, Griffin and Minchin,
Life, p. 189.

7. See letter to Chapman dated February 6, 1856, n. 1.

8. *Men and Women* actually appeared on November 10, 1855; *Aurora
Leigh*, more than a year later, on November 15, 1856.

9. See letter to Chapman dated October 31, 1855 and n. 2.

10. Within 16 months Page's picture of Browning had begun to fade. (See

—just the head—but such a work! His best, he says, and I believe. He was three months painting it and then gave it to my wife, in his princely way.

My wife desires to be most kindly remembered by you. Will you not forget to give my true regards to Macready. I heard of him, and of you from Miss Haworth—pleasant news of you all, too. Must one really leave off here, just because the paper chooses?

Ever yours affectionately, R.B.

[Victoria and Albert Museum]

To Edward Chapman

Florence, July 1, '54

My dear Mr. Chapman,

I duly heard of your prompt and kind attention to our wishes about those versicles for the charity.[1] The plan was none of ours, nor at all to our mind (between ourselves) but since it seemed auspicious to others, we did as you helped us to do—and the piper must pay himself (thankful if it is not with "fiddler's money").

And now since the proper time comes about, will you be so good as to give us the half year's account, which will be more interesting than usual, just now? We both of us have books in hand, and are anxious to know the signs of the times.[2] Will you please attend to

---

Letters, ed. Hood, p. 41, letter to Rossetti, October 29, 1855.) For the best account of the deterioration of the picture that excited Browning so much see Griffin and Minchin, *Life,* p. 193.

1. See letter of March 30, 1854.

2. The books which the poets had in hand were *Men and Women* and *Aurora Leigh.* More than a year before this date (February 24, 1853) Browning had written to Milsand that he was composing "lyrics with more music and painting than before, so as to get people to hear and see." (N. Thomas, "Deux lettres inédités de Robert Browning à Joseph Milsand," *Revue Germanique,* XII, 253.) A few days later (March 5, 1853) he told Chapman: "I shall give you something saleable, one of these days,—see if I don't." By the summer of 1854 Browning was ready with at least a portion of the "something saleable." The journey to London was planned for this time but was postponed because Mrs. Browning was not ready with her long poem. (See Leonard Huxley, "A Visitor to the Brownings," *Yale Review,* N.S., No. 2, XIII (1924), 243.) In the light of these facts it is interesting to speculate upon the reduced contents of *Men and Women* if *Aurora Leigh* had been ready. In a letter to James T. Fields of Ticknor and Fields, Boston publishers, Browning on August 25, 1854 said: "I expect to bring out in London, next season, a collection of new poems, containing about 5000 lines." (See letter published in *Century Magazine,* N.S., LXII, 130.) Since the original two-volume edition of *Men and*

this at your early leisure, for we are at a distance you know. It is not certain when we go to London. At all events, an early answer will still find us here.

We are well, and none the worse for being out of Rome.

Ever yours faithfully,
Robert Browning

Will you have the kindness to address a copy of my wife's *Poems* to be given to Mrs. Stuart of Florence on her application for it.[3]
[Note added by E. B. B.]
And will you, dear Mr. Chapman, give into the care of the same Mrs. Stuart, to our address in Florence, Mrs. Barbauld's *Early Lessons* and Miss Edgeworth's *Early Lessons*, being the *Cherry Orchard*, and the first part of *Frank*, charging them, of course, to our account?[4]

Very sincerely yours,
[Morgan]   Elizabeth Barrett Browning

To Edward Chapman

Florence, Aug. 5, '54.

Dear Sir,

I wrote to you some time ago[1] begging for the *account to the end of June*, and that you would be at the trouble to procure certain books (this was my wife's commission) and consigned the same to

---

Women contained 7,167 lines and since it is probable that Browning's estimate of 5,000 lines was based partly upon composition planned for 1854–55, it is fair to assume that only about half the lines which eventually were to make up *Men and Women* were composed before August, 1854. See above, letter dated June 5, 1854, n. 6.

3. The Brownings probably met the Stuarts in the autumn of 1849 at Bagni di Lucca. Stuart lectured on Shakespeare there and in Florence and particularly attracted Mrs. Browning to him by his frequent quotations from the works of Mrs. Jameson. (See *E.B.B.: Letters to her Sister*, p. 174.) See also below, Browning's letter of June 5, 1858 commending Stuart to Chapman.

4. Mrs. Browning's short postscript is the first of a series of requests for pamphlets and books on the rearing of children. Mrs. Barbauld's *Early Lessons*, written as a result of her efforts to rear an adopted child of her brother's, had been standard "child psychology" since its publication in 1760. "Early Lessons" by Miss Edgeworth is the general title for a series of moralized children's books variously entitled. The first of the series had appeared in 1801; sequels followed for a number of years. The seventh edition of *Frank*, a three-volume work selling for 7*s*. 6*d*., was announced in the *Athenaeum* for March 18, 1854.

1. See above, letter to Chapman dated July 1, 1854.

Mrs. Stuart who would call for them. I conclude that you supposed I wished for the *account* by the same conveyance—as it has not come by post—but Mrs. Stuart has returned without being able to call on you, not taking London by her way. Will you have the goodness therefore to send the account at once, as it particularly interests us, and leave the books till I find a fit convoy for the same? I stay here all summer.

[Morgan]

Ever yours truly,
Robert Browning

To Edward Chapman

Florence, Jan. 11, '55

Dear Mr. Chapman,

I have first to thank you for attending to our commissions so promptly—the last packet came as duly to hand as the former one. Shall I, in the next place, wear your kindness to rags by giving you a fresh list?—viz.

> *The Peep of Day*
> *Line upon Line*
> *Joseph and his brethren*—1s.
> *History of Moses.* 1s.   } Religious Tract Society
> *Great truths in simple words* 1s.
> *Orlandino*
> 3d and 4th and 5th books of *Rollo*—by Abbott (American)
> *Little Mary's Scripture lessons,* 6d.

(I can only say, my wife assures me they are only so many pamphlets,[1] tho' they seem a library.) Will you have the goodness to

---

1. All the pamphlets named in this new order are children's books, intended, no doubt, to grace the early library of six-year-old Pen Browning. *The Peep of Day* by Mrs. Favell Lee Mortimer was first published in June, 1833. A multitude of editions followed, the sixth edition in 1840 and so on until 1891 when the last edition appeared. *Line upon Line* (London, 1837). *The History of Joseph and His Brothers* (London, 1850); *History of Moses* (London, 1850); *Great Truths in Simple Words* (London, 1847); these three pamphlets were published by the Religious Tract Society. We have been able to find no information about *Orlandino.* The series of "Rollo" books was begun in 1834 and extended eventually to 28 volumes. Bk. III was entitled *Rollo at Work,* Bk. IV, *Rollo at Play,* and Bk. V, *Rollo at School.* Jacob Abbott (1803–79) was an American schoolmaster who drew attention to himself by discarding traditional disciplinary methods at his Mount Vernon School; he "appealed to the honor and conscience of his pupils" and made the school largely self-governing. "Rollo and his companions belong to that inquisitive and edifying company in ju-

send these, with a little parcel Miss Barrett will give you, to "Walter B. Cassels Esq. care of Messrs. John Peel and Co. 23 Peel St. Manchester. To be forwarded by steamer," paying the carriage to Manchester.

And finally will you be so good as to write to us, as usual, that we may see how our affairs go—what is sold and what is yet to sell? I hope to be in England next half-year, so this will be the last time we dun you—perhaps! Meanwhile, a good new year to us all! We are very well spite of some coldish weather. My wife's kind regards and thanks go with those of

Yours very sincerely,

[Morgan] Robert Browning

To Edward Chapman

Paris, 102 Rue de Grenelle
Faubourg St. Germain [1]
Oct. 31, '55

My dear Chapman,

Many thanks for your note accompanying the American letter. I have written at once to that miraculous Mr. Fields [2] who seems in

---

venile fiction which followed the Rousseauistic *Sandford and Merton* of Thomas Day." (See *D.A.B.*, "Jacob Abbott.") *Little Mary's Lesson Books* (London, 1851).

1. The Brownings remained in Florence until June, 1855, both of them at work on their poems. Mrs. Browning was behind her schedule with *Aurora Leigh;* presumably, therefore, when Browning had completed his stint of 50 poems for *Men and Women* it was decided to delay no longer the journey to London. They arrived July 12 and remained at 13 Dorset Street until October. Most of this time, except for that devoted to the renewal of old acquaintances, was spent in seeing Browning's volumes through the press. By October, the printing completed and the proofs read, the Brownings withdrew to Paris to await the issue. They stayed first in an apartment at 102 Rue de Grenelle, Faubourg St. Germain, but early winter weather drove them from these "cold and vile" rooms to the sunnier and warmer quarters at 3 Rue du Colisée. They remained at this last address until late June, 1856.

2. James T. Fields of Ticknor and Fields had met the Brownings in 1851. Browning, on the suggestion of American friends, had written to him from Florence on August 25, 1854 proposing to send to him, when they should be ready the following year, the proof sheets of *Men and Women*. The poet hoped through this means to forestall an American piracy and to insure some remuneration to himself. (Letter printed in *Century Magazine*, N.S., LXII, 130.) Fields, through Chapman and Hall, generously accepted this offer and became, naturally enough, "that miraculous Mr. Fields." The letter which Browning says he wrote "at once" has not come to light.

a fair way to canonization (i.e. Boston may be bombarded, not impossibly); unluckily my letter was posted a day too late for last week's post—won't leave till next Thursday, they tell me. I bade Fields pay you your money at once—telling him how it had come to be yours.

I am anxious to know how our affair goes on—if the trade subscribes, and all that. I observe your advertisements in the weekly papers—all prominent and eye-catching. In looking over the book, I find a few errors, and a passage or two susceptible of improvement—but I avoid calling attention to them by making a list of *errata;* still, should there be a demand, by any strange chance, for more copies than are struck off, I will send the corrections to you.

Have the goodness to send copies to the following persons:
John Kenyon Esq.—39 Devonshire Place, Regent's Park.
Miss Barrett, 50 Wimpole St.
Mrs. Surtees Cook, Wilton, Taunton Post *6*
Miss Blagden, 43 Grosvenor Place
Mrs. Paine,³ Farnham. Post *6*
Bryan Waller Procter Esq. 32 Weymouth St. (Portland Place)
Edward Moxon Esq. Dover St.
Capt Pritchard, 5 Oak Terrace, Battersea Post *6*
Coventry Patmore Esq. British Museum
P. J. Bailey Esq.
W. J. Fox Esq. M.P. 3 Sussex Place, Regt Park
Mrs. Jago, Trejago, Hammersmith Post *6*
David Ogilvy Esq. Lower Ludenham Post *6*
Alfred Tennyson Esq. (care of Moxon)
Dante Rossetti Esq. 14 Chatham Place, Blackfriars' Bridge
John Ruskin Esq. Denmark Hill, Camberwell Post *6*
Reuben Browning Esq. 9 Victoria Road Old Charlton Post *6*⁴

3. *Payne* is scratched through and rewritten as *Paine.*

4. For John Kenyon see letter of June 12, 1850, n. 2. Miss Barrett was Arabella (1812–68), fourth daughter in the Barrett family and regular correspondent with E.B.B. Mrs. Surtees Cook (1809–60) was Henrietta Barrett before her marriage in 1850 to Captain Surtees Cook. The Brownings visited the Cooks at Taunton in the fall of 1856. For Miss Isabella Blagden see below, letter of July 19, 1863, and n. 1. Mrs. Paine of Farnham, Surrey, almost literally an idolater of E.B.B., won Browning's regard through this perceptiveness and perhaps also through her statement to E.B.B. that the author of *Luria* was "the greatest dramatic genius we have had for hundreds of years." (See *Letters*

My wife is not of my opinion about the undesirableness of append
ing the errata. Of course, I should prefer by a great deal that they
were adopted. What do you say? I attach importance to the mere
stops, but there are a few blunders that affect the sense, and not
all of them my fault, neither. I subjoin the list; do what you think
best.

And believe me, dear Chapman, with much esteem yours very
faithfully,

Robert Browning

No, I won't send the list of minor blunders, for if one is altered,
all should be, but just mention two that affect the sense and are

---

of R.B. and E.B.B., II, 369. For an account of Mrs. Paine's first visit to E.B.B.
in April, 1846, and for Browning's estimate of "that good, gentle Mrs. Paine,"
see *ibid.*, II, 31, 85.)

Bryan Waller Procter (Barry Cornwall), 1787–1874, lawyer and poet, had
become known in 1836 to Browning through John Forster, and the friendship
lasted throughout Procter's lifetime. Edward Moxon (1801–58), publisher of
"Bells and Pomegranates," was introduced to Browning by W. J. Fox in 1835
and had contracted for Browning's "Essay on Shelley" as recently as 1851. "Captain Pritchard, a memorable figure in the poet's early life, lived at Battersea,
where Browning's father was born: he is mentioned in the earliest letter written by Browning, and when he died he left the poet's sister £1000." (Griffin and
Minchin, *Life*, p. 54; and *Letters*, ed. Hood, p. 1.) Coventry Kersey Dighton Patmore (1823–96) published his first poems with Moxon in 1844, and Browning
commented: "A very interesting poet has flushed into bloom this season."
(*Browning and Domett*, p. 107.) In 1846 Browning told E.B.B. of seeing Patmore at Mrs. Procter's. (*Letters of R.B. and E.B.B.*, II, 135.)

For Philip James Bailey see letter to R. H. Horne, Autumn, 1843, n. 4. For
W. J. Fox see letter to Miss Haworth, April, 1839, n. 9. Mrs. Jago was the wife
of Dr. Jago, an English doctor who, while visiting in Florence in 1847, attended
Mrs. Browning. (See *E.B.B.: Letters to Her Sister*, p. 52.) The Brownings met
Mr. and Mrs. David Ogilvy in Florence in 1847 and became very intimate
with them on a trip by *vettura* from Florence to Venice in 1851. (See Mrs.
David Ogilvy's short memoir of Mrs. Browning prefixed to F. Warne and Co.'s
edition of E. B. B.'s *Poems*, n. d.) Browning and Tennyson exchanged their
volumes of poetry from about this time to the end of their careers.

It was in 1852 that, through William Allingham, the Brownings first met
D. G. Rossetti (1828–82), a fact which makes the young Pre-Raphaelite one of
the latest of the friends in this list. The presentation copy of *Men and Women*
to John Ruskin (1819–1900) drew from him what Browning called "a dear, too
dear, and good letter." (*Letters*, ed. Hood, p. 42.) Browning's significant defense against Ruskin's charges of obscurity and unintelligibility was made in
a letter to Ruskin dated December 10, 1855. (See W. G. Collingwood, *The Life
and Work of John Ruskin* [London and Boston, 1893], I, 232–235.) For Reuben
Browning see letter of June 12, 1850, n. 1. It is apparent that this list is made
up almost entirely of Browning's oldest, most intimate friends and relatives.

the printers'. Vol II. Page 9. Line 8. you painting—*read*, I painting.
Page 47, line 12 altallissimo—*read* alt to altissimo.[5]
[Morgan]

To Edward Chapman
102 Rue de Grenelle, Faubourg St. Germain.
Wednesday E[venin]g, [December 5, 1855] [1]

My dear Chapman,

Don't think me ungrateful for your prompt and kind note of some three weeks since—I expected to have more to write about: and even now, what can I tell you? I see Galignani's table covered with papers, and a choice article in here and there a one about, what you call, the Twins; [2] the *Examiner* being the best,—as for the worst, there's no saying *that*. The serious notices are to come, it is to be hoped. How this style of thing helps or hinders the *sale*, is what you must counsel me about. Do please let me know anything you can.

Have you got your cheque from Fields? I have had another—indeed, two other American letters, guaranteeing the £75 on my wife's proof-sheets. I answered Fields' note (the enclosure in your letter) on purpose to say that you had paid me and that he must pay you—and so he has done, I trust.

Will you have the goodness to give Mrs. Jameson (who will give or send this), a copy of *Men and Women?* And finally,—you remember that notable Treatise on Bible-genealogies,[3] for which all the

5. A more substantial list of corrections for *Men and Women* may be found in a letter to D. G. Rossetti written two days before this letter to Chapman. (*Letters,* ed. Hood, p. 42.) The first correction here refers to "Andrea del Sarto," the second to "Old Pictures in Florence."

1. This letter, with only Wednesday for date, is linked with the next letter to Chapman dated December 17, 1855. In the present letter Browning says that "Mrs. Jameson . . . will give or send this." In the letter of December 17 he states: "I wrote to you more than a week ago by Mrs. Jameson." The Wednesday "more than a week"—and presumably Browning means less than two weeks—before December 17 was, for 1855, December 5.

2. This reference is obviously not to Browning's poem called "The Twins" but to some unidentified review to match the *Examiner.*

3. It may be that after William Berry's death in 1851 publishers sought the right to reissue his *Genealogia Sacra; or, Scripture Tables, Compiled from the Holy Bible* (London, 1819). There is no evidence, however, that the book was reissued nor that any other treatise on Bible genealogies was published by Longman or Murray. See below, letter of May 23, 1856, n. 2.

Publishers were tearing each other to pieces just when I left London—you never mentioned whether Longman or Murray proved the happy man. Well, I send you a fairer and improved copy of the same, which the author is desirous to substitute for the one in your possession ⁴—that's all. I write in haste—but have really said my say—and Mrs. Jameson waits.

Ever yours sincerely,

Robert Browning

I ought to add—(and it may incite your good nature to a speedier reply) that I shall leave this house on or about the 15 current, for what place is yet uncertain.

[Morgan]

To Edward Chapman

Paris, 3 Rue du Colysée

Dec. 17, '55.

My dear Chapman,

I wrote to you more than a week ago ¹ by Mrs. Jameson, but rather think, or am sure indeed, that she arrived in London too fatigued for anything but going on to bed at Ealing. By this time you may have received my note, and, above, behold my address. We are warmer and better off. I was anxious to know if Fields had duly reimbursed you; it can hardly be otherwise, however. Next, if the book continued to do well, and how well; the notices will come, I suppose, next month. Meanwhile don't take to heart the zoological utterances I have stopped my ears against at Galignani's of late. "Whoo-oo-oo-oo" mouths the big monkey—"Whee-ee-ee-ee" squeaks the little monkey and such a dig with the end of my umbrella as I should give the brutes if I couldn't keep my temper, and consider how they miss their nut[s] and gingerbread! ² I see how

4. The fairer and improved copy is probably a corrected copy of *Men and Women.*

1. Probably December 5; see preceding letter.

2. The "zoological utterances" were doubtless of a kind with the following excerpt from a review of *Men and Women* in the *Athenaeum* on November 17, 1855. "These volumes contain some fifty poems, which will make the least imaginative man think, and the least thoughtful man grieve. Who will not grieve over energy wasted and power misspent,—over fancies chaste and noble, so overhung by the 'seven veils' of obscurity, that we can oftentimes be only sure that fancies exist?" This, then, was the official greeting to Browning's bid for popularity. Browning's "dig with the end of my umbrella," though delayed

you have taken care and advertised properly, if I am any judge of that. I am sure your part has been well performed, however it may be with mine.

The notice in the *R. des deux Mondes* will be for Jan. 1, I believe; the delay was thro' the indisposition of my proper critic (a first-rate man)—and my own choice to wait for him rather than let the thing be done by another person, who had actually set to work and translated a piece or two, but I wanted my own man. He would no more suffer me to see a word of his performance, to correct a syllable of his version, than do a far meaner thing, being altogether a noble fellow, but judge whether *he* finds the writing unintelligible,—he, a Frenchman! [3]

Do please let me hear from you as soon as you can. My wife has suffered sadly from cold and vile rooms, but this place will make amends, we hope.

Ever yours very sincerely,

[Morgan]   Robert Browning.

To Edward Chapman

Paris, 3 Rue du Colisée.
Jan. 17, [1856]

Dear Chapman,

I received your letter of letters yesterday—all about nothing or next to it. The "immediate" fellow won't get an autograph out of me by his dodge, I can tell him. Ask Mr. Bailey if *his* experience confirms my surmise.[1] Fields says the book was to appear on the

---

for 20 years, was eventually given to the critic-brutes in the *Pacchiarotto* volume of 1876. (See K. L. Knickerbocker, "Browning and His Critics," *Sewanee Review* [July, 1935].)

3. It is not to be wondered that Browning wanted to reserve the *Revue des deux mondes* for a review by his sympathetic understanding friend Joseph Milsand. As early as November 15 Mrs. Browning had reported to her sister that "they are making translations of nearly half of them [poems of *Men and Women*] for the 'Revue des deux Mondes,' and Mr. Milsand told me quietly that he considered the poems 'superhuman'—mark that! only superhuman." (*E.B.B.: Letters to Her Sister*, p. 233.)

1. This sentence is scribbled in at the top of the page. Exactly what surmise Browning wanted Bailey (probably Philip James Bailey, author of *Festus*) to confirm is not quite clear. Possibly it had something to do with what Browning thought a "dodge" to obtain his autograph—a none too helpful guess since the " 'immediate' fellow" and his trick have both been lost sight of.

10th December,[2] sending some outrageous praises—preliminary from papers he had supplied with early copies. He mentions having sent you the money, and behaves handsomely altogether. This last phrase goes to somebody's heart, I hope, who has left me these two months without a word about the well or ill doing of my poems. Now do, do pray, dear Chapman, let us have the Christmas account to put a little life and heart into the end of this bleak month. I have read heaps of critiques at Galignani's, mostly stupid and spiteful, self-contradicting and contradictory of each other. What effect such "rot" would have on me, in the case of the book being somebody else's, I know exactly, but how it works with the reading public, you must tell me if I am ever to know. I suppose we are not at the end of them, and the best comes last, it is to be hoped. Your four reviews arrived safely—many thanks for them. *The British Quarterly* was just what I had not seen and would have lost most by missing.[3] I am a little curious to know what thing that is in the *Rambler*, a R[oman] Catholic mag[azine].[4] I have not seen the *Spec-*

2. Fields was the publisher of the American edition of *Men and Women*. See letter of October 31, 1855, and n. 2.

3. See *British Quarterly*, XXIII (January, 1856), 151–180, for the most laudatory of all the notices of *Men and Women*.

4. Browning was interested in the *Rambler* review because of what it might say of "Bishop Blougram's Apology," a partial portrait of Cardinal Wiseman who, in October, 1850, had been created Archbishop of Westminster and head of the Catholic Church in England. (For a complete discussion of "Bishop Blougram" see DeVane, *Browning Handbook*, pp. 213–216.) As early as 1840 Wiseman had been created bishop with the title "Melipotamus *in partibus infidelium*." Browning's lines in "Bishop Blougram" (ll. 972–974)

> . . . styled *in partibus*
> *Episcopus, nec non*—(the deuce knows what
> It's changed to by our novel hierarchy),

point directly to Cardinal Wiseman as the model from which the main features of Blougram were drawn. Browning was right in being curious, for the reviewer, Cardinal Wiseman himself, had much to say of "Bishop Blougram." A representative excerpt follows: "It is scandalous in Mr. Browning *first* to show so plainly *whom* he means, when he describes an English Catholic bishop, once bishop *in partibus*, now a member of our 'novel hierarchy,' one who 'plays the part of Pandulph,' one, too, who, though an Englishman, was born in a foreign land; and *then* to go on sketching a fancy portrait which is abominably untrue, and to draw this person not only as an arch-hypocrite, but also as the frankest of fools. It is bad enough to assign a heap of disgusting qualities to a Catholic bishop in the abstract,—though Catholics are too much accustomed to such impertinence to have their equanimity grievously disturbed; but it is far worse to attribute the hypocrisy and scepticism that he has forged in his own brain to any person whom he designates so plainly." (*Rambler, A*

tator letters,[5] and many others; if you ever like to snip out a column of these and post it hither, it will be kind in you. But kinder to ask forthwith your kind nephew [6] to make out our bill and post us *that;* so call, call, while the good thought is hot in you and take the thanks beforehand of,

Dear Chapman,
Yours faithfully,

[Morgan]   Robert Browning

To Edward Chapman

Paris, 3 Rue du Colisée,
Feb. 6, '56

My dear Chapman,

I begin to think I must have missed getting some letter of yours in reply to my last; the Post is at fault sometimes. Do pray have the goodness to let me see the Christmas account, of the old books, at any rate. As for *Men and Women* not a word have you written since the pleasant one three months ago. Here's my wife working hard at such an admirable poem—though I say it that should not say it [1]—

Catholic Journal and Review, N.S., V [January, 1856], 54–71). It is a curious fact that Cardinal Wiseman in this review writes and argues with the urbanity and facile erudition of Browning's "Bishop Blougram." (For a different opinion see W. Ward, *The Life and Times of Cardinal Wiseman* [London, 1898], II, 258, in which the author denies the resemblance.)

5. It is not clear to what *Spectator* letters Browning refers. From the context one would first suppose that they were letters referring to him or his poetry. A search of the *Spectator* has revealed no such references. There is another possibility. Browning has just referred to the *Rambler*, for he suspected that the *Rambler* would discuss his "Bishop Blougram." Now, "Bishop Blougram" contains a very powerful passage (beginning with l. 453) about war and a direct reference to the Crimean War which began in March, 1854. Possibly Chapman's last letter had referred to the publicity being given to the scandal surrounding the famous charge at Balaklava on October 25, 1854. This explanation seems tenable, for the *Spectator* for December 22, 1855 contained controversial letters concerned with the scandal.

6. Chapman's nephew was Frederick Chapman, who became a partner in the business upon the death of Hall.

1. The statement, frequently made, that the Brownings did not see each other's poetry until it was ready for the printer is shown here and elsewhere to be an exaggeration of fact. The "admirable poem," of course, is *Aurora Leigh*. In a letter to Hatty Hosmer (March 27, 1856) Browning confides that his wife "has worked like a spirit at her poem" and adds: "I have read the first six books, all transcribed and corrected in two months." (*Harriet Hosmer: Letters and Memories*, ed. Cornelia Carr [London, 1913], p. 65.)

and you ought to do your best to encourage her and yours ever faithfully

R. Browning.

I had a letter from America two days since telling us fabulous things about the sale there; to be sure, it was not from Fields himself, though the writer is his friend and intimate. I had a capital letter from Forster the other day, one from Carlyle, three from Ruskin.[2] Now for yours!

[Morgan]

To Edward Chapman

Paris, Rue du Colisée 3.
[April 12, 1856].[1]

My dear Chapman,

Will you have the goodness to give the Bearer of this, Miss Meriton White,[2] a copy of *Men and Women?*

I received a magazine last month which I ought to have thanked you for at the time. Also, I received your cheque thro' my uncle, all very duly and pleasantly. How do our affairs go on? Any news

2. The letter from Forster has not come to light. The one from Carlyle, dated December 4, 1855, is available. (See *Letters of Thomas Carlyle to John Stuart Mill, John Sterling, and Robert Browning*, ed. Alexander Carlyle [London, 1923], pp. 294–296. For Browning's reply, dated January 23, 1856,) see *Letters*, ed. Hood, pp. 43–45. The correspondence with Ruskin began with the exchange over the merits and demerits of *Men and Women*. Most of this correspondence, if extant, has not been made available in print. But see W. G. Collingwood, *Life and Work of John Ruskin*, I, 232–235, for part of it, including Browning's defense of his poetry.

1. The date of this letter is settled by a comparison of its fourth paragraph with a paragraph in one of Mrs. Browning's letters dated April 11, 1856. Mrs. Browning wrote to her sister: "Robert is going tonight with Lady Monson to see Ristori at the Italian play. He was at Dickens' last night and heard her much depreciated by himself and Macready who is in Paris for a few days." (*E.B.B.: Letters to Her Sister*, p. 244.) From this reference one may conclude that Browning's letter should be dated April 12.

2 Jessie Meriton White (1832–1906) came to know the Brownings in Florence during the Fifties. Mrs. Browning disapproved so thoroughly of the politics of Miss White, who was an advocate of Mazzini and an outspoken opponent of Napoleon III, that she wrote in February, 1858: "So indignant I feel with Mazzini and all who name his name and walk in his steps, that I couldn't find it in my heart to write (as I was going to do) to that poor bewitched Jessie on her marriage. Really, when I looked at the pen, *I couldn't move it*." (*Letters of E.B.B.*, II, 277.) Miss White married Alberto Mario in 1858. For details of the Browning-Madame Mario controversy see below, letter of May, 1859, and n. 13.

would be news indeed, but I hear from America, every now and then, and Fields wrote the other day, repeating that there was a great success there,—funny, if it were so, would it not be?

My wife's poem gets on capitally; I can answer—that is, to those who mind what I say—for six books, of between 7 and 8000 lines. The other two will be ready in time—one is about done in fact.[3] We hope to be in London in June.

The weather is true Spring. Many noticeable folks are here. I spent the evening before last at Dickens' with Macready. Milnes, my old friend, was here for a pleasant fortnight. But the great sight just now is our Italian Ristori in *Medea*.[4] You'll have it in London, I dare say.

Goodbye, my dear Chapman, I don't tell you much but you tell me nothing at all,—so, reform. With kind remembrances to your nephew,

Yours faithfully,
Robert Browning

Since writing this, I have been instructed to plague you with a commission from my wife: will you have the goodness to get Bossut's

3. *Aurora Leigh,* originally intended as a poem in eight books, was eventually extended to nine. The composition of the poem apparently continued until the summer. The manuscript of *Aurora Leigh* bears this inscription: "Read this book, this divine book, Wednesday night, July 9th, '56.—R. B. 39 Devonshire Place." The manuscript is in the Widener Library at Harvard.

4. Dickens had an apartment in the Avenue des Champs Elysées not far from the Brownings. The argument at Dickens' apartment over the merits of the Italian actress Adelaide Ristori must have been particularly interesting because of the background of personalities involved. Ristori (1822–1906) had in 1855 taken Paris by storm, in the role of Alfieri's *Myrrha*. (*Encyclopaedia Britannica*, 14th ed., "Ristori.") She had returned to Paris on April 8, 1856 to play the title role in Legouvi's *Medea*. The play ran for 19 evenings and later, as Browning predicted, opened in London at the Lyceum Theatre on June 4. (*Adelaide Ristori: an Autobiography* [Boston, 1888], p. 197.) Most of the English colony in Paris saw the play. "Dickens and Macready . . . pronounced it hopelessly bad." (John Forster, *Life of Charles Dickens,* ed. J. W. T. Ley [London, 1928], p. 612.) Mrs. Sartoris and Mrs. Jameson extolled it. The possessive phrase used by Browning, "our Italian Ristori," indicates where his sympathies lay. One may easily imagine Browning's delight in defending the feminine opinion and in taking issue with Macready, the actor-manager who had some ten years before produced with great pain—to himself, to the author, and to all persons concerned—Browning's *Strafford* and, six years later, *A Blot in the 'Scutcheon*. Mrs. Browning, however, reports that "Robert gives his verdict on Ristori midway between the contending parties. She has sensibility, he says, and not imagination." (*E.B.B.: Letters to Her Sister,* p. 244.)

French Grammar and Miss Corner's *Child's History of France*,[5] and send them here by book post? Not forgetting to put the whole to my account.

[Morgan]

To Edward Chapman

Paris, 3 Rue du Colisée.
April 21, '56

My dear Chapman,

We are very glad that another edition of E. B. B.'s *Poems* is wanted, and have turned over the various matters in our minds which you desire us to consider. We think it will be best to include "Casa Guidi" as you suggest. My wife has various poems written in Italy amounting to some thousand lines. They are in the natural advance (*I* believe) of whatever she writes now as compared with her early works; and it was her intention to make them the *nucleus* of a new volume that should succeed the *novel in verse* she is about to publish. But that novel will be a serious affair, and quite enough to occupy the public mind, or the bit of it which it bends on such trifles as poems, for a year at least; so that, say she publishes the novel next November, there would be eighteen months and over for the new volume to bear in quietness. Now, suppose we print these novelties in the third volume of the new edition, after "Casa Guidi," *as* novelties, don't you fancy it would *start* the thing advantageously,—almost as a new work, indeed? Could you not so represent the case as to get a handsome lot disposed of by the trade-subscription? Otherwise, the poems would be rather thrown away, for they ought to be attended to as new, and particularly new. The three-volume form would seem to be far better than any addition to the present size of the books,—though, from our being abroad, the contents were unequally distributed, and Vol. 1st has so many pages short of Vol. 2nd that I verily believe "Casa Guidi" would cram in there, were it advisable, which it is *not*, I am inclined to hold with you. As for the price, your own judgment must guide you there; we have a certain hankering after low prices, certainly. My wife has a notion that there is a way, and an advantage attending it, of publishing such poems as hers volume by volume, so as to allow

5. M. C. Bossut, *French Grammar* (London, 1847); Julia Corner, *Child's History of France* (London, 1852).

people to buy by degrees; they used to print Wordsworth so, she thinks. What do you say to that? [1]

I will tell you all I can about the "Novel" so that you may consider these arrangements with reference to its publication. It will be in eight books, of about 1200 lines each—say altogether between nine and ten thousand lines—not more nor less. Six of these I have read, the seventh is done, and the eighth doing. We shall hope to arrive in London all right and ready on June 16th and if you concert with Bradbury [2] beforehand, we can begin printing at once and get done as expeditiously as possible, though we must take all proper pains. My wife prefers it to go in one volume, if it can be managed. For the new edition, we can begin directly if you please, and get done before setting about the other. You have only to, 1st, send us at once a copy of E. B. B.'s *Poems* and "Casa Guidi." We will correct it throughout, and make a more equal distribution of the contents; 2dly to engage Bradbury to print away with as much expedition as possible, letting us have good *batches* of proofs at a time, which, I believe, I can make arrangements with my uncle to forward here,—for we *must* see the proofs. We will get rid of our part of the business duly and promptly, so that by the time the present edition is exhausted you can thrust a portentous *Fourth* into the purchaser's hand; 3dly you have to be so good as to tell us your mind on all this as soon as is convenient. I will write by this post to my uncle to know how far he can assist us in relieving us from the charges of carriage; but at the worst there is the book-post and the opportunities of friends' going and coming.

As to my own Poems—they must be left to Providence and that fine sense of discrimination which I never cease to meditate upon and admire in the public: they cry out for new things and when you furnish them with what they cried for, "it's *so* new," they grunt. The half-dozen people who know and could impose their opinions

---

1. All the plans suggested here by Browning were greatly simplified by Chapman, who preferred to reprint the third edition of Mrs. Browning's *Poems* and, by the addition of *Casa Guidi Windows,* to issue it in three volumes instead of two. (See Browning's note to Chapman, May 12, 1856.) The fourth edition duly appeared in the summer of this year. Moxon had published Wordsworth's *Poetical Works,* a volume at a time, in six monthly installments. (See advertisement in the *Athenaeum* for October 22, 1836.) Browning was later to use monthly installments for *The Ring and the Book.*

2. Bradbury, of Bradbury and Evans, printed all Chapman and Hall books.

on the whole sty of grunters say nothing to *them* (I don't wonder) and speak so low in my own ear that it's lost to all intents and purposes. Now, is not Ruskin a layer-down of the law in matters of art? Then, see what he says of a poem of mine, printed twelve years ago and more, in this fourth volume, but nobody will snip that round into a neat little paragraph, and head it "Ruskin on Browning," and stick it among the "News of the Week," "Topics of the Day," as the friendly method is! [3] It's a shame, ye public,—which wouldn't so much signify if you had taken the Redan!

I write this witty letter with a gum-boil big as my thumb's top just over my left eye-tooth; it's conducive to a bland treatment of the people's stupidities!

Ever yours very sincerely,
Robert Browning

I meant to apply to my uncle only with respect to the parcels of *books;* the *proofs* go for next to nothing, I am told, if described as proofs at the Post-office here. How is it with you?

[Morgan]

To Edward Chapman

3 Rue du Colisée, [Paris]
May 12. [1856].

My dear Chapman,

Here is the *1st Vol* complete; the other two of much the same size, as we have calculated, shall follow directly. We take your opin-

---

3. Browning's pride in his wife's popularity knew no shadow of jealousy. Yet, the contrast of the popular demand for a fourth edition of her *Poems* with the silence greeting any work of his, must have been galling. His chief complaint is directed usually at obtuse reviewers, "grunters," "a verminous tribe," "gooseys and ganders." In this letter, however, he is displeased with his friends, "the half-dozen people who know." Ruskin's pamphlet on Pre-Raphaelitism had saved, very recently, the group of young painters from the carping of the professional critics. In Vol. IV of *Modern Painters* which appeared in February, 1856, Ruskin quoted nearly the whole of "The Bishop Orders His Tomb at St. Praxed's Church" and praised it unstintedly; but no one took the trouble—not even Chapman—to see that the praise reached the public through the gossip columns of the weekly literary magazines. Ruskin had presented Vol. III to Browning "with affectionate and respectful regards" in January, 1856. Apparently Browning bought Volume IV, which contains no inscription. "The Bishop Orders His Tomb at St. Praxed's Church" was first published as "The Tomb at St. Praxed's" in *Hood's Magazine* in March, 1845.

ion on all the points. Let there be, therefore, three volumes, at the price you prefer, and no new poems whatever.[1]

I write in great haste, to secure the good offices of a friend starting for London.

Yours very truly,

[Morgan]
Robt. Browning.

To Edward Chapman

Paris, 3 Rue du Colisée,
May 23, '56.

Dear Chapman,

We sent you, more than a week ago, the first vol. of the next three-vol. edition; the second will go by the next opportunity, probably on Monday; [1] the third is nearly ready, so Bradbury must do his part, for my wife is anxious to get done with this business before beginning the other of the new poem.

I write now to ask you to do me the favour of trying to get me, as soon as possible, a book I particularly want: Berry's *Genealogical Tables of Sacred History*. He was author of the *Encyclopaedia Heraldica*, belonged to the Herald Office, and died about 1851.[2] It is a common book. If you will get it and send it to "R. B. 3 R. du Colisée, Paris, care of Reuben Browning, Esq., Rothschilds', New Court, St. Swithin's Lane" in one parcel with a copy of my *Men and Women* (and any notes etc.—not "presentation copies"—you may have), it will be forwarded at once, and by the same conveyance you might dispatch copy and proofs were they ready. Any news? I heard from an American friend of the great sale of my things there. Goodbye. I am obliged to break up the gossip I was beginning.

Yours very sincerely,

[Morgan]
Robert Browning.

1. See letter to Chapman for April 21, 1856.
1. Browning was writing on a Friday.
2. William Berry (1774–1851) was, as Browning notes, author of *Encyclopaedia Heraldica, or Complete Dictionary of Heraldry*. It was published in four large quarto volumes from 1828 to 1840. The volume, a large folio, which Browning requests is Berry, *Genealogia Sacra; or, Scripture Tables, Compiled from the Holy Bible*.

To Leigh Hunt [1]

Aug. 20. [1856] 39 Devonshire Place

My dear Mr. Hunt—Master Hunt, that is, as they would have addressed you in Shakespeare's time.[2] I did indeed get your letter and foolishly said nothing of the delight it gave me, from the fancy that I was to see you face to face so soon, and that there are certain points on which one is too sensitive to bear repeated touching—you put a flower in my breast which I hardly dare look at, much less finger. With respect to your own change of the evening, it also seemed obvious that you were *"padrone"* (as we Tuscans say) to give us what you would, when you would. We never expected you when the rain set in: and comes this good news of your purpose for next Tuesday week.[3] Be sure that we shall rejoice in seeing you. One thing only, one particular call from the country (*i.e. to* the country) might prevent it. In that just-possible case, you should be duly apprised.[4]

I write for my wife, or even more for her than myself—but she will soon equal me in knowledge of you. Of my books—I dare only reply to your "third" note on them, that I know they err in obscure and imperfect expression,—wishing it were not so, and trying always for the future it may be less so. And now I will forget all failure in happiest success, and frankly take the joy you give me of esteeming myself your grateful and affectionate friend,

[New York Public Library]   Robert Browning.

1. Leigh Hunt (1784–1859) had reviewed *Paracelsus* for the *Examiner* in 1835, and though the criticism of parts of the poem was somewhat caustic, the review led to a fairly warm relationship between the poets. It is probable, however, that the present letter with its formal "Mr. Hunt" is the first from Browning to Hunt and that it was occasioned by Hunt's praise of *Men and Women*. This letter is written from the London home of John Kenyon which the Brownings occupied from late June until late August, and again in October, in 1856.

2. Browning curiously insists upon the aptness of this beginning: "Dear Leigh Hunt—(It is hard to write, but you bade me do so: yet I had better say 'Master Hunt,' as they used to call Webster or Ford.")" (See *Leigh Hunt's Correspondence,* ed. Thornton Hunt [London, 1862], II, 264. The letter, dated October 6, 1857, has been republished in *Letters,* ed. Hood, p. 47.)

3. September 2.

4. The "particular call" came August 25, and the Brownings set off with Arabel Barrett for Ventnor, Isle of Wight, the country place of E. B. B.'s father. From Ventnor they moved to the northern part of the island, to West Cowes, the place of John Kenyon who was trying to recuperate from what proved to be his last illness. After his return to London Browning wrote to Hunt on October 3, 1856, attempting to make another engagement. (See *Letters,* ed. Hood, p. 45.)

To Edward Chapman

39 Devonshire Place
[*ca.* October, 1856.] [1]

Dear Chapman,

"Evelyn Hope" and "Two in the Campagna" are poems of mine, not my wife's and are to be found in *Men and Women:* in vols. 1 and 2. I send the proofs by the book-post. (Keep going!)

Yours faithfully,
R. Browning.

The poems are wanted for Mr. Wilmot's collection, no doubt.[2]

[Morgan]

To Edward Chapman

Florence, Dec. 2, '56.

Dear Chapman,

I receive by today's post *Aurora Leigh*—from you or yours, I conjecture—but no word of comment. There is always such a thing to fear in these parts as a letter's miscarrying—has that been so? If not, it's a shame of you, black and burning, not to have been at that trouble. But a letter from Mr. Procter comes too, and speaks of your needing to go to press very soon with another edition, and the book we receive *may* be sent for presumable corrections. In this case, print tomorrow, if you please. There is nothing whatever to correct, that we are able to see at present, the book having been *settled* for some time to come while we were in London for that purpose. My wife made up her mind to it as it *is,* and for the present, as I say, cannot reconsider the subject. All the "modern" passages, illustrations, are vitally necessary, she thinks,—and I think quite

1. The Brownings were at 39 Devonshire Place, Kenyon's home, from late June to late August, 1856, and again in October just before they set out for Florence on October 23. This letter, therefore, might have been written during either of these periods. If the note was written during the earlier period the proofs are those of the fourth edition of Mrs. Browning's *Poems;* if during the later period, the proofs are those of *Aurora Leigh.*

2. The Reverend Robert Aris Wilmot published a collection of poems called *Poets of the Nineteenth Century* (1857), a volume beautifully illustrated by Tenniel, Millais, the brothers Dalziel, and others. "Two in the Campagna" and "Evelyn Hope" occupy pp. 326 and 329, respectively. Mrs. Browning is represented by her poem, "Wine of Cyprus," p. 331. Browning, up to this point in his career, had not often had his poems reproduced in popular anthologies; "Ben Karshook's Wisdom," however, had been published in the *Keepsake* in 1854.

as strongly,—and could not be detached without capital injury to the rest of the poem. And for the rest, there would seem to be no verbal errors to signify; however we will look to that, and let you know or not, as it may seem worth while. But the principal thing is to pray you not to keep people waiting a moment in waiting for further notice from us (*Us*—I am the church-organ-bellows' blower that talked about *our* playing, but you know what I do in the looking after commas and dots to i's).

I saw the *Athenaeum, Globe,* and *Daily News,* that's all, hearing of eulogy from the *Lit. Gaz.* and blackguardism from the "Press"; all like those night-men who are always emptying their cart at my door, and welcome when I remember that after all they don't touch our bread with their beastly hands, as they used to do. Don't you mind them, and leave me to rub their noses in their own filth some fine day.[1]

Ever yours faithfully,
Robert Browning.

1. This, one of the bitterest of Browning's letters, was called forth by a combination of circumstances. Basically it is an expression of the mood brought on by the unexpected failure of *Men and Women*. Many though lesser pinpricks stirred the irritability of the poet. For one thing, Chapman was not the man to put in soft words of encouragement when they were needed, words which Browning thought his wife deserved while she was struggling midway in the composition of *Aurora Leigh*. Now, with the poem published, it became a shame "black and burning" that Chapman had forwarded the volume without a word of comment. It was disturbing to think that this indifference of the publisher might be an augury of the general critical response to "this divine book." The review in the *Athenaeum* should have been reassuring. Mrs. Browning is called "our greatest English poetess of any time," a measured statement, after all, when one considers the dearth of competition. The seven-column review, however, is generally laudatory. Browning, nevertheless, the "church-organ-bellows' blower," may have paused in exasperation over such strictures as this: "In brief we regret to declare that Mrs. Browning's longest and most matured effort . . . is in its argument unnatural and in its form infelicitous." It is hardly likely that the *Globe* and *Daily News* pictured *Aurora Leigh* in a more favorable light. Browning naturally was apprehensive. But *Aurora Leigh* succeeded greatly.

Mrs. Browning died and the long years passed. The neglected Browning became the favored one, the sought-after. Then as volume tumbled over volume during the Seventies, each a craggy difficulty for the reviewers of those years, the poet began to hear spiteful words again, like harsh echoes from the Forties and Fifties. In 1876 he wrote *Pacchiarotto And How He Worked in Distemper,* rough, deliberately tousled verses assaulting with the contents of a bed pot (*skoramis*) all the critical night men who stood within range of his displeasure.

Please send a copy of *Aurora Leigh* to Joseph Arnould, Esq. 35 Westbourne Place, Eaton Square.²

[Morgan]

To Mrs. William Burnet Kinney ¹

[Casa Guidi, Florence]
Friday m[ornin]g. [December 7, 1856] ²

My dear Mrs. Kinney,

You are always most kind and good: had I been aware of Mr. Kinney's calling to-day, I would have seen him gladly. My wife will be grateful for your sympathy, and happy to say so whenever she is able—just now she suffers too acutely. This has been a sudden misfortune for which she was all but absolutely unprepared. And even now it hardly seems to be more than a dream. She is better, on the whole, than I should have supposed likely, and I have no fear for the result.³

With renewed thanks to dear Mr. Kinney and yourself

Believe me,

Yours affectionately ever,

[Yale]   Robert Browning.

It is an interesting coincidence that John Kenyon died and left the Brownings £11,000 just a few days after the date of this letter in which Browning notes that the night men "don't touch our bread . . . as they used to do." Since the birth of Pen (March 9, 1849) Kenyon had settled upon the poets £100 a year. This, with the small income from Mrs. Browning's funds, plus some royalties from Mrs. Browning's books and a small amount from Browning's, constituted the yearly amount available for living expenses. The total, until after the Kenyon bequest, must have been small.

2. Joseph Arnould, an old friend, was one of the "Colloquials" of the Thirties. (See *Browning and Domett, passim.*)

1. Elizabeth Clementine Kinney (1810–89) was the daughter of David Lou Dodge. By her first marriage, to Edmund Burke Stedman, she had one child, Edmund Clarence Stedman the poet and writer. In 1847 she became the wife of William Burnet Kinney (1799–1880), journalist and diplomat, who served as American chargé to the court of Sardinia in Turin from 1850 to 1853. When his term of office ended the Kinneys moved to Florence and struck up an acquaintance with the Brownings immediately.

2. The death of John Kenyon, "the sudden misfortune" to which Browning refers below, occurred Monday, December 3. The Friday following was December 7, the most probable date of this note.

3. Mrs. Kinney, unaware of Kenyon's death, had apparently written appreciatively to Mrs. Browning about *Aurora Leigh*. Mrs. Browning was at first prostrated by the news of Kenyon's death and asked her husband to acknowledge Mrs. Kinney's letter. The same evening, however, Mrs. Browning had recovered sufficiently to write to Mrs. Kinney herself. (See *Letters of E.B.B.*, II, 244.)

To Edward Chapman

Florence, Jan. 5, '57.[1]

Dear Chapman,

I duly received your note of the 1st Nov., and you, no doubt, in the meantime were in possession of mine; so there was nothing more to say about the reprint of the Poem.[2] I perceive at last that it is announced as "nearly ready": that's well. I expected more reviews in the monthly magazines; they will follow, I suppose.

Do please let me have our account at the earliest possible moment. I shall be much poorer this year than last. (Dear Mr. Kenyon's generosity won't be available for twelve months.)[3] You have never told me a word about the new edition of E. B. B.'s *Poems*,—whether it was subscribed for, how it sells and the like: so I repeat,—the account, *do please!*

We have had a sad Christmas time, or indeed existence so far as we are concerned. Ruskin wrote at once: "I think *A[urora] L[eigh]* the greatest *poem* in the English language; unsurpassed by anything but Shakespeare, *not* surpassed by Shakespeare's *Sonnets*,—and therefore the greatest poem in the language. I write this, you see, very deliberately, straight, or nearly so, which is not common with me, for I am taking pains that you may not think, (nor anybody else) that I am writing in a state of excitement"—and now, yesterday, I had another letter "declaring my entire faith in it as the greatest poem in the English language—it has turned my head altogether and I can't talk of anything else"—and so on, again. I quote such passages from such a man, to show that I *do* feel touched and grateful when a man speaks, and do not suppose all critics to be wretched organ-grinding Ayton [4] and his like.

1. The Brownings were in Florence until late July of this year, then at Bagni di Lucca until October, at which time they returned to Florence for the remainder of 1857.

2. *Aurora Leigh* ran quickly through first and second editions and was ready for a third printing in March of this year.

3. It is to be inferred that the Brownings were poorer by £100 this year than in 1856, for presumably, with the death of Kenyon in December, 1856, the yearly allowance of £100 was suspended. Since the £11,000 inheritance from Kenyon was tied up legally for 12 months, the poets were forced to live in reduced circumstances during this period. This fact explains why all the letters to Chapman during 1857 contain requests for accounts and announcements of drafts. One may get a sketchy but fair idea of the meager returns from the Brownings' books by a careful examination of these financial negotiations.

4. Perhaps William Edmonstoune Aytoun (1813–65) whose "free and facile

The American Publisher sent his second installment like a man, and added that he and his select circle of friends had their own opinion that the poem was "a gospel," only that, which was the more meritoriously observed, inasmuch as he had not been able; even if so disposed, to take his cue from the English notices.[5]

My wife begs you to have the goodness to pack up five copies of *Aurora Leigh,* and one of E. B. B.'s *Poems,* and one of *Men and Women* and send them to us, via Leghorn, by the Liverpool steamer, paying whatever is to pay, and setting the same down to our account. Our address should be given:

Casa Guidi
1902 Via Maggio, Florence.

[Morgan]   [Signature cut off.]

To Edward Chapman

Florence, March 5, '57

Dear Chapman,

I cannot help thinking that some answer of yours to a note I sent you two months ago must have miscarried; it is so long as that since I wrote to beg for the Christmas account, which I was desirous to have *then,* and very desirous indeed to have *now.* I am also naturally anxious to hear something about the new Edition of *Aurora*—how many copies were printed and how many sold. You must not forget that we are no longer within a mile or so of each other; moreover that you promised to write now and then.

Our carnival is over, fine weather begins. How are you? and Forster? and Procter?

Thank you for the *Blackwood* and *North British* [1]—duly re-

---

pen enriched the pages of *Blackwood's Magazine"* from 1836 to 1865. Browning perhaps singled out Aytoun in this vehement way because of the review of *Aurora Leigh* in January, 1857. See letter to Chapman of March 5, 1857, n. 1.

5. The American publisher of *Aurora Leigh* was Charles Stephen Francis, president and co-owner with his brother of C. S. Francis and Co., a firm established in 1842 and dissolved in 1862. Mrs. Browning did her best to protect his rights in her poem by prefixing the following statement to the American edition: "Author's Edition: Having received what I consider to be sufficient remuneration for my poem 'Aurora Leigh,' from Mr. Francis, of New York, it is my earnest desire that his rights in this and future editions, may not be interfered with. Elizabeth Barrett Browning. London, October 21, 1856."

1. *Blackwood's Magazine,* LXXXI (January, 1857), 23–41, carried a long, gravely heavy review of *Aurora Leigh.* The *North British Review,* XXVI (February, 1857), 443–462, devoted most of its critical attention to the fourth

ceived both. (Did a letter accompany them?) Did I tell you that they paid for *Aurora* in America like men? And the success is great there, by all accounts.

My wife's kind regards and impatience go with those of

Yours faithfully ever,

[Morgan]   Robert Browning.

To Edward Chapman

Florence, Sat. March 21, '57

Dear Chapman,

You *are* late, as you acknowledge! But all the rest is very well. Quite right about the 3d edit[ion].[1] The cheque is a less safe way, I should think than a Draft on you for the same amount. I will use this, and, some fine day, draw on you for the remainder, if you please; if you don't please, say so, of course. The books are arrived at Leghorn, but I have not got them yet.[2] Will you do me the favor to get me *Instructions in the Art of Figure-Drawing* by C. H. Weigall—(a shilling pamphlet sold by Winsor and Newton, 38 Rathbone Place)[3]—and to post the same, open, to me, at your *very* earliest convenience? Another thing: will you be good enough to send *all* books, packets, and letters, etc. that may arrive, *to Miss Barrett,* 50 Wimpole St., as she will report on them. Kind remembrances from my wife. Do let us hear the news.

Yours faithfully,

[Morgan]   Robert Browning

To Edward Chapman

May 27, '57. Florence.

My dear Chapman,

I am going to draw on you this morning for the balance of our account—£44. 5. 10—at 30 days' date, so look out. Do, by way of payment of interest for the six months' use of that remarkable sum,

---

edition of Mrs. Browning's *Poems.* The articles in both magazines judicially balanced praise and mild censure.

1. Possibly a reference to the third printing of *Aurora Leigh.*

2. Books ordered in letter dated January 5, 1857.

3. *Instructions in Drawing, Figure Drawing, Shadows* issued serially 1852–56. This pamphlet was ordered possibly for Browning's own use, though one is inclined to believe that Pen, now aged eight, was to be submitted to its teachings.

tell us how things go on: when the new edition will be wanted, how the three volumes sell, and as much more news as you can put in the letter for nothing.

Will you have the goodness to send us the *Athenaeum* regularly, charging us duly with all expenses? I see it at the Reading Room, but my wife does not, and we want something of the kind.

Also have the goodness to send a copy of *Aurora Leigh* to

Miss Graham-Clarke [1]

Care of Miss Barrett

50 Wimpole St.

I am going to apprise Mr. Allingham that he will find a copy on application. Will you give it, if he calls?

Yours very sincerely,

Robert Browning

We got the packet of books etc. from Leghorn, also *National, Dublin,* and *Monthly Review.*[2] Should there present itself an opportunity don't omit to send us Procter's Book.[3]

[Morgan]

To Edward Chapman

Bagni di Lucca, Sept. 1, '57.

Dear Chapman,

Many thanks for your note and accounts, which, I agree with you in thinking very tolerable. I shall draw on you for part or the whole of the money one of these days, giving you due notice. Indeed, I will draw on you for £12, *now,* as a convenience to a servant of ours who wants to transmit so much to her family; so please, whenever

1. Miss Arabella Graham-Clarke was the sister of Mrs. Browning's mother, who was Mary Graham-Clarke. (See *E.B.B.: Letters to Her Sister,* Genealogical Table, facing p. viii.)

2. The new *National Magazine* contained in its first volume two items about Mrs. Browning, a review of *Aurora Leigh* on p. 315 and a poem by Dobell "To the Authoress of 'Aurora Leigh,'" on p. 331. In addition there is a medallion of Mrs. Browning on p. 313. The *Monthly Review,* edited by William Harrison Ainsworth, one of Chapman and Hall's authors, carried nothing in its pages about the Brownings until some six weeks after this letter was written. The *Dublin Magazine* for the months of this period has nothing about the Brownings.

3. Probably Barry Cornwall, *Dramatic Scenes,* illustrated by John Tenniel and others (London, 1857).

my order is presented, pay so much to "Ellen Wilson, or account of Elizabeth Romagnoli." [1]

I dare say you will have heard from Forster, that poor Lytton, who came here a month ago, was at once attacked by a gastric fever, laid in bed for three weeks and more, and then released in a sadly reduced state; he goes out now, but is carried up and down stairs. He was forbidden to receive letters, or, at least, be troubled with sending them; it is much on his mind that he has been utterly unable to attend to his "packet," which you refer to, and you will be sorry for the reason, now you know it.[2] All your books came safe, and you send the *Athenaeum* most satisfactorily. We have a delightful time of it here—everything green and cool. My wife is regaining strength. Please send the enclosed. "They have paid"!—like good fellows, tho' the delay looked ominous.[3] But as to delays, why—there are all sorts of such excuses at hand, eh? So no more at present from yours very faithfully,

Robert Browning

P. S. I don't understand what I ought to do in way of *stamping* the order for the £12; to be on the safe side, I shall write a bit of a note and ask you to give E. Wilson that sum. Will that not do?

[Morgan]

1. Elizabeth Wilson, simply Wilson in most of the references, was the servant brought from England by the Brownings. She married Browning's Italian manservant, Ferdinando Romagnuoli.

2. Robert Lytton went to Florence toward the end of May, 1857 to write a report on the political conditions in Italy, a kind of diplomatic service thesis to show his knowledge and grasp of foreign affairs. He fell ill on his arrival, and on invitation of the Brownings "moved to the Baths of Lucca, where he was nursed by the Brownings and their friend Miss Blagden. This illness ended in a dangerous attack of gastric fever, and his life for some time hung in the balance. . . . Not till January was he able to return to Florence to begin his studies in Italian." (*Personal and Literary Letters of Robert, First Earl of Lytton*, ed. Lady Betty Balfour [London, 1906], I, 85. For a good additional account of this period see *Letters from Owen Meredith . . . to Robert and Elizabeth Barrett Browning*, ed. A. B. and J. Lee Harlan, Jr. [Waco, Texas, 1936], pp. 136–144.) This last sentence quoted above cannot be right, for according to Browning (see below, letter to Chapman dated September 28, 1857) Lytton returned to Florence about September 12. (See also A. B. Harlan, *Owen Meredith, A Critical Biography of Robert, First Earl of Lytton* [New York, 1946], pp. 85–86.)

3. This is possibly a reference to a payment from an American publisher to Mrs. Browning for *Aurora Leigh*.

To Edward Chapman

Bagni di Lucca, Sept. 28, '57

Dear Chapman,

We leave this place, in a week or so, for Florence. You will be so kind, therefore, as to direct the *Athenaeums* to Florence. By the way, I had better mention the Reviews and Journals that we see there, so as to prevent you from sending them, in case of any article's appearance about *Aurora Leigh* etc.; they are,—*Blackwood,* the *Edinburgh, Quarterly,* and *Westminster.* We can read all these, and one dose is enough. (N.B. Our own *Revista di Firenze* of last month [1] has got a long article with translations, but we have not read it yet.)

On the 11th, I drew on you, thro' Mrs. Cordon,[2] of this place, for £40, at 30 days' date, payable therefore next 11th October. As soon as I get to Florence I shall draw for the remainder, thro' Philipson (if necessary I may draw part of it before I leave this place, but I don't think I shall.)

Poor Lytton left a fortnight ago—better but sadly reduced. I hope he is getting right at Florence.[3] I wish you would write us a word of news,—at least of our own news.

[Signature removed]

Please send *Rollo's Novels* [4] by post as before.
[Morgan]

To Edward Chapman

Bagni di Lucca, Oct. 5, '57

Dear Chapman,

We return to Florence tomorrow,[1] but having a place in an envelope to spare, I will say that I wrote to you a few days ago, and that, since then, I have drawn on you for £20, payable next Second of November. My drafts have been therefore:

1. We have been unable to find a file of this review.
2. Hostess at Alla Villa where the Brownings were staying.
3. Lytton returned to his work on Italian affairs and with a two months' extension of time was able to return to England in March, 1858, for his examination. (See *Letters from Owen Meredith,* ed. A. B. and J. ↑ Harlan, p. 120.)
4. See letters of January 11, 1855 and January 4, 1858, both to Chapman.
1. The return was actually on October 7.

Sept. 1. To Madam Romagnoli—£12.0.0
" 11. Bill to Mrs. Cordon— 40.".'
Oct. 2. " " " " — 20.".'

leaving you still accountable to me for £38, *minus* three-pence (to which amount I shall overdraw, in consideration to the Italian clerks' brains,—unless you please rather to consider it as handsome interest for the two months' waiting).[2] I shall draw for this when I get to Florence, at a month's date.

What news? Won't you say a word? Post waits, or I could add something.

Ever yours faithfully,

[Morgan]   R. Browning

To Edward Chapman

Florence, Jan. 4, '58.[1]

Dear Chapman,

A Happy New-Year to you! Please carry into effect a similar wish for myself (such as I am sure you entertain) by sending hither the Christmas account. Not a word have I heard of your goings-on since last "half." Do pray behave better this time, or I shall be confirmed in a suspicion I have that Chapman has long since dissolved partnership with Hall, Virtue, and Co.[2]

You were to send us *Rollo's Travels in Europe.*[3] Will you please do so? Also, a copy of *Aurora Leigh*—also one of that thing about "Spirit-Drawings" by Wilkinson which you are about to publish?[4]

2. The sum of £110 itemized here represents, apparently, the full royalties on the fourth edition of Mrs. Browning's *Poems* and on the two editions of *Aurora Leigh.*

1. The Brownings were in Florence until late June, 1858, when they set out upon extensive travels. They went to Paris by way of Marseilles, Lyons, and Dijon. They remained in Paris during two weeks of July and were at Le Havre from July 20 to September 20, when they returned to Paris for a stay until October 12. From October 12 to 21 they were on their leisurely way back to Florence. On November 21 they left Florence for a five-day journey by vettura to Rome, where they remained until May, 1859.

2. The name of another London publishing firm.

3. Doubtless requisitioned as preparation for the tour with Pen which was to begin in June.

4. *Spirit Drawings: A Personal Narrative* (1858) achieved a second printing in 1864. Its sequel, *The Revival in Its Physical, Psychical, and Religious Aspects* (1859), also required reprinting, in 1861. These volumes answered to the widespread interest in mediums and spiritualism, an interest devoutly shared by Mrs. Browning and cordially abhorred by her husband.

E*

All by post, if no lucky opportunity of friendly carrier should seem likely to occur.

I write in real dash this time, but with best wishes for the season (as I said) and something of a hope (as I said)—so goodbye from

Yours faithfully

[Morgan]   Robert Browning

To Edward Chapman

Florence, June 5, '58

My dear Chapman,

Will you do me and my wife a great favour? An old friend of ours, Mr. James Montgomery Stuart [1] has just gone to London. He is very able, very learned,—and variously learned too,—with as many ready accomplishments as if he were *not* learned. He is well known to distinguished persons in more countries than one, perfectly versed in German, Italian, and French contemporary literature, and with the best will to turn all these good gifts to account, he cannot get on at all *here,* because vine-bearing and olive-bearing soils don't want his wares; yet he wants something for his large family. He writes those clever letters to the *Morning Post* from "their own correspondent." I should think him fit for any amount of popular magazine-work, reviews, etc. and *lectures,* and, if any of you really care about Italian politics, he is better able to make them intelligible to the public's capacity than anybody else. He has influential friends in England and Scotland, but "while the grass grows (in Scotland)" etc. etc.[2] Now for your concern in all this: surely you will get him any work you can, will not you? Help him to any Review or Magazine? He has letters to Editors sundry but I know nothing of Editors, and trust rather in you. There! I shall not see you this year, I fear. My wife is in less than her usual health, and I am forbidden to take her to London, tho' counselled to try

---

1. Stuart lectured in Florence on Shakespeare. The Brownings heard him as early as August, 1849 and were greatly attracted to him by his frequent references to the Shakespearean criticism of Mrs. Jameson—Aunt Nina to the Brownings. Mrs. Browning in a letter to Mrs. Jameson writes of him as "your adorer Mr. Stuart." (See *Letters of E.B.B.,* I, 441.) A reference in these same letters (I, 422) indicates that the Brownings met Stuart soon after attending his first lectures.

2. "While the grasse groweth, the horse starveth."

the Atlantic breezes on the French coast, whence you'll soon enough get my accustomed half-yearly reminder.

Yours ever,

[Morgan]   R. Browning

To Edward Chapman

Paris, July 13, '58.

My dear Chapman,

Here are we arrived, for further progress to some French Bathing place, as enjoined by the doctor. My wife was very poorly and there was no such evident remedy as this,—so we did as we were bid. We don't go to England (obeying the same medicine-man) but return as soon as sufficiently salted—I suppose at the end of September.

So you won't see me. Now, pray lighten my share of that affliction by sending in our account *at once (spoken insinuatingly)*; not that I mean to help myself to the money immediately, but that I want uncommonly to know what is what and how is how about all our books; and if you want any fresh doing up of *Aurora Leigh,* now is your time, when we are and shall be within a day's reach. Do kindly send me this directly if you can, and in process of time who knows but we shall *(voice dies off mysteriously: Mr. Chapman communicates to Mr. Frederick* [1] *earnestly; Mr. Frederick turns over ledger energetically, and scene closes* with the warm applause, not to say "encore" of)

Yours faithfully ever,

Robert Browning.

Direct: 151 Rue de Grenelle
     Faubourg St. Honoré
Please send by post Rarey's Horse-taming Book pub. by Rout-ledge. [2]
[Morgan]

1. Frederick Chapman is remembered, as well he might be, "immersed in a vast account-book in a corner of his cousin's [Edward Chapman's] room." (Arthur Waugh, *A Hundred Years of Publishing,* p. 77.)
2. John S. Rarey, *Art of Taming Horses;* the first edition was probably published in 1858. See Browning's poem, "A Likeness," in the *Dramatis Personae* volume of 1864. Browning was possibly interested in pony taming, for the following year he presented Pen with a Sardinian pony.

To Edward Chapman

Le Hâvre, Maison Versigny,
Rue du Perrey 2. Aug. 8. [1858]

My dear Chapman,

Thank you for your prompt answer and the account. We agree with you that the next edition of *Aurora Leigh* [1] ought to be much cheaper, and how that may happen, we leave to your judgment. My wife, you know, has a weakness for cheap little books; not so I, who offered the public certain yellow six pennyworths,[2] which they used to look at like so many papers of jalap, once on a time! To be sure, they incline to the actual boluses no more than to the original pills.

My particular object in writing is to tell you that if you will be good enough to put those same "odds and ends, books and notes waiting me" into one parcel and forward them to *Miss Barrett, 7. Delamere Terrace, Harrow Road*—that lady will bring them to us immediately, as she is going to leave London for Hâvre, next Thursday or Friday; so your kindness to be efficacious must be energetic, and if I lose this opportunity, another may not occur.

The weather here is capital, my wife's health restored beyond my expectations. We are in a hideous angle, but the sea makes itself decidedly felt. It was right to take the journey. Why don't you go (or come) sea-faring this way? My boy bathes like a duck.

Goodbye. My wife's kind regards go with mine. What odd poem is that you have just published, of Bailey's? [3]

Yours ever faithfully,

[Morgan]   Robert Browning.

To Mrs. Sophia Eckley [1]

Le Hâvre, Aug. 19, 1858.

My dear Mrs. Eckley,

I thought I should have succeeded in recovering from the Office at Paris that letter which I am so vexed to lose: but as nothing comes

1. The "4th and cheaper edition," announced in the *Athenaeum* of January 22, 1859 as "in the Press," did not actually appear until June 11, 1859.
2. The various volumes of the "Bells and Pomegranates" series published by Moxon.
3. Philip James Bailey, *The Age; A Colloquial Satire*.
1. Mrs. Browning first mentions "Sophie Eckley" in a letter of December 27,

in reply to my application, I will write now and thank you affectionately for this last note. I am happy that your kindest of kind hearted husbands loses none of the pleasure he promised himself in giving you this particular pleasure. I thought it was best to do what could be done at once, rather than wait and risk disappointment: the portrait is not perfect certainly; the nose seems over long, and there are some other errors in the face; also, the whole figure gives the idea of a larger woman than Ba: but the artist himself was so fully aware that much was yet wanting to the line work, and not a little remaining to be comprised in it, that I wonder he allowed you to come into possession at once; when the accessories (chair and table) are added the main figure will be reduced to its proper proportion—and at our return, Ba will sit to his heart's content: but I am glad to believe, with you, that something, indeed much has been secured—and most glad, as I said, that it gives you the pleasure it *should*. I know, if *we* had, in this Hâvre, a portrait of you, equally true to our recollections, we should look many a long look at it, and say many a sincere thing.

Dear Mrs. Eckley,—what you say about its "final destination" is meant as *only you* mean such kindness—and I shall not be hindering any kindness of yours; only diverting it into its more fitting channel, when I pray you to let it be otherwise than *so:* without referring to the eventualities which are in the hands of God, let your own dear child keep one day what may remind him of a face he will have forgotten—and let it remain in America. I do not care to write much about this—but let it be so! [2]

We shall not be so very long, now, before we return: my wife has written and, no doubt, made you acquainted with our daily

---

1853. (*Letters of E.B.B.*, II, 150.) The Eckleys were frequently with the Brownings in Florence and Rome, and as Americans of means they were able to perform many kind and useful services for the Brownings.

2. The portrait referred to here is possibly an early version of Gordigiani's painting of Mrs. Browning. If so, Browning was to change his mind and request that the portrait be given to him. (See letter to Mrs. Eckley of August 7, 1859, below.) About nine years later Browning reported to Miss Blagden that Mrs. Eckley told him "she had arranged by will to give me, or Pen, every one of them [Mrs. Browning's letters to Mrs. Eckley] together with (if I did not misunderstand her) the two portraits by Gordigiani." (*Letters of Robert Browning to Miss Isa Blagden,* arranged for publication by A. J. Armstrong [Waco, Texas, 1923], p. 165.) The two portraits form item 59 of the Sotheby sale of Pen Browning's property in 1913. (See *The Browning Collections: The Catalogue of Sotheby, Wilkinson and Hodge* [London, 1913]).

ways: you know my father and sister are here, two of my wife's brothers, her sister and another brother's wife: [3] and I have a friend that sticketh closer than a brother—my friend Milsand. Ba has been a little disturbed in her progressing health by so many faces and voices—but the tumult will subside.

God bless you, dear Mrs. Eckley—together with your husband, child, and Mother. My love goes to them all.

Yours ever affectionately,

[New York Public Library]   Robert Browning

To Edward Chapman

Le Hâvre, Sept. 19, '58.

Dear Chapman,

We leave this place tomorrow for Paris—Rue Castiglione 6. Will you have the kindness to forward the *Athenaeum* to that address? We stay two or three weeks at most and then return to Italy.

I shall draw on you presently for your balance in hand—thro' my Uncle in London,[1] I suppose.

Will you please put the enclosed note into the post and be so kind as to write the direction to Mr. *Law*, Francis' agent? [2] I can't get at his address. I'll tell you moreover what it is about. I promised Francis a year ago a photograph of my wife—of which he means to make an engraving. You know, or don't know, that there have been certain horrible libels on humanity published as portraits of her in America, and I shall not be sorry to extinguish them, as the Photograph taken yesterday may be expected to do. It was executed by a clever man here, Warnod, and is so satisfactory that I keep it myself and only send a copy to Francis.[3] How say *you* to an Engraving of it

3. E.B.B.'s two brothers who joined the Brownings at Le Havre were George Barrett and (probably) Alfred Price Barrett. The sister, of course, was Arabella. The "new brother's wife" (new wife of a brother) was probably Amelia (Holland) Barrett who had married Henry Barrett on April 21, 1858.

1. Reuben Browning, a banker with Rothschilds'.

2. From "and be so kind" to the question mark is jotted in on the top margin of the letter. Law was in charge of the London agency of C. S. Francis and Co., American publishers of Mrs. Browning's poetry.

3. The fourth edition of Mrs. Browning's *Poems* contains an engraving by T. O. Barlow from a photograph by Macaire, Havre, September, 1858. Perhaps Warnod was employed by Macaire. For one of the most horribly libelous of Mrs. Browning's pictures see the reproduction of "an old engraving" facing p. 587 of Jeannette Marks, *The Family of the Barrett*.

for the next *Aurora Leigh?* Might it not be of advantage? I would let you have the original, of course, and I know they transfer these Photographs capitally in England now. Somebody put that thing of Mr. Wood's in the *National Magazine,* I remember,—the medallion thing! [4] If you see any good in this notion, write at once, please; otherwise I take the portrait with me.

I won't think of the trouble for you at present. My wife's kind regards. She is much the better for her stay here. I dare say you are at the sea-side, too. My little boy swims capitally.

Yours faithfully ever,
Robert Browning.

I had a kind and complimentary letter some time ago from the Secretary of a new Club that was to be, "the Hogarth," proposing to enroll me as an Hon. mem. Is the club full-blown or nipt in the bud? [5]

[Morgan]

TO EDWARD CHAPMAN

Paris, 6 Rue de Castiglione
25th Sept. 1858.

My dear Chapman,

Will you have the kindness to pay £35. 6. 10. (being the balance due to me up to June 30th, 1858) [1] to my Uncle Reuben Browning, who will transmit the same to

Yours very sincerely,

[Morgan]   Robert Browning.

4. A reproduction made by Henry Linton of Marshall Wood's medallion of Mrs. Browning. It was used to accompany a review of *Aurora Leigh.* (*National Magazine*, I [1857], 313.)

5. "In the summer of 1858 . . . Mr. F. G. Stephens tells us, the original Hogarth Club was founded, of which the two Rossetti's were prominent instigators,—one of the most notable of the many protestant societies that have sprung up at different times from a slightly anti-academic bias. It is interesting to find that Sir Frederic Leighton's famous 'Lemon Tree' drawing was exhibited here . . . The Hogarth Club held its meetings at 178, Piccadilly, in the first instance; removed them to 6, Waterloo Place, Pall Mall; and finally dissolved, after existing for four seasons, in 1861." (See Ernest Rhys, *Sir Frederic Leighton* [London, 1895], p. 10.) It is probable that D. G. Rossetti, a great admirer of Browning in 1858, proposed Browning for honorary membership.

1. The sum called for here probably represents the income from all the Brownings' books for a period of six months, though the account may go back to October 5, 1857, when Browning drew out £110 from his account.

To Edward Chapman

Paris, Rue de Castiglione. 6.
Oct. 7 [1858]

My dear Chapman,

I see you advertise *Aurora Leigh* with a note *4th Edit. in the press*.[1] We go away at the beginning of next week, and many a thing that could be easily managed here, may take trouble to effect from Florence or Rome. My wife wants particularly to change a word or two.

You say nothing about the portrait. I can't help thinking you might improve the looks of the book by putting it in—you know best.[2] And what form of print, and price do you decide on? Write a word, pray. I suppose your *Frederick* is an admirable book from the bits of it I have seen as yet [3]—that's right. Thackeray is here.[4] I count on leaving next Tuesday.

Yours faithfully,
Robert Browning.

[Morgan]

To Edward Chapman

[Rome], March 19, '59.[1]

Dear Chapman—Here are the last of the corrections.[2] Pray send

1. The fourth edition of *Aurora Leigh* actually did not appear until June 11, 1859.

2. The portrait insisted upon by Browning adorns the fourth edition of *Aurora Leigh*.

3. Carlyle's *History of Frederick the Second,* the first two volumes of which were issued by Chapman and Hall on September 29, 1858. In March, 1859, through a letter of Mrs. Browning, we get a glimpse of Browning reading the work: "Robert curses and swears over Carlyle's Frederick, which is a relief to my own mind too. Never was there a more immoral book in the brutal sense." (*Letters to Isa Blagden,* p. 14.)

4. William Allingham at this time records the following conversation with Thackeray, who was confined to his bed at the Hotel Bristol, Place Vendôme, Paris. " 'Browning was here this morning,' Thackeray said. 'What spirits he has —almost too much for my weak state. He almost blew me out of bed.' " (*William Allingham: A Diary,* ed. H. Allingham and D. Radford [London, 1907], p. 76.)

1. The Brownings were in Rome until May, in Florence from May to August, in Siena from August to October, back in Florence for a few days in October, and then in Rome for the remainder of the year. Some letters to Chapman for this year may be "lost." The correspondence, however, was naturally diminished through Browning's shift in interest at this time from poetry to sculpture and through Mrs. Browning's comparative quiescence between periods of illness.

2. For the fourth edition of *Aurora Leigh*.

word that they are arrived, and, generally, how things go on, and
send the proof of the portrait.[3]

Yours truly,

[Morgan]   Robt. Browning.

To Sarianna Browning

Rome, Via di Bocca di Leone, 43.

[*ca.* May, 1859.] [1]

Dearest Sis,

Yours received—to my joy. Had Reuben told me at once where
the obstacle lay, what trouble to us all would have been saved. I
had written at his desire to the Partners [2] direct,—all to no use. I
have now written and sent off a letter to Chorley, and no doubt all
will be right soon. I daresay you are anxious about us—but we
feel just as safe as usual. The English and Americans have been,
and are, rushing away with the most stupid precipitation. You
must telegraph to Naples weeks beforehand for a place, and after
all you get a chance of a strip of bare deck or a mattress there at
best—to occupy for three nights before you reach Marseilles! And
then the railroads are given up wholly to the passage of troops, we
hear.[3] The actual quiet everywhere is perfect—in Tuscany never

3. Field Talfourd's charcoal drawing, done in Rome, March, 1859, from
which G. Cook made an engraving for the fourth edition of *Aurora Leigh*.
The portrait now hangs in the National Portrait Gallery. For reproductions of
Talfourd's drawings of Mr. and Mrs. Browning see Griffin and Minchin, *Life*,
pp. 216–217.

1. The date ascribed to this letter is suggested by the contents; see nn. 3, 4,
13.

2. The word "Trustees" is struck through and the word "Partners" written
above it. These opening sentences probably refer to an investment since Reuben
Browning, the poet's uncle and financial adviser, is involved. The Chorley
mentioned here is probably John Rutter Chorley (1807?–67), secretary to the
Grand Junction Railway. Browning owned railway stocks which he was to
describe as a "nuisance" in a letter to Reuben Browning dated April 13, 1877.
(See below.) It is probable that Browning knew John Chorley through his
friendship with Henry Chorley, music critic for the *Athenaeum* and one of the
trustees for Browning's marriage.

3. On January 1, 1859 Napoleon III had publicly announced to the Austrian
ambassador that relations between France and Austria were strained. On
January 10 King Victor Emmanuel delivered a speech, the last sentence of
which had been supplied by Napoleon: "We are not insensible to the cry of
anguish from other parts of Italy." These two utterances set the stage for the
break between France and Austria over the question of Italian subordination

was there so admirable a revolution, if you can call it one; it is certain the G[rand] Duke, or rather his son,[4] ordered the commandant of the citadel to bombard the city—on his refusing, he would have taken liberal counsels, etc; of course the man he called in to advise would do nothing on such a foundation, and bade him go away— so he did, and since then all has gone on perfectly—everywhere. Here as well as in Tuscany, the people understand what folly it was to begin proceedings by bonfires, illuminations, and noise—they are quiet, and it is such again every way. I have no fear for our funded money.[5] I daresay it is depreciated enough if one wished to sell out—but one doesn't. They pay the div[idend]s 3 months or less in advance, if you prefer paying 3% interest for the advance. But people are so foolish and timid—and nowhere so much as in England, where I observe the failures have been frightful: if one sold out *there*, one would lose ten or twelve percent, and it would be no worse here. I hear the prime of the news, knowing the really instructed people. I see Lady Williams [6] and Odo Russell [7] (our diplo-

to Emperor Francis Joseph. They also produced agitation among foreigners sojourning in Italy, for war seemed inevitable. War did come on May 20 (Battle of Montebello) but ended June 24 (Battle of Solferino). The shortness of the engagement justified Browning's calm. The armistice of Villafranca by which Austria gave up Lombardy but retained Venetia had a profoundly depressing effect upon Mrs. Browning. Her despondency was no less when she later learned that Savoy and Nice were to be annexed to France as the price of Napoleon's intervention.

4. The Grand Duke, a puppet of the Austrians, thought discretion the better part of valor and left Florence during the disturbances.

5. See Mrs. Browning's letter to Sarianna at approximately this same date: "Arabel writes alarmed about our funded money, which we are not likely to lose perhaps, precisely because we are not alarmed." (*Letters of E.B.B.*, II, 311.) At the time of her marriage Mrs. Browning had £8,000 "in the funds." These were probably in the Consolidated Annuities, a form of British government stock, known as Consols. These stocks bore 3-3½% and could be redeemed at the option of the government. They were unusually sensitive to international disturbances. From a comment of Mrs. Browning it is clear that the Brownings also owned Tuscan funds: "Meanwhile we are not over anxious, or anxious at all (to speak for myself) about our funded supplies. Of course the Tuscan funds are down to the floor, but as we shan't offer to disturb our deposits, we are not likely to suffer when the crisis is over. It would have been more serious if the Grand Ducal party had indeed bombarded Florence and Casa Guidi (as it was gracious enough to intend) for in that case coupons might have perished out of the world perhaps, and we should have had to begin it again, with a very small scrip." (*E.B.B.: Letters to Her Sister*, p. 315.)

6. We have not succeeded in identifying Lady Williams.

7. Odo William Leopold Russell (1829-84), first Baron Ampthill, was a

matic agent) nearly every day (dined with them on Friday) and have heard all sorts of various things from Ld. Stratford de Redcliffe [8]—(dined with him on Wednesday after having had two hours' talk and more with him in the morning) and also am a close neighbour of Mr. Wreford, the *Times* correspondent [9]—so I am not likely to be surprized by events. We purpose leaving on or about the 25th inst. I can't say I am very apprehensive on your account; there will be every method taken to keep order in Paris, of course. I do hope you sometimes get the *Ath[enaeum]*; I posted at least *four* since I saw you and there are some three to send. I feel ashamed of this stoppage—it is thro' the peoples' keeping them instead of letting me send them to you, but it will soon be better—try and excuse it now. We will send Ba's photograph by somebody very soon. I don't think my portrait (by Talfourd) [10] will be done here, for some reason or other: Leighton's [11] will, I believe, be photo-

---

career diplomat serving with the English legation to Florence in 1859. He maintained, however, his residence in Rome. He had served under Lord Stratford de Redcliffe (see next note) at Constantinople just before and during the Crimean War. (See Stanley Lane-Poole, *The Life of the Right Hon. Stratford Canning, Viscount Stratford de Redcliffe* [London, 1888], II, 64.) In the thick of diplomatic events at Rome he was sent in May, 1859 as a member of an English mission to congratulate Francis II, King of the Two Sicilies.

8. Stratford Canning (1786–1880), first Viscount Stratford de Redcliffe, called "the Great Elchi," that is, diplomatist and ambassador par excellence. Created viscount in 1852 after a long and varied career as a diplomat, he gave up public life in 1858 when he resigned his ambassadorship to Constantinople. He spent the winter of 1859 in Rome; "in the midst of an intellectual circle, courted by the most distinguished members of foreign society, many of whom he had met in former days, surrounded by objects of the deepest interest to a mind well stored in the archives of classical antiquity, and a spectator of the beginning of that movement of *Italia Irredenta,* which has since developed into such happy results, the vexations of the immediate past were gradually forgotten." Though in retirement, he was obviously a source of special information and knowledge, and his interests would have made him especially friendly with Browning. (See Stanley Lane-Poole, *The Life of Lord Stratford de Redcliffe* [London, 1890], p. 367.)

9. Mrs. Browning wrote to Isa Blagden on March 27, 1859: "Just now I am scarcely of sane mind about Italy . . . Robert accuses me of being 'glad' that the new *Times* correspondent has been suddenly seized with Roman fever." (*Letters of E.B.B.,* II, 308.)

10. See above, letter of March 19, 1859, n. 3. The charcoal drawings of the poets by Talfourd were kept in the dining room at 19 Warwick Crescent after Mrs. Browning's death. They are now in the National Portrait Gallery.

11. Frederic Leighton (1830–96), in later years Lord Leighton (1886) and President of the Royal Academy (1878), began early to show his quality as a

graphed, and you shall have a copy also. Both the portraits of Ba are failures, I think—Leighton's certainly, thinks everybody. Ba is just about to sit once more,—to Lehmann, a clever German painter.[12] I don't hope for anything good now. In the *Ath[enaeum]* arrived yesterday, there is some more nonsense about ourselves and Miss White; it is strange there should be any possible misconception of the matter: we merely wrote to the readers and incubators of the particular report which spoke of her coming "Highly recommended by the Brownings"—which it is not pretended was true. If we had supposed she knew of, much more wrote, the thing,

---

painter. In 1848 he painted "The Discovery of Giotto by Cimabue in the Fields of Florence," a subject which would appeal to Browning. In 1852 he met the Brownings and Thackeray in Italy. "There is little doubt," says one account of Leighton, "that the presence in Rome of such persons as the Brownings, George Sand, Lord Lyons, Gibson the sculptor, and many other cultivated and refined persons, had almost as great influence as that of any artist in preparing the mind of the young man for the great position he was afterwards to fill." (*Bryan's Dictionary of Painters and Engravers,* [London, 1903] III, 201.) Mrs. Sutherland Orr, Browning's future biographer, was Leighton's sister. Leighton's best work is represented by "Cimabue's Madonna Carried in Procession through the Streets of Florence" which was purchased by Queen Victoria; "Paolo and Francesca," "The Harvest Moon," "The Daphnephoria," "Andromache," "The Bath of Psyche," and "The Triumph of Music." Leighton remained a lifelong friend of Browning. In 1864 Browning wrote verses to accompany Leighton's picture, "Eurydice and Orpheus," and in *Balaustion's Adventure* (ll. 2672-2675) he refers to Leighton as "a great Kaunian painter." (See DeVane, *Browning Handbook,* pp. 311-312.) For a full account of the painter see Mrs. Russell Barrington, *The Life, Letters and Work of Frederic Leighton* (London, 1906), 2 vols. For references to his association with Browning see I, 145-146, 149, 164, 241; II, 52, 305; and Martha Hale Shackford, *The Brownings and Leighton* [Wellesley, Massachusetts, 1942], *passim.* See also Edgcumbe Staley, *Lord Leighton of Stretton, P.R.A.* (London, 1906), pp. 31, 124.

12. Rudolf Lehmann, the painter, was born at Ottensen, a village near Hamburg, in 1819 and first came to Rome in 1839. He went to England in 1850, "little expecting to find there a second home, and to make it an abiding place." (See H. C. Marillier, *Men and Women of the Century* [London, 1896], p. xviii.) He met the Brownings in 1858. He returned to England in 1861 and married Amelia Chambers, then returned to Italy for five years before finally settling in England. He drew a portrait of Mrs. Browning on May 15, 1859, and one of Robert Browning on May 22, 1859. A formal portrait of Browning was painted by Lehmann in 1883 and now hangs in the National Portrait Gallery. A reproduction of this portrait may be seen in Griffin and Minchin, *Life,* facing p. 276. The earlier sketches of the Brownings by Lehmann were for his book, *Album of Contemporary Celebrities* (1858). For Lehmann's association with Browning see his volume, *An Artist's Reminiscences* (London, 1894), especially pp. 222-231.

we should hardly have taken that occasion to declare our "affection and esteem" for her. Now she sends a letter from Horace Greeley and others full of prosing quite beside the mark with some slight impertinences to ourselves. We have written (on compulsion) a final word confirmatory of the above, and sent it to the *Ath[enaeum]*—where you will see it in due time.[13] How sorry I am

13. In the *Athenaeum* for March 5, 1859, "Our Weekly Gossip," p. 322, the following comment appeared: "We perceive that Mr. and Mrs. Browning have been drawn into print by the proceedings of Madame Mario, better known to the English world as Miss J. Meriton White, the translatress of *Orsini Memoirs* . . . That resolute lady it appears from the joint letter of Mr. and Mrs. Browning to an American paper, is lecturing in the United States on Italian affairs, and has used their names (which we know stand high in America), and their notoriously liberal sympathies, by way of personally introducing herself, and backing her own arguments. Mr. and Mrs. Browning totally repudiate this, expressing the while personal regard for Madame Mario, and repeating their confession of liberal and democratic faith. Surely such invention of testimonials, on whatever side, in whatever cause it be made, is too unscrupulous. Mr. and Mrs. Browning have every right to the largest publicity for their temperate protest."

In the same column of the *Athenaeum* for March 12, 1859 (pp. 357-358), Frederick M. White wrote denying his sister's "unscrupulous invention of testimonials" and added, "In private intercourse my sister may have mentioned that she had enjoyed the friendship of Mr. and Mrs. Browning, but I feel confident that these gifted and generous persons never meant to raise without foundation a doubt of her personal integrity."

The *Athenaeum* for April 30 (p. 584) quoted the letter of the Brownings dated Wednesday, January 5, as follows: "Having seen a statement in the American newspapers that Madame Mario, late Miss Jessie Meriton White, has arrived in the United States, 'recommended' by the Brownings etc. etc., to lecture on 'Orsini' and 'Italian Politics,' we feel ourselves forced to explain distinctly that, with a strong personal affection and esteem for Madame Mario, and a love for liberty and democracy, still better known to all who know us, we yet entirely dissent both from her views of Orsini and her opinions upon Piedmont, considering that every attack on the Piedmontese Government is levelled also against the general Italian cause. This is the first time we have noticed a printed observation on ourselves, and only a painful sense of duty constrains us to do so now. Robert Browning, Elizabeth Barrett Browning."

This issue of the *Athenaeum* quotes a letter signed by Horace Greeley the editor of the *Tribune*, Marens Spring, Henry J. Raymond the editor of the *Times*, Harry W. Bellows, Lucretia Mott, and Henry Ward Beecher, dated April 5, addressed to the *Athenaeum:* "It seems strange that you should accuse an English woman . . . of a moral forgery, of which the American press unanimously acquitted her . . . She has never, so far as we know, spoken in her public lectures of testimonials from the Brownings, or intimated that they endorsed her views; and we do not doubt that, in all her social intercourse, she has, where they have been mentioned, frankly spoken, as some of us have heard her do at social gatherings, of their dissent from her on the Italian

at poor Mrs. Bracken's misfortune! [14] Mr. Bracken and Annette returned from Naples and are going on at once to Florence and thence
in a fortnight or three weeks to Paris. I have told her nothing about
the loss, of course: she is in very delicate health, herself. Una Hawthorne is better (miraculously, all considered).[15]

Tuesday) No fresh news of importance—rumours in plenty. Everything as quiet as possible in Tuscany. I got yesterday the engravings
of Ba's portrait—a poor thing, metamorphosed into hardly any
likeness at all from what was a very good one—but such as it is, it

---

problem; and this long before their letter appeared . . . Highly as we esteem
the Brownings, we are accustomed to judge for ourselves in political matters;
and Mrs. Browning's good opinion of Louis Napoleon will not give him a
passport to our hearts." At this point the *Athenaeum* disclaims responsibility:
"*We* have made no charge against Madame Mario. If there is an accusation, it
comes from Rome, and to Rome the explanation ought to have been addressed."
    The whole matter was then concluded by a letter from the Brownings, writ-
ten on May 7 and published in the *Athenaeum* on May 21, 1859, (p. 680): "We
request of the courtesy of the *Athenaeum* to explain for us, if an explanation
is really necessary on either side of the Atlantic, that our letter was directed to
the readers and circulators of a certain newspaper announcement (*vide* the
New York *National Anti-Slavery Standard* for the 4th of December last) of
Madame Mario's arrival in the United States 'highly recommended' by the
Brownings and others, to lecture on Orsini and Italian politics. We thought it
right to contradict this statement because, like Mr. Horace Greeley and his
co-signatories, being accustomed to judge for ourselves in political matters, we
choose, therefore, to accept the responsibility simply of our own opinions. But
we submit the terms of our letter to all reasonable persons, and inquire whether,
if we had suspected Madame Mario of any connivance with a knowledge of
the newspaper announcement, we should have used the opportunity of con-
tradicting it, to express our 'strong affection and esteem' for herself personally.
Robert Browning, Elizabeth Barrett Browning."
    For an additional comment see *Letters of E.B.B.*, II, 308, and *E.B.B.: Letters
to Her Sister*, pp. 306, 316.
    14. The Bracken family—Mr. and Mrs. Bracken, Willie (Pen Browning's
friend), and Annette—are frequently mentioned in both Mr. and Mrs. Browning's letters. The references are usually intimate and gossipy and difficult to
attach to occasions. What the misfortune alluded to here is we are unable to
say. All the Brackens bob up frequently in Browning's letters of the Sixties,
then abruptly disappear after July 19, 1871, when Browning, in enigmatic
phrases, dismisses them from his concern. (See *Letters*, ed. Hood, p. 147.)
    15. Una Hawthorne was the daughter of Nathaniel Hawthorne, who had
brought his family to Italy in 1858 and had met the Brownings in Rome. (See
Nathaniel Hawthorne, *Italian Note-books* [London, 1891], pp. 9–13.) On January 4, 1859, Browning wrote to Isa Blagden that "the Hawthornes are horribly
off, Una suffering from Roman fever, changed so that you would not recognize
her, she that never was ill before, her mother says." (*Letters to Isa Blagden*, p.
11.)

must do for the present: there is some little air of Ba in it that makes it bearable. Write to me directly on receipt of this, and I will certainly reply with even no news at all, for it must be tantalizing for you to know we are in Italy just now. Ba is very well, Peni also. I am happy to find you and Papa continue well. One sees by the permission to the Austrians to stay in France that were there even a war with England, the resident English need not leave Paris—however unpleasant it might otherwise be to remain.[16] I have other letters to write and must leave off. Love to dear Milsand.

[New York Public Library]   [No signature]

To William Johnson Fox [1]

[Casa Guidi, Florence
June 8, 1859] [2]

I put in a whole heartful of thanks, dear Mr. Fox, and am not troubled to find the phrase that implies them—"you have done just like yourself—" and what a comfort it has been to see "a word in season how good it is!" You will take advantage of every oppor-

16. In November, 1851 Robert Browning, the poet's father, retired from the Bank of England where he had long been employed and with Sarianna, the poet's sister, set up a residence in Paris in April, 1852.

1. William Johnson Fox (1786–1864), Unitarian minister and Member of Parliament from Oldham, was an eloquent speaker and a social reformer keenly interested in public questions. He preached with great effect in his chapel in South Place, Finsbury, after 1824, and assisted James Mill to establish the *Westminster Review*. He spoke and wrote strongly against the Corn Laws in 1845–46, and later in favor of Italian freedom and unity. The poet's father, Robert Browning, Sr., was sympathetic to Fox's advanced opinions and probably introduced his son to Fox as early as 1824. The young Browning was intimate with Eliza and Sarah Flower, Fox's wards, and through them Fox took considerable interest in the poet's early verses and became his "literary father" and first patron and critic. For his many services to Browning see Griffin and Minchin, *Life*, pp. 42–44, 57–58, 72, 74–75, 89, 109, 136, 198.

2. The heading of this note appears at the top of a letter from E. B. B. to Fox who as M.P. from Oldham drew profuse thanks from the Brownings for his speech in Parliament on the Italian question. In ten closely written pages Mrs. Browning, after expressing her appreciation, attempts to make him aware of "what is felt" in Italy and "how keenly it is felt." "There is a call," she wrote, "upon your great heart and eloquent voice, for England's honour's sake, still more for the sake of Italy's safety." Browning's note is a brief addendum to his wife's letter and has been printed in Edward and Richard Garnett, *Life of W. J. Fox* (London, 1910), p. 323. It is here transcribed from the original letter in the New York Public Library.

tunity, won't you? Kind regards to Tottie and best wishes to her husband [3]—with all the old gratitude and loyalty to yourself from [New York Public Library]   R. Browning

To Mrs. Sophia Eckley [1]

Siena, Villa Alberti, Marciano.
Tuesday, Aug. 2, '59.

My dear Mrs. Eckley,

I write on the part of Ba to tell you how she has borne the journey. Her suffering from that cough was extreme for the last day or two of our stay in Florence, and her weakness so great that I scarcely saw the possibility of transporting her to Siena; as, however, she had a strong impression that no change for the better would take place until she was removed from Florence, I resolved on making the experiment: she had never gone out of the two rooms. On Saturday evening [2] we managed to arrive here with the greatest difficulty. We spent two days in that apartment we all occupied a few months ago at the Agride [3] here—and yesterday evening ended so far our troubles as it brought us to this Villa. I should have mentioned that Dr. Grisanowsky [4] followed us here by the *next* train, and stayed two days at our Hôtel—most kind and zealous in his endeavor to do good—but very little good seems likely to be done by doctoring. Last night, in spite of the fresh air, which we had counted on as the remedy for that inability to breathe which causes such distress, Ba did not close her eyes the whole of the night —coughing almost without intermission. At about 5 in the morn-

3. Tottie, Fox's daughter, was Mrs. F. L. Bridell-Fox. For further information about her see below, letter of July 21, 1866, and n. 1.
    1. The Brownings were at the peak of their intimacy with the Eckleys during the winter of 1858–59 in Rome. Browning wrote to Sarianna: "The Eckleys were extravagantly good to us, something beyond conception almost." And Mrs. Browning added: "They humiliate me by their devotion." (See *Letters of E.B.B.*, II, 296, 298.) This gratitude and affectionate feeling slowly deteriorated as first Browning and then, much later, Mrs. Browning sensed that these Americans, particularly Mrs. Eckley, would not be above revealing personal information about their poet friends.
    2. July 30.
    3. On May 27, 1859, Mrs. Browning wrote from Rome: "We travel by Siena to Florence—the rapid way." (*E.B.B.: Letters to Her Sister*, p. 314.) Evidently the Eckleys accompanied them and made the stop at Siena then.
    4. Mrs. Browning's physician in Florence. See letter of August 15, 1859, and n. 1.

ing she seemed overcome by complete exhaustion and slept a little. She is now, I venture to think, better and a little stronger—having taken a cup of broth. The cough has subsided, she is dressed and sitting in a chair in the drawing room, enjoying the fine wind that is blowing the curtains about beautifully. The Villa is not the "Bargagli" which I supposed I had taken,—the proprietor of *that* raised his demands, and I took the opportunity of remaining free to choose on our arrival. Dr. Grisanowsky preferred on the whole *this* villa—which is much smaller, cheaper, and less pretentious— but very airy and sufficiently comfortable. The Storys [5] have been unremitting in their kindness. I am very glad that we decided to come here—as the one reason which induced us to leave Florence, the wish to be *cool,* will probably be better attained here than else- where: I have a dread of the damp dead heat I remember at Lucca in the middle of the day. Let Ba but get well and strong, as I trust will soon be the case, and I shall be thankful to Siena indeed. I write this as rapidly as possible in the hope that I may be able to get it sent by to-day's post. Ba bids me send her best love to you, to David and to Miss Eckley and Doady.[6] Pen associates himself with us in all this affectionateness.

I shall write again in a day or two—and soon, I hope, Ba will write for herself. This has been a sad interruption to her continued increase of health and strength since the spring. Goodbye, now— kindest love to dear David from

[New York Public Library]

Yours ever faithfully,
Robert Browning.

To Mrs. Sophia Eckley

Siena, Aug. 7, '59.
My dear Mrs. Eckley,

We received your kind note of Aug. 4th—and see that you had not received, when you wrote it, my note from this place. Ba has been very ill—more ill than you suppose, if you think her capable

5. The Storys had been intimate friends of the Brownings since 1848. They had preceded the Brownings to Siena and were established in a villa nearby. They were of great assistance to Browning in caring for Mrs. Browning and Landor. (See Henry James, *William Wetmore Story and His Friends* [London, 1903], II, 19.)

6. David was Mrs. Eckley's husband, and Doady their child. Miss Eckley was probably Mr. Eckley's sister.

of writing to bid you goodbye from Casa Guidi, or giving Pen lessons: she was so ill at Florence that Grisanowski said nothing could be done for her *but* to change the air—her strength was absolutely *gone*—she was carried down-stairs, carried into the railway-carriage, carried up to bed in the Hôtel—and she left Florence in so pitiable a state that Grisanowski set off by the next train and spent two days at the Hôtel with us to be of any use he might: he selected for us, not the beautiful Villa I had set my mind on but the least commodious of all that were to be let, on hygienic grounds for the quality of the air obtainable in it.[1] We have now been a week here but Ba has never been able to walk three steps unsupported, nor to see one human being except our own family, nor write one word—tho' her own family must be painfully surprised at her silence—which surprise, my own writing to them in her place would only change to consternation; as for Peni, I hear him his lessons. Miss Blagden who accompanied us to the station, was so impressed by Ba's illness that she chose, on her own responsibility, to telegraph to Siena that the people in the Hôtel might be ready to help, and that the Storys might be apprised and do what they could—and accordingly they were waiting and most kind in every way—but Ba has never been able to see or thank one of them ever since, tho' a week has passed. I did not tell you all this at first, knowing it would grieve you, dear Mrs. Eckley—but I cannot let you continue to suppose that she has omitted any mark of the true affection she feels for you of which she has been capable. I shall give you delight, I know, in going on to say that she is much better, tho' very slowly regaining strength: three nights ago, she coughed the whole of the night without intermission and the daybreak found her quite exhausted—but the cough is much abated now, whether with Grisanowski's multifarious remedies, or the restorative power of Siena, or its own wearing out. She does not take solids at all, only a little broth,—with a little toast since a day or two. But she is dressed daily and brought in and seated in a large airy room with wind in it at times, enough to turn a mill—and the intense quiet of the place produces its due effect, no doubt. I am very satisfied that we should have gained less in your gay place—tho' we certainly *should* have gained your neighbourhood, and all the delight that

1. The Villa Alberti was at Marciano, two miles from Siena, and the Storys and Landor were neighbors.

it implies. But you will have understood by this time how matters really stand. I trust that we shall all meet again soon happily and able to discuss the respective advantages of Lucca and Siena. Perhaps I ought to have written earlier and oftener—but I have much to do, far more than I effectually perform, I fear—and letters written at the worst and expressive of the worst would only have distressed you unavailingly—and why should I do that?

Peni thanks you warmly for your letter—thanks dear Doady for his kind memory of him and wishes [to] be nearer than circumstances have allowed and will do his best to write directly. Kindest [love] to David from Ba and myself—and to Miss Eckley. Write and tell us how you are and be sure that Ba will write the moment she can guide the pen in the little weak hand. I want to ask you a great favour, dear Mrs. Eckley: you do not like that portrait of Gordigiani's—that of Ba [2]—I do like it as I like no other: cede it to me, and try once more with some other painter of your own choice who may succeed better—I shall be glad indeed. I will also take [the] other, as companion—and sit, myself, if David likes [to] the new painter, whoever he may be,—so shall we all be [?satisfied]. I should really be most grateful to be allowed [to] do this—but I can say no more, as you see. Once more, truest love from us two to you all.

Ever yours affectionately

[New York Public Library]   Robert Browning

To Dr. E. G. F. Grisanowski [1]

Siena, Aug. 15, '59.

Dear Dr. Grisanowski,

You will be glad to know that my wife is much better: her re-

2. Gordigiani's portrait of Browning serves as a frontispiece to *Letters of R.B. and E.B.B.*, Vol. II.

1. Ernest George Friedrich Grisanowski (1824–88) was born in Königsberg, Prussia. After a brief career in the diplomatic service Grisanowski studied medicine in various universities and in 1855 took his M.D. degree at Heidelberg. He began his practice in Pisa but in 1851 moved to Florence where he took his place in the circle which included Landor, the Trollopes, Miss Cobbe, and the Brownings. He is described as exceedingly modest but gifted as a conversationalist. In later years (1879), he joined the antivivisectionists and aligned himself with a cause ardently espoused by Miss Cobbe and morally supported by Browning. (Elpis Melena, *Dr. E. G. F. Grisanowski* [Hannover, 1890], *passim*, and p. 128, for brief description of Grisanowski in Florence. For a bio-

covery seems slow, but may be all [the surer] [2] for that. The cough
is *gone* [. . .] begins [. . .] She now takes her usual diet, in diminished quantity, and no medicine. To-day she begins with asses-
milk—a remedy that has been tried successful[ly in] her case
[before . . .] outside the Villa but our sitting-room is a regular
Œolus' cave,—one only gets too much of his blustering [. . .] at
this moment [. . .] paper [. . .] Pray remember us both as most
grateful for all your goodness, my wife as well as

Yours ever faithfully

[Mrs. Margaret Tuckerman Clark]　　　Robert Browning.

To Mrs. Sophia Eckley

Thursday morning
[ca. August, 1859] [1]

My dear Mrs. Eckley,

Ba is at this moment in the throes of sitting for her portrait—
and bids me say for her that she accepts thankfully your offer.[2] Her
truest love, as ever, goes to you with that of

Yours affectionately

[New York Public Library]　　　Robert Browning

To Miss Kate Field

[Siena]
Sep[tembe]r 30. [1859] [1]

Dear Miss Field,

No letters, no *Carta di soggiorno!* I fear you have lost them. Why
do you make people so very sorry? This is the hastiest of words, for

---

graphical sketch see a review of the above-mentioned book in the *Zoophilist*
IX [November 1, 1889], 165–166.)

2. This letter, written on the four sides of a folded sheet of very small note
paper, has been torn so that most of the last two lines of each sheet have been
removed. A total of perhaps 30 words is missing.

1. There is no date on this note, but from its brief contents one may infer
that it was written after Browning's letter of August 7, 1859, in which the
proposal is made that Mrs. Eckley "cede" Gordigiani's portrait of E.B.B. to
Browning and choose another painter to do another portrait.

2. The offer was probably an acquiescence to Browning's plan outlined in
the letter of August 7, 1859. The artist was possibly Hamilton Wild, who also
painted a picture of Pen astride his Sardinian pony. (See T. J. Wise, *Bibliography of the Writings of E.B.B.*, facing p. 181.)

1. Kate Field first met the Brownings in Rome, probably in April, 1859. (See

it is very late and I want to catch to-morrow's Post. What do you mean by pretending that *we here* were not the obliged, and are not the grateful people? Your stay made us happy, you know. Make us happy again, says (or would say, but that she's asleep) my wife and says also

Yours very faithfully ever

[Boston Browning Society] R Browning.

To William Makepeace Thackeray [1]

Rome, Via del Tritone, 28

Jan. 17, '60.

Dear Thackeray,

Your note proved to be one of the *Roundabout* papers,—reaching us after a stoppage in Florence besides:[2] and now it is here, we feel embarrassed in everything but your kindness in the matter—for what do you think? On this table are two other requests from Editors to try our luck and test their liberality.[3] As for me,—I really know exactly the way to treat such compliments as they deserve and yet do the editor no harm,—have so often taken it, indeed, in my capacity of *pianiste* when pressed to contribute to the enjoyment of an evening-party: but my wife's performances have a different effect and need cause nobody to repent of their good nature. May we leave it *so*—that if she finds herself at any time provided with what is likely to suit your book, she may send it and be sure of the

Lilian Whiting, *Kate Field, a Record* [Boston, 1899], p. 93.) The Brownings, pausing in Florence after their stay in Rome, then proceeded to Siena. On September 9, 1859, Browning wrote to Isa Blagden: "Whenever you elect to come it will be a real delight to see you, and Miss Field also." (*Letters to Isa Blagden,* p. 20.) Apparently Kate Field and Miss Blagden made the visit, and the present letter is a note written to Miss Field soon after her departure.

1. Thackeray (1811–63) had been made editor of the *Cornhill Magazine,* a new publishing venture of the firm of Smith, Elder and Co., in December, 1859. Browning had refused the editorship and now declines to contribute to the magazine. Thackeray had better success elsewhere and adorned the first issues of the magazine with the names of Tennyson, Trollope, and others. That Browning was refusing a large audience is attested by the fact that the early numbers of the *Cornhill* were sold to more than 100,000 buyers.

2. The letter from Thackeray may have been sent to Siena, where the Brownings had been for the summer and fall of 1859; from Siena it apparently was forwarded to Florence too late to catch them before they set off to Rome for the winter.

3. One of these requests came very possibly from Henry F. Chorley of the *Athenaeum.*

most benignant inclination of your brow? [4] In whatever the event, take our truest thanks and best wishes. We received the extravagant gift of two copies,—or was the publisher's intent that we should not fight for *first read?*

Give your kind regards to your Daughters and tell them the boy, they and you were so good to, rides like a man.[5]

Ever yours faithfully,

[New York Public Library]   Robert Browning

To Edward Chapman

Rome, Via del Tritone, 28.
Jan. 31, [1860]

Dear Chapman,

We [received] your letter duly and the proofs two days after.[1] These last will be returned to you by the Messenger who leaves tomorrow, but I thought it might be as well to send the enclosed poem [2] at once: it is to be inserted immediately *after* the "Tale of

4. In April, 1860, Mrs. Browning "got leave from Robert to send something" to Thackeray: "A Musical Instrument," which appeared in the *Cornhill Magazine* for July, 1860. It is one of the finest of Mrs. Browning's poems. In the following year she sent Thackeray another poem, "Lord Walter's Wife." In refusing this poem Thackeray wrote on April 2, 1861: "You see that our magazine is written not only for men and women, but for boys, girls, infants, sucklings almost, and one of the best wives, mothers, women in the world writes some verses which I feel certain would be objected to by many of our readers. . . . In your poem you know there is an account of an unlawful passion felt by a man for a woman . . . so I have not published this poem." E.B.B. replied from Via Felice, Rome, on April 21 [1861] as follows: "I am not a 'fast woman'—I don't like coarse subjects, or the coarse treatment of any subject. But I am deeply convinced that the corruption of our society requires not shut doors and windows, but light and air: and that it is exactly because pure and prosperous women choose to *ignore* vice, that miserable women suffer wrong by it everywhere." She suggests "simply looking at them [evils] and calling them by their names." (See Mrs. Richmond Ritchie, "The First Number of the Cornhill," *Cornhill Magazine* [July, 1896], pp. 12–13.)

5. Thackeray and his daughters, Anne Isabella and Harriet Marion, had been in Rome during the visit of the Brownings in 1853–54. (See above, letter to Sarianna Browning, dated December 19, 1853.) Pen had been given his pony in October, 1859 in Siena, from whence it had been transported to Florence and thence, "fastened to the vettura horses," to Rome, where the little boy had a daily ride with his father.

1. Proofs of *Poems Before Congress,* a thin volume of eight poems by E.B.B. published March 12, 1860.

2. "A Court Lady."

Villafranca" and before the "August Voice." Note: we have no
proof of the "Dance" yet—of course. Also, note: this is the last
poem you will be required to add to the series, so you may calculate
exactly. Thanks for the account. I hope your cold is better. My wife
has suffered much but is recovering.[3]

Ever yours truly
Robert Browning

[Morgan]

To Edward Chapman

Rome, Feb. 6. [1860]

Dear Chapman,

[Here] is the Preface: [1] if you will engage to have it *most* carefully printed, we will trust to you, and require no proofs—as the
sending and returning these would delay publication for another
fortnight or more, and your best way is to get the book out at once:
but you must please be very painstaking, for we are nervous in such
matters. Your printing is always intelligent, however, and we don't
run much risk.

Ever yrs,
Robt. Browning

The proofs of the last two poems are not yet come and *those* we
must have. "The Dance" and "The Court Lady."
[Morgan]

To Edward Chapman

Rome, Tritone 28
Feb. 15, '60

Dear Chapman,

Here is the proof.[1] You received the preface, I hope, which I
sent some days ago. You may now print and publish without further delay—the sooner the better—sending first the proofs to

3. Mrs. Browning's chief suffering had occurred at Florence and Siena in
the summer and fall of 1859. This statement of Browning, therefore, makes
it at least possible that there had been no letters exchanged with Chapman
since the summer of 1859 and possibly no letters since Browning's of March
19, 1859.

1. The preface to *Poems Before Congress,* published with the notation:
"Rome, February, 1860."

1. Proof sheets of "The Dance" and "The Court Lady," two of the *Poems
Before Congress.* See preceding letter to Chapman.

Francis [2] as I desired. Please send *three* copies to Miss Moulton Barrett, 7 Delamere Terrace, Harrow Rd. *Three* to Reuben Browning Esq, Messrs. Roths[childs' N]ew Court, St. Swithin's Lane— with the note I enclose—a[nd to Mr.] Forster, Mr. Chorley [3] 13. Eaton Place, West Belg[rave] Sq., [W.] J. Fox M. P. 3. Sussex Pl. Reg[en]t['s] P[ark] R. M. Milnes Esq. 16. Upper Brook St. Procter. Ruskin, Denmark Hill. The rest, I will tell you about afterwards. Please write [to] let me know that the thing is done and out. [Morgan]   [Signature removed]

To Edward Chapman

Rome, Via del Tritone 28.
March 9, '60.

Dear Chapman,

I suppose the *Poems* are out by this. I must beg you to send copies, in addition to those already mentioned, to the following Londoners (or Englanders):

G. Dante Rossetti,[1] 14. Chatham Place, B[lac]kfr[iar]s B[ri]dge.
William Rossetti, 45. Upper Albany St.
Thomas Woolner Esq.[2] 27. Rutland St. Hampstead Rd.
Alex Munro Esq.[3] 6 Upper Belgrave Place S. W.

2. C. S. Francis, Mrs. Browning's American publisher, who paid for and received advance proof sheets as a protection against possible piracy in America of the English edition.

3. Henry Fothergill Chorley of the *Athenaeum,* who was to review the *Poems Before Congress,* misinterpret one of them, "A Curse for a Nation," and thereby stir up a controversy. See below, letter dated March 23, 1860, n. 1.

1. Gabriel Charles Dante Rossetti (1828–82), poet and painter, and his brother William Michael Rossetti (1829–1919), critic, had both become known to Browning as early as 1847. The elder had experimented with various combinations of his name and was G. Dante or Gabriel Dante Rossetti at the time he first wrote to Browning (October, 1847) about the anonymous copy of *Pauline* in the British Museum. Browning has unconsciously reverted to the early signature.

2. One of the original Pre-Raphaelites, Thomas Woolner (1825–92) had in 1857 come into his own as a sculptor, largely through his execution of a bust of Tennyson and medallions of Tennyson, Carlyle, and Browning. Browning's relations with him were stimulated by this contact and by his own interest in sculpturing, an interest which led him to putter about the studios of W. W. Story and Hatty Hosmer in Rome during the late Fifties.

3. In 1858 Alexander Munro (1825–71) became briefly intimate with the Brownings while making a bust of Pen.

William Allingham Esq.[4] Lane, Ballyshannon, Ireland
(by book post, prepaid)
Mrs. Jago,[5] Trejago, Hammersmhith (bookpost, prep[d])
Mrs. Ogilvy,[6] Lower Sydenham (post prep[d])
Two copies (to Mr. Browning, Messrs. Rothschilds', New Court,
St. Swithin's Lane) for Mr. Corkran [7]
and Rev. Francis Mahony,[8] Paris.
1 copy by book post, prep[d] to Miss Blagden, Villa Bricchiere,
Bellosguardo, Florence.

Six copies to Mr. Odo Russell,[9] for me (inside) thro' foreign office.
Do let us further know of any interesting notices (*really* interest-
ing). I see the *Sat[urda]y Review, Athenaeum, Thackeray*,[10] and
Macmillan—so never mind them.

Please send with the books to Rome, the three last numbers of

4. It was Allingham (1824–89), minor Irish poet, who had introduced D. G.
Rossetti to Browning in 1852. (See Griffin and Minchin, *Life*, p. 187.) The
extent of the intimacy with Browning is best revealed in *Letters to William
Allingham;* and *Letters from William Allingham [to Mr. and Mrs. Browning,
1853–1860]*, with Preliminary Note signed by Helen Allingham (1913?).

5. Mrs. Charles Trelawny Jago, whose husband was the second son of Edward Jago by Ann Darell, daughter of Edward Trelawny. The name of their
home, *Trejago*, is a memorial, of course, to the union of the Jago and Trelawny
families. Jago had been Mrs. Browning's physician in London before her marriage and afterward in Florence. (See *E.B.B.: Letters to Her Sister*, p. 52.)

6. Mrs. D. Ogilvy published, among other books, *Traditions of Tuscany, in
Verse* (London, 1851). She and her husband became intimate with the Brown-
ings at Bagni di Lucca in the summer of 1849. (See *Letters*, ed. Hood, p. 24.)
Upon Mrs. Browning's death, Mrs. Ogilvy wrote a brief memoir of the poetess.

7. John Frazer Corkran (?–1884) was for many years Paris correspondent of
the London *Herald* and *Standard*. He wrote *History of the National Con-
stituent Assembly from May, 1848* (London, 1849); *An Hour Ago; or Time in
Dreamland: a Mystery* (London, 1858); *Concise History of England in Epochs*
(London, 1859, 7th ed., 1871), and three other novels, two of them in 3 vols.
each. His daughter was Alice Abigail Corkran, also a journalist and a writer
of novels.

8. Francis Sylvester Mahony (1804–66), better known as Father Prout, was
Paris correspondent for the London *Globe* from 1858 to 1866. He had known
the Brownings from the beginning of their stay in Italy, and had earned their
gratitude, particularly Mrs. Browning's, by curing Browning of "fever and
relaxed sore throat" with an unorthodox "potion of eggs and port wine." (See
Orr, *Life*, p. 152.) He is said also to have provided Browning with the information about Cardinal Wiseman which formed the basis for "Bishop Blougram's
Apology." (See DeVane, *Browning Handbook*, pp. 214–215.)

9. See letter to Sarianna Browning [*ca.* May, 1859], n. 7.

10. The *Cornhill Magazine*, which Thackeray edited.

F

The Spiritual Magazine,[11] price 6*d*., Pitman, Paternoster Row.
N.B. If you put covers on the book, you may send the copies abroad *without them* and so save considerably in the weight. Goodbye, in great haste.

Put the names, or, from the Author, inside the books for friends.

Ever yours faithfully,

[Morgan]   Robert Browning.

To Edward Chapman

Rome, Via del Tritone, 28.
March 23, 1860.

Dear Chapman,

Please take care that the *Athenaeum* gets the accompanying note at once. You know,—and probably the friendly critic also, that there is not a word about "malediction against England" in the "sixty pages" he would fain "best give an idea of"—and that had he quoted the other half of the poem he pretends to extract, everybody else would have known likewise that it refers to the Slave-States in America, where it was printed and circulated years ago. (You reprinted it from a broadside containing poems of a similar intention by Emerson and others.) [1] Indeed, had the friendly critic

---

11. The tone and contents of this magazine may be gathered from some of the titles in the issue of March, 1860, one of those asked for by Browning: "What is the True Elixir of Life?", "Lord Bacon and Spiritualism," "Mr. Dickens and His Haunted House," "Vision of a Lady Just Deceased," "Spiritualism Among the Mormons," "Spiritualism at the Tuileries," etc. The magazine was for Mrs. Browning.

1. On March 17, 1860, Henry Fothergill Chorley reviewed Mrs. Browning's *Poems Before Congress* for the *Athenaeum*. Among other things he said that Mrs. Browning "is more political than poetical, expressing her blind faith in Napoleon the third as the hope of Italy, and flinging malediction against England,—infallible, arrogant." "Robert," wrote Mrs. Browning, "was *furious*. . . . I never saw Robert so enraged about a criticism." (*Letters of E.B.B.*, II, 366–367.) Mrs. Browning wrote the note to Chorley which Browning is here asking Chapman to deliver. On April 7, 1860, Chorley, in the column of the *Athenaeum* headed "Our Weekly Gossip," summarized Mrs. Browning's note in which she had explained that "A Curse for a Nation" was leveled at the United States and not at England. Then Chorley added: "We may be allowed to ask, in extenuation of our own hasty and incorrect inference,—why a rhyme on Negro Slavery should appear in 'Poems before Congress'?" On April 13 Mrs. Browning wrote directly to Mr. Chorley to protest both his unfair review and his refusal to make "the poor amends of printing my letter in full." (*Letters of E.B.B.*, II, 378–379.)

gone back but a single line in his citations he would have been obl[iged] to record that the poem was "sent over the Western Sea." Is England "in the *old* world's sight" I wonder, or famous for using "brand and thong" to any one,—even a friendly critic, and so he exercises his trade as you see. If it is all a blunder, why not cure such blundering even at the eleventh hour? Are all criticisms written in this painstaking, conscientious way? I have been used rather to stupidity than malignity, it seems to me,—but live and learn!

Please send a copy [2] to Lytton—I don't think I put his name in the list I made out in a hurry.

Ever yours faithfully

[Huntington]   Robert Browning.

To Sarianna and Robert Browning, Sr. [1]

[June 29, 1861.] [2]

My own Si[s], papa—you know what this means—it is all over—— I cannot say more— All unexpected, unintelligible, but with no pain, no knowledge—of what was to be— This morning, 4 ½, *29th June.* Don't come, nor send nor be anxious. I have Peny to live [for] and attend to, with her in him. I could not break this to you— I will write again and tell what I can.
[Schiff]

To Sarianna Browning

Florence, Friday, July 5. [1861]

My dearest, I rather supposed a letter would come to-day—but remember you had made some arrangements for going to Com-

2. *Poems Before Congress.*

1. Letters from the poet to Robert Browning, Sr. (1782–1866), are extremely rare; indeed, this is the only published letter from the poet to his father. Browning ordinarily wrote to Sarianna, constant companion of Browning, Sr. Apparently a few hours after Mrs. Browning died Browning telegraphed the news to his sister, then scrawled this hasty, unsigned, almost illegible note to his family. The next few letters written from Florence have more interpolations and errors than were usual with Browning.

2. The Brownings were in Rome until May of this year, then in Florence until Mrs. Browning's death. Browning stayed on in Florence settling his affairs until late in July. On July 27 he set out for Paris with his son and Isa Blagden. There they remained for a few days, then proceeded to the French coast to St. Enogat, a little place near St. Malo. Soon after the middle of September Browning returned briefly to Paris. By October he was in London, at 1 Chichester Road, his abode for the remainder of the year.

piègne, I think—for a week—if you are gone, all these things will come on you at once at your return. I wrote two letters to you, no more [1]—and am intending to write nothing more now to anyone, except anything plainly necessary. I am very well—of course I have suffered a little in my health (of course I am only speaking of *that*) but I went up two days ago to Isa's Villa for the night and have done so since, returning in the morning—and that has stopped further progress of some unpleasant symptoms, inevitable as they were. Pen was taken up from the first,—I must be here in order to do the necessary work. The funeral took place on the 1st July (at 7 p.m.). There were extraordinary demonstrations of sorrow: everybody understood. They shut up shops in our street. The coffin was carried with two great crowns, of laurel and white flowers, thro' the streets. I·send newspapers with short notices. The service was the C[hurch] of E[nglan]d. Everybody was there, I am told. I went straight from the cemetery to the Villa—and presently in the evening came the astonishing sight of the comet, which totally invisible before, it now appears had reached its nearest point to the earth on the *29th*—was first seen, next day, and on the third was over half the sky: it is rapidly going off, and on the 12th, a week hence, will be 36 million[s] of miles away.[2]

Dr. Wilson [3] assures me that she could never have recovered—

1. These are the preceding letter and the long and genuinely touching one published in *Letters*, ed. Hood, pp. 58–63.

2. The London *Times* for Thursday, July 4, 1861, p. 12, col. 2, printed a report from Bishop's Observatory concerning this comet: "Its distance from the earth on Sunday evening [June 30] was rather over 13,000,000 miles, and a little less than 15,000,000 at 11 o'clock last evening [July 2]. It is therefore receding slowly from us." *Galignani's Messenger* reported: "This new visitor has taken even Astronomers by surprise. . . . The reason why it was not observed before is that, up to the 30th ult., its distance from the pole was such to make it set with the sun . . . Its size does not exceed that of 1858. . . . the comet gave rise to an animated discussion at yesterday's sitting of the Academy of Science. [This comet may be a return of] the same that had been observed in 1556, and caused the abdication of Charles V . . . : in 1264, when it was supposed to announce the death of Pope Urban IV." But the London *Times*, under the caption, "Identity of Charles V comet and this one not admitted," reported the astronomer, M. Leverrier, as saying: "It is now positive that this is not Charles V's comet." (July 4, 1861, p. 7, col. 6.) Then on July 15 the *Times* observed: "On the morning of the 29th [of June] it [the comet] would be above the horizon at daybreak. . . . Since this date . . . it has never set, nor can it do so for at least a month from the present time." (p. 10, col. 4.)

3. See below, letter of July 1861 addressed to John Forster.

to her old state of comparative health: she would have become con-fined to the room, then the bed, no travelling, no visitors *possible*. There was no pain—the little wandering was caused by the mor-phine, in an increased dose as was necessary: nothing could have helped, all I did was right, nothing omitted. The death was caused most probably by the breaking of a second abscess [which pierced?] the trachea. The first night's attack was the breaking one in an attack of asthma: he knew it was a grave case from the first, but never expected the end would be so near,—that is, he thought there would be more lingering and pain.

I shall leave here in a few days for Paris. I stay necessarily to attend to business—not very difficult,—but I must get done with it. I then go to you directly, stay in Paris only a day or two, then go at once to Arabel for a few days,—a week at farthest. I then return to Paris, and take a lodging near you for the winter—or rather, propose first to go with you wherever you please, to the sea side or any where you like, to be quiet for the summer or autumn, and on returning I will take a lodging as I say, and devote myself to seeing what education is best for Peni and what form it should take. I shall never again "keep house," nor live but in the simplest manner, but always with reference to Pen. Pen, the golden curls and fantastic dress, is gone just as Ba is gone: he has short hair, worn boy-wise, long trousers, is a common boy all at once: otherwise I could not have lived without a maid. I can now attend to him completely myself,—so all pins, worked collars and so on, are gone and for-gotten. He behaves perfectly—has grown a dear, considerate boy of a sudden, will come to nothing but good, I am convinced. Isa Blag-den's services have been inestimable: she is going to leave Florence too and go to England directly; if I can arrange it, we will travel to-gether, but I don't know. I am going to retain a few old articles that we were used to at Casa Guidi, and leave the rest to be sold: there shall be made a photograph of the room before I move any-thing.[4] I have a perfect Photograph of Ba taken a week before we left Rome, and hope to be able to secure the plate.

I do not speak of you and Papa. You have been shocked, and alarmed for me. This must have been,—I could not spare you, that

4. This photograph was not taken, but Browning arranged to have a picture painted "of the interior of our old drawing room." (See below, letter to Sarianna Browning, July 22, 1861.)

I know. So poor Arabel will have suffered. But they are they and I am I, and you must forget your own loss when you think of mine. Dearest Papa, however, who was not well, may have been unduly grieved: I hope it is not so. Dear Milsand will be the person for whose help I shall count most presently: he will advise with me about Pen.

God bless you, dearest. I will write in a few days and tell you my ultimate arrangements. Do not answer this. I hope to be [with] you.

Ever yours affectionately

[Schiff]
RB

To Sarianna Browning

Florence, July 13, '61. Saturday.

My dearest,

You will be anxious to hear from me: I am very much better than I could have supposed possible,—and Peni is entirely well and good. I sleep up at Isa's Villa every night, returning here to breakfast. I am engaged all day in preparations for departure—it is far best to get done with them now and leave nothing on my mind—in fact, once away I don't choose to return. I wrote to you the other day and told you what I was proposing to do, and can add nothing to the little I said. I suppose I shall be ready to leave by next week's end—say on Monday week, 22d—and shall go to Paris directly,—stay a day or two only,—go to Arabel for a few days and then return. We can then all go quietly into the country together—if such a thing were possible, to the sea side: I hope it won't be too late for you. I should be able to be back again certainly by the 1st August,—the autumn remains. Perhaps this arrangement may be changed so far as the visit to London by circumstances mentioned this m[ornin]g in a letter from Arabel and George.[1] She goes to him in Devonshire, and both of them want me to go there, which I can hardly do: she insists should I not agree to this, on returning

---

1. George Moulton-Barrett (1817–95) had sided with his father Edward Moulton-Barrett in condemning E.B.B. for eloping with Browning. (See *Letters of E.B.B.*, I, 287.) Later he became one of the executors of his father's estate. Unlike his father, however, he repented his condemnation and exchanged letters with both his sister and Browning. (Browning's letters to George Moulton-Barrett have not been published but were offered for sale in Sotheby's *Catalogue, The Papers of Lt. Col. H. P. Moulton-Barrett* [1937].) See also *Twenty-two Unpublished Letters of Elizabeth Barrett Browning and Robert Browning Addressed to Henrietta and Arabella Moulton Barrett* (New York, 1935), pp. 8–11.

to meet me. It *may* thus happen that my visit will take place later: in any case, it will be only for a *few days* at any time for the *present*. I can't see friends etc. and I spend a year with you: (look out for an airy two-bedrooms and sitting room in your neighbourhood, high up, and where I can get simple attendance—I shall want nothing more.) I don't mean, do this *now*—I shall not want it till we return from the country,—but, in your walks and among acquaintances enquire, so as to have such a place in your eye. I can always get rooms in an Hôtel provisionally. I should much like some quiet place wherein to arrange my thoughts, and attend to Pen: however it will be quite time enough to talk of this when we meet. Isa goes with me to Paris—which will be a great comfort: she is one of the warmest hearted persons I ever knew—she has been invaluable to me and Pen (who stays with her always). She throws up Florence at once after this loss. Pen is changed and so good: the loss cannot be to him what it is for me—on the other hand, he could not get the comfort out of it that I do: he will have new objects, desires etc. every week and day. Well, dearest, I see that all has been for the best for her in this—in the painless end, absolute ignorance of the parting that was to be and of anxiety about [it], in the immunity from the sad dark days that *must* have followed very soon, if her health had continued to decline without this abrupt close: everything would have been miserable in that case. I have for my part, besides the consideration of this, the knowledge that my life will be easier in many important points than it might have been by never so little a variation in the circumstances of it—Pen's being just of this age, a boy, and just the kind of boy he is, will help immensely: and in my case, *writing* being the only thing I have always been used to do absolutely by myself. However, I am not too sure I shall be able to do all the wise things I profess —only, I will try—and I have done some hard things already, for which I feel the better—so now, enough of me. I have had, and continue to have, extraordinary kindness shown to me—people write with the deepest sympathy from England: Forster, Procter, Eckley etc. Here the feeling is remarkable. Yesterday Peruzzi [2]

2. Ubaldino Peruzzi (1822–91) was a decendant of one of Florence's most illustrious families. In 1861, at the time of his call on Browning, he was "ministro dei Lavori pubblici e del l'Interno" under Cavour and is described as "uno dei benemeriti del Risorgimento italiano; probo, infaticabile, gioviale e popolarissimo." (See *Enciclopedia Italiana* [Roma, 1935], XXVI, 916.)

called and said he and all the Italians were hoping I should not leave Florence—and that Peni would be brought up as a Tuscan— every career would be open to him, even if he went away for a year or two, they wished that those who had been their friends in evil days might share in the coming good fortune—he said this with real emotion and I believe I should not be deceived in taking it for simple truth:— Of course, the answer is, we are English and the beauty of Ba's effort was in its being utterly disinterested and the just zeal of a stranger for right and truth: [3] let Pen continue it. I don't see the English Papers, nor go out except to the Villa at eve- nings. I hear there are great regrets, great praises,—right for those who offer them. Arabel has been much affected, and the brothers, she says. I have just seen Wilson (Made Romagnoli) for the first time. She repeats that she saw nothing but improvement on that last night, cheerfulness, desire to get away to Siena,—she went away sure that all was well.

Truest love to Dearest Papa: I shall be able to assist you a little in devoting yourself to him now. Thank dear Milsand from my heart—his friendship remains a most precious treasure to me. I will write again and tell you exactly when I shall arrive, how, and all about it. What will be a good Hôtel near you, to arrive at? I shall however take all care of Isa, who would cut her hand off to serve Pen or myself for her sake. She had been expecting a happy summer with one of the dearest of her friends who was to visit her, but she throws up every thing. God bless you, dearest Papa, dearest Sis. I sent you two (Ital.) newspapers—not *Athenaeums,* which I think I will bring.

Ever yours affectionately,
R Browning.

I shall tell Friends to write to your address for me.
[Schiff]

---

3. Browning is referring, of course, to E.B.B.'s impassioned support of the cause of Italian unification, a support so fervid that Browning attributed a major ill effect on Mrs. Browning's health to the apparent betrayal of the Italians at Villafranca in 1859. (See *Letters,* ed. Hood, p. 59.) The inscription for Mrs. Browning placed on Casa Guidi by the Florentines was as follows: "Qui scrisse e morì/ Elisabetta Barrett Browning/ che in cuore di donna con- ciliava/ Scienza di Dotto e spirito di Poeta/ E fece del suo Verso Aureo Anello/ Fra Italia e Inghilterra/ Pone questa lapide/ Firenze grata/ 1861."

To John Forster [1]

[July, 1861.]

. . . resting before setting out for Siena. She was weak—too weak to be taken to Paris as we desired—but less than unduly weak, considering the effect of her sister's six months' illness and death last December.[2] We were both of us sure that a summer of rest and silence would remedy all that remained wrong. The weather was suffocatingly hot. There came breezes and coolness in the evenings, and she sate [?before the] window in a draft, as was habitual to her. She caught cold. "It was nothing"—but two nights after, the oppression at her chest increased and I called in the best physician here,—an acquaintance, but who attended her for the first time. He said the state of her lungs was serious—but the appearances might be of long standing, and this was an exceptional case. She said: "of the longest standing—I have heard all this years and years ago; it is one of my common attacks—not so severe as that two years ago—and is nothing." She rose every day, sate in the drawing room till evening, and so we talked. I chose to sit up at nights, to her great displeasure, to be ready with the little medicine there was to give, and to fan her: also I believe I had an instinctive alarm from *before* the beginning—tho' I could not reason it out against *her* reasons. On Friday evening we talked over our plans, and she was urgent we should take a Villa here "for three years"—we both of us conceived a sudden dislike for this poor Casa Guidi we had been happy in so long—found it hot, noisy, incommodious. Isa B[lagden]

1. The first page of this letter has been lost. Forster passed the letter on to Mr. and Mrs. Thomas Carlyle with this statement: "I wished to send you this letter of Browning's about his wife's death and his own future plans—the substance of which he permits me to tell to any friends interested in him, and I know your interest, as well as his reverence and regard for you. Dear Mrs. Carlyle, too, might care to see what he says. It is a very manly, true, and honest letter, I think: increasing one's love for Browning." (Forster and Dyce Collection, Victoria and Albert Museum.) Since the part of Browning's letter which remains is exclusively about the death of Mrs. Browning, the part that is lost must have contained whatever was said about Browning's "future plans." The "Italian good faithful maid" in this letter is Annunziata.

2. Mrs. Surtees Cook, nee Henrietta Barrett, sister of E.B.B., died of cancer after a long and painful illness. Henrietta's lingering pain probably enforced Browning's thankfulness that E.B.B. was mercifully spared a like experience. (Jeannette Marks records, apparently erroneously, that Henrietta died in August, 1860. See *The Family of the Barrett* [New York, 1938], p. 636. Date is correct in Genealogical Table, facing p. 536. See also *Twenty-Two Browning Letters* [New York, 1935], *passim*.)

F*

saw her, and talked of a friend's report of Ricasoli's identity of policy with that of Cavour.[3] I said, "I won't have talking," but while I turned my back, she whispered in her old way to her friend: "He said his policy and Cavour's were absolutely the same, only they differed as to the method of carrying it out."—"Ay, I thought so—I thought so!" Then came Ma^de Romagnoli (her old maid, you remember)—in her presence she made her usual toilette "for half an hour" quite unassisted, brushing her hair etc. Mad^e R. left saying "She is much better"—whereat the other servants attacked the Italian good, faithful maid for being "a bird of ill omen." Peni surmised something from the talk—he went to bid her goodnight: "Are you really better?" *"Much* better."—He asked twice more and was twice so answered. Then I came in, and found her "composed for the night." I sent away the two men servants, and bade the maid go to bed, which she did. Then I sate there all night. All wrong was in her *sleep:* heavy, troubled breathing, and waking with oppression—no positive pain. She was always "Better—if I would but come to bed!" At times she would wander a very little in her mind, thro' the slightly increased dose of morphine acting on the weakness of body. I would say, "Do you know me?"—"Know *you!"* (And then what I can't write.) "And you know where you are?"—"Why—not quite!"—"And you *feel?"* "Comfortable—much better!" Only once she said, "Our lives are held by God." At four o'clock I observed her feet were cold, with other disquieting symptoms. I called the maid, sent the Porter for the Physician, got hot water. She sate up, smilingly. "Well, you *do* make an exaggerated case of it!"—"And my hands too"—then she turned to me and said what must stay in my heart—but happily, smilingly,—almost laughingly. There was an incident about a familiar thing at which she laughed; at this, I said, "For my sake will you take some jelly?" (She hated it and would not be persuaded to taste it.) "Yes"

3. Bettino Ricasoli (1809–80), statesman during all of Italy's struggle for unity, was elected Italian deputy early in 1861 and succeeded Camillo Genso Cavour (1810–61) as premier when Cavour died on June 6 of that year. A bloodless revolution in Florence had forced the Grand Duke to depart on April 27, 1859. A provisional government was formed, led by Ubaldino Peruzzi, and was strengthened on May 8 by the inclusion of Baron Bettino Ricasoli, a man of great force of character, who became the real head of the administration and all through the ensuing critical period aimed unswervingly at Italian unity.

—and she took two saucers full—as much as I thought prudent to give. Then she bade, "God bless me" repeatedly till I laid her down to sleep again. "How do you feel?" "Beautiful"—and she slept at once. In a few minutes I saw there was an internal difficulty—I took her in my arms, supported her head with mine. There was no struggle, no sigh even, only a dreadful suspense for a minute or two— then a silence. I thought she had only fainted as her head lay on my arm—then there was one least contraction of the brow and Annunziata cried, "The blessed Soul has passed away!" Why should I not have tried to tell you so much of this as will give you my own one comfort in some degree and not leave you to fancy there was pain, struggling, or the consciousness of departure and separation?—She went, like God's child, into his presence with no more apprehension or difficulty than *that!* Dr. Wilson came presently— it was daylight. He says he expected nothing so sudden—it must have been a breaking of an abscess in the lungs, and there could have been no help; there was no pain.

On Monday she was buried in the Protestant Cemetery. All the few strangers, English and American, were there—the dear and noble Italians honored themselves by honoring her—their newspapers bade "all go and pay homage to the great poetess, the true friend of Italy"—and they did go. The hearse passed thro' the streets, which is never allowed—with crowns on it, laurel and white flowers—and in our street the shops were closed. I just saw once, in a sort of flash, at the grave, Italian men crying like children, Villari [4] the historian, dall' Ongaro [5] the Poet, and many others unknown to me—but I will have done with all this—only, see if they are not grateful, this traduced people! Cavaliere Peruzzi [6] called on me a week ago: he said he and the Italians all were anxious I should not leave Florence,—or if that must be, yet that Pen might continue to be "a Tuscan"; he could go away for a year or two and come

4. Pasquale Villari (1827–1917), historian and statesman, was born at Naples from which he fled to Florence after taking part in the riots of May 15, 1848. At the time of Mrs. Browning's death he had just published *La Storia di Frà Girolamo Savonarola e de' suoi tempi* (1859–61), 2 vols.

5. Francesco Dall'Ongaro (1808–73) took a prominent part in revolutionary journalism throughout his life, in Italy, then in France and Belgium, and in Italy again in 1860. His patriotic poems, *Hornelli,* though not published until 1863, were written much earlier and doubtless were known by the Brownings.

6. See letter to Sarianna Browning dated July 13, 1861, n. 2.

back—"only, let him try a career with us—we want those who were friends in our ill days to share in our coming good fortunes—every thing will be open to him!"—Of course Pen is and will be English as I am English and his Mother was pure English to the hatred of all un-English cowardice, vituperation, and lies—but so he spoke, and so I shall remember.

I sate down to write a line, and you see! But you will understand and I think feel relieved by what I have caught out of the crowd of incidents that recur to me; tell the sum of it to any friends that may have been apprehensive of worse news. I have had kind, so kind letters from many, and others who have not written feel so, I need no assurance. Should you need to find me, address at my father's *151. Rue de Grenelle, Faubourg St. Germain,*—in a week I go thither at latest. Dear Forster, dear Mrs. Forster, I am and shall be yours affectionately

[Victoria and Albert Museum]   Robert Browning

To Sarianna Browning

Florence, July 22, '61.

Dearest,

I still remain here, having been detained for no better reason than that a little picture is being painted of the interior of our old drawing room just as she disposed it and left it. I tried to get it photographed, but without success: *this* is being done so perfectly as to render my stay well worth while,—the room has not an inch in it without a memory for me, and now that I go away it will be invaluable: [1] it will be finished tomorrow and I hope to leave on Saturday next: I will write the last thing.

On asking Miss Blagden what letter you could have referred to, "wishing you to go to Florence," I find that she wrote to you on her own responsibility on Wednesday 3d and, knowing I would not have allowed it, would not ask for your address, but directed to "R. de Grenelle" simply—most fortunately it never reached you—there was no imaginable good you could have done and every possible evil to Papa and me. But you must not blame dear warm-hearted Isa who got needlessly frightened—the fact was, I stayed here, as was right, till Tuesday evening. I then became ill of course,

1. This painting of the Casa Guidi drawing room is reproduced in Sotheby, *Browning Collections.*

and had one or two sort of choaking-fits unpleasant enough—in the afternoon of Tuesday, however, I found myself of a sudden with my head on the table and sense out of it for some few moments, and I at once walked up to her Villa, and took physic: in the night I had a couple more closings of the throat, or something of the kind, and I really thought I might not get thro' the next—so I told her two or [three] things necessary to be known for Peni, and consequently, more at ease about that, got safely thro' the night, took more physic and was soon better and well. If the worst had happened, you would have been utterly unable to help ten or eleven days after, I think! But people may be forgiven the blunderings of real love and indeed devotion. I am quite well now, understand— Pen has always been so. What you say about the time when the loss would have been most felt is quite true. He has known nothing but extreme affection and indulgence, and these do not stop now. What I lose is another thing. And for Pen, it can't be helped—a woman ought to be center of a home, but God has not allowed it here. I must keep up her influence—refer him to her books and life as much as I can.

I this minute got a note from Rome: Signor Benzoni, probably before this reaches you, will deliver to you the *Packed Negative* of the Photograph taken in Rome a week before we left—about a month before the end—and *perfect*.[2] Don't touch it,—there is nothing to pay: you will see its value when you see it. There was no way of sending it to me, but it is better *so*.

Arrange just as you like about a seacoast place—of course all will be at my expense—some quiet place. Is Bretagne impossibly far?— Do as you like.

Tell dear Milsand what a joy it will be for me to see him: thank him for his dear letter to me.

God bless you and dearest Papa.
I am ever yours affectionately
Robert Browning.

I tell people to direct letters to you for me. I repeat, I will write the last thing.

[Schiff]

2. Giovanni Maria Benzoni (1799–1873) was an Italian sculptor who probably formed part of the "sculptor's circle" in the Rome of the Fifties, a circle including Gibson, Harriet Hosmer, W. W. Story, and Browning himself in his capacity as eager dilettante of the art.

For Ferdinando Romagnuoli [1]

St. Enogat
Brittany
Sept. 5, 1861.

Ferdinando Romagnuoli has been in my service for the last ten years, and only leaves it now in consequence of the calamity which puts an end to my stay in Florence. I can give him the best of characters for honesty, sobriety and kindliness of disposition: he is an excellent Cook and knows the Markets well both in Rome and Florence. He is accustomed to travel, has accompanied me to Paris and London, and can act as Courier if required. *I recommend him strongly to anyone requiring a perfectly trust-worthy servant.*
[Huntington]   Robert Browning.

To Frederick Chapman

St. Enogat, Sept. 16, '61.

Dear Chapman,

I have too long delayed thanking you for your exceedingly kind note, received six weeks ago: but the goodness which led you to write it will understand and forgive me.

I leave this place at the end of the week for Paris—where I only remain for a day or two. I shall then go to London. I have therefore to beg you to send the *next Athenaeum* to me at 151 Rue de Grenelle, Faubourg St. Germain, Paris.

You have acted very considerately with regard to the offer of any Portrait: with respect to a new Edition of the *Poems*,[1] we will arrange on my arrival. Meantime, do me the favour to send (to the address I have just given) the account—which I am anxious to see at once.

You have quite misunderstood what I meant to say about publication of new things of my own—at all events, I surely never spoke of "an advance": we will talk it over in good time.

I should accept your offer to "make yourself useful" with great pleasure—but nothing occurs to me, for the moment, beyond the

1. Romagnuoli was hired by the Brownings in 1853, and married Wilson, Mrs. Browning's maid who had come with her from England in 1846. The marriage probably took place early in 1857.
1. The collected edition of E.B.B.'s *Poems*.

commissions I have just given you. Offer my best regards to Mr. Chapman,[2] and believe me

Yours ever faithfully,
Robert Browning.

Frederick Chapman, Esq.
Your little friend is quite well and wishes to be kindly remembered to you.
[Morgan]

To An Unidentified Correspondent

1 Chichester Road, Upper Westbourne Terrace
Jan. 14, '62.

My dear Friend,

A sudden opportunity presents itself of sending the packet of photographs—but it is too sudden to admit of more, i. e. of procuring from Paris and sending the others to the other friends: yours is the "proof" I received.

I wrote to you in a bewildered way, did I not, a few days ago? My little boy was attacked by what, for some short time, (except in the bearing it!) was pronounced to be small-pox: I had only just been assured that it was simple "chicken-pock" when I scribbled a word or two to you, as in duty bound: next day I sent Mr. Miller his first instalment of proofs.[1]

May I ask the favor of your kind attention to my friend, the bearer of this, Mr. Dicey?[2] He goes among you to study and report —and there can be no better guarantee of the value of his services to truth and good feeling than you have in his good and clever Books on the Italian Question. I write very hurriedly, but your own goodness emboldens me.

Ever yours very faithfully
Robert Browning.

[Yale]

2. Edward Chapman, Frederick Chapman's uncle, was head of the publishing firm.

1. James Miller, the American publisher, who brought out *Works of Mrs. Browning* (1863–64), in five volumes.

2. Edward James Stephen Dicey (1832–1911), author and journalist, who published *Rome in 1860* and *Cavour—a Memoir,* both in 1861. In 1862 he visited the United States and recorded his impressions in magazine articles and in a book, *Six Months in the Federal States* (1863).

To Mrs. Sophia Eckley

> 1, Chichester Road,
> Upper Westbourne Terrace,[1]
> March 28, '62.

Dear Mrs. Eckley,

I must have greatly misunderstood your note in which I thought you bade me, if I found it impossible to do what you desired, think no more about the matter, or words to that effect—and I found it, most truly, impossible to even think upon such a subject; indeed, I should have done you great wrong by even attempting to do so.[2] As for a publisher, none can ever be found for poetry by a new author, of whatever pretension it may be; that is certain.[3]

Depend on it, I forget nothing and nobody—whether to my greater happiness or misfortune, I really don't know: so give my kindest remembrances and love to your husband and Doady—Pen's going with mine, and forgive all mistakes that may be made by

> Yours, as of old,
[New York Public Library]   Robert Browning.

To Richard Monckton Milnes

> 1, Chichester Road,
> Upper Westbourne Terrace,
> Apr. 4, '62.

My dear Milnes,

My word of explanation and apology will have reached you by this time. On Sunday, with all my heart! I might hardly have

1. "I shall never again 'keep house,'" Browning had written his sister Sarianna a short time after the death of Mrs. Browning. In keeping with this determination he had taken lodgings at 1 Chichester Road. From October, 1861 to April, 1862 he remained at this address; then "he exchanged the discomforts of life in lodgings for a more settled abode." (See Griffin and Minchin, *Life*, p. 226.)

2. One may surmise that Mrs. Eckley had made the request for permission to publish the letters she had received from Mrs. Browning, or, perhaps, excerpts from them. For further reference to these letters see below, letter to Mrs. Eckley dated December 4, 1869.

3. Mrs. Eckley did find publishers for her verses: *Light on Dark Days, or Meditations for Lent* (London, 1863); *Poems* (London, 1863) (this is probably the volume for which Mrs. Eckley was seeking a publisher; Longman, Green, Longman, Roberts and Green printed it); *Easter Roses* (London, 1864); *Minor Chords and Other Poems* (London, Bell and Daldy, 1869).

thought it needful to say so, but for your own amazing modesty,—should you really have supposed that one could oversleep oneself when you pleased to be up and ready [1] for

Yours ever truly

[Lord Crewe] Robert Browning.

To Richard Monckton Milnes

19, Warwick Crescent
Harrow Road, W.
May 23, '62.

My dear Milnes,

I unluckily sprained my ancle yesterday and in the evening was unable to set foot to ground. I should, however, have endeavoured to limp up your stairs for the sake of the pleasure I was sure to feel at the top of them, had I not been bound to remember that I am obliged to go into the country tomorrow to poor Mrs. Twisleton's funeral,[1] tho' I suffer any amount of inconvenience afterwards. Will you say something of this to Mrs. Milnes whom I should have been so happy to see?

Here is a letter of Landor's in answer to what I wrote at your request: I feared that he might make some such objection.[2]

Ever yours most truly

[Lord Crewe] Robert Browning.

1. Milnes was "almost the last of the race of breakfast givers." He was "astir hours before any guests had appeared on the scene." For a description of these famous breakfasts at Fryston see Reid, *Life of R. M. Milnes,* I, 461–462; II, 246 ff.

1. Thomas Carlyle describes the Honourable Mrs. Edward Twisleton as "a very beautiful and clever little Boston lady" and adds: "I well remember her affecting funeral (old Broughton Castle in Oxfordshire) and my ride thither with Browning." (See *Letters of the Hon. Mrs. Edward Twisleton, 1852–1862* [London, 1928], p. 316.) Mrs. Twisleton had come to England as a bride in May, 1852, and through Mrs. Carlyle had met the Brownings that summer. Later the Twisletons had called upon the Brownings in Florence and had made a lastingly favorable impression through their kindness to Pen (pp. 34, 311).

2. Possibly Milnes had proposed, through Browning, that Landor leave his lonely abode in Florence and return to England. Later Browning, possibly to relieve Landor's loneliness and to do something for the bereaved Mr. Twisleton, sent the latter to Florence with an introduction to Landor. Landor was delighted with Twisleton and Twisleton with Landor. Browning had further illustrated his thoughtfulness and intuitive understanding of sorrow. (See John Forster, *The Works and Life of Walter Savage Landor* [London, 1876], I, 530–531.)

To Mrs. Alicia Bayne [1]

19. Warwick Crescent,
Harrow Road.
May 26, '62.

Dear Mrs. Bayne,

I shall be happy to go to you on the 13th: [2] it has been much on my mind that I never can call of a morning. Calling or keeping away, I am however,

Yours ever faithfully

[Yale]   Robert Browning.

To Mrs. Alicia Bayne

19. Warwick Crescent, Harrow Road
June 14, '62.[1]

Dear Mrs. Bayne,

I have to beg your pardon for unfortunately being unable to keep my engagement yesterday. I was obliged to rise and accompany my Sister to London Bridge [2] at a very early hour,—other matters called for me elsewhere in the course of the day,—and by the evening I was fairly worn out and fit for nothing but to go to bed— as I did accordingly. You will forgive me, I do hope.

Yours very faithfully ever

[Yale]   Robert Browning.

1. Alicia Bayne, nee Pryme (1814–83), resided at 40 York Terrace, Regent's Park. According to Thackeray's daughter, this "kind and hospitable cousin of my father's" occupied John Kenyon's house after his death. Thackeray thought Mrs. Bayne's "dining room was the prettiest room in all London" with its "wide green windows looking across the park" and the "graceful pillars to support the bay." (Anne Thackeray Ritchie, *Records of Tennyson, Ruskin, and Browning* [New York, 1892], p. 147.) She is described as "a very warm-hearted as well as intellectual person, a cousin of Thackeray, and with a good deal of his humor in her." (Connop Thirlwall, *Letters to a Friend* [Boston, 1883], p. 56.) She edited *Autobiographic Recollections of George Pryme* (1870) and was the author with her mother (Jane Townley Pryme) of *The Memorials of the Thackeray Family* (privately printed, 1879). She married William Joseph Bayne in 1837 and had two children by this union. Her husband died in 1844. (*Letters and Private Papers of W. M. Thackeray*, ed. Gordon Ray, IV, Table II of Genealogical Tables of the Thackeray Family.)

2. In the next letter to Mrs. Bayne, June 14, 1862, Browning offers excuses for not keeping this engagement.

1. This letter is postmarked June 16, 1862.

2. Probably to London Bridge Station nearly nine miles from 19 Warwick Crescent.

To Mrs. Alicia Bayne

19. Warwick Crescent, Harrow Rd.
June 24, '62.

Dear Mrs. Bayne,

Since your goodness is inexhaustible, be it as you desire. I shall drive with you gladly on the day you so kindly appoint.

Ever yours faithfully

[Yale]   Robert Browning.

To Richard Monckton Milnes

19. Warwick Crescent, Harrow Road.
July 5, '62.

My dear Milnes,

Landor never went to Rome nor wrote the letter—and is reported to me as driving out occasionally, "going in the garden or sitting on the terrace, quite well in health and much better in temper." *Meno male!* [1]

I will see to the other matter,—the inscription etc.—before you leave,[2] if that must unfortunately be.

Ever yours faithfully

[Lord Crewe]   Robert Browning.

To Richard Monckton Milnes

Nov. 18, '62.

My dear Milnes,

How very kind you are, and how unlucky, or, if you like, ill-conditioned am I! The three months' holidays are over,[1] I represent

1. *Meno male:* literally, "less bad"; here, "the case is less bad than was supposed." A letter signed Walter Savage Landor was published in the London *Times* for June 26, 1862, p. 7, col. 3. The letter is a rambling circumstantial account of a visit to Rome, interrupted because a French bishop overbid the writer for his room. The tone of the letter is breezily anti-Catholic. As Browning's letter to Milnes indicates, Landor was not the author of it. It is probable that Browning's information was conveyed to him by John Forster who, during these last years of Landor's life, served with Browning as guardian *in absentia* of the aged poet.

2. Milnes spent five weeks at Buxton trying to rid himself of an illness first reported in the London *Times*, June 17, 1862. The inscription may be connected with Milnes' work on a jury for the Exhibition of 1862. (See Reid, *Life of R. M. Milnes*, II, 83.)

1. Early in August, Browning with his father, Pen, and Sarianna, set out for Ste Marie, near Pornic, on the Atlantic coast of France; there they stayed

stern duty in this establishment, the lessons are begun, and there's no leaving the post! [2] You know how I should have enjoyed myself otherwise. Pray say this for me to Mrs. Milnes, and, on the boy's part, to your young ladies.[3] See how well he looks in a photograph made the other day, only crossish, which he isn't.

> Ever yours most truly
> Robert Browning.

Landor is unhappily vivacious just now,—tries to plague me and succeeds somewhat.[4]

[Lord Crewe]

To Miss Isa Craig [1]

> 19 Warwick Crescent,
> Harrow Road,
> Dec. 5, '62

Dear Miss Craig,

You only do me too much honor; and I wish with all my heart I could send you any verses fit for your purpose: [2] really I have

---

until October 2. Then they returned to Paris where Browning and Pen spent a week before getting back to London and 19 Warwick Crescent.

2. Browning's attitude toward Pen's regimen, his lessons, his "progress"— mental and physical—is an arresting example of parental psychology. After two months of "stern duty" and "lessons" Pen is reported to the Storys as "growing a great fellow and a dear good boy besides," with the additional comment: "I am much satisfied with him." This was on January 18, 1863. The next day, however, Browning reported to Miss Blagden with less confidence: "Pen is quite well: there are many things that vex me—I'll tell you if I have time—but on the whole I see progress for him, work for me." (*Letters*, ed. Hood, p. 73. For the best account of Browning and Pen, see Gertrude Reese, "Robert Browning and His Son," *P.M.L.A.*, LXI, 784–803.)

3. Mrs. Milnes, before her marriage, was the Honourable Annabel Crewe, younger daughter of the second Lord Crewe. Amicia (Amy), aged 11, and Louisa are the "young ladies."

4. Landor was 88 but still capable of becoming a vexation to his patient friends, Forster and Browning. (See John Forster, *Walter Savage Landor*, pp. 516–546, for an account of Landor's last years in Florence; also, H. C. Minchin, *Walter Savage Landor, Last Days: Letters and Conversations* [London, 1934], *passim*.)

1. Isa (Craig) Knox (1831–1903), miscellaneous writer, was a friend of George Eliot to whom she presented the manuscript of her book *Duchess Agnes: a Drama in Three Acts and Other Poems* (London, 1864), now in the Rare Book Room of the Yale University Library. (See *Allibone's Dictionary of Authors, Supplement*, II, 962, for a brief biography.)

2. Miss Craig was apparently soliciting a poem for an anthology to be called *Poems: an Offering to Lancashire* (London, 1863).

nothing and can invent nothing of the kind. I always am humble
and sorry at being forced to say this when similar applications are
(now and then) made to me,—but particularly humble and sorry
in the present case, since you are the applicant.

Pray believe me
Yours most truly
Robert Browning

[Yale]

To Mrs. Alicia Bayne

19. Warwick Crescent,
Upper Westbourne Terrace, W.
Feb. 2, '63.

My dear Mrs. Bayne,
  Yes—with the greatest pleasure.[1]

Faithfully yours ever
Robert Browning.

[Yale]

To Mrs. Alicia Bayne

19. Warwick Crescent,
Upper Westbourne Terrace, W.
May 8, '63.

Dear Mrs. Bayne,
  How very good you are to remember simply to be kind to me, and
forget the long time that has gone by since I received the last piece
of kindness—the note, and tickets for the Gardens: [1] but I had to
go to Paris; [2] and find much occupation since my return. I will try
and thank you on Wednesday—for I accept your invitation with

1. This note, like several others in this volume, was jotted down while the
messenger waited for a reply. One may deduce from a comparison with Browning's letter of February 2, 1866, below, that this note accepted an invitation to
one of Mrs. Bayne's annual festivities, perhaps a birthday party.)

1. Probably the Botanical Gardens (Regent's Park) where "large flower-shows
take place on three Wednesdays in May and June, which are largely attended
by the fashionable world." (K. Baedeker, *London and Its Environs* [London,
1881], p. 222.)

2. Browning had written to Isa Blagden on January 19, 1863 that he would
"probably go to Paris for a week at the end of next month—as a change for
Pen and a pleasure to my father." (*Letters*, ed. Hood, p. 77.) The trip was
probably taken in March and extended beyond the limit of a week.

great pleasure. The Boy is as well as your goodness would have him be, and I am

Ever yours faithfully
Robert Browning.

[Yale]

To Richard Monckton Milnes [1]

19. Warwick Crescent
Upper Westbourne Terrace, W.
July 7, '63.

My dear Milnes,

I should like to put down in words what I said last night when considerably surprised and a little annoyed: you will see how mere talk gets turned aside from its purpose; and for reasons, I am somewhat susceptible on this point.

I know next to nothing of Swinburne, and like him much: I have received courtesy from him, and been told he feels kindly to me—I believe it indeed. Of his works, since his first volume,[2] I know not a line, except a poem which I looked over a long while ago at Rossetti's, and the pieces he recited the other night: I could only have an opinion, therefore, on these. I thought them moral mistakes, redeemed by much intellectual ability. They may be a sample of the forthcoming book,[3]—or just the exceptional instances—I hope so.

When I was abruptly appealed to, some days after, for my estimate of Mr. Swinburne's powers,—I don't know what I could do but say "that he had genius, and wrote verses in which to my mind there was no good at all."

If I referred,—as I probably did, to a similarity of opinion on the part of others present, it was from the reluctance I had to stand forward and throw even this cherry-stone at a young poet.

How I came by this reluctance, and keep it increasingly in spite of age ("which loses all sense of the good and the beautiful, the this and the that")—God knows! I have for thirty years had my own

1. This letter, with a circumstantial explanation has been published in K. L. Knickerbocker, "Browning and Swinburne: An Episode," *M.L.N.*, LXII [April, 1947], 240–244.

2. *The Queen Mother and Rosamund* (1860).

3. Two of the poems were probably "The Leper" and "Les Noyades," poems to be published in *Poems and Ballads* (1866).

utter unintelligibility taught with such public and private zeal that I might be excused for fancying every young man's knuckles wanted "dusting"—but I don't fancy it. Unluckily the truth is the truth, and one must speak it now and then. It was a shame in this case for Chapman to quote my blame of two or three little pieces—given on a demand for unqualified praise which was impossible—as the reason for rejecting a whole bookful of what may be real poetry, for aught I am aware: but as I am in the habit of being as truthful as I like about the quality of certain other things which he patronizes, and as I never saw their titles disappear from his advertisements in consequence—I conclude that he only uses my witnessing when he wants to cover his own conviction.

I am, my dear Milnes,
Yours ever faithfully

[Lord Crewe]   Robert Browning.

To Mrs. Alicia Bayne

19. Warwick Crescent,
Upper Westbourne Terrace,
July 17, '63.

My dear Mrs. Bayne,

I accept very gratefully on the part of Robert your kind invitation for to-morrow: he will be punctually with you at 2. o'clock.

Thank you much for the seal—the arms are altogether different from ours: [1] but, depend on it, that shall hinder nothing of your kinship, if you please, so that I shall be *proudly* as well as

faithfully yours ever

[Yale]   Robert Browning!

1. "Water-colour drawings (2) of Browning's arms, crest, and motto *Virtute*" appear as item 1237 of Sotheby, *Browning Collections*. According to Oscar Browning, Robert Browning used as his arms those of a Roman Catholic family named Byning; he describes them as "gules two bands wavy or and argent, a most beautiful crest." When he saw Pen Browning's gondoliers at the Palazzo Rezzonico at Venice decked out in "red tunics and the wavy bands of gold and silver on their arms," he wished he "could display anything so striking." (*Memories of Sixty Years at Eton, Cambridge and Elsewhere* [London, 1910], p. 6.)

To Miss Isabella Blagden [1]

19. Warwick Crescent
Upper Westbourne Terrace, W.
July 19. '63.

Dearest Isa,

We are here, you see, and mean to leave London as we did last year, on the 1st August—for the same place, Pornic or rather Ste. Marie, two miles off—if we can get the same house there—for which my sister has written. There are many advantages,—not the least being that we know the place. Mrs. Bracken and Willy mean to accompany us in all probability—we stay there two months, I suppose—and I shall much enjoy the silence and fresh air, little picturesque as the country is. You must write to my sister's next time and till the end of September,—"R. B. 151. Rue de Grenelle, Faubourg St. Germain"—in your most legible hand, if you please. [2]

Annunziata [3] called here last Monday—I was out unluckily: she promised to come again to-day, and I shall see her with very mixed feelings. Here she is. And now she is gone, poor dear thing. She looks very well, seems very comfortable,—may stay in England a long time. She was amazed at Pen's growth—he was as happy to see her as I. Next let me tell you a characteristic thing while it is in my

1. Isabella Blagden was probably the closest friend to the Brownings during the years they lived in Florence. She saw them almost daily after 1849, and frequently visited them in their summer vacations at Bagni di Lucca and Siena. She was at Casa Guidi on the day before Mrs. Browning's death and took charge of the poet and his son in the days that followed. When Browning left Florence he and she made a pact to write monthly letters to each other, she on the 12th and he on the 19th. Most of Browning's letters to Miss Blagden have been published in *Letters to Isa Blagden*, ed. Armstrong; others appeared in *Letters*, ed. Hood. The present letter was overlooked in those collections and was given to the Yale Library by William Lyon Phelps. Miss Blagden made her living by her pen; among her novels were *The Cost of a Secret, Nora and Archibald Lee,* and *The Crown of a Life*. In his break with Chapman in 1866, Browning was partly motivated by the publisher's treatment of so loyal a friend as Isa Blagden. (See Appendix C. See also William O. Raymond, "Our Lady of Bellosguardo: A Pastel Portrait," *University of Toronto Quarterly,* XII [July, 1943], 446–463.)

2. All the plans set forth in this paragraph were carried out, as Browning records in the letter of August 19, 1863, to Miss Blagden. (See *Letters to Isa Blagden,* pp. 93–96.)

3. Formerly maid to Mrs. Browning, who said of her: "Her activity and intelligence are really great, and her good nature and kindness not less. . . . I haven't a fault to find." (*E.B.B.: Letters to Her Sister,* p. 283.)

mind: sweet Sophy E. has published a volume of verses—of which I only came across one specimen in a review the other day—the *Press:* that critic, evidently knowing nothing of the author, whom he called "Miss Eckley"—said—"respect for the 'mighty dead' should have kept this lady from touching those poems of Heine's which were the *last translation* of Mrs. B."—and he quoted the attempt—actually the first of *that last translation of all.* It strikes me as more repulsive than any instance of Eckleyism [4] even I ever came

4. David Eckley, his wife Sophia, their child Doady, and Miss Eckley, had come to Italy from America in the early Fifties. Mrs. Browning was acquainted with Sophia Eckley as early as December, 1853. A warm friendship developed between the families, and the Eckleys were able to do many kindnesses for the Brownings. Browning in 1858 speaks of the Eckleys as being "extravagantly good to us," and Mrs. Browning calls them "our dear friends" and describes them as people of "enthusiasm and simplicity." (*Letters of E.B.B.,* II, 150, 296, 298.) But Browning mistrusted Mrs. Eckley, and Mrs. Browning came to agree with her husband before her death. In Mrs. Browning's *Last Poems* (London, 1862) there appeared a satire upon Mrs. Eckley, called "Where's Agnes?" Two apposite stanzas are quoted here:

> My Agnes false? such shame?
>   She? Rather be it said
> That the pure saint of her name
>   Has stood there in her stead,
> And tricked you to this blame. . . .
>
> She who scarcely trod the earth
>   Turned mere dirt? My Agnes,—mine!
> Called so! Felt of too much worth
>   To be used so! too divine
> To be breathed near, and so forth!

(We are indebted to Mr. Edward McAleer for calling our attention to Browning's identification of Mrs. Eckley as Agnes.)

In Mrs. Browning's *Last Poems* had appeared her "Paraphrases on Heine." Then in her *Poems* (London, 1863) Mrs. Eckley included her own "Paraphrases on Heine." Under this heading she paraphrased one of the poems chosen by Mrs. Browning and thereby committed an act that was repulsive to Browning. The critic for the *Press,* mentioned in the present letter to Miss Blagden, could regard Mrs. Eckley as unwise in inviting comparison with a greater poet, but to Browning Mrs. Eckley's act seemed impertinent, if indeed it was not treacherous. In a letter to Isa Blagden Browning summarizes the case against Mrs. Eckley as follows: "When Mrs. Eckley found herself discovered, she never made an effort to recover her place in Ba's liking, not to say love, still less esteem. . . . Ba wrote her *one* letter, which I read, and which, depend on it, don't figure in the book as 'finis,' and then, for the next year and a half, not a word: for "Where's Agnes?" disguised in the circumstances for my sake, who always said, 'For the husband's sake, and because *you* really deserve some punishment in the matter.' . . . Of course the letters are nothing but what it is

across—and really completing, by one black touch, the picture of that remarkable lady. You can hardly fancy a stranger doing it—unless he were translating the whole of Heine: but in a collection of rubbish, to stuff in just this!—All I can say is, *I* would not have believed it of her!

I shall not write much, for seeing A. has given me a headache. I received your note about Mrs. Freeman and called on her the next day. Her works show how decidedly artistic a turn she has, and what a deal she might have done with cultivation. Her verse, and other little things have everything but what, I suppose, it is too late for her to acquire. I hope she may succeed in selling them. She looked very well, and spoke in high praise of London, preferring it (as I understood) to Rome.[5] It will be long before I read Mrs. Brotherton's book,—but the reviews praise it, I am glad to find.[6] I cannot get Romola—spite of my repeated applications at Mudie's—and shall give up subscribing to him in consequence: his humbug is too much.[7] I found Tennyson, however, reading it in bed last Thursday—he has got an eruption—suppressed hay fever or irregularly-acting vaccination, he thinks. I dined with him the week before, and found him very pleasant: he has poems ready,—one, in particular, called "Enoch the sailor,"—which I wish he would make haste and print.[8] Yes, you may be sure I saw Mr. Conway's unwise

natural Ba should feel for 'Agnes' in her supposed perfection of purity." (See *Letters to Isa Blagden,* pp. 159–160.) There is a later exchange of letters with Mrs. Eckley. See below, Browning's letter to Mrs. Eckley of December 4, 1869, upon the disposition of Mrs. Browning's letters to her.

5. The Mrs. Freeman in this passage may be Augusta Latilla Freeman, wife of James Edward Freeman, an American painter who went to Rome in 1836 and remained there until his death in 1884. He married in 1845. His book, *Gatherings from an Artist's Portfolio* (New York, 1877), mentions many of Miss Blagden's and Browning's friends: W. W. Story, Harriet Hosmer, John Gibson, Thackeray, and many others. Browning is not mentioned. The *D.A.B.,* in the notice of her husband, describes Mrs. Freeman as a sculptress.

6. Mrs. Mary Brotherton, *Respectable Sinners* (London, 1863), 3 vols. See above, letter of November 14, 1853.

7. George Eliot's *Romola* had appeared serially in the *Cornhill* from July, 1862 to August, 1863 and was issued in book form in the summer of 1863. The book was popular, and Mudie's—one of the first and largest book-lending companies—doubtless was unable to keep all its subscribers happy.

8. Hallam Tennyson records that *Enoch Arden* was first called *The Fisherman.* (*Alfred Lord Tennyson, A Memoir* [London, 1897], I, 487.) When *Enoch Arden* was published in 1864, Browning wrote to Tennyson that the title poem "continues the perfect thing I thought it on first reading" (II, 16). See, how-

piece of picturesque narration: he means well, of course. He said
I was very intimate with the Lewes's—i.e., I dined once, and spent
two evenings there! [9] Kate Field wrote a nice letter to me the other
day with reference to some article she had written and sent—but
which I have not yet received.[10] I can't fancy she would do anything to give me pain, so shall not anticipate it. By the bye, I met
Mr. Adams,[11] the A[merican] minister, in a railway this m[ornin]g
and he told me Vicksburg was taken—no news to you by the time
you read this. Annunciata never got the book of certificates—and I
forget to whom you sent it: was it to Lucca? You told me, but I
can't remember. Cottrell wrote about the contract he had signed—
it seems a very moderately-termed and judicious one, and if the
sculptor is honest and careful, I shall be very satisfied—as I have
told him.[12] I never had any doubt as to his kindness. What do you
mean by saying that Pen "with his new friends and new objects of
interest, cannot remember you much?" All I can say is, his delight
at seeing A. just now—was edifying—he kissed her, got her wine,
etc., went with her to Miss Barrett's, and part of the way home,
and wanted to go further—in short, was just as he should have been.

---

ever, a letter to Julia Wedgwood, a confessed Tennyson heretic, in which
Browning says of *Enoch Arden:* "Could I rule the economy of the piece, it
should go thus:—" and then he invents a completely different ending for the
poem. (*Robert Browning and Julia Wedgwood,* ed. Richard Curle [New York,
1937], pp. 56–59.)

9. George Eliot (Mrs. Lewes) recorded in her *Journal* for December 16, 1862:
"In the evening Browning paid us a visit for the first time." (*The Complete
Works of George Eliot* [St. James Edition, London, 1908], X, 267.) Browning
also records this first visit in a letter of December 19, 1862: "I went the other
evening to see Mrs. Lewes . . . I liked her very much." (*Letters to Isa Blagden,*
p. 80.) Conway states in his *Autobiography* that Browning "liked to talk with
George Eliot and Lewes, but was rarely at the Priory on their Sunday evenings,
when others were usually present." He concludes that the Leweses "arranged
for private talks with Browning." (Moncure Daniel Conway, *Autobiography*
[Boston, 1904], II, 32, 165.)

10. This may be the article on Mrs. Browning which appeared in the *Atlantic
Monthly* in September, 1861. The article is not signed; but Lilian Whiting
writes of Kate Field's "series of papers in the *Atlantic Monthly* between 1861
and 1868, comprising her article on Mrs. Browning," etc. (See *Kate Field, a
Record,* p. 144.)

11. Charles Francis Adams (1807–86), American minister to the Court of
St. James from 1861 to 1868.

12. This was the contract for the monument in Florence to Mrs. Browning,
the design for which had been drawn by Frederic Leighton. Cottrell was in
charge of seeing that the design was properly executed.

You must have enjoyed Vallombrosa—Cottrell mentioned your going there. Are you going to stay at the Villa now, or go elsewhere, to Leghorn, or Siena? Tell me. I hear the weather has been very hot at Florence, and Rome: here it was oppressive, certainly—but for these last few days I have felt actually cold. My dinners, and all that, are nearly at an end—to my immense relief. I saw A. Trollope the other night at my new club, the Cosmopolitan [13]— he told me of his brother's arrival, and wanted to arrange for our meeting but it was not to be—they went to Torquay, I believe, and will return when I am far away. I had a letter from Lytton the other day—I believe he is coming to England in August. His novel seems an absolute failure—but he has got the money for it: he said, it might be surprising, but he had really expected the thing to be an advance on all he had done before. I only observed two reviews of it—two contemptuous notices.[14] He should act differently if he wants to get any permanent hold of people worth securing.

Goodbye, now, dearest Isa: I fancy you were in a hurry when you got over these two half sheets I last received—all the same, I am always glad and grateful for never so little a scrap of writing, and sometimes you are very generous. Pen came into the room just now. "Are you writing to Isa? Give her my best love!"—I wouldn't tell him you suspected him of forgetting you. Whenever I have an opportunity, I will send the photograph and the little book. I won't forget you to my Father and sister—and do you remember me to the Cottrells and other friends.

Ever yours affectionately
Robert Browning

[Yale]

13. The Cosmopolitan Club was founded in 1852 and flourished until the end of the century as the Saturday and Sunday night meeting place for a diverse group of distinguished members. (See T. H. S. Escott, *Club Makers and Club Members* [London, 1914], pp. 167–169.)

14. Robert Lytton (Owen Meredith) published the *Ring of Amasis* (London, 1863), on June 13. Browning at Lytton's request read the proofs, and then advised against publishing the book. On July 2, 1863, Lytton wrote to Browning: "Unfortunately your good advice . . . comes too late. It was not possible to stop the book. . . . I honestly thought very well of this book, and indeed fancied it an improvement in many respects upon previous work." (See *Letters from Owen Meredith to Robert and E. B. Browning*, ed. A. B. and J. Lee Harlan, pp. 214–216.) *The Ring of Amasis*, according to the reviewer for the *Spectator* (July 11, 1863), is "gaudy nonsense" written in the "meretricious style of debased art." This was probably one of the "contemptuous notices" to which Browning refers.

To Moncure Daniel Conway [1]

Chez M. Laraison, Ste. Marie, Pornic,[2]
Loire Inférieure, France.
Sept. 17, '63.

My dear Mr. Conway,

I shall have literally only five minutes to give to this note, if I would catch the next Post and save a day. I can manage, however, to reply on every point you mention—and you will understand why no more than such replies are set down. The date of the publication of each piece in the collection is printed, you will see, at the head of it.[3] No poem has been omitted, and none added to the present edition,—always excepting one very early thing, never known as mine, nor likely to be remembered by anybody.[4] There are no changes of importance in any of the poems—merely verbal corrections, nor many of these:—in the instance of *Paracelsus*, the few changes are simply a return to the original reading, which I had polished a little, in the second edition,[5] and done no good to. *Sordello* is corrected *throughout;* not altered at all, but really elucidated, I hope, by a host of little attentions to the reader: the "headlines," or running commentary at the top of the page, is added for the first time.[6]

1. Moncure Daniel Conway (1832–1907) "in 1863 went to England to lecture in behalf of the North." (*D.A.B.*) As noted in this article, Conway, because he "always came in contact with the leading men of the day," has been accused of "tuft-hunting." The present letter and others from Browning indicate that Browning appreciated Conway's interest in him and his work. Conway, for his part, consulted Browning on the strategy to use in converting the English to a more sympathetic view of the North's cause. (M. D. Conway, *Autobiography*, I, 412.) Conway's enthusiasm for Browning remained constant. In 1884 he prepared a paper on *Sordello* for the Browning Society. (*Browning Society's Papers, 1881–91,* 3 vols. [Meeting of October 31, 1884], II, 1*–4*.)

2. Browning arrived in Pornic about the middle of August and remained until early October.

3. The collection referred to is the second collected edition of Browning's *Poems*, announced in the *Athenaeum* of December 11, 1858 as a "New Edition —2 vols., 16s." (See *Letters to Isa Blagden*, p. 101, for Browning's comment on one criticism, perhaps Conway's, of this edition.)

4. The poem omitted was *Pauline*, which Browning finally reprinted in 1868.

5. There was no genuine second edition of *Paracelsus*, but the poem was reprinted with corrections in the first collected edition of Browning's *Poems* in 1849. (DeVane, *Browning Handbook*, pp. 46–47.)

6. See Browning's letter to Furnivall, written 23 years later, in which he re-

I need not add that I shall be much interested in seeing your article,[7] and that, despite your judgeship and whatever its sentence, I shall always be

Yours heartily,

[Huntington]   Robert Browning

To Mrs. Alicia Bayne

19. Warwick Crescent,
Upper Westbourne Terr.
Nov. 18, '63.

Dear Mrs. Bayne,

I am glad indeed to hear your kind voice again—Hibernicè [1]—thro' the well known hand-writing. For the invitation,—I accept it with pleasure: I already know the Professor a little, and like him much.[2]

The Boy shall be informed of your goodness, and I hope to profit by it in my degree. All regards to you all.

Yours very faithfully ever

[Yale]   Robert Browning.

peats this estimate of the amount of change *Sordello* had undergone. Yet, the 5,800 lines of the 1840 *Sordello* had been expanded to the 5,981 lines of the 1863 *Sordello*. Moreover, in the *Sordello* of 1863, the "meaning of passages is clarified, phrases are expanded into sentences, and the punctuation renovated." (For the letter to Furnivall see *Letters,* ed. Hood, p. 248; for a full account of the revisions of *Sordello,* see DeVane, *Browning Handbook,* pp. 67–68.)

7. The article was simply called "Robert Browning" and appeared in the *Victoria Magazine,* II (February, 1864), 298–316, as a review of *The Poetical Works of Robert Browning,* 3 vols., Third Edition, Chapman and Hall. Conway uses, in several ways, Browning's statements in this letter. For example, he "regrets the omission" of *Pauline,* a poem "in every way worthy" of the poet (p. 298). Of *Sordello* he says: "materially it has not been altered; but yet the mere changes of punctuation and the introduction of 'he said' or 'she said' before the quotation marks which once bewildered the reader, have removed a host of difficulties" (p. 301). The article as a whole is a warmly appreciative rational analysis of Browning's best accomplishments. It must have interested Browning to read this sentence: "In America, where the works of this poet are very widely read and studied, I have even heard of a Browning Club" (p. 298). If there were such a club it would antedate the London Browning Society by 18 years.

1. Browning is calling attention to his jest by labeling it an Irishism.

2. Mrs. Bayne's father, Professor George Pryme, had many professorial colleagues who were welcomed to Mrs. Bayne's hospitality. To which one Mrs. Bayne here refers it is not possible to say.

To Miss Elizabeth Rayner Parkes [1]

19. Warwick Crescent,
Upper Westbourne Terr.
Jan. 19, '64.

Dear Miss Parkes,

Miss Blagden's address is simply "Post Restante, Florence." She sends every day to the office, and gets the letters which would otherwise go to her Villa at night.

I don't know whether the maps I enclose may at all interest your Father,[2] but can do no harm by sending them. Would you kindly tell him further that it *was* to Mr. Taylor [3] that my Father lent my copy of the little book on the *Art of War* (a translation) with P. F.'s [4] autograph on the title-page or flyleaf—and that I shall be

1. This letter to Miss Parkes was addressed to 17. Wimpole Street. Elizabeth Rayner Parkes (1829–1925) met the Brownings in Rome during the Fifties. She had published several volumes of verses: *Poems* (London, 1852); *Summer Sketches and Other Poems* (London, 1853, 2d ed. 1855); *Gabriel* (London, 1856); *Ballads and Songs* (London, 1863), etc., and "longed to take a place among the poets of her day." (Mrs. Belloc Lowndes, *"I, Too, Have Lived in Arcadia"* [London, 1941], p. 1.) Mrs. Lowndes is the daughter of Louis Belloc (son of Hilaire Belloc) and Elizabeth Rayner Parkes Belloc. She gives a useful account of her mother's "long fight on behalf of what was to become known by the name of Women's Rights." In this fight she joined forces with Mme. Bodichon, another Englishwoman with a French husband. Browning was not sympathetic with the endeavor sponsored by these two women.

2. Joseph Parkes (1796–1865) was from 1847 to his death Taxing Master of the Court of the Exchequer. In a speech before Parliament on February 7, 1828 Lord Brougham described Parkes's *History of the Court of Chancery* (London, 1828) as "one of the ablest and most instructive books published of late years." Browning's close friend, Charles Skirrow, who was Master in Chancery, doubtless knew this work and valued Browning's relations with its author. Parkes was also a dabbler into the question of the identity of Junius and offered as his candidate Sir Philip Francis. (*D.N.B.*)

3. Probably "Mr. Taylor" is Henry Taylor (1800–86)—Sir Henry Taylor in 1869. Browning, according to Mrs. Orr, did not meet Taylor until 1872. (*Life*, p. 279.) But James Spedding in a letter dated December 14, 1871 invited the poet to a dinner with Taylor. (*Browning's Letter File*, ed. Armstrong, p. 56.) The "little book" was *The Art of War—In Four Parts. Containing I. The Duties of Officers of Horse* [by Sieur de Birac] II. *Of Officers of Foot* [by M. de Lamont] III. *Of a Soldier in General* [by M. de Lamont] . . . IV. *The Rules and Practise of War* [by Chevalier de la Valière], written in French and translated into English by an English officer, illustrated with several copper cuts. J. Morphew, London, 1707. 340 pp.

4. The initials P. F. are doubtless those of Sir Philip Francis (1740–1818), English politician and pamphleteer, who has been supposed by many, including Joseph Parkes (see n. 2, above), to be the author of *Letters to Junius*.

obliged if that gentleman will return it to me by Mr. Parkes' kind intervention.

I was prevented answering your note at once, so shall leave it myself to be sure you get it by post time.

Faithfully yours
[New York Public Library]   Robert Browning.

To Mrs. Alicia Bayne

19. Warwick Crescent,
Upper Westbourne Terrace, W.
Tuesday M[ornin]g. [March 15, 1864.] [1]

Dear Mrs. Bayne,

I begin by paying for my ticket—and hope to end by making use of it at the proper time—but as accidents may happen, I shall at worst give it to some probable purchaser. All thanks and good wishes to you!

Yours very faithfully
[Yale]   Robert Browning.

To Moncure Daniel Conway

April 26, '64.

Dear Mr. Conway,

Here are the proofs [1] which I promised; they will be published on or after 21st May. I rely on your entirely keeping them to yourself, as, with one exception, nobody has seen them.

Yours very truly
[New York Public Library]   Robert Browning

To Moncure Daniel Conway

Tuesday M[ornin]g. [May, 1864] [1]

My dear Mr. Conway,

I don't think that Tennyson is in Town still: he was at that House whither we walked together on Friday week—and a great surprise

Parkes with Herman Merivale compiled the *Memoirs of Sir Philip Francis, with Correspondence and Journals* (London, 1867.)

1. The postmark on the envelope is March 15, 1864, a Tuesday in that year.
1. Proofs of *Dramatis Personae*, published on May 28, 1864. The New York Public Library has the proofs along with this letter.
1. Conway records that "when 'Dramatis Personae' appeared, the first re-

was his presence: but I heard that, for some reason or other, nobody ought to know anything about his apparition, which would be brief moreover: he goes to friends' houses, and is hard to catch.[2]

With respect to the early sheets, they are of course only for American use [3]—if one "favoured" (as they politely call it) an English Journal at the expense of its fellows, author and publisher would have to pay for it. You can, of course, get your article ready and manage that it appear *almost* simultaneously with the book's self —and I am sure I shall be happy to see and profit by it.

You must get Howell at the Museum: it is not a very common book, as the *Letters* which are everywhere.[4]

The delay in writing was caused by my wanting to give you more satisfactory information: but you know the good will of

Ever yours most truly

[Yale]   Robert Browning.

To Mrs. Alicia Bayne

19. Warwick Crescent,
Upper Westbourne Terrace.
June 13, '64.

Dear Mrs. Bayne,

I shall be happy to go to you on the 29th if another engagement will allow—I can say no less, but, alas, not more!

Robert is too Robertish yet for Evening parties! Thank you very much for him, however.

Believe me, Dear Mrs. Bayne,
Faithfully yours

[Yale]   Robert Browning.

view of it was written by myself, from proofs Browning gave me, for the 'Morning Star.' " (*Autobiography*, II, 21.) It is apparently to these proofs that the second paragraph refers. *Dramatis Personae* was published on Saturday, May 28, 1864. This letter was probably written a short time before this date.

2. Conway, armed with a letter of introduction from Browning, went to Farringford in June, 1863 and met the Tennysons. (See Conway, *Autobiography*, II, 32–33.) Tennyson's London visit mentioned in this paragraph is not recorded in Hallam Tennyson's *Memoir*.

3. Ticknor and Fields in Boston brought out the American edition of *Dramatis Personae* simultaneously with the English edition.

4. Probably Browning refers to James Howell (1594?–1666), whose *Dendrologia, Dodona's Grove, or the Vocall Forest* (1640) is "not a very common book" and whose *Epistolae Ho-Elianae* "are everywhere" from having been reprinted many times.

To the Reverend Robert Eyres Landor [1]

London.
19. Warwick Crescent,
Upper Westbourne Terrace.
Nov. 25, '64.

Dear Sir,

In obedience to instructions from Miss Landor,[2] I beg to say that I have engaged a Packer and got a Case made for the Pictures consigned to me—and that this Case was sent this morning to the Pershore station of the Oxford and Worcester Railway—where you may at once obtain it. Every care was taken, of course, and I hope that the journey may be a safe one.

The Packer's bill,—in obedience also to those instructions,—is herewith submitted to you. And the amount may be discharged by Post order to E. G. Hambling, 9. Delamere Street, Paddington,— directly,—or the same enclosed to myself, just as is more convenient.

I congratulate myself on the opportunity which this letter gives me of assuring you, however unnecessarily, of the respect and regard of, Dear Sir,

Yours very faithfully,
[Yale]   Robert Browning.

1. Robert Eyres Landor (1781–1869) was a younger brother of Walter Savage Landor. After a successful career as scholar and fellow at Worcester College, Oxford, he became rector at Birlingham, Worcestershire, in 1829 and remained there until his death. He was an author as well as a generous and conscientious clergyman. In 1823 he published anonymously his *Count Arezzi*, which for a while was thought to be by Byron. Among his other literary productions were three tragedies, published in 1841: *The Earl of Brecon, Faith's Fraud*, and *The Ferryman*. In 1846 there appeared the *Fawn of Sertorius*, and in 1848 the *Fountain of Arethusa*. He also frequently helped W. S. Landor in matters of publication. The present letter as well as those of November 28 and December 7, 1864, in this volume were addressed to R E. Landor at Birlingham Rectory, Pershore. All of them refer to pictures which W. S. Landor, who died on September 17, 1864, wished to have sent to his brother. Browning had served unofficially as Landor's guardian from 1859 until the death of the elder poet, and with Forster had been instrumental in relieving his destitution by obtaining £200 a year from Landor's brothers with a reserve of £50 to be spent under Browning's direction. (See *D.N.B.*, "W. S. Landor," and H. C. Minchin, *Walter Savage Landor, passim*.)

2. Miss Landor is Elizabeth Sophia Landor, Walter Savage Landor's niece, who helped Browning administer the provisions of Landor's will. (See *Letters*, ed. Hood, pp. 347, 350.)

To the Reverend Robert Eyres Landor

London,
19 Warwick Crescent,
Upper Westbourne Terrace,
Nov. 28, '64

My dear Sir,

I shall not attempt to reply, as perhaps I could; you know too well with whom the generosity had rise which I have been simply privileged to assist in its course,—and I am now further privileged in being able to give you the comfort of knowing that none of that generosity failed of its proper effect,[1] and that for five years so much was contributed to the quiet and satisfaction of a man who, in spite of strange mistakings, and unfortunate hastinesses of judgment and temper, was gifted with more extraordinary endowments, as well of heart as of head, than ever met in a man before,—so far as my experience goes. The weakness is already past and forgotten, but that royalty of intellect will be increasingly perceived by the world.[2]

The amount of the charges on the Pictures, defrayed by me in Florence as well as London two years ago, I find to be £5.19.4—as specified in the enclosed Bill and Memorandum. I have just discharged the Packer's Bill, returned by you,—and the sum which you desire to pay will accordingly be

$$5.19.4$$
$$18.6$$
$$\overline{6.17.10}$$

Pray remember me, my dear Sir, as

Yours faithfully and obligedly ever,

Robert Browning

I need not add that the Bill may be destroyed forthwith, though I cannot help troubling you with it for regularity's sake.

[Yale]

1. A reference to the settlement of an annuity upon W. S. Landor by his brothers in 1859. See letter of November 25, 1864, above, n. 1.

2. Browning's estimate of Landor's endowments was consistently loyal and penetrating, and does him credit. Landor, however, knew that he would never be popular or indeed widely recognized.

To the Reverend Robert Eyres Landor

19 Warwick Crescent,
Upper Westbourne Terrace,
Dec. 7, '64

My dear Sir,

I have been stupidly culpable—and your goodness will sooner forgive me than I shall forgive myself. The Order came safely and punctually: but, instead of acknowledging its receipt to yourself, I mentioned it to Miss Landor in a letter which I had occasion to address to her on forwarding a paper just obtained from Florence. I can hardly believe in my own oversight—for "negligence" at least it was not.

I had something to say, too, of my satisfaction at your getting the picture [1] and being pleased with it. You give it rightly to Allori, no doubt: its last attribution to M. Agnolo or del Piombo did all the harm. It was not, however, refused by the Lady [2] on any other account than that of want of a place for it.

I hope—and am encouraged to believe—that if I can ever be of somewhat more use to you than in the little business of packing a picture, you will give me the gratification of letting me at least try to do my best.   Ever yours most faithfully,

[Yale]   Robert Browning.

1. The picture was one of those bequeathed to R. E. Landor by W. S. Landor and had been recently sent to him by Browning. Walter Savage Landor wasted huge sums on worthless pictures, and it was characteristic of him to ascribe an unsigned painting in his possession to the great artists, Michelangelo (1475–1564) and del Piombo (1485–1547), instead of to the less well-known Allori (1577–1621). The picture in question was probably one called "The Last Judgment," which Landor sent to Browning in London in September, 1863. In this case, however, the ascription of the picture to Sebastian del Piombo was made to Landor by an unnamed French artist. (See H. C. Minchin, *Walter Savage Landor*, pp. 165–169.) Allori was especially skillful in copying pictures by the greater masters.

2. The "Lady" mentioned here may have been Isa Blagden, a familiar figure in Browning biography. She resided at the Villa Bellosguardo, just outside Florence, and shared with Browning the burden of caring for the aged poet. It is possible, however, that the lady may have been Mrs. Lynn Linton, the novelist, to whom Landor wished to give two pictures in 1862. He was refused permission to do so, however, by Mr. Linton, the lady's husband. (See H. C. Minchin, *Walter Savage Landor*, pp. 153–154.)

To Mrs. Alicia Bayne

19. Warwick Cresc[ent].
Upper Westb[ourne] Terr.
Dec. 9, '64.

Dear Mrs. Bayne,

I was unable to get to you in time last night: one needs not apologise for one's misfortune, perhaps. Thank you heartily for your note and the invitation. Yes, I know . . that is, I have seen Mr. Digby [1] at your house—I almost fancy on that very day you mention and which I shall never forget. But I shall hope to find you at home soon, but will only say now how much I am

Yours ever faithfully

[Yale]   Robert Browning.

To Mrs. Alicia Bayne

19. Warwick Crescent,
Upper Westbourne Terr.
Jan. 30, '65.

Dear Mrs. Bayne,

Truest thanks for your invitation—but as true regrets that I am unable to accept it, having already an engagement at Mrs. Ford's: [1] you well know how gratified I was last year at being allowed to share in your festivity!

I am even more sorry, and by far, that you should find or fancy Miss Bayne's [2] health otherwise than "strong": go to Italy next year

1. Kenelm Henry Digby (1800–90), miscellaneous writer and ardent Roman Catholic convert.

1. Possibly Mrs. Walter Ford, mentioned but not further identified in *Letters of Anne Thackeray Ritchie*, ed. Hester Ritchie (London, 1924), p. 62. She may be the "Mrs. Ford" who was one of eight women members of the Burlington Fine Arts Club, an association of wealthy amateur collectors. (*Burlington Fine Arts Club: Catalogue of Pictures . . . of Mr. Robert Holford* [London, 1921–22], p. 6.)

2. Miss Bella Bayne is described by Connop Thirlwall as "all goodness—good heart, good sense, and thoroughly true and trustworthy." He adds: "From the sight of her you would hardly guess that she made quite a furore in London, by her performance in some private theatricals which poor Thackeray gave for the house-warming of his villa in Kensington." (*Letters to a Friend,* p. 56.) This triumph of Miss Bayne in a "terribly ungrateful part" brought her the nickname of "the little Trojan" from Thackeray and praise as "the greatest success of the play." (*Some Family Letters of W. M. Thackeray Together with*

by all means, and I shall have one more obligation to her if she mend whatever may be amiss.

The boy is strong and well, happily: I should much like to show you his "points," and we will manage somehow what you so kindly desire: but he works now, and I scarcely ever interfere with his play-hours or leisure.

With best remembrances to your family, Dear Mrs. Bayne,

Ever most truly yours

[Yale]   Robert Browning.

To John Ruskin [1]

19. Warwick Crescent,
Upper Westbourne Terrace, W.
Feb. 24, '65.

Dear Ruskin,

Just when you wrote last, and I replied, and all your pleasant proposal was in full prospect, the boy caught the measles and I could not decide on going out: he is now quite well again—and it is my turn to be a little out of sorts, weather aiding and abetting, I suppose. So, let us [2] wait a few days longer for a day indeed with never a drawback.

A letter, from my sister in Paris, did not bring you to my mind, certainly, but told me how properly you were placed there: [3] I can't help sending a strip of it, because it is an indirect and unintended witness to a fact I should like you to be sure of. I know and love Milsand thoroughly, and his existence to me is proof of innumerable good things which the daily rabble of rascaldom goes near to

---

Recollections by his Kinswoman Blanche Warre Cornish [Boston, 1911], pp. 56–57.)

1. Browning first met Ruskin in the summer of 1852. It was not until 1855, after the appearance of *Men and Women,* that a more personal friendship was established through a frank exchange of opinions on poetry in general and Robert and E. B. Browning's poetry in particular. (For a running account of this battle of words see E. T. Cook, *Life of John Ruskin* [New York, 1911], I, 457 ff.) The best and most significant of Browning's letters to Ruskin appears in W. G. Collingwood, *The Life and Works of John Ruskin,* I, 232–235.

2. A short word has been scratched and blotted out at this point.

3. Ruskin's visit to Paris must have been a short stay, for one of his biographers states that "In 1865, he, for once, did not go abroad, but was fairly steadily in London." (Amabel Williams-Ellis, *The Tragedy of John Ruskin* [London, 1928], p. 264.)

cast doubt upon sometimes. I hope you will see him face to face some day.

> Ever affectionately yours
> Robert Browning.

Always my truest regards to Mrs. Ruskin,[4] if you please.

[Huntington]

To Mrs. Alicia Bayne

> 19. Warwick Crescent,
> Upper Westbourne Terrace, W.
> June 1, '65.

Dear Mrs. Bayne,

Many thanks for your kindness: I am pre-engaged,—go to your neighbours the Palgraves.[1] I daresay your trip to Cambridge was a great pleasure to all concerned in it. I think I saw the sisters at Ella's [2] last week: I rejoice to hear good news of them.

> Ever yours most truly

[Yale]   Robert Browning.

4. Margaret Cox Ruskin (1781–1871), John Ruskin's mother, "tall, handsome, pious and practical." (W. G. Collingwood, *The Life and Works of John Ruskin*, I, 9–10.)

1. Francis Turner Palgrave (1824–97) the anthologist was preparing an edition of *Shakespeare's Poems* at this time. The Palgraves lived at York Gate, Regent's Park; Mrs. Bayne at 40 York Terrace, Regent's Park. Palgrave met Browning at Hallam Tennyson's christening in 1852, but "real knowledge began somewhere about 1861." (G. F. Palgrave, *Francis Turner Palgrave: His Journals and Memories of His Life* [London, 1899], p. 218.) G. F. Palgrave remembered Browning "as a frequent visitor at my father's house . . . he constantly spent Sunday afternoons with him and my mother" (p. 94).

2. John Ella (1802–88), violinist and concert director, was identified with the promotion and appreciation of music, particularly instrumental music, between 1826 and 1880. His wide acquaintance with continental musicians drew the highest talent to London and to "Ella's" afternoon and evening concerts. Three characteristics of Ella concerts gave them piquancy and prestige: the introduction of analytical programs which were printed and sent out to subscribers a few days before the concert, the centering of the artist so that his audience surrounded him, and the combining of concert and social gathering so that only by personal introduction could one secure admission. (*D.N.B.*) Browning was regular in his attendance at the annual series of Ella concerts, and it was there that he met Rubinstein and other continental musicians.

To Frederick Wedmore [1]

> 19. Warwick Crescent,
> Upper Westbourne Terrace, W.
> Nov. 13, '65.

My dear Mr. Wedmore,

Do forgive—I entreat of your good nature,—this delay of mine in replying to your note: indeed I was in hopes of being able to say something really to the purpose—but find one man is abroad, another engaged for the present. I shall wrong myself in your eyes unless I write at once. Whenever Mr. Ella [2] returns from Italy,—I believe that at my request he will lay open to you every source of information possible—give you access to his Musical Library, which should be a good one: or another person,[3] if I can manage to reach him, will do all you want. There may be fuller notices than those which I mentioned; if so, these gentlemen profess to know them. At the same time, the books in question are undoubtedly to be found at the British Museum, and there you may consult them at any time.

Had I but time myself! The want of it, however, seldom makes itself so unpleasantly felt as it did that Saturday [4] when some business, which promised to last half the time that it proved to require, caused me to miss your visit: I reached home just after your departure. I wonder whether you will indulge me so far as—when next you come to Town—after having apprised me, to dine here in my quietest of ways? So shall I recover what I must regret to have lost; or even be the gainer.

1. Sir Frederick Wedmore (1844–1921) at the time of this letter was evidently just beginning his career as an analyst of the arts. His interest, though here apparently centered on the history of music, later took the direction of art as represented by etchings, prints, genre painting, and biographies of artists. While employed by the *Daily Bristol Times and Mirror* Wedmore wrote to Browning, probably in early October, 1865, requesting information about "Abt Vogler." Browning replied "very courteously and fully." (See Frederick Wedmore, *Memories* [London, 1912], p. 52.) Wedmore proposed "to write a biographical sketch" of Abt Vogler, "nothing more ambitious than that." (*Browning's Letter File*, ed. Armstrong, p. 33.) The poet was apparently eager to help the young journalist forward by enlisting the aid of such eminent musicologists as John Ella.

2. See preceding letter, n. 2.

3. Possibly George Grove, musicologist, whom Browning had met at least as early as 1863. (Charles L. Graves, *Life and Letters of Sir George Grove* [London, 1903], p. 97.)

4. Probably, October 28, 1865. (See *Browning's Letter File*, ed. Armstrong, p. 33.)

The "Poem," you ask about, is a very long affair which I have been at work on for some time,—but as for "publishing" it,—*that* will not be done so readily: next year, perhaps.[5]

Very truly yours

Robert Browning.

[Huntington]

To Richard Monckton Milnes

19. Warwick Crescent,

Upper Westbourne Terr.

Dec. 20, '65.

My dear Houghton,[1]

Don't think me careless about these, your kind invitations, much less ungrateful. I have kept refusing pleasant calls—away from this place; till now, even if I wished to go, I could not with any decent face. Yet I like much to know that if I brought myself to break the tee-total pledge, you, for one, would be ready with a bottle of the best: thank you heartily—and herewith I pass the port.

Tennyson has been in town and lit up the blackness for us at whiles.[2]

Please thank Lady Houghton for her remembrance of me and the Boy—italicising the last word. He is getting big and looks bearded—("looks"—as the grudging somebody said of a lady— "*pretty*, well, she *looks* so!")

Another thing—who wants to buy a Botticelli,—a *Tondo*, the Holy Family, old good frame and picture intact—a fair specimen? A friend has begged me to sell it for him if I can: an old Florentine connoisseur.[3] There are works on sale at double the price. It is here if anyone wants to look at it.

Ever faithfully yours,

Robert Browning.

[Lord Crewe]

5. *The Ring and the Book* was not published until November, 1868.

1. Milnes had in 1863 accepted the title which his father had refused, that of first Lord Houghton.

2. Tennyson mentions Browning in his letter diary covering the events of this trip to London: "Dec. 12th . . . Browning was here. . . . Dec. 15th a great gathering at Woolner's. . . . Thompson the Confederate was there and Browning, and innumerable anecdotes were told." (Hallam Tennyson, *Alfred Lord Tennyson, A Memoir*, II, 32.)

3. Probably Baron Seymour Kirkup is "the old Florentine connoisseur." The picture referred to is possibly one appearing in *Botticelli Der Meisters Werke*, herausgegeben von Wilhelm von Bode (Berlin, 1926), p. 127, and listed

To Mrs. Alicia Bayne [1]

> 19. Warwick Crescent,
> Upper Westbourne Terrace, W.
> Feb. 2, '66.

Dear Mrs. Bayne,

I make haste to say that the delay in thanking you for your very kind note was caused by a misdirection of it from the Club to a namesake of mine: [2] I only get it this moment.

Although I had accepted another engagement, I consider this to be, under all circumstances, rather a summons than a mere invitation: I was delighted to be one of your guests on the same festal day the year before last,—and, last year, was only disappointed of the same gratification thro' the illness of my son. [3] I have therefore written to excuse myself, and shall gladly be present on this occasion. I remember all that is to be remembered, having been lessoned before.

I am glad to hear that you and your daughter have escaped the vile weather which is heavy upon all less happily situated.

Very sincerely and obligedly yours

[Yale]   Robert Browning.

To Frederick Chapman [1]

> 19. Warwick Crescent,
> Upper Westbourne Terrace, W.
> [February] 16, '66. [2]

My dear Frederick,

Now that the new Edition is out at last, will you kindly make all

---

on p. 149 as "Heilige Familie (falschlich zugeschrieben) (London, Privatbesitz)."

1. This letter to Mrs. Bayne was addressed to Gledlion Hall, Torquay.

2. Oscar Browning says of Robert Browning and himself: "We met frequently at the Athenaeum, where there was often confusion about our letters." (*Memories of Sixty Years,* p. 119.)

3. The letter of January 30, 1865 indicates that perhaps another invitation, not Pen's illness, stood in the way of accepting Mrs. Bayne's invitation.

1. Frederick Chapman (1823–95), a nephew of Edward Chapman, joined the firm of Chapman and Hall as bookkeeper when he was 18. Browning's addressing him directly indicates the strained relations between the poet and Edward Chapman. (See letter to Edward Chapman dated June 26, 1866 and Appendix C; information about Frederick Chapman is given in Arthur Waugh, *A Hundred Years of Publishing,* pp. 76–77 and *passim.*)

2. *The Poetical Works of Robert Browning* in three volumes appeared in

the proper calculations, and pay me what is right? I have been called on to help an old friend inconvenienced by the failure of a bank,[3] and should be glad of the money. Pray be as liberal as possible. As for the *Selections*,[4] I suppose you will have to settle with my heir,— *I* give up hopes of seeing it.

Very truly yours

[Morgan]   Robert Browning.

To An Unidentified Correspondent

19. Warwick Crescent,
Upper Westbourne Terrace, W.
Apr. 27, '66.

Dear Sir,

I was not in London when your letter with its enclosures reached me,—let this excuse the delay in replying to it. I have read the poems you are good enough to care for my opinion about: and will at least deserve your kind feeling by plainness and truthfulness. You know I have given all my life to poetry,—not a short life, now: and I have observed the procedures of my contemporaries, great and small: the result is,—I distinguish markedly between the good of having the poetical temperament, and the *not-good* of attempting to make poetry one's self, except in the extraordinary cases where there is original creative power added to the merely sensitive and appreciative,—valuable and distinguishing as these are. I have never seen an instance of success in verse,—to the extent even of selling fifty copies,—where something absolutely *new*, for good, or even for bad, was not prominent in it. I can hardly hope to please you by this frankness: and, after all, I incline too much, perhaps, to severity in criticism,—alas, what is it worth else? At all events, my practical advice would be, to continue publishing in periodicals until something more decisive is effected: the amount of publicity

---

late January, 1866, which supplies the month for this date. Someone cut it away in cutting out Browning's crest.

3. We have been unable to identify the "old friend" of this passage.

4. *Selections from the Poetry of Elizabeth Barrett Browning* appeared December 9, 1865. This may be the volume to which Browning refers and for which, though only two months have passed, he is impatient for payment. (See letter to Edward Chapman dated June 27, 1866.) It is more likely that the *Selections* represent the Procter-Forster cullings from Browning's poetry, published December 20, 1862; if so, then indeed Browning had reason for impatience.

obtained in this way,—which is, I suppose, the object in view,—will be immeasurably greater.[1]

Let me say, in reference to your postscript, that the Chevalier and I have never interchanged a word in our lives:[2] he lives next door to me, and has written more than once respecting translations etc.

I am, Dear Sir,

Yours very faithfully,

Robert Browning.

[Boston Browning Society]

To Alfred William Hunt [1]

19. Warwick Crescent,

Upper Westbourne Terrace, W

April 29, '66.

My dear Sir,

I made use yesterday of the Ticket, with which your kindness furnished me, and saw—what you please to call in your note—"the Drawing." [2] I feel proud indeed, and something better, that any poem of mine should have associated itself with the power which conceived and executed so magnificent a picture,—I weigh the word and repeat it. My own "marsh" was only made out of my

1. Browning's lifelong repugnance toward publishing his own poetry in periodicals gives a curiously negative point to this piece of advice. See his letter to Thackeray on January 17, 1860 in which he refuses Thackeray's request for a contribution to the *Cornhill Magazine*. (*Letters of W. M. Thackeray*, ed. Ray, IV, 171.)

2. Browning's neighbor, the Chevalier de Chatelain (see below, letter of May 18, 1871), was a friend of Victor Hugo and, had Browning "interchanged a word" with him, perhaps he would have had entree to the French novelist without requesting the intercession of Lord Houghton (see below, letter dated July 24, 1866).

1. Alfred William Hunt (1830–96), landscape painter, was the father of Violet Hunt, who recalls being at tea with the Brownings, Sarianna and Robert, in her early childhood. (Violet Hunt, *The Wife of Rossetti* [New York, 1932], p. xx.) Though Hunt was championed by Ruskin, he was so unfavorably treated by the Royal Academy that, after exhibiting five times under R. A. auspices from 1857 to 1862, he confined the showing of his pictures to the Old Water Color Society's Exhibition (later, Royal Society of Painters in Water Colours) from 1863 to 1870, when he resumed relationships with the Royal Academy.

2. This was Item 121, "Childe Roland to the Dark Tower Came," as recorded in *The Exhibition of The Royal Society of Painters in Water Colours* (London, 1866).

head,—with some recollection of a strange solitary little tower I have come upon more than once in Massa-Carrara, in the midst of low hills,—for I wrote at Paris: [3] somebody ought to beat me now!

I venture to add, that I was much impressed by your other admirable performances,—"Harlech," for instance, and the "Tarn." [4] Pray let me give you my hearty thanks for all these good and great things, and be remembered by you as

Yours ever truly

A. W. Hunt, Esq.   Robert Browning.

[Huntington]

To Edward Chapman

19. Warwick Crescent,
Upper Westbourne Terrace, W.
June 26, '66.

My dear Chapman,

I was prevented by various circumstances from calling yesterday, and do not know whether I can get to you to-day: so I write. I am sure I felt as much pain, as you possibly could, in taking such a step as, at first, seemed incumbent on me: and I felt as real a pleasure when your explanation proved sufficient. As for the agreement, I will sign it, of course—though it leaves matters pretty much where it finds them: for I have never complained that you did not make me a sufficient allowance on the copies printed,—nor that the payments were not made precisely at the proper time, for I never doubted but you would be ready to do so if I took the trouble to ask you; still less did I ever blame you for not giving me an exact account of copies on hand,—on the contrary you have always proposed to examine the books and report progress,—the less necessary a thing, because, once paid for an edition, I have no further money-interest in the copies on hand. Of course, absolute punctuality is best for us both; still, I repeat, my supposed grievance did

3. For a summary of details relating to the composition of " 'Childe Roland to the Dark Tower Came,' " see DeVane, *Browning Handbook*, pp. 204–207.

4. Eight of Hunt's water colors were exhibited by the Society of Painters in Water Colours at their gallery, 5 Pall Mall East. Item 160 is called "Harlech, from Llandecwyn," and Item 325 is "Stickle Tarn, Langdale Pikes." E. R. Dibdin praises Hunt's paintings for "their absolute truth, their keen conception of beauty, and the refining and delightful vein of poetic imagination." (*Bryan's Dictionary of Painters and Engravers* [revised ed., London, 1921], III, 87.)

not lie *there*—but in what I thought the fact that a publication from which we were entitled to expect considerable results had proved a comparative failure, and it did strike me that my trees of this sort would gain by changing the soil. I desire no better than that you show me I was wrong. You must do me justice to say, I neither show suspiciousness nor inordinate expectation of gain,— nor do I ever pretend to teach you on matters which you cannot but understand better than myself. But really my income may be seriously affected by affairs in Italy,[1] and I ought to care a little about what most of my fellows of the pen care abundantly for.

I don't see anything to remark on—except the obligation, in case we part company, to buy *steel plates*—are they not paid for out of the first expenditure?—*Ex. gr.* £25 in the case of the *Selections*.[2] It seems to me that the *stereotyping* [3] which is *not* so charged for (I believe)—is a different thing: am I right or wrong?

I shall wait for the account—the exact sum due to me—before I pay in the cheque: and *that* I shall be glad to have at once.

I return the letters,—which quite satisfy me as to what may be your unfor[e]seen liabilities: for the future, I am warned.

You see, poor Miss Blagden has been too well justified in her complaints; and it is a worse case apparently than I or she supposed, —though *you* are happily out of it. I sent her your letter at once.

If you tell me, when you write, that the agreement is drawn up, I will go and sign it on any day you appoint.

Very truly yours ever

[Morgan]   Robert Browning.

To Edward Chapman [1]

19. Warwick Crescent
Upper Westbourne Terrace, W.
June 27, '66.

My dear Chapman,

Nothing can be fairer, I think, than your proceedings, and I am

1. Browning wrote to Isa Blagden on May 19, 1866: "Suppose I am ruined by the loss of my Italian Rents,—how then? I shall go about and sell my book to the best bidder." (*Letters*, ed. Hood, p. 93.) The Brownings did not own Casa Guidi. Little is known about his Italian rents.

2. Probably *Selections from the Poetry of E. B. Browning* (1865).

3. Stereotypes were fixed molds made from the movable type.

1. This letter and a note written on November 11, 1867 (see below) bring

quite contented with my share of the profit. I agree to what you propose, about the abatement to be made, when the next Edition appears, of what you now pay for as to an English market, if you get an American one. I hardly expected this piece of shabbiness: Francis paid for nothing but *Aurora Leigh*,—not a *cent* for the previous poems which he has been multiplying editions of, these twenty years, and Miller paid for *Last Poems and Greek Chr[istian] Poets;* but why that is to prevent an English copy of the whole works entering America, I don't know.[2]

I hope you will do well with this Edition, I am sure. I did not require the payment for the *Selections*,[3] but it will be agreeable to get so much money at once. If you like to send it in one cheque, I will return that which I have and I will also call next week and sign the paper.

Yours very truly ever
Robert Browning.

[Morgan]

---

to an end the Browning-Chapman correspondence and, as it turned out, their business relationship. Another letter, dated June 20, in which Browning set down his grievances against his publisher, has been lost or, perhaps because of its contents, destroyed. The missing letter and these two final published letters, along with a full account of events leading to the ultimate break, are discussed in Appendix C.

2. Charles Stephen Francis (1805–87) was senior member of the publishing firm, C. S. Francis and Co., New York. From 1860 to 1880 he operated the business of the firm alone. His London agency secured for him the rights to print in America, simultaneously with English editions, the works of currently popular authors. Since international copyright was inoperative, Francis' willingness to pay for *Aurora Leigh* was so unusual as to stir Browning's praise. Francis had published as early as 1850 an edition of E. B. Browning's works, copied from the London edition. He had issued another edition in 1857, "carefully corrected by the last London edition." In 1860 he had "pirated" *Poems Before Congress* with an edition which he called *Napoleon III in Italy and Other Poems*. These pilferings were doubtless part of Browning's charge of "shabbiness." J. Miller, however, was apparently a worse offender, for in 1866 he brought out in America *Poems of Elizabeth Barrett Browning*, from the last London edition, corrected by the author, J. Miller, New York. This American edition would make it inadvisable, certainly, for Chapman and Hall to export the *Works* of Elizabeth Barrett Browning. The English edition was called: *Elizabeth Barrett Browning's Poetical Works*, Seventh Edition, In Five Volumes (London, Chapman and Hall, 1866). This was, as T. J. Wise points out, the first English edition of Mrs. Browning's collected works. (*A Browning Library* [London, 1929], p. 82.)

3. Possibly *Selections from the Poetry of Elizabeth Barrett Browning* (1865).

To Mrs. Frederick Lee Bridell-Fox [1]

19. Warwick Crescent,
Upper Westbourne Terrace, W.
July 21, '66.

My dear Tottie,

It is very kind of you to care about seeing me,—I am sure I should very much like seeing you. If I *can,* I will call on you next Sunday, —but I perhaps *cannot,*—I am just going out of Town, and, on Sundays, have to keep a particular track, where one or two friends profess the habit of expecting me,—therefore, never mind the lunch (which I never take) but let me try to call about the time you mention, and if the trial is to no purpose, forgive and understand me.

Indeed, I want to see and ask you a favour,—promised me by your Father two or three years ago: [2] he had, or once had,—so he thought, a few utterly insignificant scraps of letters and verse written by me when a boy: if you find them, do—for old love's sake,— give them to me again! I used to write to Miss Flower [3] when I was twelve or thirteen years old,—she had the vice of keeping every such contemptible thing (as she told me)—and, in consequence, whatever she thought to keep, Mr. Adams [4] or some congenial spirit now inherits. I applied for my belongings, I seem to remember, and got

1. Mrs. F. L. Bridell-Fox was the daughter of William Johnson Fox (1786– 1864). She describes her first meeting with Browning—"slim, dark, and very handsome"—as occurring on May 7, 1835 at the home of her father. (Orr, *Life,* p. 86.) She married a promising artist, Frederick Lee Bridell, in February, 1859, but the marriage was cut short by Bridell's death from consumption in August, 1863. (See Richard and Edward Garnett, *Life of W. J. Fox,* pp. 311– 312.)

2. Fox, father of Mrs. Bridell-Fox, had died on June 3, 1864.

3. Sarah Flower, later Mrs. Adams (1805–48), object of Browning's "boyish love" and recipient, apparently, of many of his effusions. (See Orr, *Life,* pp. 34–35.) As coexecutor of Benjamin Flower's will, Fox acted as unofficial guardian of Eliza and Sarah Flower after 1829. It was through Fox, who had seen and praised Browning's earliest poetry, *Incondita,* that Sarah and Elizabeth Flower had come to know, and to copy out, the verses of the juvenile Browning. (See Griffin and Minchin, *Life,* pp. 42–43.)

4. Sarah Flower married William Bridges Adams (1797–1872) in 1834. He was an inventor of devices for railways, the best known of which was a "fish" joint to secure rails to each other. In addition to his interests in civil engineering he wrote political pamphlets under the pseudonym of Junius Redivivus. (*D.A.B.*)

no answer: but if there be anything *you* can lay hands on, it will come to me, I know.[5]

Ever affectionately yours

[Huntington]   Robt. Browning.

To Richard Monckton Milnes

19. Warwick Crescent,
Upper Westbourne Terrace, W.
July 24, '66.

Dear Houghton,

I think of going to Guernsey, at the week's end,—on Friday,[1] to-wit. I don't know whether to stay a while or otherwise; but, what do you say? Could you well give me a word of introduction to Victor Hugo?[2] Be quite sure that I shall understand that "cannot" is correct—to the letter of the word, if you write it.

Ever truly yours

[Lord Crewe]   Robert Browning.

---

5. The best record of Browning's almost desperate desire to destroy all evidence of early epistolary, literary, or amorous indiscretions is found in a letter from his father to Thomas Powell on March 11, 1843: "He has destroyed all [his early poems] that ever came in his way, having a great aversion to the practice of many biographers in recording every trifling incident that falls in their way." He adds that his son "has not the slightest suspicion that any of his very juvenile performances are in existence." (See Orr, *Life*, pp. 32–33.) It was doubtless such pleas as this to Mrs. Bridell-Fox which enabled Browning to cover up his juvenile tracks.

1. On July 27 Browning proceeded to Le Croisic via Jersey, Dinard, and St. Malo and remained in Le Croisic from early August to late September.

2. Mrs. Orr recounts that Hugo was "an eminent French writer whom [Browning] much wished to know" and that "for years he carried about him a letter of introduction from Lord Houghton, always hoping for an opportunity of presenting it." (*Life*, pp. 171–172.) Hugo had occupied Hauteville House, Guernsey, since his expulsion from Jersey in 1855. Mrs. Orr states, however, that "though, in 1866, Mr. Browning crossed to Saint Malo by the Channel Islands and spent three days in Jersey," he did not meet Victor Hugo. Browning mentions writing to Frederick Tennyson on Jersey but does not refer to Guernsey at all. (See *Letters*, ed. Hood, pp. 100–101.)

To Felix Moscheles [1]

19. Warwick Crescent,
Upper Westbourne Terrace, W.
Apr. 6, '67.

Dear Moscheles,

I really wanted to give you a better chance, but there's no use in waiting: here is the stanza,—and I advise that you take the last four lines: I put in the preceding, for symmetry's sake.

> Dear, the pang is brief;
>   Do thy part,
> Have thy pleasure. How perplext
>   Grows belief!
> Well, this cold clay clod
>   Was man's heart.
> Crumble it—and what comes next?
>   Is it God?
>   In a Year. by R. B.[2]

Ever yours truly
RBrowning.

[Yale]

1. Felix Moscheles (1833–1917) was the son of the pianist, Ignaz Moscheles, described as "the greatest executant of his age." (*Encyclopaedia Britannica*, 11th ed.) Felix became a painter of some distinction and a long-time acquaintance of Browning, whom he met, he says, at the home of his cousins, the Benzons. (Felix Moscheles, *Fragments of an Autobiography* [New York and London, 1899], p. 26.) Browning provided the poetic inspiration for some of Moscheles' paintings. He sat for Moscheles in 1884; the portrait hangs now in the Ohio Wesleyan University Library. (See Grace E. Wilson, *Robert Browning's Portraits* . . . [Waco, Texas, 1943], p. 142.) The intimacy was made secure when Pen Browning decided to become an artist. Moscheles reports the following colloquy: " 'What would you advise about Pen's studies?' said Robert Browning one afternoon as we sat in my little studio, talking about his son's talents and prospects. . . . 'Send him to Antwerp,' I said, 'to Heyermans; he is the best man I know of to start him.' " (Felix Moscheles, *In Bohemia with Du Maurier* [New York, 1897], p. 27.) Browning followed this advice and was ever grateful thereafter for Moscheles' suggestion.

2. This poem appeared first as a companion piece for "In Three Days" in *Men and Women* (1855).

To Mrs. Theodore Martin [1]

19. Warwick Crescent,
Upper Westbourne Terrace, W.
Thursday. [May 9, 1867] [2]

Dear Mrs. Martin,

How gladly I would go to you on Sunday but for an engagement I have to dine with the Goldsmids! [3] I know the Professor a little and like him very much indeed, finding in his freshness and enthusiasm all the good you describe: and I was sorry to miss a Friday e[venin]g lecture of his a week ago. [4] But how much one misses in this whirling London,—and how vexatious it is that I should so often miss the delight of seeing friends like your husband and yourself! Give my truest and kindest regards to him, however, and remember me always as,—dare I venture to write it honestly down? —affectionately yours

[Huntington]   Robert Browning.

1. For Mrs. Martin's relations with Browning see letter of August 14, 1886, below, n. 1.

2. The dinner at the Martins' "on Sunday" to meet Professor Blackie (see n. 4 below) occurred on May 12, 1867. (Sir Theodore Martin, *Helena Faucit, Lady Martin* [London, 1900], p. 286.) The Thursday preceding this date would be May 9, 1867.

3. Jenny Lind (1820–87), the great Swedish singer, married Otto Goldschmidt in 1852 while touring with him in America under the management of P. T. Barnum. Goldschmidt, a German, was naturalized a British citizen in 1859 and settled in London. (*D.N.B.*)

4. A caret appears after "Professor," above which is written, in a hand other than Browning's, the name "Blackie." John Stuart Blackie (1809–95), poet, translator, and classicist, is described by Mrs. Martin in a "Journal" entry for May 12, 1867, the day she had hoped to bring Blackie and Browning together, as "fresh and clever. . . . but somewhat fatiguing to the nerves." She promised Blackie "a letter to Browning" because she wanted "to know how they assimilate." (Sir Theodore Martin, *Helena Faucit*, p. 286.) Armed with Mrs. Martin's letter, Blackie called on Browning on May 14. "He received me," wrote Blackie to his wife, "with the greatest frankness, having known me of old from the *Aeschylean* correspondence I had with Elizabeth Barrett Browning." (*The Letters of John Stuart Blackie to His Wife*, ed. A. S. Walker [London, 1909], p. 160.) The Friday evening lecture (May 3) on the subject "Music of Speech in the Greek and Latin Languages" was delivered with "dash" before "a galaxy of well-dressed ladies" and such gentlemen as Gladstone. (Anna M. Stoddart, *John Stuart Blackie* [London, 1896], p. 246.) Several of Blackie's letters to Browning are printed in *Browning's Letter File*, ed. Armstrong.

To Edward Chapman

19. W[arwick] C[rescent].
Nov. 11, '67.

My dear Chapman,

Thank you very much for your kindness and consideration.

I kept away purely for the reason I gave you,—a complimentary one altogether.[1] You should see me often enough if I could do you any real good. There may be something superfluous in this care about myself now-a-days, perhaps, but it is a care I must take.

It is over kind of you to complete your liberal present of Mr. Dyer's book: do you know I never received volume 3? [2]

Ever yours cordially

[Morgan]   Robert Browning.

To the Librarian of the Oxford Union Society

19. Warwick Crescent,
Upper Westbourne Terrace, W.
March 10, '68.

Dear Sir,

In a recent visit to Oxford,[1] I had an opportunity of observing that the Union Society had done my works the honor of including them in the Catalogue of their Library. May I be permitted,—as a trifling record of the great pleasure I experienced in attending a

1. There is tact but perhaps only a modicum of truth in this statement. Browning's real feeling toward Chapman was expressed to Isa Blagden when he explained to her why he avoided the publisher: "[I] distrust the man, without dislike of the poor good-natured fellow." (*Letters to Isa Blagden*, p. 110, letter dated February 19, 1867.)

2. Thomas Henry Dyer, *History of Modern Europe:* "from the fall of Constantinople to the end of the Crimean War." The first two volumes had appeared in 1861, the other two in 1864, with Murray as publisher. The price of 60s. for the set gives point to Browning's feeling that Chapman, with whom he had parted company, is being "over kind" in completing this "liberal present."

1. Probably February 19, 1868, in connection with Pen's impending matriculation. (*Letters to Isa Blagden*, p. 156.)

debate, on the same occasion,—to beg the Society's acceptance of somewhat more correct an edition than that which they possess? [2]

I am, Dear Sir,

Very faithfully and obediently yours

Robert Browning.

The Librarian of the Oxford Union Society.

[Huntington]

To Mrs. Augusta Harding Pym [1]

19. Warwick Crescent,
Upper Westbourne Terrace,
Apr. 30, '68.

Dear Mrs. Pym,

I am deeply obliged to you for your interesting letter,—superfluous, however, in the request it contains: for you have every right to make what use you please of those lines. I shall add, while on the subject, any other poem that may be available is equally at your service.

You know with what respect and regard I did, and shall ever, think of Dr. Harding. I was not aware that he had left us. Kind he always was to me and mine. I only saw him once since my return to England (for a moment in the quadrangle at Westminster Abbey) —but few faces remain so vividly with me as your Father's. I am glad you were a comfort to him.

My son—he ushered into the world—is nineteen, and on the point of going to Oxford: how the years fleet! May they bring you something, if they take away much from us all!

Ever most truly yours

[New York Public Library] Robert Browning.

2. Smith and Elder's six-volume edition of *The Poetical Works of Robert Browning* (1868).

1. Mrs. Pym nee Augusta Harding was the daughter of the physician in attendance at the birth of Pen. The present letter was inserted in a copy of Mrs. Browning's *Poems* (1853), signed and inscribed to Miss Augusta Harding by Mrs. Browning at Florence, November 1, 1854.

To Miss Lily Benzon [1]

Audierne, Finistère, France
Sept. 2, '68.

Dear Lily,

How good and kind of you, not only to wish me present but write this nice little letter which says so! I am sure I would very gladly be with you, were it in my power. I have told your Mama about the funny wild place in which I am: I think you would like to have a peep at it too, if but for a moment. You never saw such odd dresses, —the men, or peasants at least, wear the same sort of clothes that their great-grandfathers did, and the women, . . but I shall never be able to describe their caps, so give it up. We had a great opportunity of seeing these at a great and famous "Pardon" (as they call a Saint's Day) that was held in honour of Saint Anne on a hill by the sea, at some distance, last Sunday.[2] There was a procession,—no end to the strange figures of men, with long hair down their backs, just as long, and sometimes more curly even, than yours—but in other respects very different: some of the faces were more like an animal's than a human creature. Then the women who took a principal part in the show were perfectly wonderful in their rich attire, flowered satin embroidered with gold, I am afraid to say how much the cost was, if people told me truly. Then came a crowd of pilgrims of all sorts, who had been encamped all night round the place,—for lodging, or indeed house, there was none. The moment all this was over, they began to carouse, and on our way home we had to pick our path (that is, the horses' path) through the poor reeling, rolling people, who might better have stayed at home than end their devotions in this way. Getting back, beside, was a hard business, because our poor little Breton horses were tired to death,

1. Lily Benzon was the adopted daughter of Mr. and Mrs. Ernest Leopold Benzon whose London address was 10 Palace Gardens, Kensington. It was at the Benzons' place above Loch Tummel at Little Milton that Browning did some of his paraphrasing of Euripides for *Balaustion's Adventure*. (Griffin and Minchin, *Life*, p. 243.) Mrs. Benzon was the sister of Rudolph and Frederick Lehmann. Pen Browning was a frequent visitor to the Benzons'. (See *Letters*, ed. Hood, letters to W. W. Story, *passim*.)

2. This would be August 30. But St. Anne's Day is July 26. "It was authorized by Urban IV in 1378. In 1584 Gregory XIII fixed July 26 as date of the feast and Leo XIII in 1879 extended it to the whole Church." (Dom Gaspar Lefebvre O.S.B. of the Abbey of St. André, *St. Andrew Daily Missal* [St. Paul, Minnesota, 1936], p. 817.)

having had to perform twenty-two leagues the day before. So that they could only go fast when we went down-hill,—the country is all ups and downs,—and that seemed rather dangerous: however we had a splendid full moon, and somehow or other we got home not more than three or four hours after the proper time. Well, at this little town where we are, there is to-day a "Pardon" too, on a small scale, and they are dancing under our windows in the village-square to the music of what they call a "birrion,"—or bagpipe, such as you may be hearing now in Scotland,—only smaller and gentler, fortunately: there it is beginning again, while I write! And as it gives me the headache I will leave off. Need I say how glad I shall be to see you again, or, if that is too long off, hear from you again? Pen is well and going your way—to the north: I hope he will be lucky enough to see you. Give my kindest regards to Miss Mahlmann,[3] and continue to remember me, as I shall always remember you, dear Lily, for your very affectionate friend,

Robert Browning.

My sister also sends her best love with mine.
[Yale]

To James Thomas Fields [1]

19. Warwick Crescent
Upper Westbourne Terrace, W.
Oct. 30, '68.

My dear Mr. Fields,
I have *hardly* a minute to say that here are the corrected revises:

3. Probably Lily Benzon's governess.
1. James Thomas Fields (1817–81) in 1838 became a junior partner in the American publishing firm of Ticknor, Reed and Fields. On Reed's retirement in 1854 the firm became known as Ticknor and Fields until 1867 or 1868, at which time it became Fields, Osgood and Co. (Under date of October 29, 1868, Mrs. Fields quotes from her diary: "The firm of Ticknor and Fields no longer exists. Fields, Osgood and Co. is the new name." Mrs. James T. Fields, *James T. Fields, Biographical Notes and Personal Sketches* [Boston, 1882], p. 166. But Browning had written a letter to Fields, Osgood and Co. on July 19, 1867. *Letters,* ed. Hood, p. 113.) On November 10, 1849, Fields wrote to Miss Mitford: "I am busy just now superintending the republication of the complete poems of Robert Browning, the first American reprint. It will be issued by our house in a few weeks." (*James T. Fields,* p. 32.) In 1852 Fields had "a charming visit" with the Brownings in Paris, probably his first (p. 42). Besides the personal magnetism for which he was famous, Fields had the added advantage of being willing to pay for the right to reprint in America the works of English

the changes in the first three books are unimportant, but the remaining three are *much* affected by revision. I have no time to look thro' more than the first of these: but, should I find any error of consequence, I will write next week and give you the correction,— which cannot be much of a matter. Pray take care of me through the press.[2]

Ever yours faithfully
Robert Browning.

Of course you got, I presume, last week's sheets and letter.

[Boston Browning Society]

To Moncure Daniel Conway [1]

19. Warwick Crescent,
Upper Westbourne Terrace, W.
October 30, 1868.

My dear Mr. Conway,

I am, now even, hardly in a position to say exactly what I can do

authors. It was this endearing commercial trait which led Browning to describe him as "that miraculous Mr. Fields." (See above, letter of October 31, 1855.)

2. On July 19, 1867, Browning acknowledged acceptance of his proposal concerning publication of *The Ring and the Book* in America by Fields, Osgood and Co. but demurred about sending "anything *seven* weeks before publication" in England. (*Letters*, ed. Hood, pp. 113–114.) On August 8, 1868, the American firm proposed publication in two volumes instead of four and offered £50 for the poem. Since Browning had told Isa Blagden that he wanted "something, decidedly, for this performance" (p. 94), it is little wonder that the offer of £50 drew from the businessman-poet an exclamatory refusal: "I am very sorry that you find the arrangements of my publishers inconsistent with such as you wish to make, and that you break your bargain in consequence; so, let it be broken by all means!" In a letter on September 2, 1868, he proposed securing another American publisher (p. 127). It is likely that Fields stepped in at this point with the result that Browning was temporarily mollified, and *The Ring and the Book* went to Fields, Osgood and Co. after all. It was published by this firm in two volumes as the "Author's Edition, *From Advance Sheets.*" (See letter, below, April 15, 1870, in which Browning does seek another American publisher.) On October 30, 1868, the same day as this letter to Fields, Browning told Miss Wedgwood: "I sit waiting the revises of [*The Ring and the Book*] which are to go to America today. . . . As the Americans chose to insist on printing two [volumes] in one, I send them the second volume also." (*Robert Browning and Julia Wedgwood*, pp. 129–130.) Browning had received from Smith, Elder and Co. the sum of £1,250 for "the right of publication for five years" which was, of course, the "largest sum . . . that he had received for any of his works." (Leonard Huxley, *The House of Smith Elder*, p. 156.)

1. This letter to Conway was removed from the proof sheets of the English edition of *The Ring and the Book*.

about the sheets,[2]—still the presumption is that I may be able to let you have them in the course of next week. It is arranged that *two* volumes shall appear in the U. S. on Dec. 1: and the third and fourth, also to-gether, on March 1. Hence the publication of vol. 2 will anticipate the English edition by a month. I have, therefore, to furnish you with *the whole of the half,* if I would be of service, and I do so—on the stipulation, now obligatory,—since the property in the poem is no longer mine, on either side of the Atlantic,— that, *here,* you make no use of the *second* volume before its appearance (nor, of course, of the first)—and, in America, that you engage to give nothing that may *precede* the regular publication of reviews,—and that you will be expressly answerable for your directions on this head being obeyed by the Editor of the Newspaper which you furnish with a criticism,—on this stipulation,—if you will please to repeat it,—I will send the sheets. You know very certainly that, so far as yourself are concerned, I need no such assurance: but I should be seriously in fault if I omitted these precautions, and, by a misunderstanding anywhere, really broke my engagements,—to which it would amount. *Here* I am in no anxiety, —but it will be for you to take care,—by [3] abstaining from any premature transmission of your M.S.,—that nobody can possibly pretend to mistake your intentions, and so subject me to treatment I should least like. Will you kindly reassure me on all these points? I was sorry to miss your visit the other afternoon.

Ever most truly yours
Robert Browning.

I have said only the business—say, what I am bound to be precise about: why should I add, what you must understand so well, that, for the rest, I value properly the attention you will give, and the sympathy, to my work? My own interest that you should put these into play, as you have so often done, is so obvious, that I dwell the more determinedly on the other side of the question. Pray remember me to Mrs. Conway.

[Yale]

---

2. Proof sheets of *The Ring and the Book.* For other business arrangements concerned with *The Ring and the Book* see above, letter to Fields on October 30, 1868, and n. 2.

3. A caret is inserted here, and the words "abstaining from" written above the line.

To Mrs. Sophia Eckley

Sunday Evening
[April 11, 1869.] [1]

Dear Mrs. Eckley,

This is a hurried word to say that I shall be unable to leave London till Wednesday morning. I will call at your house as early next day as I can: but I hope you will on no account change your arrangements, if the inconvenience be considerable. I am kept by business unfortunately. All thanks for your letter. Ever yours gratefully [2]

[New York Public Library]   R. B.

To John Camden Hotten [1]

19. Warwick Crescent,
Upper Westbourne Terrace, W.
May 21, '69.

Sir,

In case I should be acting on misinformation, as may possibly be the case, I have to beg your pardon for troubling you about a

1. On April 19, 1869, Browning wrote to Isa Blagden as follows: "I called on Mrs. Eckley, who took her departure on Saturday [April 17] for London, whence she returns to America." (*Letters to Isa Blagden*, p. 168.) This note, therefore, was probably written on April 11, 1869, which was the Sunday preceding the Wednesday on which Browning departed for Paris. Mrs. Eckley's Paris address was 324 Rue di Rivoli.

2. The occasion for Browning's gratitude was Mrs. Eckley's offer to give him the letters addressed by Mrs. Browning to Mrs. Eckley. "She repeated the offer," says Browning, "that I might take it [the book in which Mrs. Eckley kept the letters] at once: I should have been harsh or rather foolish to do so." (*Letters to Isa Blagden*, pp. 159, 168.) See also below, letter of December 4, 1869.

1. John Camden Hotten (1832–73), publisher and author, established his publishing business in 1856. Ten years later he achieved notoriety by taking over publication of Swinburne's sensational *Poems and Ballads* after the book had been withdrawn by Moxon in the face of critical disapproval. For Browning's indirect part in sending Swinburne to Hotten see letter to Milnes, of July 7, 1863, and K. L. Knickerbocker, "Browning and Swinburne: an Episode," *Modern Language Notes*, LXII [April, 1947], 240–244. It is probable that Swinburne's *Poems and Ballads* had been offered to Chapman before the volume was accepted for publication by Moxon. Hotten's boldness and tendency toward unscrupulous practices tarnished his reputation, a fact which helps account for the severity in tone of the letter printed here. (See *The Letters of Algernon Charles Swinburne*, ed. Thomas Hake and Arthur Compton-Rickett [London, 1918], pp. 79–84.)

matter interesting to me. I was assured this morning that you were on the point of publishing a poem of mine: the only poem which, by any chance, can have been put into your hands, is one which I handed over to Mrs. Alfred Montgomery,[2] more than a year ago, for a particular purpose, to be printed in a particular manner: if, by any chance, this should be the poem which you intend to print after any other than the fashion originally described to me,—allow me to say that, never having dreamed of such an appearance, I should be compelled, however reluctantly, to refuse my permission.

I am, Sir,

Yours obediently

Robert Browning.

J. C. Hotten, Esq.
[Huntington]

To Mrs. Sophia Eckley

19. Warwick Crescent

Upper Westbourne Terrace, W.

December 4, 1869.

My dear Mrs. Eckley,

You have every right and reason to blame me for a silence which fairly laid me open to misconstruction. The simple truth is that your letter of 6th Dec. spoke of the volume of your *Poems*[1] which I had either received or was about to receive: I waited the post a day or two for this,—perhaps, also, on account of the almost unbearable press of work of more kinds than one, just then,—and next came the sudden illness of Robert, who was supposed to have caught the scarlet fever,—though it proved no worse than a bad

2. In 1849 Thackeray commented that Mrs. Alfred Montgomery is "pretty and clever—but Beckyfied somehow and too much of a petite maîtresse. I suppose a deal of flattery has been poured into her ears and numberless men have dangled round that pretty light little creature." (*Letters of W. M. Thackeray*, ed. Ray, II, 543.) Possibly the poem placed in Mrs. Montgomery's hands was "Hervé Riel," composed at Croisic on September 30, 1867 and first printed in the *Cornhill Magazine* (March, 1871). (DeVane, *Browning Handbook*, p. 362.) Fanny Charlotte (Wyndham) Montgomery (1820–93) was well known in literary circles and wrote, among other things, a travel book called *On the Wing: a Southern Flight* (London, 1875).

1. *Minor Chords* (London, 1869). The volume was out late in 1868, and dated 1869. Apparently Mrs. Eckley's letter was written on December 6, 1868, nearly a full year before Browning's reply.

sore throat from which he speedily recovered: and then came more work, more letters and more negligence, until your present note wakes me up effectually to a sense of my fault. This is exactly the truth, and I beg of you to forgive me.

One proof I can give you that there was not the minutest atom of mistrust in the matter: I wrote shortly after I had seen you to the person from whom came the assurance as to good intentions about the letters. I informed that person very fully of all that you stated, all that you offered, and all that you promised,—absolutely of your own accord and without the least pressure on my part,— with respect to them,—adding that I was convinced of your sincerity.[2] This was more urgent than an immediate answer to your letter, was it not?—though the answer might preferably have been sent as well, I acknowledge. As for mistrust on my own account,— lest my own scribblings should be exposed or used as autographs, —such a fancy never crossed my brain! I write as few letters as I can, —but not from any sort of care what becomes of them once written. Moreover, it is not my way, I hope, to be so unjust to "return upon my sentence," as the French would say, and change a deliberately adopted opinion without the smallest circumstance to justify such a change; and, I repeat, you left me in the opinion that you meant fully what you said, and would do what you engaged to do. In that opinion I shall continue, I trust. When I go to Paris, as I shall in all probability at Easter, I will very gladly call on you, and should business bring you to London, I shall always expect to

2. The person referred to here is Isa Blagden to whom Browning had written on December 17, 1868: "Who do you suppose visited me the other day? Mrs. Eckley, to my surprise. I told her what she was charged with in the way of exhibiting those letters [Mrs. Browning's letters to Mrs. Eckley]: she denied it indignantly. She told me she had arranged by will to give me, or Pen, every one of them. . . . she offered to give them to me *now* with every apparent sincerity. . . . she has since written offering me any *legal* assurance I might think safest, that after her death, the letters should revert to me, engaging to give them to me on my next visit to Paris (where she lives) should I doubt her. Hence on the whole, I conclude that this particular devil is not quite so black as she has been painted, by myself, amongst others." (*Letters to Isa Blagden*, p. 165.) According to the great-niece of Mrs. Eckley, Margaret Tuckerman Clark of Amherst, Massachusetts, "these letters were returned to the Browning Family but during the last year or so came up for sale at Sotheby's. . . . Sotheby sold the letters to Quaritch and the latter sold them to [Walter M.] Hill . . . for an American client." (Letter to K. L. Knickerbocker, October 30, 1939.) These letters, still unpublished, are now in the New York Public Library.

hear where I may see you—or, if you please, be seen by you in this house.

Goodbye, dear Mrs. Eckley,—I forget nothing of the Past, and you know how much memory of you is involved in that. Give my kindest remembrances and regards to Miss Eckley: it would be indeed a delight to see her again. The photograph of my poor face, which you pleased to ask for, shall be sent when I can get one. Your book is *not* come. I saw it well spoken of in a review, two days ago, if you care for that.[3]

Affectionately yours

[New York Public Library]   Robert Browning.

To Lady Castletown [1]

19. Warwick Crescent,
Upper Westbourne Terrace, W.
Wednesday M[ornin]g.
[1869?] [2]

Dear Lady Castletown,

I heard last night, to my amazement, that you "had expected me at dinner on Monday"—to meet the Motleys [3] and others. Indeed, you never said a word to me on the subject, always excepting a *half-*

3.The *Athenaeum* reviewed *Minor Chords* on April 3, 1869, and found "some poems readable . . . many others . . . 'moonshiny.' " We have been unable to locate the favorable review to which Browning refers.

1. John Wilson Fitzpatrick (1807–83), created Baron Castletown in 1869, married Augusta Mary Douglas (1810–99) in 1830. (G. E. Cokayne, *The Complete Peerage* [London, 1913], III, 101–102.) Lady Castletown is described by her son as "a remarkable woman with great personality and charm," whose salon in Portman Square "was always full of clever, interesting people. . . . She had a beautiful voice, and wonderful aptitude in reading aloud, and her rendition of . . . any poetry was worth going miles to hear." (Lord Castletown, *"Ego"; Random Records of Sport, Service and Travel in Many Lands* [London, 1923], p. 54.)

2. There is nothing upon which to base more than a dubious, conjectural date. Motley was appointed minister to England in 1869, the occasion, possibly, for being entertained by Lady Castletown.

3. Probably the family of the American historian and diplomat, John Lothrop Motley (1814–77). It is possible that Browning first met the Motleys in Rome in the winter of 1859. (Oliver Wendell Holmes, *John Lothrop Motley* [London, 1878], p. 86.) Motley, in July, 1867, reported seeing Browning at a breakfast and described him as "in great force and full of original stories and ideas as he used to be." (*John Lothrop Motley and His Family*, ed. by His Daughter and Herbert St. John Mildmay [London, 1910], p. 272.)

word, a fortnight ago, to the effect that "if you invited them and if they were able to come, you would think of me also"—which, like every other motion of yours towards me, was very kind: but as no invitation followed, I supposed the pleasant thing was not to be. After all, a moment's consideration must have made you sure that, apart from battle, murder or sudden death, such a defection on my part was impossible. I had no engagement on Monday and ate mutton in solitary state.

Ever most truly yours

[Mr. Kenneth Curry]   Robert Browning.

To Mrs. Charles Skirrow [1]

19. Warwick Crescent, W.
March 10, '70.

Dear Friend,

What will you not have thought of me? Or did your instinct let you know that because the seeing you would be an extreme pleasure

1. Mrs. Skirrow, to whom many letters in this volume are addressed, was the wife of Charles Skirrow, Master in Chancery. One letter of Browning (undated) to Mrs. Skirrow refers to Leicester Terrace as if it were their home; in 1887 they were living at 20 Sussex Gardens, Hyde Park, W., about one half to three quarters of a mile from 19 Warwick Crescent. The best account of Mrs. Skirrow may be found in W. B. Maxwell, *Time Gathered: Autobiography* (London, 1937), pp. 113–115, and *passim.* She is described as a lion hunter who "collected some remarkably good specimens" with Browning accounted "the finest head of the collection." As an indication of the character of Mrs. Skirrow and of the essential relationship between her and the poet—with also an amusing sidelight on Browning himself—we quote in full an anecdote delightfully told by Mr. Maxwell. Browning "was nearly always of the party, and, as well as being so proud of having him there, she was so joyous in showing him off, Mrs. Skirrow, as one could plainly see, had a genuine affection for him. She was watchful of his comfort, careful in giving instructions to her servants that he was to be looked after in every possible way. Of course when she had him next to her at the meal she could take care of him herself.

"Mr. Browning liked to drink port wine with his dinner and nothing else—no sherry or champagne or any wine except the port. Needless to say his taste in the matter was well understood and provided for. When the rank of other male guests made it impossible for the kindly soul to have him beside her at dinner she would send him affectionate glances from time to time. Little swift noddings, or gentle grimaces, by which he might understand that he still occupied the first place in her mind, and was not for a moment forgotten. He smiled back at her, and nodded his handsome head.

"But under these conditions one night she could not obtain the usual response from Mr. Browning. He sat there very solemn. If he nodded his head it

I put it off till I could thoroughly enjoy it? Such is the case, indeed.
I have been far from well, and harassed by various plagues, and
never quite fit to say—"Now for some comfort!"—Wait a little, and
I shall say so, I trust,—and meantime know me ever for

Yours affectionately

[Schiff]   Robert Browning.

To Mrs. Alicia Bayne

19. Warwick Crescent,
Upper Westbourne Terr.
March 28, '70.

Dear Mrs. Bayne,

I should be delighted to dine with you on the 5th but have been
long engaged for that day. How good you are to remember me!

Ever yours truly

[Yale]   Robert Browning.

To Sarianna Browning with Enclosure from E. Abbott

[April 15, 1870] [1]

Dearest Sis,

I got this today, and think it much more satisfactory to send it
than any report of its contents: though it tells nothing we do not

---

was gloomily, and never a smile came back from him. This filled Mrs. Skirrow
with solicitude, and made her very anxious before the dinner ended. What
was wrong? Then, when the ladies were leaving the room, she spoke to him,
with a hand upon his arm, expressing some hope that he had eaten his food
with appetite.

" 'You had your port wine, of course?'

" 'No,' said Mr. Browning solemnly, 'I had no port wine.'

" 'Oh, but how dreadful,' cried Mrs. Skirrow, thrown into the utmost distress. 'How could such a thing have happened! I can never forgive myself. But
you will have some now?'

" 'No, thank you,' said Mr. Browning.

"It was too late.

"Mrs. Skirrow almost wept. She repeated expressions of sorrow.

" 'Oh, pray,' said Mr. Browning, 'it does not matter in the least.'

"But of course it mattered most frightfully."

1. The heading of this letter has been cut away with the exception of the
lower half of what appears to be the word "Thursday." Toward the end of
this letter Browning mentions "a letter in the *Times* today from Robin Hedley." The letter referred to appeared on April 15, 1870, and establishes the
date of this letter to Sarianna.

know, it could not well be expected to prove more favorable; as only a fortnight's progress is recorded: [2] it does seem absurd that such miserable matters as arithmetic and grammar of that elementary kind should be hard to overcome if a will to overcome them is really present, as would seem to be the case. I shall write presently to Pen—having some bad news for him: Alfred writes that Sept is suddenly dead,—of heart disease, it is supposed.[3] "The last letters from him were dated the 13th March and written in the highest spirits and full of a prosperous future: four days later"— came the end. In a letter George wrote in reply to mine, he mentioned that Sept had just been made a member of the legislative council, or some such-named institution. I only remember seeing him once in my life—indeed, I doubt whether it was he, even then. But the loss will be felt by his brothers, and what Storm will do, I don't know. George might well employ his time there, one would think.[4] You got Pen's letter I sent yesterday or the day before. There

2. The following note from Pen Browning's tutor accompanied Browning's letter:

Ollerton
April 13, '70.

Dear Sir

I think it is nearly a fortnight since I wrote to you: therefore I write again, though I have not much to add to what I then said.

I find your son deficient in those parts of his work which depend on application and accuracy; on the other hand, where taste and thought is required, he does well. Thus his Latin Prose is far from bad, and his Translation at times elegant. In neither has he anything to fear in his next Exam^n. On the other hand his Arithmetic, and Grammar, more especially the former is inaccurate. He has been helped too much, and done too little for himself. I am trying to teach him to work for himself, and trust to his own powers.

He is very kind in doing what I wish him to do: and really works very fairly. He seems quite aware of his deficiencies and anxious to remedy them.

Believe me

Very sincerely yours
E. Abbott

Pen Browning had failed to pass the entrance examinations for Balliol and was now preparing for a try at Christ Church.

3. The words "they had" have been scratched through before the quotation.

4. This passage mentions four of Pen's uncles, all brothers of his mother. Alfred Price Barrett (1820–1904) was one of the three Barrett children who dared to marry before the death of their father. He married his cousin, Georgina Elizabeth (Lizzie) Barrett, in 1855 and immediately thereafter received a sympathetic letter from E. B. B. (*Letters of E.B.B.*, II, 207.) Sympathy was well placed, for he was immediately disinherited through a codicil to his father's will. (Jeannette Marks, *The Family of the Barrett*, p. 598. Most of the dates

came a letter evidently from Nicholas,—I opened it and found that Mrs. Paget [5] could not take her, but recommended her to somebody else: the object in writing was to ask if you would receive a fresh applicant: I replied that you were away, but might be written to, and I would apprise you that you might expect such a letter. Locker [6] asked for your address yesterday and I gave it: he has been *very* ill, and his wife (still in Paris) is not well. I engaged to go and drink tea last e[venin]g with Miss Smith [7] to meet a Miss Martin, a

---

in this paragraph have been taken from the genealogical tables in Miss Marks's book.) This tie of having shared Mr. Barrett's paternal wrath is sufficient explanation of the correspondence with Browning. Septimus (Sept) James Barrett (1822–70), trained as a lawyer, had gone to Jamaica to manage the family estate, and had died in the family manor at Cinnamon Hill. George Goodin Barrett (1817–95), of the Inner Temple, barrister at law, had at first joined his father in casting off Elizabeth Barrett after her marriage to Browning. A letter from Browning in 1851 had brought about a reconciliation, and in 1857 it was George Barrett who in an "affectionate letter" apprised E. B. B. of the death of her father. (*Letters of E.B.B.,* II, 19, 263.) Charles John (Storm) Barrett (1814–1905) gained the epithet of the "family fool" by committing such quixotic indiscretions as marrying a native Jamaican woman who falsely claimed to be pregnant by him. (Jeannette Marks, *The Family of the Barrett,* pp. 614–615.) Though Browning may not have known this story, he did know that Storm, on another occasion, had attempted to throw away half an estate simply for the pleasure of making "an immense sacrifice." (*Letters,* ed. Hood, p. 79.) Storm managed, however, to live out a very long life in Jamaica. One notes that among "missing" letters of Browning must be counted those which he wrote to his wife's brothers.

5. Nicholas possibly had been in the service of Sarianna as a maid. Lydia North married James Paget in 1844. Her husband, surgeon to royalty, was knighted in 1871, after which, of course, she became the Lady Paget of later reference in Browning's letters. (See letter of September 5, 1888, below, n. 2.)

6. For note on Frederick Locker-Lampson see below, letter dated July 6, 1879. Locker's acquaintance with Sarianna Browning was closest in 1860 while she was living with her father in Paris (151 Rue de Grenelle) and while Lady Elgin, Locker's mother-in-law, maintained a popular salon in the Rue de Lille. (Orr, *Life,* pp. 15–17.) Two of Sarianna's rare letters are published in Augustine Birrell, *Frederick Locker-Lampson: A Character Sketch* (London, 1920), pp. 105–106.

7. Annie Egerton Smith was part proprietor of the Liverpool *Mercury* and had therefrom "considerable means." She had become acquainted with the Brownings in Florence. After the death of Mrs. Browning and Browning's return to London Miss Smith became the poet's constant companion to almost all London had to offer in the way of serious music. Sarianna, Miss Smith, and Browning spent four summer vacations together, 1874–1877, during the last of which Miss Smith died suddenly. (Griffin and Minchin, *Life,* p. 255; Orr, *Life,* and *Letters,* ed. Hood, *passim.*)

H

German Pianiste, Sutton Corkran, and Mr. Ball: [8] I went much against my will as I came home tired: and on arriving found—that Miss Martin having been prevented from coming, Miss Smith had sent a telegram to Mr. Ball to bid him stay away lest he should be disappointed,—and as for Sutton,—when she found she could get me and Mr. Ball she thought she would ask him another time! Consequently the tea and coffee were for me only, so I drank three cups of each. I will send you the *Ath[enaeum]* and *Ill[ustrate]d News* to-morrow. Pen wants the latter and the *Field*. There is a letter in the *Times* to-day from Robin Hedley, in reply to that assertion of Lady M. Douglas (just like the usual lies!) that in her convent no letters were ever refused to the nuns: he says that when he wrote to his sister, in that very convent, his letter was returned to him as a thing she could not receive.[9]

Good bye, dearest—love to Milsand.

Ever affy yours
RB.

The owl is better, I think, though very helpless still: he seems paralysed in some degree. I feed him against his wish, poor fellow.[10]
[Schiff]

8. We have been unable further to identify Miss Martin. Sutton Fraser Corkran was Paris correspondent for the London *Morning Chronicle,* at which time he and his wife, Henrietta, became "dear friends" of the Brownings in 1852. (*Letters,* ed. Hood, p. 39.) Corkran in the Eighties became a translator from the German of George Taylor. "Mr. Ball" may be John Ball (1818–89), a scientist and politician, who was to participate in a Moroccan scientific expedition in 1871. (*D.N.B.*)

9. A Mr. Newdegate had introduced into the House of Commons a bill requiring that monastic institutions be subjected to government inspection on the ground that they systematically violated civil liberties. Lady Gertrude Douglas, daughter of the Marquess of Queensberry, wrote to the *Times* on April 12, 1870 opposing this bill on the basis of her own experience as a Sister of the Black Veil, an experience during which she had had, she said, complete freedom in contacts with the outside world. Robert Hedley replied that his sister, after becoming a "pervert to Rome," was not allowed to receive any communication from him. (London *Times,* April 15.)

10. "His pet owl was not unknown to visitors at Warwick Crescent" is an understatement about Browning's well-known bird. (Griffin and Minchin, *Life,* p. 36.) The owl, this one, may have been a gift from Mrs. Skirrow. She did give him an inkstand topped with the figure of an owl. (See below, letter dated Jan. 2, 1872.)

To An American Publisher [1]

19. Warwick Crescent,
Upper Westbourne Terrace, W.
Apr. 15, '70.

Gentlemen,

I have just published an edition of the works of E. B. Browning, in five volumes, in which I have given my utmost endeavour to ensure correctness throughout: there can be nothing comparable to it, for completeness and accuracy, in the current American reprints; nor does it admit of further help from me in a line or letter.[2]

I should greatly like that wherever my own poems are published,

1. As indicated above, Browning was dissatisfied with Fields, Osgood and Co. because of their handling of *The Ring and the Book*. (See letter dated October 30, 1869, n. 2.) James T. Fields retired from the company in 1870, a fact which may have spurred the effort to find another publisher and thereby to carry out a threat which he had made in 1868. (See *Letters*, ed. Hood, p. 127.) This letter attempts to make good that threat. To what American publisher it is addressed is uncertain. James Miller, New York publisher, brought out a thick one-volume edition of the *Poetical Works*, with a Memoir and illustrations, in 1871. On the title page is the statement: "Corrected by the Last London Edition." T. Y. Crowell and Co. published the identical edition, omitting the memoir but including the same illustrations. On the reverse of the title page is recorded: "Entered according to act of Congress, in the year 1870, by James Miller." It is doubtful that Browning's offer, to whomever made, was accepted. Certainly, Browning's own works continued to be published by James R. Osgood and Co. *Balaustion's Adventure, Fifine at the Fair, Red Cotton Night-Cap Country,* and *Aristophanes' Apology* all appeared as "Author's Editions from Advance Sheets." Domett records on December 9, 1875 that Browning "congratulated himself on having got rid of his American publishers, who had neglected to send the money they had agreed to pay for his last work [*Aristophanes' Apology*] for a considerable time after it was due. He had now had the pleasure of telling them that the *New York Times* had paid him double the money they offered him for the new poem [*The Inn Album*], and he could do without them. It appears accordingly in that paper, seven columns of it at a time." (Quoted in Griffin and Minchin, *Life*, p. 257.) Nevertheless, James R. Osgood and Co. did publish *The Inn Album* and *Pacchiarotto*, without, however, the claim that either was "Author's Edition, from Advance Sheets."

2. Elizabeth Barrett Browning's *Poetical Works*, Eighth Edition In Five Volumes London: Smith Elder and Co., 15 Waterloo Place 1870. Although numbered "Eighth Edition" this is an exact reprint of the "Seventh Edition" brought out by Chapman and Hall in 1866. Smith and Elder bought the stereotype plates from Chapman and Hall and simply issued a reprint. American publishers had had the seventh edition to guide them for the past four years. It is perhaps a bit disingenuous for Browning to imply that recent editing had improved the available text of Mrs. Browning's poems.

those of my Wife should be obtainable also. Are you inclined to reproduce the present edition? As regards my right to propose that you should do so, let me mention that for no poem previous to *Aurora Leigh* was any payment whatever made to the Author: that work, and some of the following few, received remuneration— which, I should hardly suppose, would pretend to bar any arrangement after so many years.

If you accede to this proposal, and will inform me of the price you are prepared to pay, I will at once forward the five volumes.

I am, Gentlemen
Obediently yours
Robert Browning.

[Boston Browning Society]

To Miss Kate Field

19. Warwick Crescent, W.
July 5, '70.

Dear, Miss Field,

I wish I could do what you request of me, but it is doubly impossible: in the first place, I know next to nothing of the places, dates and circumstances you want: and, were it otherwise, my mouth would be stopped for reasons strong enough which I can't explain now.[1] The Works, and what of the Life you had the opportunity of becoming acquainted with, are quite within your competency to lecture upon—and I need no assurance that the feeling with which you will treat them is as good and kind as ever.

Come to England, as you promise, and you will gratify few more than your old friend

Robert Browning.

Many and cordial thanks to your Mother for the regards which I beg to reciprocate.[2]

[Boston Browning Society]

1. On March 3, 1869, Kate Field made her "*début* as a lecturer at Chickering Hall," Boston, on the subject: "Women in the Lyceum." (Lilian Whiting, *Kate Field*, p. 211.) She developed two other lectures, one on a "Trip Through the Adirondacks" and one on "Charles Dickens." It is apparent that she wished to get from Browning information about Mrs. Browning from which she could construct a lecture. His reply evidently put an end to the idea of a lecture on E.B.B.

2. Mrs. Field and Miss Field sailed for Liverpool aboard the SS *Russia* on May 17, 1871. Mrs. Field died aboard ship on May 26 with the vessel still three days out of port.

To Richard Monckton Milnes

19. Warwick Crescent,
Upper Westbourne Terrace, W.
Dec. 7, '70.

Dear Houghton,

If there is no other reason for your choice of the 24th rather than the 19th than the goodnatured one of the "shyness" to be avoided by a visit in company of your friends,—have no apprehensions on that score and let the 19th be the hospitable day,—as my son, I find, may be wanted elsewhere in the last week of the month. Should any inconvenience have arisen, you shall be kind to him on some other occasion. *I* nourish "animosity to country houses"?— who spent all last autumn in some dozen, one after one! Like Damascus of old "it is too delicious." [1] Oblige me by a word in reply and believe me ever yours truly

[Lord Crewe]   Robert Browning.

To Richard Monckton Milnes

19. Warwick Crescent
Upper Westbourne Terrace, W.
Dec. 21, '70.

My dear Houghton,

I understand the kindness of your suggestion: but there is no need to interfere with the original plan of arriving on the 24th. Robert will enjoy Christmas nowhere better than with you; and I rather wish him enjoyment, that he has been doing well, and working hard,—lately. Don't trouble yourself about any thought of a youth quite able and willing to amuse himself—make him play to the young ladies if they like music, for one thing. So, all best wishes of the season to you and yours from your old friend

[Lord Crewe]   Robert Browning.

1. "Despite various drawbacks, her rich streams, bursting as they do, on the very edge of the desert, and creating a delicious verdure, have won for Damascus the name of the earthly Paradise of the Arab world." (*Encyclopedia Biblica* [London, 1899], Vol. I, col. 988.) But on August 19, 1870, Browning *had* expressed animosity for country houses in a letter to Isa Blagden: "I shall escape if I can all visits in England this year . . . the country-life does not suit me, and I prefer the utter roughness of this hamlet [St. Aubin] to the finery of that and the other great place where I might be." (*Letters*, ed. Hood, p. 141.)

To Richard Monckton Milnes [1]

19. Warwick Crescent, W.
Old Year's Day. [1870]

Dear Houghton,

I expected you and your family would be kind to Robert,—but you have been miraculously kind, he says. Your reward must be in his thorough sense of it. He is a grateful and loyal boy and sure to remember you all gratefully through life.

Best new-year wishes to Lady Houghton, and Fryston generally: one may even bring in France—trusting with Horace—"Nil desperandum—auspice Ducrot." [2]

Ever truly yours

[Lord Crewe]   Robert Browning

To Mrs. William Burnet Kinney

London, 19. Warwick Crescent,
Upper Westbourne Terrace, W.
Jan. 6, '71.

Dear Mrs. Kinney,

You and your husband are just as fresh and distinct in my memory as when, some dozen years ago, yourselves used to be so pleasantly in my eyesight and hearing. I meant to talk a little on paper about that good time, but a note from your friend Sir K. James [1] informs me that you require an answer at once: so I will confine my words (for the present, at least) to the matter in hand. I should so thoroughly like to comply with any request of yours, that you must

1. This letter is published, without comment, in Reid, *Life of R. M. Milnes,* II, 244. We reprint it in order to complete the sequence of letters concerning Pen's Christmas entertainment at Lord and Lady Houghton's.

2. Auguste Alexandre Ducrot (1817–82) had fought at Sedan where he was captured but managed to escape. Back in Paris he organized the defense of that city and led sorties against the enemy. Before one of these sorties (November 28, 1870) he issued the following proclamation to his troops: "Pour moi, j'y suis bien résolu, j'en fais le serment devant vous, devent la nation tout entière, je ne rentrerai dans Paris que mort ou victorieux!" A commentator adds that this proclamation "devenue célèbre, et qui le couvrit de ridicule lorsqu'il rentra dans Paris très vivant, mais vaincu." ". . . auspice Ducrot" failed, for on January 19, 1871 he was overwhelmed at Buzenval. (*La Grande encyclopédie,* XIV, 1195.)

1. Sir John Kingston James (1815–93), knighted in 1854 before inheriting a similar title from his father in 1875.

understand how much it vexes me that I dare not break my now somewhat-old rule in this respect: I have been repeatedly solicited to allow letters to be published,—and in more instances than one have had to threaten the recourse to law-procedure before I could stop the publication. In this particular instance, I the more object to it, that I should thereby give the unmitigated scoundrel in question a right as well as opportunity to retaliate, after his natural fashion, by a fresh vomit of lies such as he printed five years ago in a *Spiritual Magazine*—wherein, referring to this very "séance," he attributed all my unbelief to my "ludicrous jealousy of my wife,— whom the Spirits crowned as 'The Poet,' passing over—me!" [2] If I ever cross the fellow's path I shall probably be silly enough to soil my shoe by kicking him,—but I should prefer keeping that disgrace from myself as long as possible. Indeed, I have got to consider such a beast as the proper associate and punishment of those who choose to shut their eyes and open their arms to bestiality incarnate. Let me sweeten my imagination by returning to you,— assuring you how much I value your remembrance, and what a de-

2. The episode referred to here was first recounted in the *Spiritual Magazine* for July, 1864 as a review of "Mr. Sludge, the Medium" and reprinted in D. D. Home, *Incidents in My Life*, 2d ser. (New York, 1872). The heart of the incident was reported on pp. 105–107, as follows: "Previously to the arrival of Mr. and Mrs. Browning some of the children had been gathering flowers in the garden, and Miss Rymer and I had made a wreath of clematis. The wreath was lying on the table, at a little distance from that at which we were sitting. The wreath was afterwards put on the table at which we were sitting, but whether naturally or by spirit hands I do not remember. During the *séance* this wreath was raised from the table by supernatural power in the presence of us all, and whilst we were watching it, Mr. Browning, who was seated at the opposite side of the table, left his place and came and stood behind his wife, towards whom the wreath was being slowly carried, and upon whose head it was placed, in full sight of us all, and whilst he was standing close behind her. He expressed no disbelief; as indeed, it was impossible for any one to have any of what was passing under his eyes, whilst Mrs. Browning was much moved, and she not only then but ever since expressed her entire belief and pleasure in what then occurred. It was the remark of all the Rymer family, that Mr. Browning seemed much disappointed that the wreath was not put upon his own head instead of his wife's, and that his placing himself in the way of where it was being carried, was for the purpose of giving it an opportunity of being placed upon his own brow." Browning's anger was further increased by Home's report of a second meeting with Mr. and Mrs. Browning during which Mrs. Browning apologized for her husband's actions: "She placed both her hands in mine, and said, in a voice of emotion, 'Oh, dear Mr. Home, do not, do not blame me. I am so sorry, but I am not to blame.'"

light•it will be if I am ever able,—in this world of wonders,—to see you again and say so. Meanwhile consider me ever Yours affectionately

[Yale]   RBrowning.

To Arthur William Edgar O'Shaughnessy [1]

Jan. 11, '71.

Dear Mr. O'Shaughnessy,

I am indebted to you for a very remarkable volume of poetry which, I am glad to see, had met with prompt recognition on the part of the critics.[2] I received Mr. Payne's book at the same time.[3]

1. Arthur William Edgar O'Shaughnessy (1844–81) earned his living as an assistant in the zoological department of the British Museum but gave his leisure to the writing of lyric poetry. He produced four volumes: *Epic of Women and Other Poems* (1870); *Lays of France* (1871); *Music and Moonlight: Poems and Songs* (1874); *Songs of a Worker* (1881). With his wife Eleanor (nee Marston) he published a volume of children's stories called *Toyland* (1875). The first of these volumes, and the most successful, he presented to Browning with the inscription: "Robert Browning, Esq., with the author's entire homage, Oct. 1870." (Sotheby, *Browning Collections*, item 959.)

2. O'Shaughnessy dedicated his *Epic of Women* to John Payne, and Payne in turn dedicated *The Masque of Shadows* to O'Shaughnessy. It was appropriate, therefore, for the *Athenaeum* (November 5, 1870) to review the poets together under the caption "Two Young Poets." Of O'Shaughnessy the critic said: "the volume before us is a work that raises high expectations." With Payne the critic had more fault to find but saw promise in him too. Browning could find in this review the familiar statement that "Tennyson occupied the highest place" while he himself was still "denied even . . . the title of poet."

3. John Payne (1842–1916) was a young barrister who published a number of volumes of poetry including: *The Masque of Shadows and Other Poems* (1870); *Intaglios: Sonnets* (1871); *Songs of Life and Death* (1872); *Lautrec: A Poem* (1878); *New Poems* (1881). In addition he translated François Villon, the *Decameron*, and the *Thousand and One Nights*. The first four of these volumes of Payne's own poetry were presented to Browning "with the author's homage to a great poet," "with the author's compliments," or "with kind regards." (See Sotheby, *Browning Collections*, items 975, 976, 977, 978.) "Browning acknowledged the receipt of his copy of *The Masque of Shadows* on 11 June, 1871, describing the poems as a gift indeed to be thankful for.'" (Thomas Wright, *The Life of John Payne* [London, 1919], p. 36.) Late in life Payne told his biographer, Thomas Wright, that "Browning was the delight of my boyhood, and I still treasure and love the two little volumes of the original edition (1855) of *Men and Women*, which, to my taste, contains all his worthiness" (p. 14). Apparently the two men did not meet, though Payne, on Browning's invitation, once approached Browning's door in De Vere Place, saw carriages before the house and through timidity refused to enter (p. 37).

There will be many eyes turned to such "lucida sidera," and none more gratefully as well as hopefully than those of

Yours most cordially

[Huntington]   Robert Browning.

To the Chevalier de Chatelain [1]

19. W[arwick] C[rescent].
May 18, '71.

Dear Chevalier and Neighbour,

I thank you very much indeed for your gift of the translation of *Othello*. We ought all to be grateful to you—who show such sympathy with,—and intimate knowledge of,—our greatest writers' greatest works.[2] At all events, I am proud to subscribe myself

Yours gratefully

[Huntington]   Robert Browning.

To Miss Kate Field

19. Warwick Crescent,
Upper Westbourne Terrace, W.
June 21, '71.

Dear Miss Field,

The lodging-house strongly recommended to me is kept by Miss Jack, 8. Dorset Square:[1] use the names of Mrs. Sutherland Orr and Mrs. Hardman.

1. Jean-Baptiste François Ernest de Chatelain (1801–81) was a French journalist and literary man who took up permanent residence in London in 1842 and was naturalized in 1848. His home was for many years next to Robert Browning: Castelnou Lodge, 20 Warwick Crescent. (*D.N.B.*) Browning said in a letter on April 27, 1866, above, that they had never spoken, though they exchanged notes.

2. This is a reference to the Chevalier's best-known book, *Beautés de la poésie anglaise* (1860–72), five volumes of translations from English to French comprising over 1,000 selections from Chaucer to Tennyson. (*D.N.B.*)

1. Kate Field landed at Liverpool, May 30, where she was met by friends who took care of funeral arrangements for her mother (see letter of July 5, 1870, n. 2). A Mrs. Taylor put her up at Notting Hill, Kensington, while she sought "a boarding house." In a letter of June 5, 1871, Browning had promised to refer her to "a particularly comfortable boarding house . . . if necessary." (Lilian Whiting, *Kate Field*, p. 266.) In a letter to Isa Blagden dated July 19, 1871, Browning says: "By the bye, I have seen next to nothing of Kate Field . . . I want heart to go and find her in the middle of Mrs. P. Taylor and Co., Women's Rights, Anti-Contagious-Disease agitation and so forth . . . I regret

Whenever you please to appoint I shall be delighted to see you here:—next week, I should add—as I go away on Saturday—Monday.

Ever yours most truly

[Boston Browning Society]   Robert Browning.

TO WILLIAM HEPWORTH DIXON [1]

19. Warwick Crescent, W.
July 27, '71.

My dear Hepworth Dixon,

I shall, in all likelihood, be out of London, long before the 15. August.[2] If you simply want to put my name along with the rest, I need not say you can do so,—for I find that any protest of mine against such a proceeding is supposed to mean nothing at all,—and really the matter is of little importance to anybody—including myself.

Pray believe me, ever,
Yours very truly

[Huntington]   Robert Browning.

———

it, this time, for I really like Kate Field . . ." (*Letters,* ed. Hood, p. 147.) He is, in another letter, "glad that Kate Field had no wrong notion of my indifference to her visit." (*Letters to Isa Blagden,* letter of August 19, 1871, p. 191.) Lilian Whiting records that Browning "called often to see her [Miss Field], renewing their friendship of a decade before." (*Kate Field,* p. 274.)

1. William Hepworth Dixon (1821–79), editor of the *Athenaeum* from 1853 to 1869, organized the National Shakespeare Committee in 1863 with the immediate purpose of conducting the Tercentenary Shakespeare Festival in Stratford. (*Letters of W. M. Thackeray,* ed. Ray, IV, 416. Professor Ray tells of Thackeray's exclusion from Dixon's committee.) The idea of a Shakespeare memorial apparently grew out of the National Shakespeare Committee. (See *Harper's New Monthly Magazine,* LVIII [May, 1879], 886.) The memorial was erected between 1877 and 1879. Browning had an aversion for the kind of promotion Dixon had undertaken, and the tactlessness in Dixon which had caused the trouble with Thackeray may partially account for the sharpness of Browning's reply.

2. Browning left London early in August for a stay with the Benzons at Little Milton above Loch Tummel, then on to Loch Luichart, Louisa Lady Ashburton's estate in Scotland, and, afterward, perhaps, to other country houses until after the middle of October when he returned to London.

To An Unidentified Correspondent

Allean House,
Pitlochry A.B.[1]
Sept. 14. '71.

Dear Friend,

Thank you heartily for the way you convey to me and even,—no matter how needlessly,—enforce Lady Marian's invitation for *to-morrow!* It is impossible for me to profit by anything except the kindness of it, so far am I away just now: [2] but do thank her very much. I hope you have such weather in the South as delights every nerve of me while I write.

Ever affectionately yours

[Yale]   Robert Browning.

To An Unidentified Correspondent [1]

19. Warwick Crescent, W.
Oct. 20, '71.

Dear Madam,

In answer to your inquiry respecting "the antecedents of the journey from Ghent to Aix"—I have to say that there are none but the sitting down under the bulwark of a ship off the coast of Tangiers, and writing it on the fly-leaf of Bartoli's *Simboli;* the whole "Ride" being purely imaginary.[2]

I am, Dear Madam,
Very faithfully yours

[Huntington]   Robert Browning.

1. Browning and his son were visiting Ernest Benzon at his newly acquired place at Little Milton in the hills above Loch Tummel, a mile or two from Pitlochry.

2. Pitlochry in Perthshire, Scotland, lies more than 300 miles north of Lady Marian Alford's place in Belton, England.

1. The letter which brought forth this note from Browning is symptomatic of a slow but sure awakening of learned and semilearned curiosity about the materials from which Browning made his poems. *Browning's Letter File,* ed. Armstrong, shows that the trickle of such inquiries began in the middle Sixties, reached a sizable stream during the Seventies; then in the Eighties, as a logical growth from these beginnings, came the organized curiosity of the Browning societies.

2. Almost ten years later Browning was to be asked the same question concerning the historical background of his poem, "How They Brought the Good News From Ghent to Aix." He made substantially the same reply. (See *Browning Society's Papers,* I, 49.)

To Sarianna Browning

Offington, Worthing.
Monday. [1871?] [1]

Dearest Sis, poor Mr Gaisford [2] is still confined to his bed, nor very likely to [be] well soon: it seems right therefore to go away: and I shall do so to-morrow: I leave by the 12. (something) train, and shall hope to be at home in the course of the afternoon.

Ever affy yours

[Schiff]   R B.

To Mrs. Charles Skirrow

Jan. 2, '72.
Tuesday Night

Dear Friend, What on earth (or under it) *can* you mean by "fearing your owl is a vexation to me"? I poured out all my heartful of the truest thanks that ever were, for the most charming gift that ever was,—and Mrs. Gray engaged to give them faithfully to you. This letter, and indeed any sort of letter I can hope to write, will be a poor substitute for the living words which I thought would do me more justice, and therefore please you better. As it is,—you must take this colder assurance that I am entirely glad and grateful too. I don't quite engage to put ink in so beautiful a thing,—it seems a desecration,—but, as long as I live, it shall be as near me as if it

1. Browning scribbled this note on a single sheet of stationery upon which "Offington, Worthing" is embossed. Clues for dating this letter are meager. D. G. C. Elwes writes that Offington, "now an inconsiderable manor . . . has been recently purchased by Thomas Gaisford, eldest son of Dean Gaisford, the eminent Greek scholar." (*History of the Castles, Mansions, and Manors of Western Sussex* [London, 1876], pp. 52–53.) One may simply conjecture that Browning's visit occurred probably at some time during the Seventies, possibly early as the remainder of this note may indicate. An entry in a guidebook of the period may be quoted as follows: "*Worthing* (Pop. 8641) . . . *Offington* (T. Gaisford, Esq.), the ancient residence of the Lords de la Warre, lies about ½ m. W. of the village. The house has been much altered. It contains a valuable library, and is surrounded by fine trees." (R. J. King, *Handbook for Travellers in Sussex* [London, 1877], p. 71.) The library of an eminent Greek scholar could well have been the reason for Browning's visit since his concern for Greek was particularly keen during the early Seventies.

2. Mrs. Orr mentions that Browning "stayed with Mr. and Lady Alice Gaisford at a house they temporarily occupied on the Sussex downs." (See *Life*, p. 289.) She places this visit, somewhat vaguely, as occurring "somewhat later" than the "earlier part of the decade" of the Seventies.

were blackened all over, and suggest far more pleasant thoughts than I could actually dip out [of] it: if, however, you *do* insist on the ink,—*sarà servita,* you shall be obeyed, as is but reasonable.[1]

All best wishes for you, this and other and many New Years! Sarianna wishes them as cordially as do I. Thank you too for Lord Westbury's delightful flattery: if my whole works have the effect on him which his one speech,—that I heard at Jowett's Dinner,— had upon me, it will be success enough.[2]

Ever affectionately and gratefully yours

[Schiff]   Robert Browning.

To Mrs. Alicia Bayne

19. Warwick Crescent, W.
Jan. 15, '72

Dear Mrs. Bayne,

You are absolutely welcome to use my poor name for whatever purpose may seem of the slightest service [1] to you,—and as for a "character,"—I hope I give you of *that* as much as I safely may without impertinence, whenever I happen to mention *your* name to anybody unacquainted with it,—and, consequently, with all the

---

1. "A brass Inkstand, the lid shaped as an owl's head with glass eyes" apparently was Mrs. Skirrow's Christmas gift to Browning. (Sotheby, *Browning Collections,* item 1283.)

2. Richard Lord Westbury (1800–73) was Lord Chancellor from 1865 to 1868. Mrs. Skirrow's husband, Charles Skirrow, was an intimate of Lord Westbury and is credited by T. A. Nash with having provided "useful information with regard to Lord Westbury's professional career." (Thomas Arthur Nash, *The Life of Richard Lord Westbury* [London, 1888], I, viii.) In a letter from Jowett to the daughter of Lord Westbury, Mrs. Adamson Parker, the dinner mentioned by Browning is described: "I made his [Lord Westbury's] acquaintance . . . on the occasion of a dinner which was given by my old friends and pupils at the Albion Tavern to celebrate my election as Master of Balliol. . . . The speech which your father made on that occasion, in returning thanks for the distinguished strangers, will never be forgotten by those who heard it. . . . The grave and earnest and pathetic tones of the speaker are still ringing in my ears. But this seriousness, which was never laid aside, was only the veil of as much fun and mischief as could well be concentrated in a speech of twenty minutes duration." Jowett became Master of Balliol on September 7, 1870. The dinner occurred in February, 1871. Guests included Robert Lowe (Chancellor of the Exchequer), Lord Cardwell (Secretary of State for War), Lord Houghton, and Browning, besides Dean Stanley, who was chairman for the occasion. (Evelyn Abbott and Lewis Campbell, *The Life and Letters of Benjamin Jowett* [London, 1897], II, 5.)

1. The word "use" has been altered to "service."

kindness possible. But I cannot promise you any sort of success for your quoting me to the Blackwoods,—at least, in their quality of magazine-proprietors,—since they have never, so far as I know, been aware of my existence: perhaps my opinion may prove all the more weighty! [2]

You very well know how proud (for want of a better word) the notice of the Bishop makes me,—certainly I value his good word beyond any amount of ordinary commendation. I beg you to assure him of my gratitude for his message about my little book.[3]

Here is beginning another year, dear Mrs. Baine [sic]: I wish you and yours every enjoyment of it, and myself more frequent enjoyment of your company than I have been privileged with of late,— for which I have to blame my own indolence rather than anything else. But the new year is a proper time for good resol[ves] and I have made at least one which will dispense with the necessity of merely assuring you that I am,

Ever most truly yours

[Yale]　　　　　　　　　　　　　　　　　　Robert Browning.

To Mrs. Charles Skirrow

19. W[arwick] C[rescent]. Monday, Jan. 29, '72.

Dear Friend,

Have you thought hardly of me? Y-e-s! Then, listen! For once, I was forced to go elsewhere than to the Procters',[1] at 2 o'clock, to bid

2. Perhaps it is just as well that *Blackwood's* virtually ignored Browning or that Browning thought that he had been completely ignored. From 1850 to 1872 the magazine mentioned him three times: "there is no getting through the confused crowd of Mr. Browning's *Men and Women*" (LXXIX [February, 1856], 135); *The Ring and the Book* was accounted a "wonderful poem" which the critic hoped was to be "the longest" (CIX [April, 1871], 442); the same poem was used as a prime illustration for an article on "Prolixity" (CIX [June, 1871], 616–630). With the publication of *Aristophanes' Apology, Blackwood's* began reviewing some of Browning's books. The aforementioned *Apology* is called a "wilds of confused wordiness" (CXVIII [July, 1875], 91); *Agamemnon*, "an ugly dried flower" (CXXVI [October, 1879], 423 n.), etc. Mrs. Bayne does not appear in the pages of *Blackwood's*.

3. Probably *Balaustion's Adventure,* which appeared in August, 1871.

1. Browning climbed to the fifth floor of Albert Mansions, 13 Upper Harley Street, to visit the Procters regularly each Sunday afternoon. His habit in this respect was well known to many people. (There is a long account of Mrs. Procter and her Sunday salon in Kegan Paul, *Memories* [London, 1899], pp. 319–333; there is a briefer glimpse in Rudolf Lehmann, *An Artist's Reminiscences,* p. 225.)

a friend good bye, before departure of that friend for the country: I could not get to you in time: in the evening I was obliged to go out again. To-day I breakfasted with the Attorney-General and accompanied him to the Court,[2] whence I came back tired enough, but determined to say at least a word for myself, and explain why, with every wish to call, I found it impossible to do so.

Ever affectionately yours

[Schiff]   Robert Browning.

To Miss Kate Field

19. Warwick Crescent, W.
Apr. 26, '72

Dear Miss Field,

How sorry I am! The 4th of May is precisely the day of the Academy Dinner—a feast to be greatly observed, and whence there is no dispensation obtainable. My sister is also engaged. We can only regret our own fortune and augur well of yours![1]

Ever affectionately yours

[Library of Congress]   Robert Browning.

2. John D. Coleridge (1821–94) was Attorney General from 1871 to 1873. (Richard C. Mitchell, *Chronicle of English Judges, Chancellors, Attorneys General, and Solicitors General* [Oswego, New York, 1937], p. 91.) The famous Tichborne trial, begun on May 12, 1871, was in the final part of the first stage, and Coleridge was in the midst of his address to the jury, an address which lasted from January 15 to February 23, 1872. It was a case "in which everyone took sides, and the interesting, the popular, the pleasant side to be on was that which favoured the cause of the claimant." (Ernest Hartley Coleridge, *Life and Correspondence of John Duke Coleridge* [New York, 1904], II, 184.) Browning's curiosity about the trial was doubtless stimulated by the technical resemblance to his own handling of *The Ring and the Book*. This resemblance is recognized by Ellis Yarnall in a letter to Coleridge, dated April 7, 1872, about a month after the conclusion of the Tichborne case: "Surely there has never been," he says with reference to Coleridge's summation to the jury, "a more copious setting forth of any single matter, the freshness of the story being, at every presentation of it, the same. Somehow I was reminded of *The Ring and the Book*, as, again and again and again, I was confronted with the same villainy, and yet each picturing had its own novelty and interest." (*Forty Years of Friendship*, ed. Charlton Yarnall [London, 1911], p. 139.) Carlyle's facetious remark that "Browning *will* very likely do the [Tichborne] Claimant by and by" was perhaps not so far from a possibility as one might suppose. (*William Allingham: A Diary*, under date of May 13, 1873. See also DeVane, *Browning Handbook*, p. 342.)

1. This was the annual banquet of the Royal Academy of Arts which served as a private opening of the current exhibition of pictures. The dinner, "sumptu-

To Mrs. Charles Skirrow

Alton Towers,
Cheadle.[1]
May 2⅗, '72.

Dear Friend, You are infinitely good to me; but I don't consider myself bad because, knowing that you want no words of mine to tell you as much, I have a repugnance to these poor ineffectual words. I never feel so little as when I am considering all about it with a view to a proper setting-forth of the same. I am certain it is quite otherwise with you: so, there might be worse arrangements between us than that I should only take, and most gratefully, the good I get from every letter of yours, and not attempt to pay you back again in such coin as you are now going to get. Yes, I was really tired and bilious last week, and wanted exactly the warm mudbath of laziness I am up to the neck in, now and for a few days longer. The people are most kindly, the place is different enough from my usual exercise-ground, and the life realizes the ideal sea-side pleasure of Hood, consisting as it does of "drinking, eating, eating, drinking, and vexing not our heads with thinking." This is the famous "dream of Pugin come true," the Muriel Towers of Dizzy, who fitted his "Lothair" into all the peculiarities of the place.[2] The guests are

ous and elegant in all its appointments," was served to "a numerous and distinguished company." Browning's friend of other years, John Forster, responded to the toast to Literature. Though Browning was doubtless present, his name does not appear in the *Times's* account of the banquet. (London *Times*, May 6, 1872, p. 9, col. 3.) The augury of good fortune for Miss Field was doubtless in connection with her lecture on Dickens, at Willis's Rooms, May 6, 1872, a lecture which was preceded by an informal reception. (Lilian Whiting, *Kate Field*, p. 285.)

1. Alton Towers, Cheadle was the country home of the nineteenth Earl of Shrewsbury, "now a popular resort." (Baedeker, *Great Britain* [1927], p. 285.) Cheadle is in Staffordshire just north of a direct line from London to Liverpool.

2. Augustus Welby Pugin (1812–52) is described by A. E. Richardson as "one who offered no resemblance to any other Victorian architect." (*Early Victorian England*, ed. G. M. Young [London, 1934], II, 217.) The nineteenth Earl of Shrewsbury (1830–77) commissioned Pugin to design Alton Towers but, unlike others who engaged this unorthodox architect, the earl allowed Pugin complete freedom in carrying through his ideas. The result is described in *Lothair*, by the Right Honourable B. Disraeli (London, 1870), particularly in vol. II when Lothair first visits Muriel Towers which "crowned a wooded steep, part of a wild, and winding, and sylvan valley at the bottom of which rushed a foaming stream" (II, 54). Muriel Towers consisted of "a number of

nowise lovely nor admirable, but good natured and happily unpro-
vocative of those exalted mental efforts which you deplore in their
effect on my fine face, which is at least dog-rose-tinted delicately
already. I return with the family on Monday, will see you directly
after, and we'll have tea, and talk, and you shall forgive this admirable epistolary performance—so exactly what you have a right
to expect from

Your affectionatest est est

[Schiff]   RB.

TO MRS. BLANCHE RITCHIE CORNISH [1]

19. Warwick Crescent, W.
Nov. 24, '72.

Dear Mrs. Cornish,

Only yesterday—the very Saturday's self,—and at 5 o'clock,—did
I go to the Club [2] and find your invitation: for, you must know, I
have been kept at home by something of a cold and cough this
fortnight and more, and never guessed what was waiting for me all
the while. Thank you most truly for the kind thought of the invitation, which in some sort I rejoice to have only got when it was
too late for the exposition—since I should have assuredly teazed
myself with rebellious designs to go and so behave badly to the
Doctor. It is a true, deep, and abiding delight with me that the

---

courts and quadrangles . . . , all of bright and fantastic architecture, and
each of which was a garden, glowing with brilliant colours, and gay with the
voice of fountains or the forms of gorgeous birds" (II, 62). Descriptions of
Muriel Towers continue *passim* throughout the remainder of this three-volume
novel.

1. Mrs. Blanche (Ritchie) Cornish (*ca.* 1847–1923) was the daughter of William Ritchie who, at the time of his death in 1861, was Legal Member of Council in Lord Canning's government. She married Francis Cornish (1839–1916)
in 1866. (Vaughan Cornish, *A Family of Devon* [St. Leonard's-on-the-Sea, Sussex, 1942], Table III of the Genealogical Tables of the Cornish Family.) In
*Some Family Letters of W. M. Thackeray, Together with Recollections by
His Kinswoman Blanche Warre Cornish* there is a good incidental account of
Mrs. Cornish's relations with the Thackeray girls and their father. In addition
to this slender volume on Thackeray, Mrs. Cornish produced two novels:
Alcestis (London, 1873) and *Northern Cloisters* (London, 1882). Both were pub-
lished anonymously. (Halkett and Laing, *Dictionary of Anonymous and
Pseudonymous English Literature*, new and enlarged edition by Kennedy,
Smith, and Johnson [London, 1928], I, 53; IV, 196.)

2. Doubtless the Athenaeum, to which Browning had belonged for the past
ten years.

month at St. Aubin was signalized by your appearance,—that of your whole party, I mean: and it makes the sky bluer and the sea brinier and the little house bigger in my memory. I mean to use my advantages and never let any of you escape me again if I can help it. So thank you again and again. Give my kind remembrances to Mr. Cornish, and make Miss Thackeray keep me a little in mind: how I keep her in mind, she is going to see, if I may be so honored when my piece of work is done.[3]

My sister begs to send her kind regards. Believe me

Ever yours truly

[New York Public Library]   Robert Browning.

To the Chevalier de Chatelain

19. Warwick Crescent, W.
Jan. 23, '73.

My dear Neighbour,

You confound me by your generosity as well as by your ability and versatility. I mean to read your translation [1] as soon as I am somewhat more at leisure: it will interest me exceedingly. Believe that I shall value as it deserves this evidence that,—at the age to which you have so happily attained on the day you made me the present,—in the words of the Bible "the eye was not dim nor the natural force abated." [2] May it long continue so with my excellent neighbour—of whom I beg to subscribe myself the friend, and admirer also,

[Huntington]   Robert Browning.

3. *Red Cotton Night-Cap Country, or Turf and Towers* was published the first week in May, 1873 and dedicated simply "To Miss Thackeray." The dates on the manuscript in the Balliol College Library indicate that Browning began the poem on December 1, 1872. (DeVane, *Browning Handbook,* p. 329.) The implication of this letter is that he had begun writing the poem some time before that date.

1. *"King Lear" de Shakespeare,* publiée par le Chevalier de Chatelain 19 Janvier, 1873.

2. Deut. 34:7. The birthday of the Chevalier de Chatelain was January 19, the day on which his translation of *King Lear* appeared and on which he made the presentation of the copy to Browning.

To George Smith [1]

March 8, '73

Advertisement [2]

I premise, and wish to have distinctly borne in mind by any reader of this poem, that it is no more nor less than a mere account treated poetically, of certain problematic facts taken just as I find them given, by parties to a dispute, in the published pleadings of their respective legal advocates and the formal decision of a Court of Law. Each and every such statement, therefore, affecting the conduct of either party, must be considered as depending absolutely upon public authority and pretending to no sort of guarantee for its truth obtainable from private sources of information—into none of which have I the will or power to enquire. My business confines itself to working a sum from arbitrary or imaginary figures: if these be correct, the result should follow as I give it—not otherwise. Nor would I attempt the working at all, had not the parties themselves begun by proposing the figures for examination. No fact has been purposely changed, although conversations, declared and described, could only be re-produced by a guess at something equivalent. Either party may—and one must have—exaggerated or extenuated

1. George Smith (1824–1901) assumed control of Smith, Elder and Co., publishers, upon the death of his father in 1846, and moved the business to 15 Waterloo Place. Under his care the company published the works of many eminent Victorians: Ruskin, Charlotte Brontë, Darwin, Wilkie Collins, the Brownings, Matthew Arnold, Harriet Martineau, Trollope, and Mrs. Humphrey Ward. In 1860 Smith established the *Cornhill Magazine* under the editorship of Thackeray. In 1865 he founded the *Pall Mall Gazette*. His most important venture was the publication of the *Dictionary of National Biography* in 66 volumes, begun in 1882 and completed in 1901. Smith became Browning's publisher in 1866 after the poet's break with Chapman (see Appendix C). His treatment of Browning was generous and wise. He took Browning's work without insisting upon a preliminary scrutiny of the poet's manuscript. (See *Letters*, ed. Hood, p. 226.)

2. Browning completed *Red Cotton Night-Cap Country* on January 23, 1873, and placed the manuscript in the hands of his publisher, George Smith of Smith and Elder. "When the poem was in first proofs, Mr. Smith . . . held it back for fear of a libel suit from some of the participants of the tragedy which is the material of the narrative." (DeVane, *Browning Handbook*, p. 329.) Apparently Browning outlines his first defense against a libel action in this "Advertisement," prepared, one may assume, as a foreword to *Red Cotton Night-Cap Country*. The argument is that he has used public records only and has stuck to the facts. See, however, the next letter to Smith, March 15, 1873, below.

or invented: my concern is exclusively with these presumable exaggerations and extenuations and inventions as they were presented to and decided upon by the Court of the Country, as they exist in print, and as they may be procured by anybody.

[Yale]   R.B.

To George Smith

19. Warwick Crescent, W.
March 15, '73.

My dear Smith,

We neither of us had the least doubt that the law was exactly as the letter states it to be.[1] But,—as yourself observe,—the vital point is,—can a Foreigner use that power in an English Court, which certainly an Englishman possesses? *Is there one such case in the Books?* If we were ignorant as to what the parties could do, being English instead of French, I suppose every sessions could furnish an instructive example. But I want an instance of [2] the other procedure, and I have just written to the Attorney-General [3] for his opinion on this particular point—all the rest is beside the question. Thank you exceedingly for all your goodness and trouble.

Ever yours truly

[Yale]   Robert Browning

To Mrs. Margaret Raine Hunt [1]

19. Warwick Crescent, W.
March 22, '73.

Dear Mrs. Hunt,

How can I be other than surprised, and gratified by such an honor as you propose doing me? I doubt whether it will conduce to

1. This letter was a reply from the first lawyer Browning consulted about possible libel in connection with *Red Cotton Night-Cap Country*. As can be seen, Browning is now concerned, not so much with whether or not his poem is libelous (see above, letter of March 8, 1873) as with the technical or practical possibility of a Frenchman seeking redress in an English court.

2. The word "of" appears in the manuscript twice at this point.

3. The Attorney General, John Duke Coleridge, an old friend of Browning, had gained wide fame through his participation in the Tichborne trial. His answer to Browning's question appears as a footnote to the next letter to Smith dated March 26, 1873.

1. Mrs. Margaret Hunt, nee Raine (1831–1912), wife of the water colorist, wrote many novels under the nom de plume of Averil Beaumont, beginning with *Magdalen Wynward; or the Provocation of the Pre-Raphaelite* (London,

the advantage of your book,[2] but the generosity will be the more conspicuous. And I want no preliminary taste of proof-sheets to be quite assured that your indulgence for me will be the one thing symptomatic of weakness in your book.

My sister still keeps her room, but is recovering though slowly. I shall certainly call—with her, if possible,—and see whatever you are good enough to show us.

With all regards to Mr. Hunt, pray believe me very cordially yours

[Huntington]   Robert Browning.

To George Smith

[March 26, 1873] [1]

Dear Smith,

What do you think of it? I have gone through the whole poem, softening the roughnesses, and taking out all direct sting—I don't think there will be anything to apprehend now,—nor will you, when you see the proofs. General Schenk [2] (Lawyer) told me last

---

1872) and ending with *Mrs. Juliet* (London, 1892). Only a few of Mrs. Hunt's novels are available in America. One of these, *Barrington's Fate* (1884), opens with a quotation from Browning's "A Likeness" and proceeds immediately to a description of a male character "lying on a sofa reading Browning's *Dramatis Personae* in perfect contentment of body and mind."

2. The book was possibly Mrs. Hunt's second novel, *Thornicroft's Model* (1873). Mrs. Hunt's habit was to use quotations from various poets as headpieces to the chapters of her novels. Perhaps she had told Browning of her intention to use quotations from his poems in this manner. On the other hand, she may have proposed dedicating the book to him, though dedications were not customary with her.

1. This note of Browning addressed to Smith is written in pencil at the end of the following letter from John Duke Coleridge, the Attorney General, to Browning. Coleridge's letter expresses an opinion on the possibility of a libel suit resulting from the publication of *Red Cotton Night-Cap Country*.

1 Sussex Square, W
26th March. 1873.

My dear Browning

You ask me a question which I have no special means or faculties for answering—and which [either?] you or Spottiswoode can answer just as well as I can. I can only say that if I were you (which is I suppose the sort of position you wish me to take) I would alter the poem rather more if I felt I could do so without serious injury to its intention and conception and [?] art. I don't believe the risque is practically great and the damages if one can suppose any given could not I think be large.

Ever sincerely yours.
J D Coleridge

night he would give me a Bill ot Indemnity against any results in America.

In all haste, yours ever

[Yale]   RB

To George Smith

19 Warwick Crescent, W.
March 31, '73

My dear Smith,

Thank you for your note. I am prevented from calling on you to-day and, probably, to-morrow so write to say that I have just got the corrected proofs [1]—which you too can obtain; and I really think I have reduced the offence to a minimum. If you think so too—you may at once transmit the copy wanted in Boston,[2]—taking care that *one* of the very few and minute corrections still to be made, *is* made in such a copy—I mean the change of name at page 129. for Antoine read Léonce.[3]

I am going to read the poem, or as much of it as proves digestible at a sitting, to Miss Thackeray [4] this morning. I saw the Attorney-General for a few minutes at the Club Saturday: he evidently thinks there is no danger at all, after the alterations I described to him—only insists on a presentation-copy as his fee! [5] I will call on Wednesday: but if you decide favorably, you may despatch the American copy at once and so save time. With truest thanks for all your care and kindness

Ever yours
R. Browning.

2. Robert Cumming Schenk (1809–1890), American military officer, diplomat, and poker player (author of *Draw Poker* [New York, 1880]), was minister to Great Britain from 1870 to 1876. He was commissioned a brigadier general at the beginning of the Civil War and rose to major general in command of the 8th Corps at Baltimore.

1. These were proofs of *Red Cotton Night-Cap Country*.

2. Ticknor and Fields were to publish the American edition of *Red Cotton Night-Cap Country*.

3. The specific correction is added as an afterthought, crowded in after "p. 129."

4. Browning, after reading the poem to Miss Thackeray, dedicated the work to her.

5. The Attorney General, John Duke Coleridge, and Browning possibly met at the Cosmopolitan Club of which both were members.

On considering, it will be even more expeditious if I send *you* the corrected proofs—which you will deal with as you please—and, *if* you please, send to the Printer. *The last page 281. has not been sent to me, however.*

[Yale]

To George Smith

19 Warwick Crescent, W.
March 31, '73

Dear Smith,

Will you please correct in the proofs page 124. line 6. *Antoine Mellerio* to *Léonce Miranda?*

and

p. 256. line 5—after Church insert *of* [1]

Ever truly yours

[Yale]   R Browning.

To Reuben Browning

19 Warwick Crescent, W.
Apr. 27, '73.

Dear Reuben,

I was very sorry that I missed you yesterday: had I known you were coming I would have done my best to be at home. Thank you very much for the trouble you have taken about the E. C. Stock: [1] please relieve yourself and me from the business, by selling the Stock at once; if you transmit the money to me, I will add it to some savings of mine, and, in a few weeks, I hope, invest the whole in whatever seems best. It shall be as you and your son recommend —though I still believe in Italian 5%. [2]

Ever affectionately yours

Robert Browning.

1. These are last-minute corrections for *Red Cotton Night-Cap Country.*
1. English Consolidated Annuities, a stock issued by the British government which paid a steady rate of 3 to $3\frac{1}{2}\%$ interest during most of the nineteenth century.
2. It is likely that Reuben Browning accepted Browning's preference and invested in Italian securities, for Browning's will refers to "all my stocks and properties in the Italian Public Debt." (London *Times*, February 22, 1890.) Furthermore, the amount of income derived from his Italian investments during 1886–89 has been recently disclosed in the significant little book: Roma

You shall have my new book ³ at the week's end.
[Yale]

To George Smith

19 Warwick Crescent, W.
May 9, '73

My dear Smith,

Here is a note I return to you as rather for your consideration than mine: but it gives me the opportunity of saying that Mrs. Orr has pleased to write another article on the new Poem,—which the *Fortnightly,*—to which it was highly commended by Mr. Lewes,—don't want: ¹ I have not read a word of it, of course,—but on every account I should be glad if there were any way to its appearance: it seems only my duty to such disinterested zeal (and considerable intelligence too) that I should bring the fact that there *is* a paper of the kind going a-begging—under your notice: so the duty is done.

Miss Thackeray has written to me, somewhat mysteriously, but so as to give me the impression that she has taken some of the Mrs.-Trimmerisms in the *Daily News'* article as offensive to *her:* I should be sorry indeed if that were the case, and, on that account, would like Mrs. Orr's notion of the morality of the poem,—which I need no examination to accept as fair and favourable,—to be put in evidence ²—

Ever truly yours
Robert Browning.

King, *Robert Browning's Finances from His Own Account Books* (Waco, Texas, 1947). This book shows Browning's considerable investment in both English and Italian stocks (see pp. 16–17). It is possible, therefore, that Browning's uncle Reuben advised retaining the English Consols and buying Italian securities with his "savings."

3. *Red Cotton Night-Cap Country,* which appeared during the first week of May, 1873.

1. Mrs. Orr reviewed *Red Cotton Night-Cap Country* in the *Contemporary Review,* XXII (June, 1873), 87–106. The *Contemporary Review* was edited by James Thomas Knowles (see letter of November 25, 1873) and published by Strahan. Browning apparently wanted Smith to accept Mrs. Orr's article for the *Cornhill Magazine* or for the *Pall Mall Gazette,* the newspaper of literary interests which Smith had founded in 1865 and still controlled. George Henry Lewes (1817–78) had relinquished the editorship of the *Fortnightly Review* to John Morley (1838–1923) in 1867.

2. The *Daily News* (May 5, 1873) had found that the theme and the motive of the poem (*Red Cotton Night-Cap Country*) were outside the sphere of true

I see there *are* a very few corrections to make,—punctuation, etc.—
which require a day's notice, should we be fortunate as to the sale
and need ³ a new edition ⁴—
[Yale]

To George Smith

19 Warwick Crescent, W.
Saturday, May 10, '73

My dear Smith,

Here is the M.S. of Mrs. Orr: ¹ if you can do nothing for it, please
return it as soon as convenient, as she may try her luck (and mine)
in other quarters.

Do you see the *Athenaeum?* There is evidently some regularly
reported Trial which everybody can refer to: I am told there is a
similar statement of facts in yesterday's *Echo.*²

Ever yours truly

[Yale]

Robert Browning.

---

and healthy art. Mrs. Sara Trimmer (1741–1810), a "woman of great piety," conducted from "1802 to 1806 the *Guardian of Education,* a periodical to criticize
and examine books for children and books on education, so that only good
ones might spread abroad." (*D.N.B.*) Mrs. Orr indulged in no Trimmerisms in
her review (see previous note) but found Browning's new poem "surpassing
as a work of art anything he has yet done." Throughout the review she defends
the morality of the poem.

3. Something has been stricken out after the word "sale," and "and need"
written above.

4. No new edition of *Red Cotton Night-Cap Country* was called for.

1. Browning apparently sent with this note the manuscript about which he
had written to Smith the day before.

2. The *Athenaeum* for May 10, 1873 reviewed *Red Cotton Night-Cap Country.* The reviewer, for two columns, gives the facts of the case and then says:
"It is upon this well-known story of violence, called in France the Mellerio
Debacher case, that Mr. Browning's poem is based, and the disguise is so thin
that it would be false delicacy in us if, being well acquainted with the facts of a
story so easily accessible in the French law reports, we should follow Mr. Browning in his alteration of names."

To Mrs. Coddington [1]

19. Warwick Crescent, W.
May 24 [1873?] [2]

Dear Mrs. Coddington,

It will give me great pleasure to dine with you on the 14th as you so kindly propose.

With best respects to your Family, pray believe me

Very sincerely yours

[Library of Congress]   Robert Browning.

To Mrs. Charles Skirrow

19. Warwick Crescent, W.
June 4, '73.

Dear Friend,

I called yesterday to say—what is harder to write—how very happy I am that you are going to be,—or actually are,—happy at last: I wish it and rejoice in it with all my heart and fewer words than are at my pen's point—did I let it get the better of me.[1]

You were never "out of mind" for me. I got a letter from Nice expressly mentioning that anything sent there "within ten days" would find you, especially the *Atlantic Monthly*. Now, they never sent me a number till some six weeks afterward, when I found they also forwarded the next month's number—for economy's sake, I suppose. When I referred to your letter for advice, I found no other word in it than those above-mentioned. I therefore,—having no means of informing myself further,—sent the magazines to Rome at once. The *next* arrival was by last night's post only—and you shall have *that,* of course. As for my poem,—thereby hangs a long

1. Mrs. Coddington was the mother of Fannie Coddington, whom Pen was to marry in 1887 after a lapse of 15 years between his first and second proposals.

2. The Coddingtons were settled in London for several years after 1868; they returned to New York in November, 1873, where both Mr. and Mrs. Coddington died without returning to London. Browning refers in a letter of October 30, 1887, below, to knowing them "fifteen years ago." The present note must have been written in one of the later years of their acquaintance; and since in 1872 Browning was at Alton Towers, Cheadle (see above, letter of May 23, 1872), the most probable year date is 1873. See also below, letter of November 14, 1873.

1. A reference to the acquisition of a new home by the Skirrows? See above, letter of March 10, 1870, n. 1.

tale: it appeared three weeks ago: ² the moment I get to see Smith,³ your copy shall pay its respects to you,—equally of *course!*

There! I am delighted to think that you are so near and that I may see you as of old—may I not?

My sister sends her very kindest of loves, most abundant of good wishes. She returned from Paris last week, having gone to recover her health, and I hope with success.

You must commend me—far beyond my deserts, as a friend should,—to Mr. Skirrow, and believe me ever, dear friend,

Affectionately yours

[Schiff]   RBrowning.

To Mrs. Alicia Bayne

19. Warwick Crescent, W.

June 25, '73.

Dear Mrs. Bayne,

I am sure I feel,—and so does my Sister,—great disappointment at having been unable to go to your pleasant entertainment yesterday. I was obliged, after Ella's concert,¹ to go and bid goodbye to Dr. Chambers: ² my sister had to follow a friend home,—while

2. *Red Cotton Night-Cap Country.* If this is to be taken as an accurate time reference the poem appeared May 14, 1873.

3. George Murray Smith (1824–1901), senior member of the publishing firm, Smith, Elder, and Co., and long a friend of Browning. He met him in 1844 or 1845 at the home of Thomas Powell. "They soon formed a cordial friendship." In 1847 or 1848 the publishing firm was nearly ruined by an embezzlement of £30,000. At this moment Browning "sent Henry Chorley—the critic of the *Athenaeum*—with a message to George Smith, asking if he would undertake the publication of his books. Much as he would have liked to become his friend's publisher, his business affairs were too involved to let him undertake new responsibilities, and he was constrained to say 'No,' without giving the reason. Twenty-one years passed before the desired chance was renewed." (Leonard Huxley, *The House of Smith Elder*, p. 155.)

1. John Ella organized the Musical Union in 1845 and was its guiding spirit until 1880. The concert referred to here was advertised in the London *Times* for June 23, 1873, as follows: "Musical Union. Jaell and Auer on Tuesday, half-past 3, June 24ᵗʰ. Trio, C Minor, Mendelssohn; Quartet, D Minor, Haydn; Kreutzer Sonata (by desire), Beethoven; solos, Prelude and Polonaise, C Minor, Chopin. Jaell last time this season. Tickets 10s., 6d., each; family tickets for three, one guinea."

2. William Chambers (1800–83), of the Edinburgh publishing firm of W. and R. Chambers, was the uncle of Amelia (Chambers) Lehmann, the wife of Browning's close friend Rudolf Lehmann, the portrait painter. Chambers had

Robert was at the Windsor review.[3] Pray accept our best thanks for the kindness of your invitation, as well as some particular thankfulness on my sister's part for your extension of it in her behalf: and believe me ever

Dear Mrs. Bayne,
Yours most truly

[Yale]   Robert Browning.

To Mr. Coddington [1]

19. Warwick Crescent, W.
Nov. 14, '73.

My dear Mr Coddington,

I heard of your kindness in calling yesterday, and was almost fortunate enough to find you,—so soon did I return after your visit. With regard to the invitation, what can I say but that I should be happy to accept it were I able to fix a day next week for my return from the country; my stay depends altogether on circumstances about which I am as yet in the dark, and, while it may only last for a day or two, may, just as possibly, extend over the week.[2] If you were certainly going away before then, I would consider *that* tantamount

been granted an LL.D. by the University of Edinburgh in 1872 and was perhaps in London, along with thousands of other Britishers, to see something of the festivities attending the state visit of the Shah of Persia.

3. The Windsor review was part of a lengthy series of ceremonies which began on June 19 with the arrival of the Shah of Persia and which were designed to reveal to the eastern potentate the might of England on sea and land. The reporter of the review which Pen witnessed observed that "although it may be very true that we are a Naval rather than a Military Power, the Review of troops in Windsor Park yesterday presented a scene as thoroughly and peculiarly English as the Review of Ships at Spithead the day before." (London *Times,* June 25, 1873.)

1. Specific information about the Coddingtons is meager. They resided in New York City. They first visited London in 1866 and came to stay for several years in 1868. Browning met them through Dean Stanley, and Pen proposed marriage to Fannie Coddington in 1873. (See *Letters,* ed. Hood, p. 274.) In a letter of September 30, 1887, below, Browning mentions the Coddingtons as "our friends" and says that Fannie has "ample means." For other letters involving the Coddingtons see three letters to Marie, Fannie's sister, in *Letters,* ed. Hood. When Pen and Fannie met again in 1887, the courtship was renewed, and they were married on October 4, 1887. See *Some Memories of Robert Browning,* by his daughter-in-law Fannie Barrett Browning (Boston, 1928), *passim.*

2. See next letter. The circumstances appear to be whether or not the party at Lord Carnarvon's would be pleasant enough to justify staying for a week.

to an obligation for my return in any case: but I have still the occasion of seeing you before the 25th and you need not fear that I will forego such a privilege. Pray offer my best thanks and kindest regards to Mrs. Coddington whose goodness to me and mine I shall ever remember gratefully, and believe me

Dear Mr. Coddington,
Yours most truly
Robert Browning.

[Library of Congress]

To Sarianna Browning

Highclere Castle
Newbury [1]
Thursday M[ornin]g
[November 20, 1873] [2]

Dearest Sis,

Yours came safely; the packet is four more numbers of the Chicago Railway Guide; [3]—the letters are requests for autographs.

1. A picture of Highclere Castle is reproduced in Sir Arthur Hardinge, *The Life of Henry Howard Molyneux Herbert, Fourth Earl of Carnarvon* (London, 1925), II, facing 34. After seven years' repairing on this thirteenth-century house was completed in 1850 "Highclere soon became a gathering place where intellectual interests and sport were equally enjoyed" (I, 66).

2. The dating of this letter depends upon matching Browning's account of his doings with an account recorded by Lady Knightley in her *Journals* under the dates November 18–21, 1873. Lady Knightley mentions as present everyone named by Browning, plus, of course, Browning's own name. She writes (November 19) of being "divided between Count Beust and Mr. Browning all day." She records (November 21) the arrival of Lady Portsmouth for luncheon. There are numerous other details which establish the fact that Browning and Lady Knightley were writing of the same occasion at Lord Carnarvon's. (*The Journals of Lady Knightley of Fawsley*, ed. Julia Cartwright [London, 1915], p. 251.)

3. F. G. Kenyon records as a "most curious proof" of Browning's popularity in America "the California Railway time-table edition of his poems." (Orr, *Life*, p. 333, n. 2.) The *Chicago Railway Guide* apparently also printed Browning's poems for the amusement of its patrons. The issue for September, 1873, probably one of those sent to Browning, contains this preamble: "Official Guide of the Chicago and Alton Railroad . . . Containing Time Cards, Advertisements, and Part of a Reprint from the Latest English Edition of the Complete Works of Robert Browning ... . 10,000 Copies for Free Distribution, Monthly." Then the editor of the *Guide* adds: "This plan of combining high class literature with railway time-cards is adopted in the belief that the traveling public will prefer works of permanent value, and which appeal to the highest culture and most refined taste, to scraps of current rail-

There are here Ly. Dorothy Nevill,—Pen's friend, her daughter [4] (who begs to be remembered by him, and hopes to meet him next season), Henry Cowper,[5] the Holfords,[6] and others.[7] Ct. Beust [8] left yesterday—after inviting me very civilly to dine with him next Monday to meet Ld and Ly. Granville.[9] Ld Carnarvon was so exceedingly warm in his manner last evening,—*kind* he can't help be-

---

road history. . . ." There is no doubt that this form of distribution did provide Browning a potentially large reading public, a public, too, with the leisure of travel aboard the Lightning Express which was scheduled to negotiate 126 miles in five and a half hours. Bk. V of *Sordello* was available in the issue of the *Guide* from which we have quoted—sturdy reading, indeed, for a traveling public!

4. Lady Dorothy Nevill (1826–1913) has left several volumes of chat about her life and the people she knew. She mentions "having myself known Browning," but she does not elaborate upon this experience. (*The Reminiscences of Lady Dorothy Nevill*, ed. Ralph Nevill [London, 1906], p. 232.) Typical of contemporary testimony about Lady Dorothy is Lady Knightley's tribute that she "is always amusing." (*The Journals of Lady Knightley*, ed. Cartwright, p. 367.) Lady Nevill's daughter, Miss Meresia Nevill, grew up to be an active worker in the conservative political organization called the Primrose League. (*Reminiscences of Lady Dorothy Nevill*, ed. Nevill, pp. 290–291.)

5. Henry Frederick Cowper (1836–87) was the second son of the sixth Earl Cowper. He was M.P. from Herts, 1865–85. (Frederick Boase, *Modern English Biography* [London, 1892–1921], I, 729.)

6. Robert Stayner Holford (1808–92), art collector and M.P., built Dorchester House in London—"itself a work of art"—and Westonbirt in Gloucestershire. "For an English country house he felt the fascination of youth . . . as is evidenced by several primitives and Pre-Raphaelites from Westonbirt." Holford was an original member of the Burlington Fine Arts Club, an amateur collectors' club. His son, later Lt. Col. Sir George Holford, was possibly one of "the Holfords" at Highclere. (For a sketch of Holford as a collector and builder see the preface to *Catalogue of Pictures and other Objects of Art Selected from the Collections of Mr. Robert Holford* [privately printed for the Burlington Fine Arts Club, London, 1921], particularly pp. 10–12.)

7. "Others" included Cockerell, Morier, Sir Rainald and Lady Knightley, Townsend, editor of the *Spectator*, and General Scott, "a great authority on sewage." (*The Journals of Lady Knightley*, ed. Cartwright, p. 251.)

8. Count Friedrich Ferdinand Beust (1809–86) was the Austrian ambassador to Great Britain, a "typical *homme du monde*," observed Lady Knightley, "pleasant enough . . . when you can stir him up, which is not always an easy task." (*The Journals of Lady Knightley*, ed. Cartwright, p. 251.)

9. George Leveson-Gower, second Earl of Granville (1815–91), statesman, married, after the death of his first wife, Castalia Rosalind Campbell in 1865. From 1870 to 1874 Lord Granville was Foreign Minister in the cabinet of Lord John Russell. (*D.N.B.*) Lord Granville and the Count von Beust first met in Paris "thirty years previously" when Granville's father was the English ambassador there and Beust was Secretary to the Austrian legation. (*Memoirs of . . . Count von Beust* [London, 1887], II, 305.)

ing,—seemed so pleased at my consenting to stay—that I arranged to
stay the week out and return next Saturday.[10] The weather has been
not amiss—dry always, if dull and grey—but today is sunny, mild
and pleasant: I have been walking in the park,[11] and, after luncheon, shall begin again. The main party of men are gone out to shoot
—(since writing the last word, Ly. Portsmouth and her daughter
are arrived to Luncheon).[12] I need not say how glad I am to hear
that Pen is employed, and keeps up his music a little: young Primrose [13] is here (out shooting now) and he is taking lessons of
Schnegelsberg [14] (lessons of harmony!)—in consequence of my
recommendation. If Pen were here, and *played,* he would carry all
before him: some horrible girls' performance gets devout thanks.
The notion of raising the vases a little is a very good one. Every sitting room in this house has one or more screens just like ours in
shape (with pillars, etc.) but with tapestry instead of the carving,
and, consequently, not half so pretty. There are two such in this

10. Henry Howard Molyneux Herbert, Fourth Earl of Carnarvon (1831–
1890), made Highclere "one of the first houses to adopt the week-end party."
Genial and courteous, he gathered together people "eminent in literature,
politics, and administration" and by "his delightful ease and humour" put
his guests "on the best terms not only with their host but with each other."
(Personal recollections of Col. Sir Herbert Jekyll as quoted in Hardinge, *Life
of . . . Carnarvon,* III, 323.) Browning, named as one of Carnarvon's intimate
friends, is described as "most genial of poets" (III, 316).

11. An excellent description of Highclere Park as "the prettiest park I have
ever seen" is quoted from Cobbett's *Rides* in Hardinge, *Life of . . . Carnarvon,*
I, 65–66.

12. Eveline Herbert, two years younger than her brother, Lord Carnarvon,
married Isaac Newton Wallop, the fifth earl of Portsmouth, in 1855. The estate
of Lord Portsmouth was close to Highclere, convenient for a social interchange
between families. (Hardinge, *Life of . . . Carnarvon,* I, 68.) "Lady Portsmouth,
like her brother, had very catholic tastes. She gathered around her scientists,
philosophers, and poets, such as Huxley, Herbert Spencer, Jowett, Matthew
Arnold, and Robert Browning; and her adaptibility enabled her to enter with
equal heartiness into the tastes of her husband and his friends, who found the
turf and the hunting-field more congenial than the study and the library" (III,
11).

13. The Right Honourable Sir Henry Primrose (1846–1923), Pen's contemporary, apparently did not continue seriously his study of music. He attended Balliol, a fact which may have made Browning wince, and then for a
time became secretary to the Viceroy of India, Lord Ripon. He held other posi-
tions in the government and possibly needed little of what Schnegelsberg had
to teach him of harmony. (*Who Was Who, 1916–1928.*)

14. We have been unable to find any further information about Schnegelsberg.

room: an infinity of beautiful things all over the house of course. Take care of our dining room chairs—Chippendale: they are pronounced to be invaluable.

Goodbye, dearest two of you, R. B.

I enclose a line for Procter to-morrow.[15] If Pen were to accompany you, it would delight the old man.

5 o'clock/ Day's sport (5 guns)—218 pheasants, 40 hares, 20 rabbits, 1 partridge.

[Schiff]

To James Thomas Knowles [1]

19 Warwick Crescent, W.
Nov. 25, '73.

Dear Mr. Knowles,

I am quite of your opinion that the excision of the two Letters, and accompanying matter which you have marked, will benefit Horne's article. This morning's post brought, with your packet, another "proof" from the author: and I rejoice to see that the mistakes in the printing—which were confounded and confounding in your uncorrected copy, are tolerably removed in Horne's paper with an effect you will appreciate. If he could fill up the half-line in which he mentions my permission to publish, with some half-dozen words about my having done so without seeing the letters—and in confidence that he would do harm to nobody,—I should like such an acknowledgement, and will tell him so.[2]

15. Bryan Waller Procter (Barry Cornwall), 1787–1874, poet and successful conveyancer, was one of Browning's oldest friends.

1. James Thomas Knowles (1831–1908) was from 1870 to 1877 editor of the *Contemporary Review*. In 1877 he became founder, proprietor, and editor of the *Nineteenth Century*. He was knighted in 1903.

2. Horne's article is a series of four articles entitled: "Letters from Elizabeth Barrett Browning to the author of 'Orion' on Literary and General Topics." The four installments appeared in the *Contemporary Review* for December, 1873 (pp. 146–161), January, 1874 (pp. 281–302), February, 1874 (pp. 447–461), and April, 1874 (pp. 799–813). Browning's request concerning the acknowledgment to him was precisely granted: "I asked permission of my friend, Mr. Robert Browning, for their publication; and this was granted at once, and in terms that enhanced the favour as much beyond my means to express, as it would be beyond his wish that I should make the attempt. He had never seen the Letters, but trusted in my good feeling." (p. 147.)

The letters are insignificant beside hundreds that I possess,[3] but there was no notion of glorifying their writer in the permission I gave,—only the willingness to benefit her friend.

I may say, while I have the opportunity, that Mrs. Orr will be glad to write the article you suggested,[4] as I shall be abundantly satisfied with whatever she pronounces. If you would like to see her—she will always be cheerfully visible at 11. Kensington Park Gardens, W.

> Ever truly yours
> Robert Browning.

In the note I am about to write to H. I shall say that you propose to omit the Letters, and that I entirely agree with you.

[Yale]

To Mrs. Charles Skirrow

> 19 W[arwick] C[rescent]. Monday night
> [December, 1873?] [1]

Dear Friend,

Consider me,—in Mormon phrase,—"sealed" to you and Mr. Skirrow for Friday Dec. 12th and very glad to find myself so "engaged."

> Ever truly yours

[Schiff]   Robert Browning.

To Mrs. Arthur William Edgar O'Shaughnessy [1]

> 19 Warwick Crescent, W
> Feb. 6, '74.

Dear Mrs. O'Shaughnessy,

Thank you very much for your kind invitation. I have unluckily

---

3. These letters are, of course, the letters from E.B.B. to R.B. in 1845–46, published with his letters to her, in 1899.

4. The *Contemporary Review* for May, 1874 printed a long article (pp. 934–965) on "Mr. Browning's Place in Literature" by A. Orr. Mrs. Orr sketchily reviews Browning's long career and justifies his ways to his generation.

1. The date "Friday Dec. 12th" occurred between 1870 and 1889, three times: 1873, 1879, 1884. The earliest of these three years is selected as a conjectural date because of the fairly formal complimentary close.

1. Mrs. Eleanor (Nellie) O'Shaughnessy (?–1879), wife of the poet A. W. E. O'Shaughnessy, was the elder daughter of Westland Marston, the dramatist, who in 1842 "as a youth of twenty-two" was "already a friend of Browning."

I

a standing engagement for all Sunday evenings.[2] Will you give my kindest remembrances to your Father and Husband, and believe me,

Dear Mrs. O'Shaughnessy
Yours most truly
Robert Browning.

[The late Mr. Arthur E. Case]

To Mrs. Charles Skirrow

19. W[arwick] C[rescent]. July 30, '74.

Dear Friend,

First, (the old story) forgive me! Next,—let me lunch with you to-morrow, Friday, at 1/4 2, and I'll tell you all I can in excuse. We leave Town next Tuesday, and I shall be as delighted to see you before then as your goodness deserves.

Ever affectionately yours
RBrowning.

[Schiff]

To Mrs. Sara Jane Clarke Lippincott [1]

19. Warwick Crescent, W.
June 28, '75.

Dear Mrs. Lippincott,

I very well remember you, and the good days, and shall greatly enjoy seeing you when I can manage it: just now, I am quite be-

(Griffin and Minchin, *Life,* p. 115.) Doubtless, Browning came to know all of Marston's talented but ill-fated family—Philip Bourke Marston, the blind poet, Cicely, the younger daughter, and Nellie, described by Richard Garnett as "a lady of considerable literary accomplishment." (*D.N.B.*) Their home near Regent's Park was a meeting place, according to Mrs. Louise Chandler Moulton, "where Browning and Thackeray and Dickens and Rossetti and Swinburne and many more of the best and brightest men and women of the time were frequent visitors." (Louise Chandler Moulton, "Biographical Sketch of Philip Bourke Marston," prefixed to *The Collected Poems of P. B. Marston* [Boston, 1892], p. xxii.)

2. Sundays were socially patterned days for Browning. His standing engagement with the Procters was well known. When Henry James sent the American poet, Emma Lazarus, an introduction to Mrs. Procter, he assured her that on Sunday afternoons Browning would be there. (*Letters of Emma Lazarus,* ed. R. L. Rusk [New York, 1939], p. 53.) He also is reported as "constantly" spending Sunday afternoons with the Palgraves. (G. F. Palgrave, *Francis Turner Palgrave: His Journals and Memories of His Life,* p. 94.)

1. Sara Jane (Clarke) Lippincott (1823–1904) is described by Mrs. Newton Crosland (Camilla Toulmin) as "a charming writer of stories and poems and an able journalist." (See *Landmarks of a Literary Life* [London, 1893], p. 220.)

wildered by the various calls on my time. I will try hard to see you
on the first occasion that presents itself—and, if it is too backward
in such self-presentation, will somehow make one by force. The
young *Florentine* [2] is twenty-six and abroad just now.

Ever truly yours

[Yale] Robert Browning.

To Mrs. Charles Skirrow

19. W[arwick] C[rescent]. July 16, '75.

Dear Friend, I am going to do what I possibly can to get to you this
evening, but I am so much afraid of what seems too likely that I
write early to say that I am really very unwell,—having a strange
oppression at my chest, quite new to me, which seems either bilious-
ness, or rheumatism, or both. I have to dine out,—with old Lord
Stratford de Redcliffe,[1] and were it in my power I would put him
off, but I can hardly venture to do *that,* as I have never called even
once this season—which, thank Heaven, is drawing to a close. I well
know how these excuses may be disbelieved in,—they are no nonsense in the present case, however.

My sister too has a bad cold, and will have great difficulty in
dragging herself out. We are a "poor lot," spite of a little scribbling! [2]

Nothing could exceed your Husband's kindness to Miss Smith—
and nobody could be more grateful than she: these troubles were
wearing her fast away, and I anticipated another attack: the last
was formidable enough.[3]

Ever his and yours affectionately

[Schiff] RBrowning.

Mrs. Lippincott had in 1844 adopted the nom de plume Grace Greenwood, and
under this name she published numerous magazine articles and about a dozen
books. Her first tour of Europe (1852–53) resulted in one of her best-known
books, *Haps and Mishaps of a Tour in Europe* (1854).

2. Pen Browning.

1. Stratford Canning (1786–1880), created Viscount Stratford de Redcliffe in
1852, was nearly 90. He had ended his public career in 1858. During these later
years of his life he became keenly interested in poetry and religion. His book
Why Am I a Christian? (London, 1873) had gone into five editions. Browning
had known him since the early Fifties when they had met in Rome.

2. Possibly on *The Inn Album* which appeared in November, 1875. Domett's
Diary for July 24, 1875, records that Browning "had finished nine-tenths of a
new poem already." (Quoted in Griffin and Minchin, *Life,* 257.)

3. Doubtless a reference to some sort of legal help from Mr. Skirrow. (See

To Sarianna Browning

Villa St. Ange, Villers-sur-mer.
Wednesday E[venin]g
[August or September, 1875.] [1]

Dear Sis, I was very glad to get your letter this morning,—which has crossed mine to you,—and to hear of Milsand's good opinion of Pen's work: of course, he knows what imperfection there must be in a photograph which gives the due amount of *yellow* to be found in my face,—and certainly his approval would not be lessened by seeing the picture itself.[2] My main object in writing now is to supply an omission in my letter: I had promised Miss Smith to ask Milsand whether he knew of any advantageous way of getting good and cheap Vin Ordinaire from Caen: Miss S. would like to get little casks, as at Mers. This is her question and not mine. I bathed to-day, and found the distance and publicity (of going) less formidable than I expected. The water was *hot* rather than warm. Miss S. has a nice little carriage by the month, and we went in the afternoon to Buzeval, which I recognized at once—notably, the Protestant church there.[3] You are very hot, I suppose, in Paris. I have no news. Good night, dearest. I am tired and shall go to bed. All love to Milsand.

Ever affy. yours
[Schiff]   Robert Browning.

To Samuel Ralph Townshend Mayer [1]

19. Warwick Crescent, W.
Oct. 30, '75.

My dear Mr. Townshend Mayer,

Your kindness and delicacy are just what I should expect of you:

below, letter of September 15, 1877, in which Browning describes the sudden death of Miss Smith and mentions again the progress of her lawsuit.)

1. Browning left London for Mers near Tréport, France on August 4 and spent August and September in that French village.

2. This is Pen Browning's portrait of his father done from a photograph. It was executed at Dinant, Belgium in 1874. (Wilson, *Browning's Portraits*, pp. 97-99.)

3. Perhaps Beuzeval, which is described as "formant avec Houlgate, qui en dépend, une rue longue de 2 k." and as containing among its sights a "temple protestant." Houlgate is about four miles from Villers-sur-mer. (*Dictionnaire géographique et administratif de la France* [Paris, 1890], I, 435.)

1. Samuel Ralph Townshend Mayer (1840–80), miscellaneous writer, was in

take my true thanks for them. You must not suppose that Horne has done a single thing which I did not, once for all, sanction when he asked and obtained my leave, under most exceptional circumstances, to avail himself of the right to publish letters addressed to him at a time when I was a stranger to the writer.[2] Indeed, they could not have been so published unless by my permission. I only mentioned—what I ought not to seem boastful by repeating unnecessarily—that I would have given no other person, under no other circumstances, leave to do what I so assuredly dislike. Whatever favour I have conferred, I do not pretend to limit by objecting to its natural consequences,—and must not avail myself of your offer—however I appreciate it—of withdrawing from any service to Horne—which service has been my only satisfaction in the affair.

My wife had a very sincere regard for Horne, and the admiration for his genius which is or ought to be inevitable: and I dare not pretend to blot out—so to speak—any sort of demonstration she chose to make before her life was connected with mine.

Ever truly yours

[Huntington]   Robert Browning.

To John Forster

19. Warwick Crescent, W.

Dec. 2, '75.

My dear Forster,

If you "require no notice," your letter at least exacts the most grateful of recognitions, and more than one of these. During those forty years you allude to, I have been constant in remembering— and, when occasion was, declaring—that as you stood forward my very first critic, so you remained, to my apprehension, the best— the most competent, although not, perhaps, to me the most im-

---

1875 proprietor and editor of the *St. James's Review*. His wife, nee Gertrude Dalby, was an intimate in the home of B. W. Procter. (*D.N.B.*) Possibly through this mutual connection Browning became acquainted with Mayer.

2. Richard Henry (later Hengist) Horne (1803–84) corresponded with Elizabeth Barrett between 1839 and 1846, at a time when Browning was "a stranger to the writer." *Letters of E.B.B. Addressed to R. H. Horne*, with comments on contemporaries and a connecting narrative by R. H. Horne, was edited by S. R. Townshend Mayer and appeared in 1876 with the title-page date of 1877. The same volume was published in New York in 1877 with a preface and memoir by Richard Henry Stoddard.

partial.[1] I was repeating this only last Monday to a friend of a new generation who partook of what I find is something like a common belief—that *Paracelsus* was welcomed with the warmest acknowledgements: I told the true story of everybody's silence or condemnation till the *Examiner* spoke up for it.[2] So long as my poems last they will continue to record that fact and its consequences—their fitting preface. It would be strange indeed if I were not proud at in any way pleasing you in my last work.[3] I have written a good deal of late years, and it could hardly be hoped that attempts in various and opposite directions should always equally hit the mark. I think, however, that you will have been sure of my sincerity of purpose, and that is enough. That in this instance you can do more than this, and estimate my performance as you do—makes me proud, I repeat. But I want no such word, or feeling which it expresses, when I say simply I am happy you recall our old days and conversancy— my own friendship was too vital to succumb at the interruption of *that*.[4] Nor have I at all doubted of your good will to me. I see books in the shelves before me, as I write here, which I have not opened this long while: but I know well their contents, and no modern pamphlet supplants them in my heart and mind.

I won't try and say more. I wish you had not spoken of "dark days that come to you." I make no complaint of my own sky, unless when some shadow from without affects the general quiet, if not brightness.

God bless you!

[Victoria and Albert Museum]   R. Browning.

1. Tact again gets the upper hand of strict truth. W. J. Fox was certainly Browning's "very first critic," his "literary god-father," to use Browning's own phrase, later modified. It is certain that Browning regarded Milsand as his best critic.

2. Forster's review of *Paracelsus* was the first, but not the last, to praise the poem. (For a summary of the critical reception accorded *Paracelsus* see DeVane, *Browning Handbook*, pp. 52–54. See below, postscript of letter to Grove, February 4, 1876.)

3. *The Inn Album*, published in late November, 1875.

4. The interruption in the friendship between Forster and Browning occurred, as is well known, when Browning offered to pitch a "bottle of claret" at Forster's head if Forster offered any further doubt concerning the veracity of a lady whom Browning was quoting. Frederick Lehmann, who relates this story, adds that "immediate apology or reconciliation were in vain. A kind of peace was, however, patched up before Forster's death." (*Memories of Half a Century*, compiled and ed. by R. C. Lehmann, pp. 112–114.)

To George Grove [1]

19. Warwick Crescent, W.
Feb. 4, '76.

My dear Grove,

Thank you exceedingly, and thank Mr. Bradley too.[2] I only want fairness, and when I get good will also, as I do in this criticism, there is little or nothing to complain of: besides, I have been knocked about all my life, and taught patience under a tap or two. Probably I get a few more, on this account, than my more susceptible brethren of the craft.

Ever cordially yours
Robert Browning.

Poor Forster! Mr. Bradley may not know that "in the days when I wrote *Paracelsus*" that poem was treated with the utmost contempt by every weekly and daily journal without a single exception till Forster, wholly a stranger to me, wrote a generous article in the *Examiner*—forty years ago. I am glad that I reminded him of it,[3] in reply to his telling me, on the publication of *Inn Album:* "I yield to an impulse too strong to resist, and send a word—requiring no notice from you—to say how profoundly it has moved and affected me. There are things in it than which even you have done nothing

1. Sir George Grove (1820–1900), musicologist and editor of *Grove's Dictionary of Music and Musicians*, was editor of *Macmillan's Magazine* from May, 1868 to April, 1883. He was knighted at Windsor on May 22, 1883. It was probably at the home of Frederick Lehmann in Westbourne Terrace that Browning and Grove first became acquainted, certainly as early as 1863. (See Charles L. Graves, *Life of Grove*, p. 97.) Browning supported Grove's candidacy for membership in the Athenaeum Club in February, 1871, and stated to Lehmann: "I simply oblige myself in so doing" (p. 191).

2. Browning sent a copy of *The Inn Album* to "Grove, the Orientalist, the Schubertian, the Literate in Ordinary and extraordinary, and the old valued acquaintance . . . into the bargain." (Graves, *Life of Grove*, p. 215.) Grove acknowledged receipt of the book and perhaps promised that a review of it would appear in *Macmillan's Magazine*. Professor A. C. Bradley (1851–1935) wrote a thoughtful, generally condemnatory review for Grove. He softens his comments, such as that "his earlier style has degenerated into mannerism . . . Browningese," by reminding readers of their great debt to the earlier Browning. (A. C. Bradley, "Mr. Browning's 'The Inn Album,'" *Macmillan's Magazine*, XXXIII [January, 1876], 347.)

3. See letter to Forster dated December 2, 1875 and n. 1.

finer." Such "bread" could one who certainly "cared for poetry"
extract from Mr. Bradley's "stone"! [4]
[New York Public Library]

To Mrs. Charles Skirrow

19. Warwick Crescent, W.
March 3, '76.

Dear Friend,

I confess a painful amusement on reading your note—with its
assurance that "a *word* from me would get this picture of Frascheri's
accepted by the Academy." [1] I have the most decided experience
that my best endeavours can do nothing of the kind. The year before last, a picture by Heyermans, Pen's master, received all the
honours of "the Line." [2] Last year, he sent a very good successor,—
which I was most anxious should be as fortunate, and I ventured to
recommend it to all the Academicians I knew. It found no place—
"not"—I was told—"thro' any lack of merit, but because, by a new
rule, only *eight* works by foreign artists are admissible—and there
were eight with presumably superior claims." (Observe, that foreigners *resident in London,* enjoy the privileges of natives,—Lehmann, [3] Tissot, [4] and others; the rule was intended to limit the num-

4. The last sentence of Bradley's review of *The Inn Album* was put into the
form of a question: "May not those who care for poetry in England appeal to
him [Browning] for something fitter to stand with those works for which they
can never cease to be grateful, even though he should again give them for
bread such stones as *Red Cotton Night-Cap Country* and *The Inn Album?*"
1. Giuseppe Frascheri (1809–86) exhibited in London in 1872 at the Suffolk
Street Exhibition. (Algernon Graves, *Dictionary of Artists Who Have Exhibited
Their Works in the Principal London Exhibitions from 1760 to 1893* [3rd ed.,
London, 1901], p. 103.) His painting of Salvini was apparently not accepted by
the Royal Academy. (For a brief biographical notice of Frascheri see *Allgemeine
Lexikon der bildenden Künstler* [1916], XII, 392.)
2. Jean-Arnould Heyermans' picture was Item 658, "The Doctor's Visit: A
Dutch Interior," shown at the Royal Academy in 1874. (Algernon Graves, *The
Royal Academy of Arts* [London, 1906], IV, 93.) Heyermans' pictures were
not accepted again by the Royal Academy though he did exhibit at Grosvenor
Gallery and elsewhere. (Algernon Graves, *Dictionary of Artists . . . in the
Principal London Exhibitions from 1760–1893* [London, 1901], "Heyermans.")
3. Wilhelm August Rudolf Lehmann (1819–1905), brother of Frederick Lehmann and of Mrs. Benzon, was born in Hamburg and after some years spent in
Rome, where he first met Browning, settled in London in 1866. (R. C. Lehmann, *Memories of Half a Century*, p. 255.) He executed drawings of both the
Brownings in Rome in 1859. (Rudolf Lehmann, *An Artist's Reminiscences,*
pp. 226–228.)
4. James Joseph Jacques Tissot (1836–1902) was born in Nantes, achieved

ber of absolute strangers who take up the room required for our own artists—probably to the disadvantage of the latter! Such is the *rule*. Mr. Frascheri must take his chance and run his risk. Undoubtedly the portrait is an interesting one—and Salvini [5] is very well known to everybody here: but the work must be left to its own merits—and these, again, may fail to obtain it a place should they be ranked *ninth* in order. Heyermans' picture was exhibited at once (at the Brussels Exhibition) and was both admired much and sold promptly.

I will take luncheon with you very gladly next Wednesday,— having a great desire to see and talk with you again.

Ever affy. yours,

[Schiff]   RBrowning.

To Mrs. George Henry Lewis [1]

19. Warwick Crescent, W.
May 9, '76.

Dear Mrs. Lewis,

It was some time before I could properly read Mr. Fosbroke's poems: [2] and I confess to having delayed a little the expression of

popularity as an artist in Paris, but after the Franco-Prussian War took up residence in London, where his paintings were frequently exhibited by the Royal Academy. (*D.N.B.*)

5. Tommaso Salvini (1829–1916), the Italian actor, played in London from April 1 to July 16, 1875, principally in the leading roles of *Othello* and *Hamlet*. Browning's congratulation to the actor for his interpretation of Hamlet is printed in *Leaves from the Autobiography of Tommaso Salvini* (New York, 1893), p. 170. Salvini was back in England March 1, 1876, touring the provinces (p. 171). Frascheri doubtless counted on this current publicity to attract attention to his picture.

1. George Henry Lewis (1833–1911), senior member of Lewis and Lewis, a firm of solicitors, after the death of his first wife married Elizabeth Eberstadt of Mannheim, Germany, in 1867. He was knighted in 1893 and created baronet in 1902. (*Burke's Peerage* [1940], "Lewis of Portland Place.") Mrs. J. Comyns Carr recalls that the Lewises "did much to break down the very definite barriers which still separated the fashionable and the Bohemian branches of society . . . she opened her doors, not only to writers and painters, but also to actors and actresses." (*Mrs. J. Comyns Carr's Reminiscences*, ed. Eve Adam [London, 1926], p. 243.)

2. John Baldwin Fosbroke was apparently one of the writers to come under Mrs. Lewis's wing. He published *Rheingold, A Romantic Legend* (London, 1872), with a new edition in 1873, and *Erlinthule, King of Ithol, and Lyrics of Greenwood Tree* (London, 1873). (*English Catalogue, 1872–1880* [London, 1882], p. 164.) These volumes are in the British Museum, but apparently no copies are available in the United States. A critic of *Rheingold* indicates that

how they strike me. It is hard indeed to have to seem niggardly of praise when one would so gladly give it, to any amount not quite incompatible with telling the truth—as one *sees* the truth, you must remember. For I wish everybody that cares to ask my opinion about poetry to bear in mind that my own claims to be a poet have always been strongly contested, and not altogether by people I despised: so, there is always an appeal from me to a more favourable and presumably competent judge. I cannot expect any great success for the author of these two volumes—that is, success of the kind worth having from the critics worth consulting: there is plenty of the superficial glitter of language, and profusion of figure, to attract another kind of taste: and throughout there is abundant evidence of acquaintance and sympathy with what I should call "poeticalness";—and these qualities suffice for very many readers—as the extracts from the periodicals, which are appended, prove sufficiently. But somehow it is found that such success neither goes deep, nor strikes root: only creative power does that,—and I cannot, with all the will in the world, see creation here—nor indeed in one out of the dozen volumes of verse which come to me in this way. The misfortune is, that the writers are probably superior in endowment to nine-tenths of their neighbours: they have cultivation, a pictorial and musical faculty, high and fine aims—and yet the wings for actual flight are rudimentary and only distinguish them from the groundlings without availing to make them at their ease in the air. Pray tell this, in your own better—*not* kinder—form to Mr. Fosbroke, with sincere thanks for the honour he did me in wishing for the opinion I give with great reluctance: and believe me, Dear Mrs Lewis,—

Yours very sincerely
RBrowning

[Yale]

To Mrs. Charles Skirrow

19. Warwick Crescent, W.
May 20, '76.

Dear Mrs. Skirrow,

I am confounded at your goodness. Salvini,[1] however, is not the

---

the poem is a "narrative in cantos," then cites such errors as having a "young lady of the robber baron period" say: "Bach was not made for lovers," on which note he gives the poem up after a one-paragraph review. (*Athenaeum*, August 31, 1872.)

1. See above, letter of March 3, 1876, n. 5. Salvini arrived in London from

only person "overwhelmed with engagements." I have none for the 18th and, in joyfully accepting your invitation for that day, I promise myself the first holiday I have had these seven months.[2] I fully meant to call and say this for myself this morning, but it is already too late. All regards to Mr. Skirrow from

Yours affectionately ever
R Browning.

Salvini made me a long call—most pleasant, but hence the lateness of writing.

[Schiff]

To Mrs. Charles Skirrow

19. W[arwick] C[rescent]. Aug. 3 [1876] [1]

Dear Friend,

A word of true thanks and earnest good bye. We start this evening for Arran [2]—a trial of novelty, to be judged of by success or the other thing.

I can only thank you and good kind Mr. Skirrow for all your goodness to

Yours affy ever

[Schiff]   R Browning.

his tour of the provinces on May 15, 1876. He performed *Othello* seven times, then "fell seriously ill," was visited by the Prince of Wales's "own physician," and told that his "days were numbered"; whereupon he recovered and set out immediately for Italy. (*Leaves from the Autobiography of Tommaso Salvini*, pp. 171–172.)

2. This would be from November, 1875, the month in which *The Inn Album* was published. Fresh from this work, Browning turned to the composition of most of the miscellaneous poems which make up the *Pacchiarotto* volume of July, 1876.

1. As indicated in this note, Browning began the journey to the Isle of Arran on August 3. He was back in London on October 23 or 24.

2. The full address was Blairbey, Lambech, Arran, N.B. Browning refers to "beautiful Arran" in a later letter, but did not choose this place again for a summer vacation.

To Gordon Smith [1]

London, 19. Warwick Crescent, W.
Jan. 16, '77.

Dear Sir,

Pray allow me, by your intervention, to return my warmest thanks to the "Burns' Monument Committee" for the honor of their request that I should be present at the Unveiling of the Statue, and subsequent Banquet.[2] It is a matter of deep concern to me that circumstances over which I have no control oblige me to forego a gratification which I would so willingly accept were it in my power. How much I sympathize with and admire the popular feeling of which you give ample evidence, it is unnecessary to say.

I passed this last Autumn in sight of Ayrshire. How can it have happened that the Poet never bestowed on beautiful Arran the one additional charm of which it is susceptible—the magic of an association with his name?

Pray believe me, Dear Sir, with renewed thanks and regrets,

Yours very truly
Robert Browning.

Gordon Smith Esq.
etc., etc., etc.
[Yale]

1. Apparently Gordon Smith was secretary of the Burns' Monument Committee, the chairman of which was Baillie Wilson of Glasgow. The committee was probably formed early in 1876, for the London *Times* for October 25 of that year reports that a bronze statue of Burns was cast the day before, for erection in Glasgow at a later date. (See next note.)

2. "A statue of Robert Burns, subscribed for by the working classes of Scotland . . . was unveiled by Lord Houghton. . . . In the evening the event was celebrated by several banquets, at the chief of which Lord Houghton presided. . . . Laudatory speeches were delivered, and the proceedings were characterized by the greatest enthusiasm." (London *Times,* January 26, 1877, p. 10.)

To John Hullah [1]

19. Warwick Crescent, W.
Jan. 25, '77.

Dear Mr. Hullah,

You have done my poem much honor by setting it to music.[2] Of course you are quite at liberty to print what I shall be happy to see when printed.

Ever truly yours

[Baylor]   Robert Browning

To Sidney Colvin [1]

19. Warwick Crescent, W.
Feb. 15, '77.

My dear Colvin,

I had already received Mr. Browning's [2] invitation, and replied affirmatively to it, when your second letter reached me yesterday. I shall be altogether at your disposal, therefore, and most willingly, till Friday morning—when I much fear I ought to return. I have also provided myself with a Ticket for the Concert, which promises

1. John Pyke Hullah (1812–84) was one of a musical circle which included Sir George Grove and John Ella from among Browning's acquaintances. A few months before writing this letter he had received an honorary LL.D. from the University of Edinburgh as "an accomplished modern linguist . . . admirable musician and literary man." (Frances Hullah, *Life of John Hullah* [London, 1886], p. 207.) In 1877 he published *The Song Book; Words and Tunes from the Best Poets and Musicians.* None of Browning's poems is included in this collection.

2. The poem referred to is "The Lost Leader." Two copies of the music for this poem are in the Browning Library at Baylor University. One of these is an "original manuscript . . . written in pen and ink." The other is a photostat of the printed version which "covers nine pages" and was published by L. Cock, 63 New Bond Street, W. (Information for this note was kindly provided by Dr. A. J. Armstrong in a letter to K. L. Knickerbocker, August 18, 1947.)

1. Sir Sidney Colvin (1845–1927), critic of art and literature, became a fellow of Trinity College, Cambridge in 1868 and was elected Slade professor of fine art at Cambridge in January, 1873. Colvin became acquainted with Browning in the early Seventies, at Naworth, the country home of George Howard who gathered about him, says Colvin, a "varied company of talents and distinctions . . . in art, literature [and] politics." (E. V. Lucas, *The Colvins and Their Friends* [New York, 1928], pp. 73, 101.)

2. Oscar Browning (1837–1923) had been a master at Eton until 1875 when he went to Cambridge as lecturer in history and political science. He and Robert Browning met occasionally at the Athenaeum Club.

to be thronged by London visitors.[3] You must instruct me in the decencies to be observed at the ceremony of conferring the Degree: at Oxford they dislike certain cuts of coat and colours of neck-tie, you know: and forewarned is forearmed.[4] But a word about this, any day before the actual Wednesday, will suffice.

With renewed thanks, dear Colvin,

Yours truly ever
[Huntington]   Robert Browning.

To Reuben Browning

19. Warwick Crescent, W.
Apr. 13, '77.

Dear Reuben,

I received the B[an]k Div[idend]: many thanks! Pray don't forget,—if there be any means of selling the Railway shares,—to do so, and extinguish this nuisance, once for all.

We remembered your Birthday, and agreed a good and gallant Seventy-Four had, indeed, been launched on April the Eleventh. Long may it continue the A.1. we know so well! [1]

Ever affy
[Baylor]   R.B.

3. Joseph Joachim conducted the first performance of his overture in commemoration of Heinrich von Kleist and also a new symphony in C minor by Johannes Brahms. In addition he performed Beethoven's violin concerto and two excerpts from Bach's sonatas in C. (London *Times*, March 9, 1877.)

4. The degree of doctor of music was to be conferred upon Browning's favorite violinist, Joseph Joachim (1831–1907), described in *Grove's Dictionary of Music and Musicians* as the "greatest master of the violin of his generation." The degree was conferred on March 8, 1877, and the concert, performed by Joachim, was presented the next evening. In a letter of March 10, 1877, Browning said that the ceremony, the concert, and association with Joachim were "'each and all' worth the trouble of the journey." (Orr, *Life*, p. 297.) The scene witnessed by Browning during the ceremony of conferring the degree is, in part, described by the London *Times*, March 9, 1877, as follows: ". . . the impatience of the undergraduates was more than once manifested by inane observations directed to the officials" and with the beginning of the Latin oration "a running commentary of senseless observations commenced and some bronze coins were insultingly thrown before the public orator." This experience, and perhaps others, with Oxford undergraduates may have helped prepare Browning for his own experience of having a red cotton nightcap dangled above his head during the ceremony of receiving the honorary degree of D.C.L. from Oxford. (Griffin and Minchin, *Life*, p. 271.)

1. Reuben Browning, nine years older than his nephew, Robert, was 74

To Mrs. Charles Skirrow

Sunday Afternoon
[June 3, 1877.] [1]

Dear Friend, it is very hard to say you nay in this matter: but I should so exceedingly like to see and hear the last of Rubenstein [sic] to-morrow, that I feel it impossible to forego the Crystal Palace —for which I must start at 1 o'clock.[2] I am sure I want to see you and your Husband quite as much as you can care about seeing my poor self. Will you let me go to your Richmond Dinner next Sunday?—If you *will*, I consider that I am justified in giving up the earlier engagement. Pray be as kind as you can in the case of

Yours affectionately ever

[Schiff]   Robert Browning.

To Mrs. Charles Skirrow

19. W[arwick] C[rescent]. July 19, '77.

Dear Friend,—again I am unhappily engaged, or should delight in going with you to Mr. Jefferson's.[1] I ought to have written this note

years old on April 11, 1877. The reference is a playful one to the great battle-ships of Nelson's day—ships carrying 74 guns, such as Nelson's flagship, the *Vanguard*, at the blockade of Cadiz in 1797-98. In naval operations in the Napoleonic wars the ships of 74 guns, while not the largest afloat, were the standard size for the British fleet. (See William L. Clowes, *The Royal Navy, A History from the Earliest Times to the Present* [London, 1899], IV, *passim*, but especially p. 203.)

1. The notation "Ap–June 1881" appears in a hand other than Browning's in the upper right corner of this letter. It is probable, however, that it was written on June 3, 1877, for Rubinstein's final concert in 1877 occurred on Monday, June 4. (London *Times*, June 4, 1877, advertisement, p. 1, col. 6: "Crystal Palace—Rubinstein Concert, this day (Monday) at 3. Rubinstein's last appearance in England this Season.") Though Rubinstein was in London for other seasons, including the season of 1881, his final appearances in other years did not occur on a Monday.

2. Browning doubtless met Rubinstein, possibly in April, 1877, at John Ella's, 9 Victoria Street, during one of Ella's famous musical evenings. (One meeting between Browning and Rubinstein is recorded in Catherine D. Bowen, *"Free Artist: The Story of Anton and Nicholas Rubinstein* [New York, 1939], p. 261.)

1. Joseph Jefferson (1829–1905), creator of the title role in *Rip Van Winkle*, was in July, 1877 ending his London stay with "a brief season of farces, *Lend Me Five Shillings*, and *A Regular Fix* at the Haymarket Theatre." (William Winter, *The Life and Art of Joseph Jefferson* [New York, 1894], p. 189.) Jefferson himself recalls "a memorable lunch at the Star and Garter" with "Charles

last evening, but unaccountably forgot to do so. I am very grateful for your goodness, though I cannot enjoy it as I am sure I heartily desire.

Ever affy yours

[Schiff]. RBrowning.

To Mrs. Charles Skirrow

La Saisiaz, Sept. 15, '77.

Dear Friend, I got your gay and kind letter yesterday. How did it find me, can you suppose? Poor Miss Smith, who had been the evening before in exceptionally good health and spirits, and, after taking a pleasant walk with me, had arranged for an excursion the next day, was found dead in her dressing-room—where, a short time before, her maid had left her full of hopes about the weather, and the little events of the journey which was to begin at 10; perhaps half-an-hour after, or less, I returned from my usual walk to breakfast at 9: and, failing to see Miss Smith about the house or grounds I spoke to her maid, who was at the breakfast-table, and heard that Miss Smith had not left her room yet. "Quite right," I said, "she reserves her strength for our expedition": and made the same remark to my sister who was in the balcony above, as I went up to her. I then walked to the windows of Miss Smith on the other side,—was surprised at not having a recognition and good-morning; and observed thro' the thin curtains that no figure was dimly visible in the bed-room,—as, when the outside shutters were open, must needs be the case. I stepped to the next window,—and was struck by the same still more remarkable absence of a figure—for *there,* in the dressing-room, she was sure to be. I looked through an opening in the curtain, and saw her kneeling on the ground—which her poor head had touched. I called my sister, who ran in—cried to me—and brought me to her side. She was quite warm—but dead. The servants tried the common remedies, in vain. I sent for a Doctor to Geneva—failing to find one at the next two villages—and he arrived after some delay—but no sort of assistance would have been of any avail: it was a case of the most thorough "apoplexie fondroy-

---

Kingsley, Robert Browning, and George Augustus Sala." (*The Autobiography of Joseph Jefferson* [New York, n.d.], p. 360.) The date of this lunch is not given, but apparently it occurred during Jefferson's second long stay in London, June, 1875 to October, 1877.

ante": she must have died *standing*, and fallen as we found her. So, have I lost one of the most devoted friends I ever had in my life—a friend of some five-and-twenty years standing: I have been much favoured in friendships—especially from women: no one ever was more disinterestedly devoted to me who grieve to remember how little I was ever able to do in return for so much.

I telegraphed to Mrs. Castle, her sister—who, fortunately, was at Paris—and by return of telegram, had her promise to start immediately for this place—where I am now expecting her (11 1/2 a.m.) every minute. Her arrival will relieve me from much anxiety and responsibility. The formalities to be observed here are precise and troublesome, but I believe I have arranged tolerably.[1] I wrote to Mr. Rowcliffe [2]—who is in the thickest of the law suit: his last accounts of its progress were quite re-assuring. See what Life is, dear friends—for this I communicate to Mr. Skirrow as well as yourself: it is needless to say. I write confusedly perhaps, which you will forgive yours ever affy

Robert Browning.

I shall leave here for Paris the moment I am able—possibly even to-morrow: the place is detestable to me and my sister. You will not answer this, therefore. I hope to call at your Hôtel.
[Schiff]

To William G. Kingsland [1]

19 Warwick Crescent, W.
Nov. 10, '77.

My dear Mr. Kingsland,

I make haste to assure you that I never heard till this moment of your calling here—which needed no kind of apology: I shall al-

1. The account given here of Miss Smith's death is much fuller than that recorded by Domett, as reported to him by Sarianna Browning. (See Griffin and Minchin, *Life*, pp. 263–264.)

2. Probably Miss Smith's solicitor.

1. Browning first wrote to W. G. Kingsland on November 27, 1868, to thank him for "his intelligence and sympathy" and for "a very gratifying letter." (*Letters*, ed. Hood, p. 128; four other letters from Browning to Kingsland appear in Hood's volume, the last one dated July 7, 1889.) Kingsland became an original member of the London Browning Society and published in 1887 *Robert Browning: Chief Poet of His Age, an Essay Addressed Primarily to Beginners in the Study of Browning's Poems*. A new edition of this book was issued in 1890 with a preface in which Kingsland printed a letter from Browning ex-

ways be delighted to see you, and so will my Sister—on whom, if I am away, you may generally count. But we were, both of us abroad for two months—all August and September—and your visit may have occurred during our absence.

I well know your kind sympathy and generous zeal: it has been very good of you to speak up for me so boldly. That omitted line has been long observed and regretted by me—it happened thro' the printer's leaving out the previous leaf, as it stood in the original edition: and *this* edition being stereotyped does not allow of the insertion I would gladly effect: should I be able in a future edition to replace the line, I will certainly do so.

This is a hurried note,—as I am obliged to go out,—but it answers its purpose if it repeats my thanks—and induces *you* to repeat your visit to

Yours cordially ever

[Yale]   R Browning.

To Mrs. Louise Chandler Moulton [1]

19. Warwick Crescent, W.
Feb. 24, '78.

Dear Mrs. Moulton,

Thank you very much for the present of your *Poems:* they need no "generosity," and get mere justice when I say that, having begun the book,—somewhat more than "five minutes" ago,—I close it only where needs I must—at page the last, with music in my ears

---

pressing gratitude for Kingsland's continuing efforts on his behalf. One of Kingsland's letters to Browning is available in *Browning's Letter File,* ed. Armstrong, pp. 87–88.

1. Ellen Louise (Chandler) Moulton (1835–1908) began her literary career in Boston at the age of 15. Soon after her marriage to William U. Moulton in 1855 she established a Friday salon to which were invited Boston's leading literary men: Lowell, Whittier, Longfellow, and others. In 1876 Mrs. Moulton began her annual summer-autumn trips to Europe and "was introduced to London life by Lord Houghton at a breakfast to which Browning, Arnold and others only less prominent had been bidden." (Jessie B. Rittenhouse, "Louise Chandler Moulton and Her London Friendships," *Bookman,* XXVIII [February, 1909], 601, 602.) The story is told that at this breakfast Mrs. Moulton asked, in an aside to her neighbor, which gentleman was Robert Browning. The neighbor announced the question and "at this the poet turned and striking an attitude of obsequious gallantry, bowed low, exclaiming, '*C'est moi!*' Thus began a friendship which lasted without interruption until Browning's death."

and flowers before my eyes,—not without thoughts across the brain.[2]
Pray continue your flights, and be assured of the sympathetic observance of

Yours truly

[Library of Congress]   Robert Browning.

To Lady Combermere [1]

19. Warwick Crescent, W
March 15. 1878.

Dear Lady Combermere,
Pray allow me to thank you exceedingly for the kindness of your
invitation, and to say how sorry I was to find myself unable, by
reason of previous engagements, to obey it as I would otherwise
gladly have done.

Believe me, Dear Lady Combermere,
Yours very sincerely

[Baylor]   Robert Browning.

To Richard Monckton Milnes

19. Warwick Crescent, W.
March 26, 1878.

My dear Houghton,
You have always been kind in your enquiries about my son. His
picture has just arrived, and,—without venturing to encroach on
your time of which I know the value,—I cannot help saying that,
should any chance bring you this way, it would greatly gratify me
could you bestow a minute on the thing—any time, any day this

2. Louise Chandler Moulton, *Poems* (Boston, 1878). Mrs. Moulton's letter
dated February 13, 1878 accompanying her *Poems* accounts for the language
and tone of Browning's reply: "Dear Mr. Browning: It is certainly presumption
in a poor little swallow to want to sing to a great poet—but great poets can
afford to be generous, so perhaps you will let my swallows perch under your
friendly eaves, and listen, sometime, for an idle five minutes to their song.
Yours sincerely, Louise Chandler Moulton." (*Browning's Letter File*, ed. Armstrong, p. 75.) The page facing the table of contents of *Poems* shows a swallow
singing, presumably in full-throated ease. There are poems about "Mayflowers," "Morning Glory," "Roses," enough to place flowers before a reader's
eyes.

1. Robert Wellington (1845–98), third Viscount Combermere, in 1866 married as his first wife Charlotte Anne Fletcher, who apparently is the Lady
Combermere addressed in this letter. (*Burke's Peerage*, p. 633.)

week, Sunday included.[1] If you are unable—as you may well find
yourself—be assured I shall quite understand.

         Ever yours
[Lord Crewe]   Robert Browning.

To Mr. [William?] Morris

       19. Warwick Crescent, W
       Apr. 6. 1878.

My dear Mr. Morris,

 I very heartily agree with the desire expressed in the Memorial,
and have signed it accordingly.[2] Thank you much for your kind
note which brought it under my notice.

         Ever truly yours
[Baylor]   Robert Browning.

To Richard Monckton Milnes

       19, Warwick Crescent, W.
       May 6, 1878.

My dear Houghton,

 I have managed to inform myself tolerably well of the kind words

1. Pen's picture is probably the one described as item 20 in Sotheby, *Browning Collections*. The picture, painted by Pen in 1878 and exhibited at the Grosvenor Gallery and at Manchester in 1879, represents a "Saint in a Desert, looking at a skull, which he is holding in both hands." The painting is entitled "The Unanswered Question." Browning arranged a private showing of the picture at 19 Warwick Crescent and wrote personal invitations to influential friends. Carlyle, among others, helped to "inaugurate most auspiciously Robert's first appearance as a would-be painter." (See *Letters*, ed. Hood, pp. 183, 186.)

1. Possibly William Morris (1834–96), the poet, who did not move within the orbit of Browning's close acquaintances and whose poetry, along with that of the other Pre-Raphaelites, was a "weariness" to Browning. (*Letters*, ed. Hood, p. 134.) The present brief note apparently concerns one of Morris' crusading schemes. See next note.

2. Morris founded in 1877 a Society for the Protection of Ancient Buildings. On April 17, 1878, he wrote a letter to the London *Times* protesting against a scheme for "the wholesale removal of City Churches." He cited as his reason for writing, the admission by the Bishop of London—when queried by Lord Houghton in the House of Lords—that such a scheme was on foot. It is probable that Morris had requested Browning to sign a Memorial urging protection of London's ancient structures, and that, as indicated by this note, he was one of "the eminent men" who joined on the basis of a personal appeal from Morris. (See J. W. Mackail, *The Life of William Morris* [London, 1899], I, 342.)

you used Saturday in alluding to the Picture.¹ You cannot suppose I ever was or shall be indifferent to any commendation of me or mine: but I was unfortunately placed at the greatest distance from you possible, with very talkative surroundings; and though I did hear much that you spoke, and certainly caught some of the expressions which I now ascertain the exact purport of,—I could only be sorry that I had no assurance on the matter. Without such assurance, our long intercourse would warrant me in believing that the kindly feeling you have always shown me, would find vent whenever an occasion presented itself for obliging your old and affectionate friend

[Lord Crewe]   R. Browning

To Courtney Peregrine Ilbert ¹

19. Warwick Crescent, W.
May 9, '78.

Dear Sir,

I heartily wish Professor Smith the success he deserves, and of course my name, whatever it may be worth, is quite at his service should you care to append it to the Committee list.² I was about to ask for the favor of a voting-paper: perhaps you can kindly procure me one.³

Pray believe me, Dear Sir,

Yours very truly
Robert Browning.

C. P. Ilbert Esq.
[Huntington]

1. See letter dated March 26, 1878, and n. 1.
1. Sir Courtenay Peregrine Ilbert (1841–1924), after a brilliant career at Balliol where he was an intimate friend of Benjamin Jowett and afterward his literary executor, became parliamentary draftsman under Sir Henry Thring. (*D.N.B.*)
2. Henry John Stephen Smith (1826–83), mathematician, was like Ilbert and Browning a fellow of Balliol College, Oxford. "In 1878 Smith unsuccessfully contested the parliamentary representation of the University of Oxford in the liberal interest. He was a ready and telling speaker, but his candidature was urged on academic rather than on political grounds." (*D.N.B.*)
3. In the upper left corner in another hand are the words: "Answ. and papers sent—M. B."

To Mrs. Alicia Bayne

19. Warwick Crescent, W.
June 3, '78.

Dear Friend, I was intending, in any case, to go to you with my Sister on Saturday. I accept this new invitation with great delight. You do me no more than simple justice when you recognize my deep and affectionate interest in the fortunes of your Son: I wish him every happiness from the bottom of my heart. It will be indeed a satisfaction to tell him so—though the assurance is superfluous enough—just as it is superfluous—though most gratifying—that *you* communicate to me your pleasure in the success of my own child.

Long may it be permitted to us to exchange such congratulations! Whether long or short the period,—while it lasts I shall be ever, Dear Friend,

Yours affectionately and gratefully
[Yale]   Robert Browning.

To Mrs. Margaret Raine Hunt

19. Warwick Crescent, W.
June 4, '78.

Dear Mrs. Hunt,

I suppose my little word of criticism on your book [1] will go to you the most tardily of all: certainly it will be as appreciative and encomiastic as any that can have preceded it. I was fairly delighted by the freshness and nature of that old-world north-country life,— about which I knew so absolutely nothing, though I am familiar with it already. The first two volumes indeed are so charming that they rather wrong (in my eyes, at least) the surprises and adventures of the third: for I could have wished the schoolmaster to remain just what he seemed, and the Captain,—well, I suppose such a man would conceive and carry out such a piece of villainy as you very properly make choke him: but what I altogether enjoyed and shall enjoy are the village-days, so pathetic and beautiful. I was not able

1. Probably *The Hazard of the Die* by Averil Beaumont (London, 1878), 3 vols. Averil Beaumont was the nom de plume used by Mrs. Hunt for all 11 of her novels published in England. American editions of some of her works named the author as Mrs. A. W. Hunt. This book is not, we believe, available in the United States.

to read the three volumes at once,—at once, I mean, on their arrival: but when I had an uninterrupted morning or two I meant
to make the most of my leisure—and that I have done so—leaves
me very grateful. I shut up the book (for a time) to scribble this
—thanking you most truly, and begging you to remember me as
ever

Gratefully yours

[Huntington] RBrowning.

To Mrs. Louise Chandler Moulton

19. Warwick Crescent, W.
June 14, '78.

Dear Mrs. Moulton,

It would give me real pleasure to accept your kind invitation for
the 19th, but I am unfortunately engaged the whole of the evening.
It is very good of you to remember me.

Pray believe me, Dear Mrs. Moulton,

Yours very sincerely

[Library of Congress] Robert Browning.

To Mrs. Charles Skirrow

[July–August 1878?] [1]

Dear Friend,—I have seen Irving in the *Bells*,—and admired him
duly: [2] but I have so persistent a cold—or rather cough—that it
will be wiser for me to stay at home,—I having been out last night,
and none the better for it. I have an engagement for this evening
which I shall not keep.

You know whether I do or do not estimate your goodness aright!

Ever affy. yours,

[Schiff] RB

1. The notation "1878 (?)" is penciled in a hand other than Browning's in
the upper right corner of this note. This is probably the correct year date. For
the month date see next note.

2. *The Bells* by Leopold Lewis, first produced in November, 1871, was re-
vived on July 8, 1878 and ran until the third week in August. (Austin Brereton,
Life of Henry Irving [London, 1908], I, 242–243.) Irving left London in the
autumn to tour the provinces in *Hamlet*. Since Browning left London for
Switzerland about mid-August (see next letter), it is reasonable to assume that
this letter was written between July 8 and August 15, 1878.

To Mrs. Charles Skirrow

Hôtel Bodenhaus
Splügen, La Suisse
Sept. 12, '78.

Dear Friend, I have never forgotten that you bade me write to you, —and, by this time, I fancy, you are all but at home again, if not already. Will you tell me all about yourself and Mr. Skirrow in return for the abundant nothings I am going to bestow on you? For there is nothing to say beyond this—that I and my Sister left hot London for hotter Paris, and made up our minds that whenever we came to a cool place—there we would stop and be thankful: whereupon we set out and stopped just *here*—4757 feet above the sea: and finding exactly what we wanted, here have we been staying nearly a month. The little village has not a single shop in it,—much less a habitable house: but the Hôtel is exceedingly good—and we are lodged in a huge building called the "Dépendence," alongside of the Hôtel proper, and are truly "monarchs of all we survey," being the sole tenants. We are in the midst of exquisite scenery, in which we walk daily for some four or five hours at a stretch—generally managing seventeen miles about, in that time. The weather has been most favorable—and the effect upon us both was at once so unmistakable that we determined to make the most of it. The heat is daily reported "excessive" in Italy by what portion of the travelling world we hear converse at the dinner-table,—the only occasion when we see a soul: and we have plenty of experience of what the sun can do when we brave him (umbrellas over head) at mid-day: but the keen mountain-air and never-ceasing wind temper all that: and both of us are "renewed like the eagles." [1] Our favorite trudge is up the St. Bernardine-road, to Hinterrhein, a village above eight mi[les] off, where, from a glacier on the mountain-top close by, the Rhine springs. Nothing can exceed the beauty of the valley,—as deeply green at this moment, as if Spring were just begun. Our other achievements have been—the top of the Splügen pass— which gained, you are in Italy: and the fine Via Mala where we spent this morning.[2] No pla[ce] ever agreed with me so well,—and

1. "They that wait upon the Lord shall renew their strength; they shall mount up with wings as eagles; they shall run and not be weary; and they shall walk and not faint." Isaiah 40:31.

2. This was Browning's nearest approach to Italy since his departure from it in 1861.

henceforth, whether I get it or no,—shall be assured that mountain-air,—and not the sea-bathing,—is my proper resource when fagged at the end of a season. We passed you[r] Ragatz,[3] I must tell you,—whatever its advantages may be they are neutralized, for our purpose, by the crowd of visitors there—our train deposited enough to frighten one. The Engadine,[4] too, seems to have been choke-full of English: no, this sort of savagery is the sui[t]able thing. We have newspapers, however, good cookery, absolute cleanliness, and *such* quietude! The end is, we shall stay some ten days longer, and then make for Venice—which I have a yearning to see again. My Sister has never been in Italy at all, and I shall be glad of her enjoyment. So, Venice revisited, and such of the Lombard cities as lie not too much out of the way, we shall go back by some other route. Have I tired you, dear friend? No,—your goodness holds out even on greater provocation: be good and, first of all, give my kindest love, and that of my Sister, to Mr. Skirrow,—take your share in the largess,—and *pray* write and tell me what you can of your two selves. If I should be off and away, the letter will follow me to Venice. All happiness to you both from

Yours affectionately ever

[Schiff]   Robert Browning.

TO MRS. CHARLES SKIRROW

19. W[arwick] C[rescent]. Oct. 29, '78.

Dear Friend, I shall be most happy to see you again on Saturday, and as often after as good fortune will allow. I fully intended to write from Venice,—and cannot excuse myself for having—not neglected to do so, but suffered a press of little matters to get between my intentions and their fulfilment. I sent your address (at the Hôtel) to Pen—who called on you immediately, and was informed that you had gone elsewhere, but *where* they knew not,—you had however been in communication with them, and would get his card in due time—which may or may not have been the case.

---

3. "Bad Ragaz or Ragatz (1696'), with 2200 inhab., at the entrance of the narrow valley of the boisterous Tamina, which falls into the Rhine E. of the station, is one of the most frequented watering-places in Switzerland." (Baedeker, *Switzerland* [London, 1938], p. 84.)

4. The Engadine is a valley 60 miles long, east of Splügen, and bounded by Maloja Pass on the north and the Tyrolese frontier on the south. St. Moritz, its most famous resort, was later to attract Browning to it for a vacation.

We are (my Sister and myself) exceedingly well, and have got some compensation this time for the sad last year's experience: [1] but I will tell you on Saturday. Till then, and then, and ever and always after then, you know I am—with much love to your husband—

[Schiff]

Yours affectionately
RBrowning.

To Richard Monckton Milnes

19. Warwick Crescent, W.
April 3, '79.

My dear Houghton,

I only this moment became aware,—by a notice including your name, which occurs in the newspaper,—that you have probably been in Town last week. I was assured to the contrary, and so may have lost the gratification of a visit to the house where I [intended] to show Robert's new pictures: [1] at least I could have tried for a repetition of that kindness which was so much laid to heart last year. Indeed, this present writing is unnecessary enough,—you know my feeling on the subject: still, it shall go to you from

[Lord Crewe]

Yours ever most sincerely
Robert Browning.

1. The vacation of the previous year had been interrupted, and to a great degree spoiled, by the death of Miss Annie Egerton Smith. (See above, letter dated September 15, 1877.)

1. Pen sent some new pictures to his father in 1879. They probably included those described in Sotheby, *Browning Collections* as items 26, 27, and 28—all pictures of scenes at Dinant, Belgium. Once again Browning made an occasion of his son's showing. George Smith, Browning's publisher, allowed the use of an empty house at 11 Queen's Gate Gardens, South Kensington, for the display. Formal invitations were engraved for the occasion. (See *Letters,* ed. Hood, for facsimile of one of these invitations, facing p. 186.) The pictures were shown from Friday through Monday of the last week in March, from 2 till 6 P.M.

To Frank Harrison Hill [1]

19. Warwick Crescent, W.
Apr. 8, '79.

Dear Mr. Hill,

I will certainly vote for you: and, if you get in the Club [2] and attend there occasionally, I will manage to increase my visits in number,—they being at present, on an average, two in five years.

Ever truly yours

[Mr. Earl Leslie Griggs]   Robert Browning.

To William Hale White [1]

19. Warwick Crescent, W.
May 2, '79.

My dear Sir,

Few more gratifying occurrences than the reception of your letter have rewarded my work this many a year. So, I have had a friend without knowing it!—and a lover of Bunyan too, the object of my utmost admiration and reverence.[2] I will not deprive your wall of

1. Frank Harrison Hill (1830–1910) had joined the staff of the London *Daily News* in 1866 and had become editor-in-chief in 1870, a post which he held until 1886. It was to Hill that Browning recounted, in 1884, his relation with Macready in the production of *A Blot in the 'Scutcheon*. (Orr, *Life*, pp. 110–116.)

2. Probably not the Athenaeum Club, which Browning frequented and to which Hill was elected in 1889. (Francis G. Waugh, *Members of the Athenaeum Club* [printed for private circulation, London, 1894], p. 70.)

1. Though the name "N. Hale White" appears at the bottom of this letter in Browning's hand, the recipient is certainly William Hale White (1831–1913), critic, novelist, and philosophical writer. Under the pseudonym of Mark Rutherford he wrote *The Autobiography of Mark Rutherford* (1881) and *Rutherford's Deliverance* (1885), as well as the novel *The Revolution in Tanner's Lane* (1887). Under his own name he published a translation of Spinoza's *Ethic* (1883) and wrote, among other things, *Emendation of the Intellect* (1895) and *Examination of the Charge of Apostasy against Wordsworth* (1898). In 1905 he produced a study called *John Bunyan*. He wrote this letter to Browning after reading "Ned Bratts" in *Dramatic Idyls*, 1st ser., published on April 28, 1879.

2. While at Splügen in the Swiss Alps during the late summer and fall of 1878 Browning wrote "Ned Bratts" with "the story of 'Old Tod,' as told in Bunyan's 'Life and Death of Mr. Badman' . . . distinctly in . . . mind." (*Letters*, ed. Hood, p. 209.) On returning to London he purchased the *Works of John Bunyan* (Edinburgh, 1771). (Sotheby, *Browning Collections*, item 530, p. 85.)

its decoration—the portrait: though I thank you gratefully for your offer, and,—I repeat,—for making known to me that I am richer, by the possession of your sympathy, than I could have supposed, and have a right to bid you remember me as, Dear Sir,

Cordially yours ever
Robert Browning.

N. Hale White, Esq.

[Huntington]

To William Hale White

19. Warwick Crescent, W.
May 9, '79.

My dear Sir,—What am I to say on receiving, as I do this moment, your gift?—which, valuable in itself, is made precious indeed by the circumstances under which you bestow it on me. Indeed I never dreamed of depriving you of what you cannot but greatly miss: your own generosity must reward you. The admirable portrait [1] shall grace this room wherein I write, by the side of Spenser and Milton,—and my eyes will never fall on it without bringing to my mind the donor.[2] Might I hope one day to see the donor's self? My Sister and myself take an early luncheon at 1 o'clock: if you have, by good chance, any occasion to come our way, and may be induced to apprise me by a written word, that gratification will complete whatever seems wanting from this present one—great as it is. In any case, believe me ever, Dear Sir, most cordially and

gratefully yours

[Huntington]   Robert Browning.

To William Black [1]

19. Warwick Crescent, W.
June 6, '79.

Dear Mr. Black,

Thank you exceedingly for your kind note and the journal which followed it—and from which I got much information concerning

---

1. The words "of Bunyan" are inclosed in parentheses and appear above the line, over a caret, written in a hand other than Browning's.

2. The portrait of Bunyan does not appear in Sotheby, *Browning Collections.*

1. William Black (1841–98), novelist and biographer of Goldsmith for the

matters I was in ignorance about. Can "Browning's" faculties be in as satisfactory a state as his biographer flatters him by supposing, when he never remembers having gone to school at Dulwich, nor living at Richmond, nor having for father a banker, nor the said father counselling him to care for "guineas and half-guineas" rather than for "poetry" [2]—in which he himself was a perfect adept—though of an earlier bygone school—and,—had he possessed a particle more vanity and less generosity,—might have beaten hollow his son and your friend

[Mr. Frederick W. Hilles]   Robert Browning.

TO FREDERICK LOCKER [1]

July 6, '79.

My dear Locker, I have transcribed the three stanzas with great willingness: I fear however I have failed to observe your directions in three minute points—fortunately minute. I forgot to make the Alexandrine begin a little in advance of its predecessors,—for-

---

"English Men of Letters" series (1878), probably is the person to whom this letter is addressed. Several social notes from William Black to Browning are printed in *Browning's Letter File,* ed. Armstrong. The first of these, dated February 12 [1880], is familiar and friendly enough to indicate more than a brief previous acquaintance (see p. 82). Browning's letter, too, is written in a vein which argues a previous intimacy with the recipient.

2. The journal referred to is the *University Magazine* (a sequel to the *Dublin University Magazine*), the issue of March, 1879, pp. 322–335. In it, as part of "A New Series of Contemporary Portraits," is an article on "Robert Browning," accompanied by an excellent photograph by Elliot and Fry. Browning refers to the following statements in this article: "Till his fourteenth year he was educated at a school in Dulwich" (p. 324); "In 1832 . . . he was living at Richmond, Surrey" (p. 324); "with humorous reference to the kind of wealth with the chink of which the banker was most familiar, he [Robert Browning, Sr.] is reported to have said they [Browning's poems] do not bring in many sovereigns" (p. 324). This was the first of two articles on Browning, the second appearing in April, 1879, pp. 416–443.

1. Frederick Locker (1821–95), Locker-Lampson in 1885 and thereafter, apparently first became acquainted with Browning about 1859, the date of Locker's *London Lyrics.* (See Browning's letter to Locker dated July 26, 1858, in Augustine Birrell, *Frederick Locker-Lampson: A Character Sketch* [London, 1920], p. 101.) He was on intimate terms with Browning's father and with Sarianna, a relationship fostered by Locker's and the senior Browning's love for old prints, particularly those of Hogarth. In a letter dated March 7, 1890, Sarianna wrote to Locker of her appreciation for his "expressions of affection for Robert." She added: "You know how much he loved you and valued your friendship—the feeling lasted unabated to the end" (p. 105).

got to leave out the vowel in the unaccented endings,—and forgot to put in an illogical stop or two as they appear in the printed copy.[2]

Ever yours truly

[Huntington]   RB.

To Mrs. Charles Skirrow

19. Warwick Crescent, W.
July 30, '79.

Dear Friend, will it suit you to have me next Friday at 1 1/2? I shall be delighted, if it will: or Saturday, at the same hour,—just as you direct. I have been oppressed with engagements—all happily ending, so far as I know, with to-day—when I have three invitations to dine, and two to go into the country.

Ever yours affectionately
Robert Browning.

Of my plans, when we meet.
[Schiff]

To C. W. Deschamps [1]

19. Warwick Crescent, W.
May 10, '80.

Dear Mr. Deschamps,

You were good enough to promise to come and see my son's picture, one day. If by chance you should be able to look in at 11,

2. It is probable that Locker had requested some of Browning's verses for the collection of his daughter, Eleanor. Apparently he was practicing on Browning a variant of the device, described by his son-in-law, Augustine Birrell, of copying out "in his own clear hand, on loose sheets, his daughter's favourite poems; and then [having] the leaves stitched together and clad in red morocco; and if any of the authors had the luck to be alive, getting them to add their names at the foot of their verses" (p. 69). "Rabbi ben Ezra" may be the poem from which Browning was to copy three stanzas. In this poem an alexandrine, a rare line in Browning, ends each stanza and is printed "a little in advance of its predecessors."

1. C. W. Deschamps was connected with the Hanover Gallery, 47 New Bond Street. (See below, letter dated October 4, 1881.) This gallery held fairly continuous exhibitions with emphasis upon "pictures and drawings which will meet the requirements of all purchasers." (Advertisement in London *Times*, November 28, 1881, p. 1, col. 3.) Deschamps' relations with Browning were restricted to the business of exhibiting and otherwise exploiting Pen's pictures. Apparently he performed satisfactorily, for he was still acting as caretaker of Pen's pictures—varnishing, crating, uncrating, shipping, hanging—as late as

Queen's Gate Gardens next Wednesday between 4. and 6. p. m., I shall be there and happy to show it to you.[2]

Pray believe me, Dear Mr. Deschamps,

Yours very sincerely
Robert Browning.

[Yale]

To C. W. Deschamps

Venice, Oct. 19, '80.

Dear Mr. Deschamps,

My absence from England will explain the cause of the delay in replying to your kind letter to my Son—for whom I am always empowered to act. The Inquisition picture is quite at your service for the Exhibition you propose: the only difficulty is where to find it. I sent it to Liverpool—where I suppose its size prevented its being hung,—as only the other large picture "Solitude" [1] appears in the catalogue. If you can ascertain where it is and get possession of it (for which the present letter will be your warrant) I beg you do so. Messrs. Smith and Elder, 15 Waterloo Place, will give you any more particular information concerning its whereabouts. I furnished them also with the proper title of the picture, "The Delivery to the Secular Arm"—together with a quotation from Calderon, and a translation of the same, which may be inserted in your catalogue.[2]

Believe me, Dear Mr. Deschamps,
Yours very truly
Robert Browning.

[Yale]

1889. In that year Browning wrote to Pen: "I wrote to M. Deschamps—giving him the dimensions again: these people like making themselves of importance." (*Letters*, ed. Hood, p. 307.)

2. This is a continuation of the private annual showings of Pen's pictures—a device by which Browning successfully stimulated his son's productivity. These private showings were also for professionals, such as Deschamps, who could see, judge, and decide on the advisability of a public showing.

1. This picture and two others, "Watching the Skittle Players" and "A Tan-Yard, Dinant," were exhibited at the Royal Academy in 1880. (Graves, *The Royal Academy of Arts; A Complete Dictionary . . . 1769-1904*, I, 320.) "Watching the Skittle Players"—a portrait of a pig accompanied by an apropos stanza beginning, "With meditative grunts and much content"—was still in Pen's possession at his death, as was also "A Tan-Yard, Dinant." (Sotheby, *Browning Collections*, pp. 9, 13.)

2. Preserved with the letter is the paper which Deschamps got from Smith and Elder; it has the following quotation and translation, written in Browning's most careful hand, and is dated on the back, "28/7/80":

To C. W. Deschamps

Nov. 8, '80.

Dear Mr. Deschamps,

I returned to London last night, and had intended to call on you in a day or two. I have just received the favor of your Card of Admission, and see there is no time to be lost—therefore take the quickest method of saying that my Son is delighted that you like and exhibit his picture: [1] but *he entreats most earnestly that you will get it previously varnished,*[2]—I need not say, at my expense. He attaches so much importance to this, that I am sure you will have the kindness to see that the thing is properly done by a competent person. I told him he might rely on you for thus obliging him.

Your goodnatured interest in the progress of a comparative beginner will be pleased to know that I was assured by a French friend on whose opinion I set a high value (as do all who know him) that the works completed during the last six months in Belgium (which my friend went expressly to see, a fortnight ago) show a very marked progress—as they ought to do.

Pray believe me,
Dear Mr. Deschamps,
Yours very truly
Robert Browning.

[Yale]

The Delivery to the Secular Arm: a scene during the existence of the Spanish Inquisition at Antwerp, 1570.

Así la mano de Dios	Therefore the hand of God
Tu sentencia con el dedo	Thy sentence with His finger
Escribió, y esta justicia	Hath written, and this tribunal
La remita por derecho	Consigneth it now straightway
Al brazo seglar.	Unto the Secular Arm.

Calderon.

1. "Hanover Gallery, 47 New Bond Street . . . The Winter Exhibition of Oil Paintings by British Artists and of original drawings for Punch will be opened Monday, 15th inst." (London *Times,* November 13, 1880, p. 1, col. 6.) The exhibition closed on Saturday, January 8, 1881. Deschamps did exhibit Pen's massive picture, "The Delivery to the Secular Arm." (See letter of November 10, 1880.)

2. See letter of November 13, 1880.

To Mrs. Charles Skirrow

19. Warwick Crescent, W.
Nov. 10, '80.

Dear Friend, I am back again since a couple of days, and anxious to see you, and to thank you for your letter, and to excuse as well as I can my disgusting self for merely feeling grateful and not saying so with pen and ink. Meantime I want to say that Pen's Inquisition Picture will be exhibited at the Hanover Gallery next week, and I am anxious that you should see and like it, if possible: will you?— by help of the Ticket I enclose?

Love to your Husband. My Sister, as well as I, come back quite well—though I had a little indisposition on arriving,—caught,— but I will hold my tongue about it: I had promised to go to last night's Dinner, and thereby was able to disengage myself from what began to frighten me: court-dress, for one thing! [1]

[Schiff]

Ever affectionately yours
Robert Browning.

To C. W. Deschamps

19. Warwick Crescent, W.
Nov. 13, '80.

Dear Mr. Deschamps,

I have just had a letter from my Son in which he begs me so earnestly to see that the Picture is varnished that I have in turn to beg you to get it done. He says many parts were sunk in when he saw it six months ago. He also says that the canvas wants tightening somewhere by a tap of a hammer on the pegs. Pray oblige me by attending to this at once.[1]

[Yale]

Yours sincerely
Robt Browning.

1. This was the banquet held at the Guildhall to celebrate the inauguration of the Right Honourable William M'Arthur, M.P., as Lord Mayor of London. The attendance at the banquet "numbered upwards of 1000," and the chief address was delivered by Gladstone. (The London *Times* for November 10, 1880, prints over five columns describing Lord Mayor's Day and the banquet at the Guildhall.) Browning throughout his life had an almost morbid fright of such occasions and once left town "to avoid the Academy dinner" where he might have been "called on to return thanks for—literature!" (*Letters to Isa Blagden*, p. 169.)

1. See above letter of November 8, 1880.

K

To Mrs. Charles Skirrow

19. Warwick Crescent, W.
Jan. 6, '81.

Dear Friend, the stupid mistake was mine: I had to write a similar word of excuse to Miss Lawrence who asked me to dine on the 21st when I am engaged. Unluckily I am also engaged on the 19th to the "President, Council, and Professors of London University" [1]— which *day* I had in mind, altho' the *other* date got repeated.

Pen desires to thank you exceedingly for your invitation—that of *tomorrow*—which he accepts with greater pleasure that he will be gone before the day you first appointed. Expect him punctually —and gratefully—at 1/4 8, to-morrow, Friday.

In great haste—but as great
affection, yours
RBrowning.

[Schiff]

To C. W. Deschamps

19. Warwick Crescent, W.
Jan. 14, '81.

Dear Mr. Deschamps,

My Son,—who left last evening for Belgium,—is very desirous that his picture at the Hanover Gallery should be photographed while there, to avoid the trouble of removal to the Artist's house. I called two days ago to ask for your permission that this may be done. Will you be kind enough to let me know if I may communicate with Mr. Hollyer, who has photographed other pictures satisfactorily?

Believe me, Dear Mr. Deschamps,
Yours sincerely
Robert Browning.

[Yale]

1. The dinner scheduled for January 19 "was put off in consequence of the severity of the weather and will now be held about the middle of February." (London *Times*, January 20, 1881, p. 10, col. 6.) The dinner was rescheduled for February 16. "On the invitation of the President, members of the Council, and Professors of University College, Gower street, a large number of gentlemen distinguished in literature, science, art, and the learned professions dined together last night in the library of the college to celebrate the opening of the New North wing of the college buildings." Browning's name appears fourth in an unalphabetical listing of the distinguished persons present. (London *Times*, February 17, 1881, p. 6, col. 6.)

To Mrs. Charles Skirrow

19. Warwick Crescent, W.
Jan. 22, '81.

Dear Friend, I am sorry indeed to know—(what I might have expected)—that you are physically "snowed up," as materially are houses and lands. How much I hope you will "weather" it all, you know without assurance of mine. Indeed I *have* felt the cold as an aggravation of the cough I got from my attendance on that sad day.[1] On Tuesday I was to have dined at Lincoln's Inn with the Benchers,[2] but felt uncomfortable at the look of things, and sent an excuse: to which it was replied by the Treasurer next day that almost everybody had kept away, and that many of the faithful were the worse for their fidelity. Next day's dinner was considerately put off by telegraph—(my notice taking four good hours to reach me)— but I should have kept at home all the same in any case. A dinner to which I was bound last evening was put off for the same good reason. I am glad to think I have no engagement now for many days to come. Let me fix on Friday the 11th for your Lunch, since you so kindly give me leave: I have something to do on the afternoon of the other days. If you agree, please let me have a word, and the *time*.

Yes, Pen,—after being very poorly for a week,—seeing that the weather was likely to be worse instead of better, made a rush on Thursday (last week) and got safely over: he writes—what I receive only this morning from Dinant—that he will probably return to Antwerp this day. He brought four pictures—which I shall be happy to show you: they are at the same house as that you visited in the Spring:[3] but there is no sort of cause for hurry, as they will remain where they are for the next two or three months. His largest picture was in peril from the floods at Dinant, and could only be

1. The funeral of George Eliot on December 29, 1880, which Browning attended in the company of Herbert Spencer. The procession began at 11 A.M. and reached Highgate Cemetery at 12.30. "During the whole of the proceedings the rain was falling steadily." (London *Times*, December 30, 1880, p. 6, col. 3.)

2. "Lincoln's Inn . . . the Benchers entertained at dinner yesterday [January 18], being Grand Day in Hilary Term, the American Minister [James Russell Lowell], the Treasurer of the Middle Temple," . . . (London *Times*, January 19, 1881, p. 8, col. 1.)

3. 11 Queen's Gate Gardens, South Kensington. (See letter of May 10, 1880, above.)

removed from the house by the waterside after Pen had left for London: the lower part was submerged actually, but I fancy no serious harm has been done. In the letter received this morning is a photograph of Dinant, turned into Venice, with the river many feet above the ground-floor, and Pen himself, punting in a wash-tub, engaged in carrying bread to the captives in the higher storeys, —cut off as these were from other access. But I must end. All love to you all from yours affectionately ever

[Schiff] Robert Browning.

To Mrs. Charles Skirrow

19. Warwick Crescent, W.
[*ca.* February 1, 1881] [1]

Dear Friend, I have the misfortune to be hopelessly engaged this evening—you know how much I regret it.

M. Dourlans [2] is with me—and, at this moment is out with my sister. It just occurs to me that you *might* have no one in view for your place,—and in that case it is impossible but that it would greatly gratify him to see you and the play to-gether: but I shall say nothing of it when he returns unless I have had some intimation from you: this is just a chance shot, understand. I dined with Tennyson last Saturday, and felt foolish at not having anything to say about what interests him so much. [3] I take this opportunity of saying that Pen's five new pictures will be on view at 11, Queen's Gate Gardens next Saturday, Sunday, and Monday, from 2. to 6. p.m. and you *must*—and any of your friends *may*—come and see them.

Ever affectionately yours

[Schiff] Robert Browning.

1. A notation in a hand other than Browning's appears in the upper right corner of this letter "1881 (?)." N. 3 below gives the basis for the conjecture that this letter was written in early February, 1881.

2. Gustave Dourlans, an intimate of Joseph Milsand and through him of Browning and his sister. (Orr, *Life*, p. 176.)

3. See below, letter of February 20, 1881. The play was probably Tennyson's *The Cup*, which opened at the Lyceum, January 3, 1881 with Henry Irving and Ellen Terry in the leading roles. (Austin Brereton, *Life of Henry Irving*, I, 327.) Browning had witnessed the first performance of Tennyson's *Queen Mary* (I, 208) and was embarrassed to be with Tennyson before he had seen *The Cup*. After seeing the play he "was loud in praise," according to Hallam Tennyson, who printed a note of thanks, dated February 8, 1881, from his father to Browning. (*Tennyson, A Memoir*, II, 258.)

To Mrs. Charles Skirrow

19. Warwick Crescent, W.
Feb. 18, '81.

Dear Friend, I am most unluckily engaged this evening—have to dine at Ld Airlie's to meet no less a personage than Dizzy: [1] so that I can only thank you very heartily, as I am sure I do.

Ever affectionately yours

[Schiff]   RBrowning.

To Mrs. Charles Skirrow

19. Warwick Crescent, W.
Feb. 20, '81.

Dear Friend, of course I will go to you on Friday since you wish it. After all, the obstacle you foresee is no such very serious one. Sarianna thanks you, but is forced to attend her Committee of some kind for some purpose or other.

Yes, I should have greatly enjoyed seeing *the Cup* [1] with you: I was amused with my own entertainment nevertheless.[2] All love to you and your Husband, from yours affectionately ever

[Schiff]   Robert Browning.

1. Browning had been to a dinner at which Disraeli was present on a previous occasion, described by Disraeli in a note to Lady Bradford, dated April 4, 1878: "The Dinner yesterday at P[ercy] Wyndham's was of an aesthetical character; Pss. Louise, De Vescis (of course), etc., etc., and Browning, a noisy, conceited poet; all the talk about pictures and art, and Raffaelle, and what Sterne calls 'the Correggiosity of Correggio.' " (Monypenny and Buckle, *The Life of Benjamin Disraeli* [London, 1929], II, 1155.) Disraeli, say his biographers, attended the dinner "at Lady Airlie's on Friday the 18th [1881] . . . After dinner at Lady Airlie's he had a talk with Matthew Arnold . . . whom he complimented now as the only living Englishman who had become a classic in his lifetime" (II, 1474). Browning is not mentioned, and one may assume that Disraeli's attitude remained that which is summarized by Sir Stafford Northcote in his *Diary* under date of July 11, 1880: Disraeli "was contemptuous over Browning (of whom, however, he had read very little)" (Andrew Lang, *Life, Letters, and Diaries of Sir Stafford Northcote* [Edinburgh, 1890], II, 1455.)

1. Tennyson's *The Cup*, with Henry Irving as Synorix and Ellen Terry as Camma, opened to a brilliant audience on Monday, January 3, 1881. (Austin Brereton, *Life of Henry Irving*, I, 327. See also above, letter of February 1, 1881, n. 3.

2. See above, letter of *ca.* February 1, 1881, and n. 3.

To Madame Bessie Rayner Belloc [1]

19. Warwick Crescent, W.
March 18, '81.

Dear Madame Belloc,

Thank you—and thank Miss Kellog [2]—for the Tickets which,— I am sorry to say, neither my Sister nor myself can profit by, this time, through engagements we are held to. Here they are—returned for the benefit of more lucky people.

I do indeed regret deeply the conception, execution and publication of those memoirs, equally unwise in their praise and unworthy in their blame: but I knew the extraordinary limitations of my dear old friend—and of his "woman" too—just as well forty years ago as to-day.[3] His opinions about men and things one inch out of his own little circle never moved me with the force of a feather— or I should hardly have lived five minutes of my whole life as I have done, and, for the remainder of it,—please God,—shall do. But we must not ourselves prove ingrates for a deal of love, or at least benevolence, in deed and wish,—I must not, anyhow,—so, instead of "burning Carlyle and scattering his ashes to the winds," I am on the committee for erecting a monument to "True Thomas" [4]—

1. This letter is printed in Bessie Rayner Belloc, *A Passing World* (London, 1897), pp. 27–29. Madame Bessie Rayner (Parkes) Belloc (1829–1925) possibly met Browning in Italy as early as 1857. (See *In a Walled Garden* [London, 1896], chapter on "In Rome with Mrs. Jameson.")

2. Unidentified.

3. Browning refers here to J. A. Froude's edition of Carlyle's *Reminiscences,* which was published in March, 1881, within a month of Carlyle's death on February 5. This letter to Madame Belloc represents a tiny facet in the controversy which began at once over Froude's book. Browning's judgment of the "revelations," as "equally unwise in their praise and unworthy in their blame," has been supported by later students of Carlyle's life and works. On the other hand, it has been strongly implied that because Browning found Mrs. Carlyle a "hard, unlovable woman," he was "inclined to be too favourable in judging Carlyle." (See Waldo H. Dunn, *Froude and Carlyle, A Study of the Froude-Carlyle Controversy* [London, 1930], p. 265.) It seems obvious that Browning is expressing to Madame Belloc his exact feeling about Carlyle and estimating his debt to the author of *Sartor Resartus.*

4. "True Thomas" is of course Carlyle. In 1881 a committee was formed to honor the sage of Ecclefechan, as a countermeasure to the effect caused by Froude's *Reminiscences,* which to many seemed to exhibit a false view of Carlyle. Carlyle had written the *Reminiscences* in a mood of self-blame and depression after his wife's death in 1866. A statue by Boehm, belonging to Lord Rosebery, a replica of which has been erected on the Chelsea Embank-

whose arm was laid on my shoulder a very few weeks ago. He confessed once to me that, on the first occasion of my visiting him, he
was anything but favorably impressed by my "smart green coat"—
I being in riding-costume: and if then and there had begun and
ended our acquaintanceship, very likely I might have figured in
some corner of a page as a poor scribbling-man with proclivities
for the turf and scamphood. What then? He wrote *Sartor*—and
such letters to me in those old days! No, I am his devotedly and—
if you permit me—yours cordially
[Yale]   Robert Browning.

To Mrs. Charles Skirrow

19. W[arwick] C[rescent]
Apr. 9, '81.

Dear Friend,
Since you exact them—here are the helps [1] to that generosity you
are minded to inflict on your undeserving but very
[Schiff]   grateful RB.

To [Mrs. Charles Skirrow?] [1]

19. Warwick Crescent, W.
June 20. '81.

Dear Friend, this replies tardily to your kind invitation, since I
have only just returned from Oxford.[2] I will do my best to avail
myself of your kind invitation aforesaid,—but if I find myself unable, you will be sure of my regrets—as of the constant regard of
Yours truly
[Baylor]   Robert Browning.

---

ment near Carlyle's old home, is what the committee upon which Browning
served succeeded in doing for Carlyle.

1. Information to aid Mrs. Skirrow in her purchase of a birthday gift for
Browning, a faithfully performed yearly duty.

1. The formal complimentary close of this letter makes it highly dubious that
Mrs. Skirrow was the recipient.

2. Browning apparently returned from Oxford before Commemoration
Day, which he usually attended. This year it fell on June 22. (See London
Times, June 23, 1881.)

To Kegan Paul [1]

19. Warwick Crescent, W.
July 15, '81.

Dear Mr. Kegan Paul,

I want your goodnatured intervention in a little matter. You must know, I received, perhaps many months ago, a little book— *Dorothy, a Country Story.*[2] By whatever the chance, it escaped my

1. Charles Kegan Paul (1828–1902), publisher, biographer, and intimate of many literary men of his time, carried out quickly and faithfully Browning's request that he transmit to the author of *Dorothy* Browning's high opinion of that poem. Paul evidently sent Browning's letter to Munby (see next note) with the request that the letter be returned. After copying the letter Munby did return it. Munby's copy is now in the Rare Book Room at Yale, inserted in a volume of *Dorothy*. Although there is no evidence of a second English edition of *Dorothy*, it is clear that Paul made good use of Browning's letter in stimulating an American market for the poem. It was published in Boston by Roberts Brothers in 1882 and soon after by Munro for the Seaside Library in a ten-cent edition. Reviewing the Roberts Brothers' edition in April, 1882, P. B. Marston wrote as follows: "No author's name was upon the title page, but it was an open secret that it was written by Arthur J. Munby. Browning and a half dozen other poets received this work with enthusiasm." ("A Realistic Poet," *Atlantic Monthly*, XLIX, 514.) It is probable that the secret became open after Paul and Munby saw the advantage in making use of Browning's energetic espousal.

2. Arthur J. Munby (1828–1910) published *Dorothy, A Country Story in Elegiac Verse*, London, C. Kegan Paul and Co., Paternoster Square, 1880. The complimentary copy of the poem sent to Browning by Munby is item 948 of Sotheby, *Browning Collections*. On the half title of this item appears in Browning's autograph: "Robert Browning, with the compliments of the author, unknown." With the volume at the sale of the Browning collections was a "long A.L.s. of the author," doubtless a letter from Munby acknowledging Browning's praise. Other letters were exchanged between Browning and Munby; but that the two poets did not become well acquainted is evident from a letter of Munby to Furnivall, dated November 7, 1887, the first paragraph of which follows: "A lady to whom I am under some small obligation asks me for an autograph of Mr. Browning. I have several letters from him to myself, but I shan't part with them, so I must look elsewhere; and I can't ask the autographer himself. Have you any odd signature of his, that you would give me for the lady?" That Furnivall forwarded this request to Browning is clear, for the letter was found in Browning's file of letters. (See *Browning's Letter File*, ed. Armstrong, pp. 120–121.) Munby's career as a poet began in 1852 with the publication of *Benoni: Poems* and ended in 1909 with the publication of *Relicta: Verses*. He was, therefore, a sporadically practicing poet for a period of 57 years, during which time he produced ten small volumes of verse. (See *Cambridge History of English Literature*, XIII, 559 for a list of Munby's works.) Saintsbury in writing there of the "Lesser Poets of the Middle and Later Nineteenth Century" speaks of Munby as "an eccentric poet of rather wasted

notice altogether until a few days ago when I withdrew it, by accident, from a pile on the table—and, finding the leaves cut, dipped into the middle: a minute's reading sent me back to—not the Preface, but line the first—whence I proceeded to the last with a surprise of delight as rare as it was thorough. Then, enquiring about the mysterious adventurers with the paper-knife, I found to my confusion that my Sister had anticipated all my experience, and that my Son,—short as his stay with me was, had pronounced the poem to be, over and above the literary charm, "a perfect picture-gallery." "It was impossible" my sister thought "that I could be unaware of their praises"—but, all the same, unaware I certainly was: and that everybody else should remain so, seemed such a wrong that I at once carried the book to our friend Mrs. Orr,[3] and yesterday finished a reading which, in its effects, justified all my expectations of success. Now,[4]—the book was consigned to me "with the compliments of the Author," as the printed form ran: and I cannot help begging you to say for me to that Author that it is literally years since I have admired and enjoyed a poem *so much*—and I am carefully sober in professing no more.[5] I have never seen the minutest notice in the periodicals,—of course I make no sort of guess at who the Author may be: but from some signal exquisiteness of observation, I almost fancy the fine hand must be *feminine:* if I mistake, my blunder is one tribute the more to a consummate male craftsman.

There,—I have somewhat discharged my mind, despite the hot

---

talents," whom, however, some critics would place at the head of the minor poets of this period; "nor," observes Saintsbury, "would this estimate lack arguments to support it" (p. 210 n.).

3. There is nothing in Mrs. Orr, *Life* about this episode.

4. There is a word scratched out here.

5. It is difficult to know what Browning found so attractive about Munby's poem. The theme is that woman can be noble even though subjected to the hardest kind of physical labor. The poem was an attack on paternalistic legislation which would make illegal any sort of physical toil for women. Hard, calloused, horny, large hands represent the lower, laboring class of women; soft, delicate, small hands stand for the idle, aristocratic women, the only sort of women with whom Browning associated. A few representative lines (pp. 9, 10) follow:

"Dorothy—who is she? She is only a servant-of-all-work . . .
Oh, what a notable lass is our Dolly, the pride of the dairy . . .
Stalwart and tall as a man, strong as a heifer to work:
Built for beauty, indeed, but certainly built for labour—
Witness her muscular arms, witness the grip of her hand!"

weather which might incline "expressive silence to muse the praise" [6] which I have put down αμωσγέπως. [7] Will you help it along? and believe me

Ever truly yours

[Huntington]   Robert Browning.

To Mrs. Charles Skirrow

Lans, par Grenoble, (Isère,) France.
[ca. September 1, 1881] [1]

Dear Friend,

I said I would write a word or two, since you care so kindly to receive them: and if the letter could carry with it some little suggestion of the pleasant hamlet I write from, it would be worth sending. Nearly three weeks have S. and I spent in the most rural and unsophisticated place we ever saw in our lives: a few cottages, one pretence at a shop, no tradition of an English tourist, utter roughness, abundant geniality, and such scenery, such mountains, and woods, and pastures, as make it sufficient delight to just live and let all else alone. We walked three hours and a half this morning without meeting even a peasant. There is a gorge close by, the Furon Pass, which exceeds in grandeur the Via Mala: but indeed the beauties are innumerable. We are in no mind to depart yet, though our faces will be turned towards Italy. All the same, I cannot fancy a single London acquaintance of mine who would endure the rough living for a moment: rough *lodging*, I should say: the *fare* being singularly good and plenteous: but a room like this in which I write, with bare walls, bare floor,—not even a chest of drawers to allow of the portmanteau's discharge of its load! The air is divine —and my tallow-coloured cheeks glow as with wine. Now, don't tell the spoilers of this jewel of a retreat: one hôtel-proper, and perhaps a Villa or two, would do the business effectually: and we

---

6. "Come then, expressive silence, muse His praise." James Thomson, *Hymn,* l. 118.

7. "In some way or other."

1. Browning and his sister Sarianna first visited the region of the Grande Chartreuse in 1881. In a letter dated September 15, 1881, Browning wrote that "today ends our five weeks' stay." (*Letters,* ed. Hood, p. 197.) They must, therefore, have arrived at Lans about August 11. The present letter mentions a stay of "nearly three weeks" at Lans, which would indicate a date near September 1.

thought some calamity was impending last Sunday, when took place the solemn "Ouverture de la Chasse": one would think, by the look of the country, that game abounded: there are bears on the hill-tops, and black game ought to abound like sparrows in London: so, on the Saturday, arrived the "Chasseurs," from Grenoble, with guns, dogs, and a promise of doughty performance. They rose at 4. next morning, with noise befitting the first of a campaign: I had misgivings notwithstanding: and, at supper, questioned our Land-lady as to the result of the day. "Monsieur,—un *tout*-petit lièvre!" Next day, one successful sportsman presented us with two "pieds-noir"—birds of bumble-bee bigness: and the most redoubtable Nimrod of them all furnished for our supper two veritable quails —so ended the "Chasse"—all taking leave on the Monday, guns on shoulder, dogs *en laisse,* and hugely-fringed bags at waist.

But I have not told you of our visit to the Grande Chartreuse, during our couple of days' stay at Grenoble. Very interesting,[2]— journey, visit, and all—to me, at least, for S. was not allowed inside the walls. I dined capitally on the Convent's allowance, inspected a cell, and fancied I could manage to inhabit such an one, with the Library (a good one) at my disposal. I shall not forego the *petit verre* of their liqueur as I have been apt to do, after coffee. Enough of this, surely! But it is your own fault, Dear Friend. Where may you be, I wonder? At some gay Casino—most properly—where Mr. Skirrow can renew his strength like an eagle. I hope it with all my heart. If our purpose holds, we shall not return to London till later in the Autumn than is our wont: we shall stay where we are till Italy cools, and then go here and there as the circumstances suggest. Now, if you want to delight me altogether, you will write as much about yourself as you can afford to do, and send it here—say, within the next fortnight. I will carry your letter into the woods, and read it under a fir-tree, sitting on aromatic herbs,—with a huge grass-hopper, every now and then, jumping upon my hat. Do, now! Sarianna, whose health was far from satisfactory, is quite herself

2. Browning's noncommittal response to the romantic wonders of the Grande Chartreuse—"very interesting," he says—stands in contrast to the whole ro-mantic tradition and to the attitude of his contemporaries, particularly Mat-thew Arnold. Though Browning traveled much and saw many natural wonders, he rarely if ever became exuberant over what he saw, and it never would have occurred to him, as it did to Arnold, that the Grande Chartreuse could be a symbol, an inspiration for a poem.

again. She reminded me (unnecessarily, to be sure) that I had engaged to write to you. Her love goes with mine to you and my dear friend your Husband. Pen,—you will like to know,—is hard at work,—paintin[g] much and—if I may trust other report than his own—well. Good bye, dear friends both. You have no more affectionate brother-in-love than yours ever

Robert Browning.

Look out for the proper envelopes when I get home again!
[Schiff]

To C. W. Deschamps

Albergo dell'Universo, Venezia.
Oct. 4, '81.

Dear Mr. Deschamps,

I got this morning an application for pictures, from the Hanover Gallery: but I see no mention of your name. As I understood from you that you intended to be connected with that enterprise, it may happen that, for whatever the reason, you give your services elsewhere: and since my promise with regard to my Son's pictures was made to yourself, I should be obliged if you would let me know (to the above address) [1] as soon as possible how the case stands. There are two unexhibited pictures, and a portrait painted only last May (not the one you saw) which I can contribute to the Gallery, if you advise.[2]

Yours sincerely,
[Yale]   Robert Browning.

To Mrs. Charles Skirrow

Venice, Oct. 30, '81.

It will indeed be a scrap of a scribble that I can write today, dear . . . (Oct. 31.) See now! I was cut short at the very beginning: and, this last morning of all, when I have a world of worries to endure preparatory to our departure to-morrow, I can only stammer out a word or two of thanks for your dear letter of yesterday, with the

1. The parenthesis has been inserted above the line with a caret.

2. The two unexhibited pictures may be "Still Life, Dinant," (sunflowers and tray with peaches and melons) and "Disturbed Life" (a picture of owls) both painted in 1880 and exhibited at the Grosvenor Gallery and at Manchester in 1881. (Sotheby, *Browning Collections*, items 24, 25.)

pleasant news it contained. We hope to pass Tuesday night at Turin,
—that of [Wednesday at] [1] Macon, next,—and last comes Paris, and
Friday's passage home: at home, not long will I be without the
sight and hearing of you, *se Dio vuole*. Poor Mrs. F. G. has just told
us, and doubtlessly *you* also—of the death of her Son, a much-to-be-
wished close of a sorrowful life.[2] My Sister loves you and Mr. Skirrow, and so say we both of us to both of you.

Ever affectionately yours

[Schiff]   Robert Browning.

To John W. Field [1]

19. Warwick Crescent, W.
Dec. 20, '81.

My dear Mr Field,

Long ago I had your very kind letter and should have answered
it at once but that the old "business before pleasure" adage came
into my mind; business-matters having increased with me of late.
But I will take my pleasure now—and a real and thorough one it is
to thank you for all your goodness to me and my sister which made
the unpropitious weather at Venice as warm as that Roman season
you describe so temptingly. You meant to give us as much delight
as you could—and how completely you succeeded I shall long remember. The *Fanfulla* [2] arrives regularly to our great satisfaction,

1. Possibly the "stammer" caused the omission here.
2. Sarah Anna Elizabeth Purefoy Jervoise of Shalstone Manor, Bucks (1809–
99), married in 1832 Thomas FitzGerald (d. 1860). There were six sons and two
daughters of this union. The son referred to here was Robert Allen FitzGerald
(1834–Oct. 1881), a barrister-at-law. (*Burke's Landed Gentry* [London, 1939],
"Purefoy of Shalstone," p. 1868.)
1. John W. Field, virtually an expatriate American from Pennsylvania, was
"a man of singular friendliness, of whom Lowell, shortly after making his acquaintance, wrote:
'Few things to charm me more can nature yield
Than a broad, open, breezy, high-viewed Field.' "
(*Letters of James Russell Lowell*, ed. C. E. Norton [New York, 1894], I, 339 n.)
Field was part of the Anglo-American coterie which found a common meeting
ground at Mrs. Arthur Bronson's in Venice. At the beginning of November,
1880, the coterie dispersed, Browning heading for London, Field and Lowell
for Rome, where, joined by another mutual friend, W. W. Story, the three "idle
about, telling over old stories and reviving old associations" (II, 264).
2. *Fanfulla della Domenica,* a paper published at Rome, had carried a series
of articles on Browning by Professor Nencioni, described by Mrs. Bronson as
"the only Italian who has thoroughly mastered the difficulties of Browning's

and gives a touch of Italy to the whole week. Had the Storys—all of them—been where we expected to find them—why—the arrangement would have been too perfect: I rejoice to hear they are well; give them, and the dear brace of painters, my best love and that of my sister.[3] From Mrs Bronson I hear every now and then—always with fresh gratification.[4] Lowell is here—and made the choicest of all possible speeches at the Chapter House-meeting this day week, when the poor Dean was commemorated.[5] And I must tell you another pleasant thing connected with your country. Don't you remember Mrs Bloomfield Moore, whose ways were talked over at Venice? She appeared in London, some weeks ago, and wrote to me that she wished to see Pen's handiwork—the immediate result of which was that she purchased the large picture of the "Inquisition," which I showed you, for the Philadelphia Academy of Fine Arts; and, for herself, a picture you cannot have seen, one of his last, "A Belgian Market-woman"; and this with [6] so much *heartiness* and liberality that the procedure was doubled in value. I put a moderate price on the larger work—knowing the unsaleable nature of such canvases: and she was at pains to discover what had been the original estimate at the Gallery where it was exhibited last year—which was none of my doing—and wanted to increase

---

poetry." Browning told Nencioni that he "subscribed to the paper at once . . . after reading your first kind notice of me." (Katherine de Kay Bronson, "Browning in Venice," *Century Magazine,* LXIII, 579.)

3. "The Storys, whom Browning had anticipated meeting in Venice, had gone to Vallombrosa, where their daughter (the Marchesa Peruzzi di Medici) had a villa. . . . Mr. Story's two sons, the painter and the sculptor, both had studios in Venice at the time, and Mr. Browning often strolled into these." (Lilian Whiting, *The Brownings* [Boston, 1911], p. 229.)

4. Mrs. Arthur Bronson, whose relations with Browning are described by Miss Whiting as "one of the most beautiful of the friendships of the last decade of the poet's life." (*The Brownings,* p. 242.) Certainly Mrs. Bronson, "a very cultivated and charming American woman who for more than twenty years made her home in Venice," was extremely generous in her care for Browning. The best account of Browning's Venetian sojourns is contained in Mrs. Bronson, "Browning in Venice," *Century Magazine,* LXIII, 578 ff.

5. James Russell Lowell had been in Venice in the autumn, during the latter part of Browning's stay there. (*Letters of James Russell Lowell,* ed. C. E. Norton, II, 261.) The speech referred to was made in "the Chapter House of Westminster Abbey in Commemoration of Dean Stanley, 13 December, 1881." The speech emphasizes the close spiritual tie between the United States and England. (J. R. Lowell, *Democracy and Other Addresses* [1887], p. 57 ff.)

6. "For herself" has been struck through and the phrase "and this with" written above the line.

her payment accordingly!—out of the question, of course: Pen recognizes, as do I, the great advantage of becoming known in America, and is more than satisfied.[7] He arrives to-morrow,—having finished various pictures which, I am assured, show continued progress—as does this writing of mine, having just enough room to, yet once more, load you with our affectionate regards and best Christmas wishes. Dear Mr. Field keep us in mind—and believe me—for my part—ever yours gratefully

[William C. DeVane]   Robert Browning.

To Sidney Colvin

19. Warwick Crescent, W.
Jan. 16, '82.

My dear Colvin,

I return the letter—an interesting one, but mainly so, to me at least, from the introductory account of the wife's demeanour and professions when neither were of any use—though commendably decent.[1]

Ever yours truly
Robert Browning

7. Mrs. Clara Sophia (Jessup) Bloomfield-Moore (1824–99), author of poems, children's stories, a book of etiquette, and proponent of Keely's discoveries, joined the large group of Browning's devoted women friends in 1879 when the poet called upon her at London's Claridge Hotel even before, as she recalls, she had "found time to deliver a letter of introduction." She adds: "Our friendship dates from that first evening of our meeting." (Clara Bloomfield-Moore, "Robert Browning," *Lippincott's Magazine*, XLV, 685.) She gives a full account of why she bought Pen's pictures: it was to settle a debt she owed to Mrs. Browning for the inspiration of her poetry. "When I heard that her son was an artist I determined to give him an order for some portraits . . . but, finding that some of his pictures remained unsold . . . I proposed to buy one for the Philadelphia Academy of Fine Arts . . . I . . . asked the price. His father at once gave me the picture . . . on the ground that it would benefit his son to have it placed in a gallery in America. I refused to accept the picture as a gift, and, remaining firm, Mr. Browning finally named the moderate sum which I paid for the picture. At a later date I purchased the two pictures that I gave to the New York and Boston Art Galleries, thus carrying out my desire to evince to the son my gratitude for the enjoyment and help I had found in his mother's poems" (p. 689). There are subtle differences of emphasis in Browning's and Mrs. Bloomfield-Moore's accounts of this transaction.

1. Colvin published a *Life of Landor* (1881) for John Morley's "English Men of Letters" series. In the prefatory note he wrote: "To Mr. Robert Browning in particular my thanks are due for his great kindness in allowing me to make use of the collection of books and manuscripts left him by Landor, including

With respect to the admirably dramatic *endings* of many of the dialogues,—besides the "Bacon and Hooker," notice the closing lines of "Peter and his Son," "Elizabeth and Mary"—"Johnson and Horne Tooke"—but you will have noticed and appreciated these and other examples—as that of "Tasso and his Sister." [2]
[Huntington].

To Mrs. Charles Skirrow

19. Warwick Crescent, W.
Feb. 28, '82.

Dear Friend,

"Engaged"—sad to say—on the 19th of March—need I say more? unless that I am ever

affectionately yours
[Schiff]   R. Browning.

To Sidney Colvin

19. Warwick Crescent, W.
March 21, '82.

My dear Colvin,

I entirely agree with you as to the propriety of spelling Landor's words in the usual way. I don't think the subsequent modifications of his system, in books latterly published, came from himself: they were mainly coaxed out of him by Forster's desire to help the poems by removing so obvious a stumbling-block—and so especial a godsend to the critics of his day who would thankfully devote half of an article on "Gebir" to merriment over "messager," or some such word, which occurred there.[1] At the same time, I would leave on

---

Landor's own annotated copies of some of his rarest writings, and a considerable body of his occasional jottings and correspondence." It was to Browning, therefore, that Colvin submitted a letter which, one may assume, presented Mrs. Julia Landor's defense against what was being said of her relations with her husband, Walter Savage Landor.

2. Colvin was preparing *Selections from the Writings of Walter Savage Landor,* which was to be preceded by a critical preface. It is this preface which Browning has in mind in asking that Colvin consider the dramatic quality of many endings of Landor's *Imaginary Conversations*. The *Selections* appeared in 1882.

1. Colvin in preparing his *Selections from the Writings of Walter Savage Landor,* about which he is here asking Browning's advice, used Forster, *The Works and Life of Walter Savage Landor,* as the authority for his text. (See *Selections,* p. 355.)

record his practice—rational, in the main, and desirable as it really was—only, this generation does not desire it, and yet need not lose all the delight and instruction they may nevertheless get from his poetry relieved from perfects-in-t.

I am happy to hear of a second edition: *I pede fausto!* [2]

Ever yours sincerely

[Huntington]   Robert Browning.

To Mrs. Charles Skirrow

19. Warwick Crescent, W.
Apr. 18, '82.

Dear Friend,

I am vexed indeed to have to say—I can find the *dies* nowhere. They were always in one drawer of this desk—which drawer I have vainly ransacked. Can it be that they remained with the Stationer? If so, well: if not—your kindness must content itself with blanks where the impressions used to be.[1]

Yes, my toothache was removed after a day or two of pain enough. You ought to have had a more substantial holiday, but these spring days may in a manner supplement its deficiency. *I* get not one day out of the year, except the Autumn *outing,*—and even *that,* if we have to remove just then,[2] we shall hardly get, poor S. and

Your affectionate
R Browning

All love to the Husband.

[Schiff]

To An Unidentified Correspondent

19. Warwick Crescent, W.
Apr. 21, '82.

Dear Sir,

I am sorry that I can give you no information as to where the numbers of the original edition may be procured. You may oc-

---

2. Probably Colvin's *Life of Landor* for the "English Men of Letters" series, published in 1881. The verso of the title page of the copy in the Yale Library bears the words "Fifth Thousand," enough certainly for a "second edition." The Italian phrase Browning translates elsewhere as "Go ahead."

1. The dies were used to make letterheads for Browning's stationery, which was to be provided him this year as a birthday gift from Mrs. Skirrow.

2. See below, letter of August 30, 1882, n. 4.

casionally find some of them in Booksellers' Catalogues, I believe—at an absurd price.[1]

Yours obediently
Robert Browning.

[Huntington]

To Mr. and Mrs. Charles Skirrow

19. Warwick Crescent, W.
May 8, '82.

My two dear, very dear Friends—I could not be taken by surprise when the present arrived which your kindness had so long prepared me for: [1] and yet when it *did* arrive, and at this moment when I have just finished laying it away in my desk, the wonder is still as fresh as ever that you should be *so* kind to me—who, I will not say have so little deserved of you—for I have no wish to consider you as otherwise than altogether generous—whereby I may feel myself altogether, dear Friends,

Yours gratefully and
affectionately ever
Robert Browning

and your name too, Dear Mrs. Skirrow, is in that wonderful book of names of the donors of the wonderful Bookcase and Books which came to glorify my birthday yesterday.[2] Well,—let who may find "Life not worth living." *I* have had reason enough to enjoy it!

[Schiff]

1. Scribbled on the manuscript of this note in a hand other than Browning's are the words "re Bells and Pomegranates."

1. See letter of April 18, 1882, above, n. 1.

2. "On the poet's seventieth birthday he received, from the Browning Societies of Oxford, Cambridge, Cornell University, and others, a gift of a complete set of his own works, bound in olive green morocco, in a beautifully carved oak case, with this inscription: 'To Robert Browning on his seventieth birthday, May 7th, 1882, from some members of the Browning Societies. These members having ascertained that the works of a Great Modern Poet are never in Robert Browning's house, beg him to accept a set of these works which they assure him will be found worthy of his most serious attention.'" (Lilian Whiting, *The Brownings*, pp. 243–244.) This is item 458 of Sotheby, *Browning Collections*, p. 80. The presentation statement quoted there differs considerably from the one reported by Lilian Whiting. Probably her statement was taken from the "small volume containing autograph signatures and letters of the subscribers."

To Mrs. Charles Skirrow

19. Warwick Crescent, W.
May 10, '82.

Dear Friend, I shall be delighted to see you—but don't come till I let you know, in a day or two,—because a work of Pen's is to arrive which I should like you to see: it is due already from Paris.[1]

Yes, joyfully on the 11th and meanwhile and ever all love to you and your Husband from

Yours affectionately ever
RBrowning.

The case is the prettiest thing possible, and altogether I never had more gratification from any kindness at all of the same nature in my whole life.[2]

[Schiff]

To Mrs. Charles Skirrow

19. Warwick Crescent, W.
May 29, '82.

Dear Friend—I am *yours*—in the dining way as well as any other —on the 20th—as on the 11th. You did not write, but I remembered your verbal invitation,—being glad to have this confirmation of it, all the same.

Love to you both, and all best wishes from

Yours affectionately ever
Robert Browning.

The statuette—misdirected from Paris—has arrived long ago—at *the Station,* where it remains in a "box": we hope to get it tomorrow, and, any day afterwards, you can see it here.[1] Geo. Smith has carried off the new portrait, and I suppose you may see that also, should you care to take the trouble, at *Waterloo* Place: I wish you would.[2]

[Schiff]

1. Doubtless the bronze statuette of Dryope, 38 inches high, signed "R.B.B. 1882." (Sotheby, *Browning Collections,* item 1272; see letter of May 29, 1882, below.)
2. See letter of May 8, 1882, above, n. 2.
1. See above, letter of May 10, 1882, n. 1.
2. George Smith of Smith, Elder and Co., Browning's publisher, whose offices were at 15 Waterloo Place. The portrait is probably Pen's second oil paint-

To Mrs. George Washburn Smalley [1]

19, Warwick Crescent, W.
July 25th '82.
5 p.m.

Dear Mrs. Smalley,

I cannot help telling you at once that I have just seen Gen[era]l Merritt [2] who has in the kindest—(I may say, simply, American)— manner promised to get the little business—which yet would have been no little trouble to me—managed by to-morrow. This I owe your goodness, and do believe in the gratitude of

Yours affectionately
[Kenneth L. Knickerbocker]   R. Browning.

To Mrs. Charles Skirrow

Hôtel Vivard, St. Pierre de Chartreuse, Isère, F.
August 30, '82.

Dear Friend, I should certainly have written to you although in ignorance of where my letter would find you: now that I know how

---

ing of his father, done in 1882. The first, showing Browning in academic robes, went to Balliol College; the second is in the possession of Mrs. Reginald Smith, whose husband became a partner in the firm of Smith, Elder and Co. (Wilson, *Browning's Portraits*, pp. 132–133.)

1. Phoebe Garnaut, adopted daughter of Wendell Phillips, became Mrs. George Washburn Smalley in 1862. Her husband (1833–1916), American journalist, reported the campaigns of the army of the Potomac and possibly came to know General Wesley Merritt (see n. 2 below) at this time. Smalley organized the London bureau of the New York *Tribune* in 1867 and remained abroad as the *Tribune's* European correspondent until 1895. Smalley "knew everybody of importance in both England and America" and "did excellent service to the cause nearest his heart, the cementing of Anglo-American friendship and understanding." (*D.A.B.*) Browning's note to Mrs. Smalley attests to the helpfulness of these Americans. Smalley in his *London Letters* (1890) has much to say about Browning.

2. Wesley Merritt (1834–1910), American army officer, became a brigadier general of volunteers in 1863. He was assigned to frontier duty from 1866 to 1879, then was sent to England as Consul General, to serve with Lowell, who was United States Minister. On September 1, 1882 he became Superintendent of the U.S. Military Academy at West Point. Merritt has been described as a "fine looking man of strong will and wide experience . . . highly competent, and at the same time modest and agreeable." (*D.A.B.*) Apparently the favor Browning had requested of General Merritt through Mrs. Smalley was the obtaining of consular certificates. A letter closely antedating the present note of thanks and making the request for similar aid from the Smalleys, was with one other note to Mrs. Smalley, sold in December, 1949 to an unidentified purchaser by Robert K. Black, rare-book dealer of Upper Montclair, New Jersey.

to send a word or two straight to the aim, I do so joyfully. I forget whether you were informed of our projected visit to Ischia, where Mr. Cholmondeley has been residing of late.[1] I like him very much, and expected great pleasure from the beautiful place which I have only seen afar off, and so a month was to pass: perhaps you may have noticed in the papers the sad accident to Miss Wade—a guest of his, together with two of her brothers. C. wrote to me about it in great distress—saying that he should be obliged to go to England, but that his Villa was still at our disposition—and making various suggestions for our comfort should we incline to proceed there, which we have no mind to do under the circumstances. The poor girl must needs climb the Epomeo—a mountain he describes as "splendid but frightfully dangerous"—"to see the sunset and make sketches": at night, as she did not return, the brothers and many attendants with torches searched for two hours, and found her insensible in a ravine beneath a nearly perpendicular rock over which she must have fallen: there was plenty of help, but she died next morning, never having recovered her senses. Her father and mother were summoned from the Engadine, arrived in time to bury her,— and the establishment broke up as I tell you. It is useless now to observe on the strange carelessness of allowing a lady to go unattended on an evening expedition up a mountain known to be "frightfully dangerous": after the event one sees such a mistake only too clearly. Canon Wade was just about to officiate when the telegram with its news reached him—in the vestry of the chapel,—and he preached his sermon all the same, I hear.[2] Apart from my concern for Cholmondeley, and sympathy with the Wades,—neither my sister nor myself greatly care for the change in our journey: we shall take the old road to Venice, stopping a little at such towns as

1. Mr. Cholmondeley is described in the London *Times* account of the death of Miss Wade (see below) as "an elderly gentleman" who had leased Villa Sauvé as a vacation home for himself, "two young men and their sister, . . . a part of the family of the Rev. Canon Wade, . . . rector of St. Anne's in London and Canon of Bristol Cathedral." (August 26, 1882, p. 6, col. 3.) Mrs. Orr records that Browning included "Mr. Cholmondeley of Condover" in his rounds of country-house visiting. (*Life*, p. 289; see also *Burke's Landed Gentry*, "Cholmondeley of Condover," p. 405.)

2. The accident occurred on Saturday, August 12. The London *Times* account, cited in the previous note, reported that Canon Wade and his wife arrived "on Tuesday after the Saturday when the distressing accident occurred." The funeral took place at dawn of the following day.

we have left unvisited—Bergamo and Vicenza, for instance.[3] Of this little rough wild quiet and beautiful hamlet, there is nothing new to communicate: some few changes in our "Hôtel's" administration are for the better,—an experienced mother-in-law having taken the place of her baby-encumbered daughter, and the *cuisine* feels the difference: the great loveliness of the scenery, and still peacefulness of the solitary country remain unsurpassable, so far as my experience goes. The weather is fairly good,—judging by what one hears of it from every quarter: we had a magnificent week, to begin with,— then followed occasional rain and cold: but our walks have suffered little interruption, and at this moment the sun is bright, and I have climbed a bit of a mountain (no Epomeo!) and tramped over the ridge for two hours about, as my way is before breakfast. S. is taking her morning exercise at this moment,—and, after the arrival of the Po[st] we shall march together and earn our dinner. And, thus vegetating, we are in the middle of our fourth week of residence: we may stay a fortnight longer. That "Bill" for abolishing our poor little house has finally received Royal assent, and out we must go—where *into* is a mystery, which I shall be troubled to solve on my return: but we somehow manage to "fall on our legs" generally.[4] And now for *you*—after all this talk about our important selves: I am very glad that both of you enjoy your holiday so much —are so comfortably housed and in such good company: of "company" we have nothing to boast—a couple of purely French families, from Grenoble, who come for the good reason that they want mountain-air: an Englishman has never wandered this way,—the Grand Chartreuse being more accessible from other parts of the country. If the George Smiths are still with you, give them my love and tell them we shall expect to see them at Venice,—which was not so likely to be the case when we were bound for Ischia. As for Lady

3. Browning and his sister were balked in their attempt to reach Venice this year. Browning wrote to Mrs. Bronson expressing his regret: "As for the failure to get to Venice, we, my sister and I, have only regretted it once, that is, uninterruptedly ever since. . . . Besides the adverse floods and bridge breakings I was, for the first time in my life, literally lamed by what I took for an attack of rheumatism." (Katherine de Kay Bronson, "Browning in Venice," *Century Magazine*, LXIII, 576.)

4. This "Bill" was the Regent's Canal Bill. (Orr, *Life*, p. 375.) Browning was not to leave 19 Warwick Crescent until 1887 when a "threatened railway near the front of the house—an innovation never carried out—drove him away." (Sir Walter Besant, *London North of the Thames* [London, 1911], p. 150.)

Wolseley—one dares not pretend to vie with her in anxiety just now,—but my own pulses beat pretty strongly when I open the day's newspaper—which, by some new arrangement, reaches us, oftener than not, on the day after publication. Where is your Bertie? I had an impassioned letter, a fortnight ago, from a nephew of mine, who is in the second division of the Black Watch; he was ordered to Edinburgh, and the regiment not dispatched, after all,—it having just returned from Ind[ia]: the poor fellow wrote in his despair "to know if I could do anything!" He may be wanted yet: though nothing seems wanted in Egypt, so capital appears to be the management.[5] Well, I have given your goodnature plenty of exercise in this letter full of nothings—but you drew them on yourself: I daresay our vivacious old friend furnish[es] her due *quota:* she has been fully a fortnight at hom[e] and I can hardly suppose she will stay there in qui[et] much longer. She is full of the praises of that Italian C[ount]—whatever was the name—whom I sat by at Greenwich las[t] year, and who has been entertained at Shalstone.[6] Dear f[riends] both,—all love to you! S. is still out, but I may safely ad[d] her best wishes for you to those of yours ever affectionate[ly . . .]

[Schiff]   Robert Browning.[7]

5. On June 12, 1882, a riot in Alexandria resulted in the death of over 50 Europeans. On July 11 Admiral Seymour opened the fire of a British squadron upon the harbor fortifications of Alexandria and put the garrison to flight. "Sir Garnet Wolseley was sent out to Egypt before July was over, with an expeditionary force, the line taken being the necessity of protecting the Suez Canal, as the Egyptian troops were practically at large in the Delta." (R. H. Gretton, *A Modern History of the English People* [London, 1913], p. 88.) Browning's approval of the British intervention in Egypt was shared by most of his countrymen who knew little about the occasion for this strong-handed policy. In another letter Browning expressed the "sincerest hopes Wolseley may get done as soon, and kill as few people, as possible,—keeping himself safe and sound—brave dear fellow—for the benefit of us all." (Orr, *Life,* p. 344. This extract is taken from a letter to the Skirrows and represents the only letter from Browning to the Skirrows used by Mrs. Orr which is not among the present collection of Browning's letters to the Skirrows. Mrs. Orr has printed a portion of the present letter: from "If the George Smiths" to "management." Pp. 321–322.) Browning's particular worry over events in Egypt possibly involved thoughts of Pen and possible military service.

6. "Greenwich and Richmond are, classically, the two suburban dining-places." (Henry James, *English Hours,* with illustrations by Joseph Pennell [Boston, 1905], p. 161.) Shalstone Manor, Buckingham was the home of Mrs. Thomas Fitzgerald, who, doubtless, is the "vivacious old friend."

7. The bottom of the signature and a whole line of the complimentary close are cut away. The right margin of the last page of this four-page letter has been clipped so close that many of the margin-words are only partly visible.

To Mrs. Charles Skirrow

19. Warwick Crescent
Oct. 28, '82.

Dear Friend,

I was prevented from calling on you yesterday; and to-day—little as I expect you will safely be able to go and greet Sir Garnet [1]—I am bound to stay away. I write therefore to beg you to keep my belongings till I call for them—and (better still) for a five-minutes' talk with you—and to say that I will gladly dine with you and your Husband on the 11th.

All love to you both from

Yours affectionately ever,

[Schiff]   Robert Browning.

To Frederick James Furnivall [1]

19, Warwick Crescent, W.
Nov. 5, '82.

My dear Furnivall,

I return Mr. Symons' letter and the annexed Poem [2]—of which,

1. Sir Garnet Wolseley (1833–1913), after a brief but successful Egyptian campaign, returned to England a hero, first to Dover, then to London, where "in spite of wet, cold, and muddy streets, crowds assembled outside Charing-Cross Station on Saturday evening [October 28] to see and cheer" the conqueror of the rebellious Egyptians. (London *Times,* October 30, 1882, p. 8, col. 1.)

1. Frederick James Furnivall (1825–1910), Chaucerian and Shakespearean, founded the London Browning Society, the first meeting of which was held on October 28, 1881, with 300 persons in attendance. At this meeting Furnivall declared his feeling for Browning in these terms: "Browning is the manliest, the strongest, the life-fullest, the deepest, the thoughtfulest living poet, the one most needing earnest study, and the one most worthy of it." This came as an anticipatory answer to any who might say, as someone did, "My dear Mr. Furnivall, I think it is 300 years too early for a Browning Society." (*Frederick James Furnivall, a Volume of Personal Record* [London, 1911], pp. lxiv–lxv.) Furnivall became an intermediary for some of the many persons who wished to meet Browning, to ask him questions, or to submit samples of their work to him. The present letter is an example of such an intercession.

2. Probably Arthur Symons (1865–1945) who was to publish *An Introduction to Browning* in 1886. The preface to Symons' book of criticism expresses thanks to Browning for providing "almost inaccessible prefaces to some of his earlier works" and to F. J. Furnivall "for permission to make use of his *Browning Bibliography*." What the poem was which Symons submitted to Browning through Furnivall we are unable to say.

—pray assure him,—I never heard before and never wrote a word of—nor indeed have had the patience to read even now: it is a "holy fraud" apparently.

Ever truly yours
[Huntington]   Robert Browning.

To Miss Emily Henrietta Hickey [1]

19. Warwick Crescent, W.
Dec. 18, '82.

Dear Miss Hickey,

Thank you very much for the pretty dress you have given my play—just the appropriate one, I think, for your purpose [2]—which I wish, with all my heart, it may serve in any degree.

I and my Sister reciprocate your kind Christmas wishes. For myself,—you best know—yet I seem to guess at,—the infinite obligations I am under to you. You must be sure I am

Yours truly ever
[Yale]   Robert Browning.

To Mrs. Charles Skirrow

19, Warwick Crescent, W.
Feb. 9, '83.[1]

Dear Friend,—I am sure *I* was not sorry to find you were out on the day I called, and, moreover, to hear that you regularly went to fetch

1. Emily Henrietta Hickey (1845–1924) was the cofounder with F. J. Furnivall of the Browning Society. "In 1881 Miss Hickey expressed to Furnivall her admiration for the work of the noble Victorian poet; he decided that she ought to know Browning and took her to see him on July 3. She and Furnivall discussed the formation of a Browning Society and mentioned the project to Browning, who did not refuse permission." (*F. J. Furnivall: a Volume of Personal Record,* p. lxiii.) She became first honorary secretary of the Browning Society, a member of its committee, and laborer in the elucidation of Browning's works.

2. "The Tragedy of *Strafford* was studied during the Easter term by about three hundred pupils of the North London Collegiate School for Girls; and the interest shown in the Play was great enough to induce Miss E. H. Hickey to ask Mr. Browning's leave to make an annotated edition of it." (*Browning Society's Papers* [Second Report, July 6, 1883], I, x.) See letter to Miss Hickey on March 24, 1883. These two letters, taken together with the foregoing quotation, indicate that Miss Hickey may have prepared the preliminary text for school use.

1. In 1883 Browning was in London from January 1 to possibly mid-May; Paris, possibly mid-May to May 30; London, May 30 to soon after August 13;

Mr. Skirrow as usual. *That* was better than finding you on the sofa,
and fancying him alone in his glory "When the long hours of the
Public are past, and he thinks in the Brougham to be cosy at last!"
But to the immediate business: you know how gladly I go to you
at all times: I am much out of sorts, however, having caught a bad
cold some ten days ago, which obliges me to be careful: now, on
Wednesday I am obliged to dine with people to meet other people
I needs must see: and I do feel that your luncheon would stop that
proceeding altogether; for, even under the most favorable circumstances, I cannot manage two such outings in one day; and just now
either would task my strength sufficiently. I know you will understand and forgive

Yours affectionately ever
Robert Browning.

[Schiff]

To Frederick James Furnivall

19, Warwick Crescent, W.
March 1, '83.

My dear Furnivall,—These new remittances from America should
properly go to you [1]—Dulce decus et præsidium meum—(not that
the verse quite runs thus.) [2] I return your own kind and pleasant
letter: don't return what I myself send. I shall write to Prof. Moss.[3]

All regards to Miss Meta and to you—from yours ever

[Yale]   Robert Browning

Gressoney in the Swiss Alps including journey thereto, from soon after August
13 to about October 1; Venice (Palazzo Giustiniani-Recanati) including journey
thereto, about October 1 to December 8; en route to London via St. Gothard
and Bâle on December 9, Paris on December 10; London, December 12 for
remainder of the year.

1. The founding of the Browning Society did two things to encourage the
sale of Browning's works in America: it stimulated the founding of Browning
societies in all the chief cities; it reduced Browning's books "to less than half
their former price." (*Browning Society's Papers* [Third Report, July 4, 1884],
I, xvii.) It was also instrumental in securing a reliable publisher in America
for Browning's works, Houghton-Mifflin and Co.

2. "Mæcenas atavis edite regibus
   O et præsidium et dulce decus meum." Horace, *Odes* I, 1, ll. 1–2.
   Wickham's translation: "Mæcenas, in lineage the child of kings, but
   oh! to me, my protector, pride, and joy."

3. Unidentified.

To Miss Frances Power Cobbe [1]

19, Warwick Crescent, W.
March 3, '83.

Dear Miss Cobbe,

I am going presently to the Club and will write there, as energetically as I decently can, to the Members for Marylebone, for their vote.[2] I say "from the Club" because I can find their address in the Directory there—not having it here.

Ever truly yours

[Huntington]   Robert Browning.

To C. W. Deschamps

19, Warwick Crescent, W.
March 17, '83.

My dear Mr. Deschamps,

With respect to the International Fisheries' Exhibition,[1] I beg to say that my Son's picture,—which you so kindly recommended to

1. Frances Power Cobbe (1822–1904) became acquainted with the Brownings in Florence in 1858. A glance through the index to the *Life* of Miss Cobbe indicates her life purposes: "Reformatories and Ragged Schools," "The Sick in Workhouses," "Workhouse Girls," "The Claims of Women," "Claims of Brutes." She was, as she describes herself, "a willful woman," eager to make, one may add, her will the will of all. (*Life of Frances Power Cobbe by Herself* [New York, 1895].)

2. This note of Browning is in reply to the following request from Miss Cobbe: "Office of the Society for Protection of Animals from Vivisection, . . . March 2, 1883. Dear Mr. Browning: Now is the moment when, if you will send a line to Sir Thos. Chambers and W. D. Grant, expressing your wish that they should vote for Mr. Reid's bill on the *4th April*, you may do us very great service. A word from you will be worth 10,000 other voters. Ever yrs, most truly, Frances Power Cobbe. I enclose a leaflet to send with letter to M.P.'s." (*Browning's Letter File*, ed. Armstrong, pp. 95–96.) Browning's poem, "Tray," published in *Dramatic Idyls* in 1879, had shown his abhorrence of vivisection.

1. The International Fisheries Exhibition was held in London at the Gardens of the Royal Horticultural Society, South Kensington. It opened May 13, 1883. C. W. Deschamps was fine art superintendent in charge of setting up the art exhibition and handling "all communications respecting the purchase or sale of pictures." (*International Fisheries Exhibition, Official Catalogue* [London, 1883], p. xcii.)

the Melbourne Exhibition,[2] two years ago,—is already accepted by
the Committee and in print in their Catalogue.

Pray believe me, my dear Mr. Deschamps,

Yours sincerely,

[Yale]   RBrowning.

To Miss Emily Henrietta Hickey

March 24, '83.

Dear Miss Hickey,

I beg pardon for a little delay in answering your pleasant note—
which I managed to mislay but have found. I was much interested
in the Examination Papers, and glad that my play could be put to
such good use. You are quite welcome to edit and annotate *Strafford*
as you propose.[1] If there is any fresh printing to take place, you will
kindly treat with the Publisher—as before: [2] and the author will
know how to behave himself—as before—remaining as he did before and shall ever continue—

Yours most truly

[Huntington]   Robert Browning.

To Mrs. Margaret Raine Hunt

19, Warwick Crescent, W.
May 6, '83.

Dear Mrs. Hunt,

I did indeed both see the one beautiful picture and marvel that
I nowhere saw the other. If I understand you rightly that admirable

2. Pen exhibited "Stall in a Fish Market at Antwerp," a picture shown previously at the Royal Academy in 1879 and, as indicated here, at Melbourne in
1881.

1. *Strafford,* with notes and preface by Emily H. Hickey and an introduction
by S. R. Gardiner (London, 1884). "In annotating this play," Miss Hickey
wrote in the editor's preface, "I have had before me the probable needs of
students and the possible needs of teachers." With her request for permission
to edit *Strafford* Miss Hickey had evidently sent the examination on the play
set for the North London Collegiate School. See above, letter of December 18,
1882, n. 2; and *Browning Society's Papers,* I, 454.

2. This may refer to a school text of *Strafford,* or Browning may be identifying Miss Hickey's editing with the work of the Browning Society. Furnivall
had reprinted Browning's "Essay on Shelley" after getting "leave from the
Writer and the representatives of its Publisher." ("Foretalk," *Browning Society's Papers* [1881], p. 3.) Moxon was the publisher treated with "as before."
Smith, Elder and Co. held the rights to *Strafford.*

"morning on the Thames" was absolutely *rejected* [1]—not excluded for want of room,—and *that* I *do* understand to be—well, past understanding! As the Spanish proverb has it—"Patience, and shuffle the cards!"

For my own motto—glorified by its application—I am properly grateful.

Yours truly ever
Robert Browning.

[Huntington]

To Mr. and Mrs. Charles Skirrow

19, Warwick Crescent, W.
May 9, '83.

Dear Friends, all the waiting in the world will do no good; and, two days after the reception of your most valued of presents and kindest of letters,[1] I find myself just as far from being able to thank you properly as I was at the moment. You do not want the expression of the love and gratitude which you must well know exist and always will continue to do so in the case of

Yours affectionately ever
Robert Browning.

[Schiff]

To Mrs. Charles Skirrow

19, Warwick Crescent, W.
May 31, '83.

Dear Friend, I only returned from Paris last night—hence the delay in replying to your kind letter and its invitation. All next week I see no escape from one engagement or another: will it suit you to have me on Tuesday 12th? If so—I shall enjoy seeing you, and be glad to meet any friend of yours. S. is at Shalstone [1] for the moment, but will be back immediately.

Ever, with love to you both,
Yours affectionately,
Robert Browning.

[Schiff]

1. A. W. Hunt's picture called "A North Country Stream" (with descriptive verses: "Summer redundant, Blueness abundant") was exhibited by the Royal Academy in 1883. (Graves, *The Royal Academy of Arts: A Complete Dictionary* . . . *1769–1904*, IV, 196.)

1. It was the custom of the Skirrows to mark Browning's birthdays (May 7) with gifts and greetings.

1. The home of Mrs. Thomas FitzGerald, who is described by Mrs. Orr

To Mrs. Charles Skirrow

19, Warwick Crescent, W.
[June–July, 1883?] [1]

Dearest Friend,—I meant to call myself with the book which I have quite done reading. I send with it the Homeopathic work you wished to see. I have been far from well,—hence the delay. Mrs. Procter engages to do what is requisite in the matter of the introduction to the redoubtable Lady [2]—who leaves town this morning for a few days: on her return, all will be managed.

Ever affy. yours,

[Schiff]   RB

To Mrs. Charles Skirrow

19, Warwick Crescent.
July 20, '83.

Dear Friend,

I am always yours—and shall be particularly yours on the 30th as you have the goodness to desire. I got home excellently on Saturday, and so properly wound up a delightful evening's entertainment, thanks for which to my two beloved friends whose

I am, affectionately ever,

[Schiff]   Robert Browning.

---

as one of Browning's "constant correspondents." Mrs. Orr makes use of what must be only a small part of the total correspondence. (*Life*, p. 295.)

1. Above the letterhead in a hand other than Browning's is written "1884(?)." But see below, n. 2.

2. Probably Emma Lazarus (1849–87), an American poetess and controversialist, who received a letter of introduction to Mrs. Procter from Henry James dated May 9, 1883, a few days before Miss Lazarus sailed for England. James advised that the visit to Mrs. Procter should be made on a Sunday afternoon so that "Browning would be sure to be there." In early June, 1883, Mrs. Procter wrote to Miss Lazarus inviting her for "Sunday 24th" and added "I will engage Mr. Browning to come and meet you." (*Letters to Emma Lazarus*, ed. R. L. Rusk, pp. 53–54.) Apparently the meeting took place, and on the same day (June 24, 1883) Browning invited Miss Lazarus to visit him on the following Saturday (p. 65). The adjective "redoubtable" describes Miss Lazarus' vigorous militant defense of the Jews which won for her "everywhere tokens of an international reputation" (*D.A.B.*). See Browning's reference to the death of Miss Lazarus in 1887 from cancer. (*Letters*, ed. Hood, p. 277.)

To Felix Moscheles

19, Warwick Crescent, W.
Aug. 4, '83.

My dear Moscheles,

What illustrations can you find better than the two first lines of that Poem of Shelley's which your pictures suggested to me yesterday? Call the combined pictures "The Cloud"—then write over No. 1.

I bring fresh showers to the thirsting flowers
From the seas and the streams.

and over its companion,—

I bear light shade for the leaves when laid
In their noonday dreams.

"Dispersing the clouds" (No. 1) would bring a shower.
"Compelling them" (No. 2) brings a shade, surely! [1]

Ever yours,

[New York Public Library] R.B.

To C. W. Deschamps

19, Warwick Crescent, W.
Aug. 13, '83.

Dear Mr. Deschamps,

I am just on the point of leaving London, and may not return before the Fisheries' Exhibition closes.[1] Should that be the case, will you have the kindness to see that the "Fish-Stall" [2] is carefully re-

1. In his *Fragments of an Autobiography*, pp. 327–329, Moscheles tells of the episode leading to the writing of this letter: "I was at work on one or two companion pictures which, for want of a better title, I had called 'The Cloud-Compeller' and 'The Cloud-Dispeller.' In the first a deep-toned figure gathers the rolling clouds together; in the second a brighter child of the skies peeps out from behind them.

" 'You might take some lines from Shelley's "Cloud" for those pictures,' suggested Browning. . . .

"And . . . he recited the whole poem. . . .

"The next day I received a letter from Browning indicating the particular passages from Shelley's poem which he thought would be suitable to my pictures."

1. The exhibition closed on November 1, 1883 while Browning was in Venice.
2. Pen's picture "A Stall in the Fish Market at Antwerp." Pen received a gold medal for exhibiting the best of four still-life pictures. (*International Fisheries Exhibition*, Awards of the International Juries, p. 63.)

moved to the place whence it was taken,—21, Queen's Gate Place, S.W,—?

Yours very faithfully

[Yale]   Robert Browning.

To Mr. and Mrs. Charles Skirrow

Hôtel Delapierre, Gressoney, St. Jean,
Val d'Aosta, Italia.
[August 30, 1883] [1]

Dear Friends, I might have written somewhat earlier than I do,—but, on our arriving at this place, there were some reasons for apprehending we might need to go elsewhere. These are gone by, however—and in all likelihood we shall stay here at least a fortnight longer, and then keep to our original plan of spending a month at Venice. Now, where is Gressoney? Why, simply the most beautiful little cluster of cottages nested in a valley or rather pass through the Alps, just under Monte Rosa: we reached it in the only possible way—on mules, even our luggage being so (literally) "lugged" up a break-neck ascent—seven hours of continued clambering once at the top—or nearly,—for there is another Gressoney-la Trinité up higher still,—there is a [very] comfortable *Pension*, with a delicious Padrone, and everything to moderate heart's desire, though we are [5]ooo feet above the sea. Of all the retreats [I have made] acquaintance with, this is clearly the [most] eligible, and it appears to be all but unknown to the English—only resorted to by Italians in search of healthy coolness during the fierce heats below —and fierce enough we found them a fortnight ago at Turin [and] Ivrea, the towns by which one gets here: and, by all accounts, even now the life there is intolerable, while this morning sees our mountains white with last night's snow. Of course Monte Rosa is one huge white from crest to base. A little rapid river—the Lys—runs in the mid valley, white like the glaciers that feed it—and all round as far as one knows is *such* quiet and loveliness! It cannot lie hid forever. They purpose a carriage road, and are even now laying the telegraph wires: after all, there is some inconvenience in being

---

1. Browning and his sister arrived at Gressoney on August 22, 1883. A comparison of this letter with a note written to Furnivall on August 29, 1883 indicates that this letter to the Skirrows was probably written about August 29 or 30, 1883. (See *Letters*, ed. Hood, pp. 220–221.)

forced to send for—a dose of medicine, say—to Pont St. Martin—
a seven hours' journey. The air is all that one imagines perfect in
mountain-air, and it is doing me—and I hope, S.—abundant good:
we walked for two hours before breakfast this morning, and shall
presently get an appetite for dinner by the like means. When the
snow comes in good earnest we shall descend as we mounted, and
make for Venice. Is not this a pretty contrast to your gay life and
surroundings, pray? We get newspapers regularly, however, and
I have a book or two, and the days go by only too quickly. Talking
of newspapers,—you saw, I daresay, last week's *World* with its Letter. I cannot conceive what has made Mr. Yates so persistingly kind
to me ever since I have known him: it was never in my power to do
him the least service, social or literary,—yet he never lets slip an
occasion of saying a kind word—and, this time, much more than a
word about me: I am sure I am not ungrateful, however unable to
repay him for his goodness. If he did not himself write the Letter,
he inspired it—or at least allowed it, and I feel all the gratification
he can have wished to bestow—not the least part of it being that
Pen reads the paper regularly.[2] Pen's news are very pleasant too: he
has been hard at work at Dinant; finishing three large Landscapes,
—of which I hear good accounts, and,—as I hope to be assured by
to-day's post,—well forward with a subject from Shelley which
promises to be equally satisfactory. I wish I had been able to show
you, in those last hurried London days, his Statue of "Dryope fascinated by Apollo in the form of a Serpent"—it is successfully cast
in plaster, and will be produced in bronze at the end of the year.[3]
—Of course, by "Statue" I mean the photographs [from] the clay.
He gives me much delight, dear fellow! And much delight give,
and have given, and will give me the two dear friends I am probably
teazing with all this about me and mine: they will not so easily
teaze *me* however if they tell me—as I count on their doing—
equally minute details of their own adventures. How are you both?
How is the foot? Is Mr. Skirrow getting the rest he deserves? Is the

2. Edmund Yates (1831–94), novelist and journalist, founded the *World:
A Journal for Men and Women*, the first number of which appeared on July
8, 1874. (*D.N.B.*) On November 8, 1881, he sent Browning a note saying: "I
have taken the liberty . . . to send you a *World* every week, thinking it may
amuse you." (*Browning's Letter File*, ed. Armstrong, p. 90. See below, letter of
December 4, 1883, and n. 5.)

3. See below, letter of December 4, 1883, and nn. 2 and 3.

L

Bertie *ménage* [4] flourishing in all its branches? What old friends
have you met, what new ones made? I have not a single soul in London or England considerate enough to feed my hunger with gossip,
—everybody is away, and—in most cases—is I don't know where:
but I hold you, dear Mrs. Skirrow, to your word, and shall expect
liberal things in as many days as it will take you to reach me. The
very outside of your letter will bring back the banquets at the
"Ship," [5] and the Dinners, and the Luncheons, and the years' round
of such favors as never were! Well, I must leave off. S. sends her true
love to you both, and for me—what can I send that you have not
already and long ago got?—my most affectionate regards and best
wishes of all kinds—being as I am ever yours

[Schiff]   Robert Browning.

To William James Linton [1]

Venice, Oct. 29, '83.

Dear Sir,

I am obliged to refer you to Messrs Smith and Elder for the permission to publish the poems you mention.[2] They exact a Fee in
every instance.

I remain, Dear Sir,
Yours obediently
[Yale]   Robert Browning

4. Albert Edward, Prince of Wales, known in "the family circle" as "Bertie."
(Sidney Lee, *King Edward VII* [London, 1925], I, 7.) During the late years of
the century-the Prince spent three weeks of August in Wiesbaden or Homburg.
Mr. and Mrs. Skirrow regularly spent their vacations in Homburg.

5. There is a pen drawing of The Ship, Greenwich, a "celebrated hotel" on
the banks of the Thames, by Joseph Pennell in Henry James, *English Hours,*
facing p. 162. Henry James describes the dinner at Greenwich as "the most
amusing of all dinners." "It begins," he says, "with fish and it continues with
fish: what it ends with . . . I hesitate to affirm . . . We eat all the fish of the
sea, and wash them down with liquids that bear no resemblance to salt water.
We partake of any number of those sauces with which, according to the French
adage, one could swallow one's own grandmother with a clear conscience" (pp.
161–162).

1. William James Linton (1812–97), wood engraver, poet, and anthologist,
was born in London but in 1866 moved to America where he remained until
his death. He established the Appledore Press in Hamden, Connecticut, in
1878. He was, while in England, an intimate of R. H. Horne, E.B.B.'s great
friend.

2. *English Verse*, ed. W. J. Linton and R. H. Stoddard (New York, 1883)
consisted of five volumes of selections. In the volume entitled *English Lyrics*

To Miss Emily Henrietta Hickey

Palazzo Giustinian-Recanati,
Venice, Nov. 30, '83.

Dear Miss Hickey,

I return the "Proofs," corrected as far as possible,—having, besides altering errors, changed a word or two, so as to strengthen the verse a little.[1] Observe,—I have only received the thing, and consequently corrected it, up to page *64:* there occurs a gap which ends at the *slip 73.* If you send the missing part—and, if you please, the *notes,*[2] I will return them at once. Never scruple,—pray,—to ask for such easy service from one you have so greatly obliged as

Yours truly ever

[Huntington]   Robert Browning

To Mr. and Mrs. Charles Skirrow

Palazzo Giustinian-Recanati,
Dec. 4. '83.

My two dear Friends,—yes, it *is* the 4th—and on the 4th of October did we arrive here for "a short stay": but as to going away,—*that* was too hard, with such kind compulsion from our Hostess,[1] and a

---

of the XIXth Century E.B.B. is represented by seven poems (including four sonnets) and Browning by three poems, all short, and two stanzas from "In a Gondola." In the introduction Browning is described as "the subtle dramatist who has poured his own heart's blood into Sebald and Ottima, Colombe and Valence, and a score of other live men and women" (p. xxvii). A scene from *Colombe's Birthday* appears in the volume called *Dramatic Scenes and Characters.*

1. See letter of March 24, 1883, above, and nn. In the editor's preface to Miss Hickey's edition of *Strafford* Browning is thanked "for his readily given permission to issue this edition of *Strafford;* for his explanation of three or four passages . . . and for his revision of the text." (*Strafford . . . by Robert Browning* [London, 1884], p. vii.) Miss Hickey's edition of *Strafford* really represents a text with notes, all of which had received Browning's own editorial sanction.

2. Browning evidently received the notes, read them carefully, and gave Miss Hickey suggestions for improving them. She expresses special debt "to him for most of the note on V. 2. 40."

1. Mrs. Arthur Bronson, who describes the Palazzo Giustinian-Recanati as "in some respects worthy of a poet's sojourn" with its long history and its "fine façade, with Gothic windows looking out upon a court and garden, and a southern exposure." (Katherine deKay Bronson, "Browning in Venice," *Century Magazine,* LXIII, 580–581.)

continuance of wonderful weather,—weather unexampled, say the inhabitants. During these long months—one rainy day and no more! On all the others we took our usual walk; and, three days ago, there were butterflies enlivening the garden-plants still in flower: it is cold now,—and there is an end to the insects: but still-fine weather, to my mind: indeed on Sunday we were witnesses of a *baruffa* or "row"—a posse of women screaming for *water*—which the Municipality was bound to supply their *quartieri* with,—all its wells being dried up. And you have fancied, I dare say, my own little well of memory and gratitude somewhat low and scanty of tribute: but, from week to week, I have been uncertain as to what course was to be determined on,—and only now is it certain,—if one may say so,—that next Saturday is our doomsday. This sounds wickedly—for I have abundant reason for wanting to be at home, (after four months' absence)—and no few friends to make my return joyful enough: but only a poor creature has just one side to his soul. We take the St. Gothard route, —a novel experience,—sleep at Bâle, and reach Paris on Tuesday,— no, Monday evening, Tuesday we spend there with Pen, and—if his pleading for "at least two clear days" can be resisted, we are in our own beds on Wednesday night. Pen has much to show us,—besides himself,—his statue of "Dryope" [2] has gone to be cast in bronze, but he sends me four different views of it in photograph, by which I see the work he has bestowed on it even since it was rendered in plaster: he has made also two new Busts—photographed also,—really good original things: and has brought to Paris his summer studies at Dinant, three large landscapes which are attracting much attention from people whose criticism is worth notice.[3] The dear old fellow is not idle, you see!

I ought to have written earlier were it only to say—what however "goes without saying"—that I will most readily put my name— whatever its worth may be—to any petition in favour of Mrs. Dutton Cooke: it could not be done by proxy, of course: but if you let me have the paper as soon as I return, it shall go back to you an hour

2. First done as a statuette. It is item 1271 of Sotheby; *Browning Collections,* p. 149, described as follows: "A large bronze Statue of Dryope fascinated by Apollo, in the form of a serpent; 6 *ft.* 4 *in.* high. Exhibited at the Grosvenor Gallery, 1884, on the intercession of the artist's father, after being rejected at Burlington House."

3. One of these busts is probably item 1273 of Sotheby, *Browning Collections.* The landscapes are possibly items 27, 30, and 32.

after I have signed it.[4] I see nothing, by the way, of the business in which Mr. Yates is concerned, and sincerely hope that the adversary is tired of his proceedings—so uselessly vindictive.[5] Bless us, if there were a prosecution imminent on all reported gossip in Venice! One of the gondoliers of our house here—or rather his wife—obliged the population by contributing three babies to it,—short-lived things: and we heard the other day that, during their life and (I rather think) after their death, they were exhibited daily at our dinner-table. Poor Don Carlos went, out of curiosity and good-nature, to see—and fee—the mother,—and at once got credited with the paternity: and the mother herself was said to have been all but slain by the scent of his pocket-handkerchief.

I could perhaps amuse you by some better scribbling,—but I am pressed for time, this afternoon—the little matters that ought to have been done long ago, pressing all at once to be dealt with—and S. is waiting for me to go with her to a shop "just at the foot of the Rialto." This will be enough if you know by it that she and I are never consoling ourselves for leaving Venice without remembering that our dear Friends are in London. So, with her love and mine to you both, I am ever

Affectionately yours,

[Schiff]   Robert Browning.

4. Edward Dutton Cooke (1829–83), dramatic critic, died suddenly of heart disease on 11 September 1883. (*D.N.B.*) He was survived by his wife, Linda (Scates) Cooke who had studied piano at the Royal Academy and had become a well-known pianist. It was doubtless through this talent that Browning became acquainted with the Cookes. The petition was probably circulated to provide some kind of aid for Mrs. Cooke.

5. "In January, 1883, there appeared in the *World* a libellous paragraph referring, though not by name, to the Earl of Lonsdale." (*D.N.B.*) Suit was entered against Yates in December, 1883. (London *Times,* December 10, 1883, p. 4, col. 1.) On April 2, 1884 he "was found guilty of criminal libel . . . and after the failure of an appeal, was in January 1885 sentenced to four months' imprisonment. He was released after seven weeks, but the incident left a permanent mark on him." (*D.N.B.*) While his appeal was being acted upon he wrote a note of appreciation for Browning's sympathy on May 17, 1884: "Our friend Mrs. Skinner [Skirrow?] tells me of your kind expressions of sympathy with me in my present trouble, for which I am heartily obliged." *Browning's Letter File,* ed. Armstrong, p. 98.) See above, letter of August 30, 1883, n. 2.

To [MRS. FRANK HILL?] [1]

19, Warwick Crescent, W.
Dec. 17, '83.

Dear Friend, it was a real vexation to me that I found myself unable to go to you yesterday as I had hoped I might. I arrived three days ago—but have to pay a visit in the country this afternoon: next Sunday I shall hope to see you,—hear all about you, and tell [?] as much of my own news as you may care to know.

With all regards to Edith, believe me

Ever affectionately yours

[Baylor]   Robert Browning

To MISS EMILY HENRIETTA HICKEY *

To MISS EMILY HENRIETTA HICKEY

Hatfield House, Hatfield, Herts [1]
Dec. 19, '83.

My dear Miss Hickey,

I suppose we may preferably read "The Rights we claimed"—returning the capital letter, to show the particular claim: and, at page 7., one might change "Bill" to simply "prayer." [2]

Ever yours truly

[Huntington]   Robert Browning.

1. On the reverse of this letter, perhaps in the handwriting of Sarianna Browning, appears this notation: "Mrs. Frank Hill, 3, Morpeth Terrace, Victoria Street, Westminster, S. W." (Information provided by Dr. A. J. Armstrong of Baylor University.)

* The letter to Miss Hickey dated December 17, 1887, printed on pp. 353–354, below, was misdated by Browning and should be read here.

1. Hatfield House—one of the country homes "more like a palace"—was the property of the third Marquess of Salisbury, Robert Arthur Talbot, who became Prime Minister in 1885. This magnificent establishment is described in detail, with floor plans and pictures of the exterior, in *Victoria History of the County of Hertford*, ed. William Page (London, 1912), III, 92–101. It was here that the Shah of Persia was entertained during his visit to England in July, 1889. (London *Times*, July 6, 1889.)

2. The change of "Bill" to "prayer" occurs in I, i, 204.

To Mrs. Charles Skirrow

19, Warwick Crescent, W.
Dec. 22, '83.

My dear Friend,

I did get your letter to Portland Place,—but I was just on the point of starting for the Country,[1] and foolishly have delayed saying, —what, however, needs no saying at all,—that I was sure of the kindest of welcomes from you, and as sure that my greeting was quite as sincere. Yes,—I will gladly dine with you on the 6th. Sarianna is as well and as loving "to-you-wards" as ever,—and I am yours and your Husband's ever affectionate

[Schiff] Robert Browning.

To Mrs. Louise Chandler Moulton

19, Warwick Crescent, W.
Dec. 25, '83.

Dear Mrs. Moulton.

I am only just returned to Town,—hence a delay, for which I apologize, in replying to your letter of three days ago. I make haste to say that, should the day and hour suit your convenience, I shall be happy to see you here on Thursday at 3. p.m. If you are already engaged, pray mention a time which allows you to call—as you so kindly propose to do.

Believe me, dear Mrs. Moulton,

Yours very truly

[Library of Congress] Robert Browning

To Miss Mary Gladstone [1]

19, Warwick Crescent, W.
Dec. 28, '83.

Dear Miss Gladstone,

In common with everybody, I read while abroad Mr. Gladstone's translation of Cowper's Hymn, and noticed a prefatory remark that

1. See letter of December 17, above. Portland Place was the London home of Mr. and Mrs. George Henry Lewis. (See letter of May 9, 1876, above, n. 1.)

1. Mary (Gladstone) Drew (1847–1927), daughter of the Prime Minister, apparently met Browning in 1870, at which time she described him a "very agreeable" but "not an altogether remarkable person to look at." (*Mary Gladstone . . . Her Diaries and Letters,* ed. Lucy Masterson [New York and Lon-

there existed few or no Hymns, original or translated, in Italian—
so much, at least, was implied, if I remember rightly. In Venice, I
attended the interesting Waldensian Service held there, and fancied
that Mr Gladstone might care to look over the Hymnal in use—of
which I venture to send a copy.²

Pray believe me,—with all good wishes proper to the Season,—
Dear Miss Gladstone,

[Huntington]

Yours very sincerely
Robert Browning.

To Frederick James Furnivall

19, Warwick Crescent, W.
Jan. 11, '84.¹

My dear Furnivall,

The little things have come at last, and here they go begging
your acceptance—old Venetian, or rather Bassanese Majolica.² They
will be, at all events, conspicuous in your room—therefore, "When
these you see, Remember me"—who am

[Mrs. Olive M. Furnivall]

ever affectionately yours
Robert Browning.

---

don, 1930], p. 53.) In 1877 she speaks of him as "old Browning . . . with his
dreadful voice" and tells how he "places his person in such disagreeable
proximity with yours and puffs and blows and spits in yr. face" (pp. 116–117;
entry under March, 9, 1877). In 1880 she still "was bored by Browning" (p. 191;
entry under March 29, 1880). On August 7, 1880, she wrote to Browning thanking him for his "warm-hearted letter." *Browning's Letter File,* ed. Armstrong,
p. 83.) From this time forward Miss Gladstone showed a growing warmth and
sympathy for Browning and called his death "an ungetoverable loss." (*Diaries,*
p. 411.) On July 20, 1880, she heard Browning read "the Russian idyll, 'Up in a
Villa' and 'Andrea del Sarto'" at Lady Airlie's and found his voice "worse
than I thought, but certainly he acts it well" (p. 204).

2. Mrs. Bronson records that Browning "on each one of his arrivals in
Venice . . . took up his life precisely as he had left it. On Sunday morning he
always went with his sister to the same Waldensian chapel, in which they
seemed to take great interest." ("Browning in Venice," *Century Magazine,*
LXIII, 581.)

1. In the year 1884 Browning was in London from January 1 to April 14; in
Edinburgh from April 14 to 20; in London again until early in the week of
August 11; at St. Moritz until October 1; and in London again from October
3 until the end of the year.

2. Bassano, an ancient walled town in the Vicenza province of Italy, became
famous as early as the fifteenth century for its manufacture of very colorful
majolica.

To Mrs. Charles Skirrow

19, Warwick Crescent, W.
Jan. 16, '84.

Dear Friend, do forgive the hurry in which I wrote this morning—
all through a fear of detaining your servant: I never observed the
postscript of course. Sad to say, I have already disposed of next Sunday evening,—no need to add how much I wish I could give it you.

Ever affectionately yours
Robert Browning.

I called this afternoon on the very charming lady whose recitation
I missed.[1]

[Schiff]

To Miss Emily Henrietta Hickey [1]

19. Warwick Crescent, W.
Feb. 15, '84.

Dear Miss Hickey,

I have returned the Proofs [2] by post,—nothing can be better than
your Notes—and, with a real wish to be of use, I read them carefully that I might detect never so tiny a fault,—but I found none—
unless (to show you how minutely I searched) it should be one that
by "thriving in your contempt" I meant simply "while you despise
them, and for all that, they thrive and are powerful to do you
harm." [3] The idiom you prefer—quite an authorized one—comes
to much the same thing after all.

You must know how much I grieve at your illness—temporary
as I will trust it to be. I feel all your goodness to me—or whatever in

1. Probably the American recitationist, Cora Urquhart Potter, who was to
dedicate her volume *My Recitations* to Browning in 1886. (See below, letter of
September 3, 1886, n. 5.) There is a full-length photograph of "the very charming lady" as frontispiece in *My Recitations*.

1. This letter was published in Orr, *Life* (p. 335). We republish it here from
the original manuscript in order to complete the record of Browning's dealings
with Miss Hickey about *Strafford*.

2. The proofs were those of Miss Hickey's annotated edition of *Strafford*
with an introduction by Samuel R. Gardiner, prepared under the auspices of
the London Browning Society. See above, letters of December 18, 1882, March
24, 1883; and below, December, 17, 1887.

3. *Strafford*, II, ii, 188–189.
   "A breed of silken creatures lurk and thrive
   In your contempt."

my books may be taken for me—well, I wish you knew how thoroughly I feel it—and how truly I am and shall be

Yours affectionately

[Yale] ·   Robert Browning

To Mrs. Anne Thackeray Ritchie [1]

19, Warwick Crescent, W.
Feb. 15, '84.

Dear Mrs. Ritchie,

As the sailors said in answer to Nelson's sublime "England expects etc."—still more sublimely in a tantrum—"Do our dooty? Why, o'coorse we will!"—I hardly thought Mr. Cornish, who wrote to apprise me there was duty to do, would need assuring that I shall be there on Monday to vote and—what I can—help: I put down my name on his paper a week ago—"o'coorse." [2]

Ever truly yours

[Huntington]   Robert Browning

To Mrs. Charles Skirrow

[March 2, 1884] [1]

Dear Friend, kindest of the kind, extend your kindness, if possible, to forgiving me the delay in replying to your letter yesterday—I was away from home all day. I am wholly yours and Salvini's [2] on the 16th— On the 12th I see I am unluckily engaged. How magnificent *Lear* was last night!

Ever, in utmost haste,
Yours affectionately

[Schiff]   RB.

1. Anne (Thackeray) Ritchie (1837–1919), had been known to Browning since 1853, when she was a girl of 16, and amused Pen Browning by drawing pictures for him. (*Letters of Anne Thackeray Ritchie*, ed. Hester Ritchie, pp. 56–57.) The playfulness of this letter may be traced to their early association in Rome.

2. Blanche (Ritchie) Cornish—after 1896 Warre-Cornish—was Anne Thackeray Ritchie's sister-in-law. It was through this relationship that Mrs. Ritchie requested Browning's vote at the Athenaeum Club. Mr. Cornish was elected to the club in 1884.

1. This letter bears the note in a hand other than Browning's: "Ap. 1885(?)," but it is obviously the first of a sequence of notes in which Browning creates and then attempts to straighten out a confusion over a date with Mrs. Skirrow to see Salvini in *La Morte Civile*. Browning mentions "Lear . . . last night" in this note. Salvini's first performance of *Lear* occurred on March 1, 1884 (London *Times*, March 3, 1884).

2. See letter of March 4, 1884, below, n. 2.

To Mrs. Charles Skirrow

19, Warwick Crescent, W.
March 3, '84.

Dear Friend:

I was engaged, since a fortnight, to the Boughtons [1] for the 16th —but I do consider I have cause, in this instance, to appeal for an excuse to their kindness,—and I am doing so. I shall therefore be with you,—and greatly enjoy it,—next Sunday week.

Ever affectionately yours
Robert Browning.

I wrote yesterday to the Committee of the Athenaeum and again proposed Salvini as a guest,—and no doubt shall obtain their invitation: it is a social distinction perhaps,—hardly more in his case. [2]
[Schiff]

To Mrs. Charles Skirrow

[March 4, 1884] [1]

Forgive over and over again, Dear Friend—it *was* the 14th I meant for *La Morte Civile* [2] and not the 16th which is yours also. [3] Yes,

1. George Henry Boughton (1833–1905), printer and illustrator, was an exhibitor at the Royal Academy from 1863 to the time of his death. In 1865 he married Katherine Louisa Cullen. Boughton, doubtless, was one of the "artist friends" whom Browning found it "a never-failing pleasure to visit." (Felix Moscheles, *Fragments of an Autobiography*, p. 324.) "George Boughton and his audacious little wife were also devotees of the *bal masqué*, and many an amusing evening was spent at the house of this clever *genre* printer." (*Mrs. J. Comyns Carr's Reminiscences*, ed. Eve Adam, pp. 31–32.)
2. Browning had performed this service for the Italian actor before. In 1875 Salvini records that "the celebrated Browning proved his friendship by securing my admission as a guest to the Athenaeum Club." (*Leaves from the Autobiography of Tommaso Salvini*, pp. 169–170.) See following letter.
1. The note "1883(?)" has been penciled at the top of this letter. The reference to Salvini and the invitation to the Athenaeum Club, however, make it clear that this letter is an immediate sequel to the letter of March 3, 1884, above.
2. Giacometti's *La Morte Civile* with Salvini in the leading role was presented "for the first time in England" on March 7, 1884. "The prevailing gloom, unreality, and longwindedness of the author's sentiment failed to make much of an impression on the house." (London *Times*, March 8, 1884, p. 12, col. 3.) The result was that Salvini did not play this piece again during his stay in London. On March 14 he substituted Soumet's *Gladiator* for *La Morte Civile*. Browning saw this performance (see *Letters*, ed. Hood, p. 228) played at Covent Garden, which Salvini recalled as "an ice-house" with the audience sitting "in their overcoats and furs, the men with their collars turned up, and the women with their heads wrapped in shawls." As for Salvini, dressed for the

Salvini was magnificent indeed.[4] I sent him this morning a renewed invitation from the Athenaeum to be its guest during his stay.

All love!

[Schiff]   RB

TO AN UNIDENTIFIED CORRESPONDENT [1]

19, Warwick Crescent, W.
March 7, '84.

Dear Sir,

The incident of the "Ride" is altogether imaginary. I wrote the poem at sea, off the African coast, after many weeks' parting with a certain good horse "York," on whose back I would fain have found myself—hence the suggestion of a gallop in relief of an invested town whereto access, by a certain road hitherto impracticable, was discovered to be open for once. As I had no map, and wrote swiftly on the inside-cover of a book I was reading, the places mentioned were remembered or guessed at loosely enough.[2]

Commending this account to the indulgence of your young gentlemen, I beg to remain, Dear Sir,

Yours very faithfully

[Huntington]   Robert Browning.

---

fourth act in "silken tights," his "teeth chattered" before he went on stage. (*Leaves from the Autobiography of Tommaso Salvini*, pp. 220–221.)

3. Browning "got" Salvini for Mrs. Skirrow on Sunday evening, March 16 and apparently was importuned to get him for another London lady. (See below, letter dated March 16, 1884.)

4. Salvini opened a repertory season in London with *Othello* on February 28. He played *King Lear* on Saturday, March 1, and *Othello* again on Monday, March 3. (London *Times*, February 28, March 1, 3.)

1. As indicated in the complimentary close of this letter, the person here addressed was probably a teacher, seeking background for one of Browning's poems. The formation of the Browning Society in 1881 encouraged this sort of esoteric interest, an interest flattering enough to elicit, for the most part, cheerful replies from the poet.

2. Browning had already written two explanations of "How They Brought the Good News from Ghent to Aix" to inquirers. One of these, to Charles D. Browning (March 22, 1883), is a short account of the poem. (*Letters*, ed. Hood, pp. 215–216.) The other is the well-known account which appeared in the *Literary World XII* (March 12, 1881), 104, and which names "the book" as Bartoli's *Simboli*. See also William Clyde DeVane, *Browning's Parleyings: the Autobiography of a Mind* (New Haven, 1927), pp. 50–55.

To An Unidentified Correspondent [1]

19 Warwick Crescent, W.
March 16, '84.

Dear Friend, all thanks for your pleasant greeting. As for getting Salvini for either you, myself, or another Lady [2] who also witnessed as you did and wanted exactly the same thing,—I will do what I can, but confess that I despair of it. I have not yet seen him (off the stage) for I was unluckily out of the way when he called here last Sunday—he told my sister that every moment of his short stay here was engaged. I shall certainly see him this evening, however: and if I can with decency ask a second visit from him, I will assuredly do so: you understand the difficulty of the thing. The other Lady would have him dine with her. If he were going to remain a little longer, such pleasures—or pains—might easily be! But he goes, and is little likely to return, more's the pity!

Ever truly yours
Robert Browning.

Go and see him as often as is yet possible, and don't read the prigs in such corners as the *Saturday Review!* [3]
[Yale]

[To Mrs. Charles Skirrow?] [1]

19, Warwick Crescent, W.
March 25, '84.

Dear Friend, I need not say how greatly I shall value seeing the great and dear artist once again, if it is in my power to do so: I

1. This letter was printed, unannotated, by W. L. Phelps in the London *Spectator,* September 23, 1938. It is here transcribed from the original manuscript. Possibly this letter was addressed to Mrs. Eustace Smith. (See below, letter dated July 17, 1884, n. 1.) Salvini's season in London had begun at Covent Garden "at the end of February." The theater, like "an ice-house," had "constrained many to stay away" with the result that Salvini shortened his London stay. See *Leaves from the Autobiography of Tommaso Salvini*, pp. 220–221.

2. Mrs. Charles Skirrow most probably.

3. The critic for the *Saturday Review* (March 8, 1884) regrets that "the Italian tragedian" is not all "that his ardent admirers declare that he is" and then proceeds to attack his performances in *Othello* and *King Lear.*

1. This letter was printed, unannotated, by W. L. Phelps in the London *Spectator,* September 23, 1938; it is here transcribed from the original manuscript. A sheet of writing paper pasted to Browning's letter contains part of the last sentence of a letter ("quite right in not allowing him to go to the

accept therefore provisionally—because Pen has just arrived, while his works in painting and sculpture are delayed on the way,—and we are pushed into a very unpleasant corner, by the sending-in-day's close approach: the moment I know what time I can spare, you shall hear how I am circumstanced, depend upon *that!*

Pray send in the Italian lines at once to Ld. Wolseley: they are (to my notion) more lengthy than strengthy and I do not "take to" translating them successfully at this present: but I shall retain your copy, and if I *can* manage to make even a decent cotton purse out of a ——, you shall have my performance by Monday.

Ever affectionately yours

[Yale]
Robert Browning.

To Mrs. Charles Skirrow

19, Warwick Crescent, W.
March 31, '84.

Dear Friend, I would not send you a mere Circular to tell you that Pen's works will be on view to-day and till Tuesday, because I wanted to say something besides, and therefore have missed the Post, and only write this morning. First, then, I shall gladly accept your kindness to-morrow and be with you by 2. o'clock.—Pen, I believe, wih accompany me,—but he is loaded with work and may find it too hard—having to be back at the Studio by 3 p.m.—which, till 5 o'clock, is the reception time, at Miss Montalba's Studio, 11. Campden House Road *Mews:* [1] so that you need only consider him as a "squeezer-in," to be disposed of in a corner.

I am the more anxious to say this *now*, that this afternoon *may* possibly be the best time for you to come and see—as I know you will do if you are able. There are *no* stairs to climb, the Studio being on the ground-floor. Of course I hope for the delight of seeing

---

funeral") and the close: "yours sincerely, C. F. Skirrow." Below, on the same sheet, is this note: "The 'Great and dear artist' referred to is Salvini. Pen refers to his son Robert Barrett Browning."

1. Henrietta Sherritt Montalba (1856–93) was the youngest of the four artist daughters of Anthony Rubens and Emeline Montalba. She lived most of her life with her parents in Venice. Her sister Clara did the drawings for Mrs. Bronson's article, "Browning in Venice," *Century Magazine*, LXIII, 572 ff. She herself produced a terra-cotta bust of Browning which was exhibited at the Grosvenor Gallery, 1883. (*D.N.B.*)

dear Mr. Skirrow. There is the Statue,—with two Busts and three landscapes, with one large figure-picture.[2]

Ever yours affectionately
Robert Browning

I just hear that it is very unlikely Pen will be able to do more than "just look in."

[Schiff]

To Mrs. Anna Lea Merritt [1]

19, Warwick Crescent, W.
April 2, '84.

Dear Mrs. Merritt,

I was disappointed in my hope of being able to get away from my Son's Picture-show on Sunday and Monday.[2] He was here mainly to help me in that and similar matters: but there were too many friends of whom he was ignorant, and I was forced to stay—to my real regret.

Pray believe me, Dear Mrs. Merritt,

Yours very sincerely
Robert Browning

[Yale]

To Joseph Joachim [1]

19 Warwick Crescent, W.
April 5, 1884.

Dear Joachim, will this trifle answer the purpose? It is all I could do in so short a time, and has only its truth to recommend it. Take it, such as it is, with the love of yours ever

Robert Browning.

2. See letter of December 4, 1883, above, nn. 2 and 3.

1. Mrs. Anna (Lea) Merritt (1844–1930) was the daughter of a Quaker, Joseph Lea of Philadelphia. In 1865 she began a European tour which lasted for three years, and studied art with Henry Merritt. She first exhibited at the Royal Academy in 1871, and painted many portraits in London. She married Merritt (1822–77), art critic and picture cleaner, just a few weeks before his death. She was busy writing her memoirs at the time of her death. (*D.N.B.* "Henry Merritt"; *Who Was Who, 1929–1940,* "Anna Lea Merritt.")

2. See above, letter of March 31, 1884.

1. The verse appears, with signature and date, on the first page of the letter, the note, on the back. It was printed, unannotated, by W. L. Phelps in the London *Spectator,* September 23, 1938.

The Founder of the Feast

"Enter my palace"—if a prince should say—
"Feast with the Painters! See, in bounteous row,
They range from Titian up to Angelo!"
Could we be silent at the rich survey?
A host as kindly, in as great a way,
    Invites to banquet,—substitutes, for show,
    Sound that's diviner still, and bids us know
Bach like Beethoven; are we thankless, pray?

Thanks, then, to Arthur Chappell,—thanks to him
    Whose every guest henceforth not idly vaunts
"Sense has received the utmost Nature grants,
My cup was filled with rapture to the brim
    When, night by night,—Ah, memory—how it haunts!
    Music was poured by perfect ministrants
By Hallé, Schumann, Piatti, Joachim!" [2]

[Yale]

2. These lines were written in homage to Arthur Chappell and were first printed in the *World* on April 16, 1884. They have been reprinted in *Browning Society's Papers* [Meeting of January 30, 1885], Pt. VII, 18*; by Nicoll and Wise, *Literary Anecdotes of the Nineteenth Century* (1895), Vol. I; and in the Cambridge Edition (1895), p. 947. Browning, on a clipping from the *World*, deleted l. 9 and altered l. 10. This revised version appears in *New Poems by Robert and E. B. Browning*, ed. F. G. Kenyon (New York, 1915), pp. 49-50. Five persons are honored in this short poem, and all were intimately associated with the Popular Concerts at St. James's Hall. Arthur Chappell (d. 1904), part proprietor with his brothers of the music firm Chappell and Co., directed the Popular Concerts from their beginning in 1859 to the time of his retirement nearly 40 years later. It was his policy to present the best in classical music and to bring back, year after year, such distinguished musicians as Hallé, Clara Schumann, Piatti, and Joachim. The second of these policies produced, as Hermann Klein observes, "the warmest ties . . . between those who performed and those who listened." Klein adds that the latter included "some of the most prominent poets, painters and *littérateurs* of the Victorian era." (*Grove's Dictionary of Music and Musicians* [1935], IV, 229.) From the many pianists who appeared at St. James's Hall Browning chose for homage Sir Charles Hallé and Clara Schumann. Hallé (1819-95) was best known to Londoners for his performance of Beethoven's sonatas. Clara Josephine Schumann (1819-96), a superb pianist, came first to England in 1856, a few weeks before the death of her composer-husband, Robert Schumann (1810-56). She made annual visits, with few breaks, from 1867 to 1882, a period during which Browning was one of the most devoted supporters of the Popular Concerts. Alfredo Carlo Piatti (1822-1901), the greatest violoncellist of the nineteenth century, won acclaim on his first visit to England in 1844. From 1859 to 1898 he was a regular performer at the Popular Concerts and, along with Joachim, gave continuity to

To Mrs. Charles Skirrow

19, Warwick Crescent, W.
May 8, '84.

Dearest Friend, the first use I make of your munificent gift is to shew you, by its help, on what beautiful paper my next year's letters will be written, however they may come short of the beauty in their black character. You know that I never take up a sheet, nor fold and fasten it, without thinking of you and thanking you most heartily. I am sure I wish you and the dear Husband as much happiness,—almost,—as if I were not daily the happier for it: all which you know very well,—though I cannot resist saying it once more. As for the invitations,—that to the Theatre, and the other to the Richmond festivity I can and do accept with delight: the one about which I continue to be in doubt, will soon be mine to accept or regretfully forego, and you shall not be kept in suspense any longer than I can avoid, depend upon it!

All love to you both from
Yours ever gratefully

[Schiff]

Robert Browning.

To Mrs. Charles Skirrow

19, Warwick Crescent, W.
May 13, '84.

Dearest Friend, I delayed writing until I could say for certain whether the 28th was or was not mine to dispose of—and—as I thought would be the case— [1] I find that it is *not,* and I must keep another engagement. I shall be with you on the 16th and on the 15th of June,—and, if I could, would gladly see you every day of the year.

What can I say for the envelopes? You cannot listen to what I

the string quartet which year after year brought the best of chamber music to St. James's Hall. Joseph Joachim (1831–1907) has been called "the greatest master of the violin of his generation." He was "the presiding genius" of the Popular Concerts from the beginning "when he introduced the Rasoumowsky quartets of Beethoven and the chaconne of Bach." Thenceforward "his interpretations of Beethoven's concerto and of Bach's sonatas were universally recognised as models." (The facts for this note are taken from *Grove's Dictionary:* for Hallé see II, 498–499; for Joachim see II, 778–780; for Piatti see IV, 171–172; for Schumann see IV, 645–648. See also Popular Concerts, IV, 228–230, and St. James's Hall Concert Rooms, IV, 501.)

1. A word has been scratched through at this point.

shall say (to myself) whenever I use them—always with a fresh feeling of love for you and your Husband. Bless you both!

Yours affectionately ever

[Schiff]   Robert Browning.

To An Unidentified Correspondent

19, Warwick Crescent, W.
June 11, '84.

Dear Friend:

You know how delighted I should be to go to you on Sunday, were it in my power, but unfortunately I am engaged to spend the early afternoon at Richmond.[1] I need not say a word about my regrets,—nor assure you that I am ever

Affectionately yours

[Library of Congress]   Robert Browning.

To Mrs. Charles Skirrow

19, Warwick Crescent, W.
July 17, '84.

Dear Friend,

I have again and again wondered whether you were not out of town—it was stupid in me to leave that point so long uncleared up. I am very sorry you have been harassed as you inform me. On the 23d. I have promised to dine with Mrs. Eustace Smith,[1] or I would gladly go to the Play in your most pleasant companionship. Whenever I see you next you [shall][2] have the Photograph certainly. All love to your Husband and yourself as ever from

Yours affectionately

[Schiff]   Robert Browning.

---

1. Browning had been pledged to Mrs. Skirrow at Richmond for Sunday, June 15 since May 13, and possibly longer; see letters of May 8 and May 13.

1. Mary Eustace Smith was apparently another of London's lion hunters. On May 31, 1876, she wrote a desperate appeal to Browning asking "Can you explain what has happened to Salvini?" She adds, "I am in despair . . . I was looking forward with much pleasure to his dining here . . . which he had promised to do." (*Browning's Letter File*, ed. Armstrong, p. 68.) She was the wife of Eustace Smith (1835–1914), physician to H.M. the King of the Belgians and to the East London Hospital for children. He published three pioneering works on the diseases of children. (*D.N.B.* and *Supplement to Allibone's Critical Dictionary of English Literature*, ed. J. F. Kirk [Philadelphia, 1891], II, 1357.)

2. "Have" appears in the manuscript of this letter twice at this point. Browning repeats the word "have," instead of writing "shall have."

To Mrs. Charles Skirrow

19, Warwick Crescent, W.
Aug. 10, '84.

Dear Friend,—it is needless to say how much I should enjoy one more Greenwich Dinner [1] with you, but my days and hours here are numbered, we go to St. Moritz early next week, and I have only too much to do on Monday. I bid you farewell for—I trust—a short while only—assuring you and the dear Husband that I love you with all my heart, and shall never forget your kindness. My Sister sends her very best regards to you both, and I am ever affectionately yours

[Schiff]   Robert Browning.

To Mr. and Mrs. Charles Skirrow

Villa Berry, St. Moritz, Engadin[e]. S.
Sept. 13, '84.

Dear Friends,—if I did not write before, it was on account of the uncertainty about our movements just at the time when a letter ought to have been written. You know how we came to choose this place rather than Gressoney [1] where we did so well last year: the fear of a seven days' Quarantine effectually hindered us from entering Italy at once— S., you remember, was in no condition to bear much hardship: and our kind Mrs. Moore interposed help at the right time, and pressed us so warmly to be her guests that there was no refusing: we came accordingly, and passed a very pleasant week or ten days, when suddenly Mrs. M. was obliged to leave for America—to her great annoyance: there was plenty of telegraphing and being telegraphed to, and the end is that she went away a week ago, and must have started yesterday for New York.[2] She was very unwill-

1. "The month of August is so uncountenanced in London that," writes Henry James, "going a few days since to Greenwich, that famous resort, I found it possible to get but half a dinner. . . . All well-bred people leave London after the first week in August." (*English Hours*, pp. 161–162.)

1. Gressoney, in Val d'Aosta, is in the Italian Alps.

2. Mrs. Bloomfield-Moore records an interesting scene of parting from Browning: "To one of his chosen friends who said to him in parting (when most unexpectedly called away from the place where with Miss Browning they were passing the season together), 'Remember, I have loved you with the best and most enduring love—soul love,' he wrote,

Not with my Soul, Love!—bid no soul like mine
Lap thee around nor leave the Sense room."

It is apparent, of course, that Mrs. Moore herself is the "chosen friend" alluded

ing to leave this Villa, which she has taken till December, and where her poor daughter (whose mind is affected at times and whom we never see) remains with a couple of attendants—and hardly less unwilling was she to leave us,—but since it needed to be done, she made every possible arrangement for our convenience, and we remain her guests, in every sense of the word, as long as we please: we shall however not stay longer than to the end of the month, and hope to be at home in three weeks: the quarantine-difficulty is at an end—but our Venetian friend,[3] whose hospitality we were expecting to enjoy, is on her way to Paris and London. So, having got great good out of this beautiful place,—the like of which neither S. nor myself ever experienced,—we seem to have done our duty, and I shall be interested in passing an Autumn in London, although our travels are cut short by some six weeks. I suppose you know this St. Moritz. During the stay of Mrs. M. we made daily excursions to all the most picturesque passes and glaciers: since she went, we have walked long walks on the mountain and about it. The weather soon broke up—but to mend again: to-day is, I think, the worst specimen we have had,—the mountains snowed upon, and the plains drenched with heavy rain: but to-morrow may be as propitious as was yesterday, when we took every advantage of a real summer sun tempered by the wind fresh from the hill-tops. There have been many friends and acquaintance[s] here, but we don't come precisely for sociality: I was thoroughly glad to meet—some time ago—Mrs. Bancroft,[4] charming as ever: Mrs. F. G.'s [5] cousins, good-

to. Then she adds, quite rightly, that "Browning had more friends among noble-hearted women than fall to the share of many." (Mrs. C. J. Bloomfield-Moore, "Robert Browning," *Lippincott's Magazine*, XLV, 690.)

3. Mrs. Arthur Bronson. See above, letter of December 20, 1881, n. 4.

4. Mrs. Elizabeth (Davis) Bliss Bancroft (d. 1886) became the second wife of George Bancroft (1800–91), the American historian, in 1838. They spent much time abroad. Mrs. Bloomfield-Moore records that she requested Browning to write a quatrain, which she would cable, on Bancroft's eighty-seventh birthday. He did so "quick as thought." (Mrs. C. J. Bloomfield-Moore, "Robert Browning," *Lippincott's Magazine*, XLV, 686.) Bancroft's biographer says that the quatrain was accompanied by a note from Browning: "I chose a short metre with a view to saving your charges for the cable despatch!" (M. A. De-Wolfe Howe, *The Life and Letters of George Bancroft* [New York, 1908], II, 309.) The quatrain may be found in F. G. Kenyon, *New Poems of Robert Browning* (1914) and in the Macmillan edition in one volume (1914).

5. Mrs. FitzGerald of Shalstone Manor had one aunt, Mary Purefoy, who married the Reverend Francis Ellis. Ellis through his wife came into possession of Herriard Park and by royal license changed his name to Francis Gervaise.

natured ladies, are close by: so is Ly. Galway: [6] but the "company"-proper disappeared a fortnight ago, and the Baths, lower down, are a solitude,—shops shut and hotels empty. It is not impossible that on our way home we may pass through Brussels: the Triennial Exhibition [7] there, a considerable show, having treated Pen so handsomely. His Dryope could not be obtained from the Grosvenor till the beginning of August—and they excluded all works from the Exhibition after July the 25th yet on his sending the Committee a photograph, they "unanimously" granted him a delay: and have given the statue a capital place in the gallery. He is hard at work,—says a letter received yesterday,—painting in the open air "backgrounds of subjects he has in his head." See how I rely on your goodness for bearing with what interests myself considerably, but is hardly important to anybody else! Well, your goodness may be relied upon, and so may that of dear Mr. Skirrow. Both of you have my true love, as both of you know. S.—quite herself again—sends (orally, this time) her love along with mine. I shall send this to London,—though you may be still from home.

Ever affectionately, Dear Friends, yours

[Schiff]   Robert Browning.

To Barnett Smith [1]

19 Warwick Crescent, W.
Oct. 6, '84.

Dear Mr. Barnett Smith,

I returned to town on Friday Night,[2] though I was ignorant, till your letter informed me this morning, that any notice had been

Children of Mary Purefoy and Francis Gervaise of Herriard Park would be Mrs. FitzGerald's cousins. (*Burke's Landed Gentry,* "Gervaise of Herriard Park.")

6. Lady Galway (?–1891) was Henrietta Elizabeth Milnes before her marriage to the sixth Viscount Galway in 1838. She was the daughter of Robert Milnes and sister of Richard Monckton Milnes, first Lord Houghton.

7. "I am occupied this very day [August 7, 1884] in sending his statue of Dryope to Brussels, where the exhibition will give it a chance of being judged by better knowledge than is found here." (*Letters,* ed. Hood, p. 229.) Browning did not go to Brussels but left St. Moritz on October 1 and arrived in London on October 3. (See letter of October 6, below; and letter of September 28, *Letters,* ed. Hood, p. 230.)

1. George Barnett Smith (1841–1909), author and journalist, apparently became acquainted with Browning in the early Seventies and cemented a pleasant relationship by producing in 1876 "a memoir of Elizabeth Barrett Browning in

taken of the circumstance. My Sister and myself are in excellent
health, as you kindly desire may be the case.

With this, will also go to the Printer's the last revises of the Poem,[3]
—including a request that I may have at once a clean copy of the
whole: when this arrives, you shall have it immediately, with whatever information I can give about the time of publication—when
I get it from Mr. Smith,[4] whom I shall see as soon as I can. There
may be the greater delay in publishing that there are negotiations
going on in America about a simultaneous edition there,—and in
no case can the [5] publishing be done before Nov. 1, I believe.[6]

I hope that nothing but an attentive perusal is necessary to the
understanding of the book: but there are a few Persian names, and
allusions which you might like to be explained, and I will make a
note of these: any question you put to me on particular points requiring elucidation, I will try to clear up.

By all means give the *Times* [7] the preference—as you say, for the
book's sake as well as your own.

With kind remembrances from my Sister, and many regards to
Mrs. Smith, believe me

Yours very sincerely

[Huntington]   Robert Browning.

the ninth edition of the *Encyclopaedia Brittanica*" which so thoroughly satisfied
Browning of the honesty and capability of such a biographer that he made it
a "custom to send Smith proofsheets of his later volumes in advance, to enable
him to write early reviews." (*D.N.B.*)

2. October 3.

3. *Ferishtah's Fancies*, which appeared on Friday, November 21, 1884. (*Letters*, ed. Hood, p. 232.)

4. George Murray Smith, of the firm of Smith, Elder, and Co., Browning's
publishers from *The Ring and the Book*, in 1868, on.

5. The word "the" occurs twice in the manuscript at this point.

6. Houghton Mifflin Co. had through the good offices of the Browning Society become Browning's official publishers in America. This note appears on
the page facing the contents of the American edition of *Ferishtah's Fancies*:
"London, *October* 31, 1884. Messrs. Houghton-Mifflin and Co. are the authorized publishers of 'Ferishtah's Fancies' in the United States. Robert Browning."
The English edition appeared "simultaneously with the American edition."
(*Letters*, ed. Hood, p. 232.)

7. A two-column review of *Ferishtah's Fancies* appeared in the London
Times, November 18, 1884 (p. 4, cols. 5–6). What questions Smith put to Browning, if any, we do not know, but the reviewer probably had this letter in
mind when he wrote: "The thin disguise of Persian names and allusions which
the reader will encounter here really cover no deep-hidden purpose in the
poet's mind."

To Norman MacColl [1]

19, Warwick Crescent, W.
Oct. 13, '84.

Dear Mr. MacColl,

You were good enough to ask—now some months ago—whether I could let you have a copy of my forth-coming poem so that it might be put into good hands in time. I expect every day a clean set of "Proofs," and if you still wish so to dispose of them, I shall send them with great pleasure—trusting to your kindness which, I know, will not let me suffer from the critical Brotherhood who only receive the book in the regular way after publication. [2]

Ever truly yours

[Huntington]   Robert Browning.

1. Norman MacColl (1843–1904), reviewer for the *Athenaeum*, on hearing from Furnivall that Browning was about to publish a new poem (*Pacchiarotto*, 1876) proposed to the poet that proofs be sent so that a timely review might appear. Browning on June 13, 1876, gracefully refused. (*Letters*, ed. Hood, pp. 172–173.) By 1881, however, he had a working agreement with MacColl to give preference to the *Athenaeum* in information concerning his forthcoming poems, in return for cooperation from the *Athenaeum* in the way of helpful gossip about his son's pictures (pp. 203–204.) The present letter is the first indication that Browning had reached the point of sending proofs to MacColl and thereby attempting to "work the oracle" by favoring him, with Barnett Smith, above others of "the critical brotherhood."

2. MacColl's review of *Ferishtah's Fancies* appeared in the *Athenaeum* for December 6, 1884, in spite of Browning's word that the book would be released on November 21, Friday, the day on which the *Athenaeum* was published weekly. (*Letters*, ed. Hood, p. 232.) The delay may have been occasioned by MacColl's full-length treatment which ran to nine columns. Ironically, the best Browning achieved by favoring MacColl was the reviewer's admission that "Mr. Browning's admirers will welcome this volume." Otherwise, the poet is chided for such a line as: "Till she believes herself Simorgh's mate" because "Ferishtah, being a Persian, should have remembered Simorgh is not a male bird, but a 'right royal hen.' " MacColl then states the heart of his objection to the volume: "If the pessimism of the present day is to be confronted and answered, it is not by such an optimism as this."

To Mrs. Charles Skirrow

19, Warwick Crescent, W.
Oct. 30, '84.

Dear Friend,

I accept for the 15th with all the pleasure possible. I am delighted to think you are at home again, and that I shall so soon see you.

With love to your Husband,
Ever affectionately yours
[Schiff]   Robert Browning.

To Sir Theodore Martin [1]

19, Warwick Crescent, W.
Nov. 10, '84.

My dear Sir Theodore,

I received a Telegram, this morning, which apprised me of the signal honour offered by the Students of Glasgow,[2] and could only repeat the sorrow I have again and again felt at being obliged to—what shall I say?—"put it by." (In the middle of the last line, I was interrupted by a Telegram to the same effect from the United Clubs.) I was once as good as elected for your St. Andrews,[3] all the other Candidates pleasing to retire in my favour: and, the same year, I was assured of success at Aberdeen.

What I feel at all these proofs of kindness and respect, I find difficult to put into words,—nor indeed shall attempt it. And to you—and to dear Lady Martin—there is scarcely need that I should

1. Sir Theodore Martin (1816–1909), man of letters, published the *Bon Gaultier Ballads* in collaboration with Aytoun, but gained greatest royal attention and favor through a five-volume life of Prince Albert. He was knighted in 1880. Through his wife, Helen Faucit, whom he married in 1851, he had known Browning for more than 30 years. It was near the Martins' home in Wales, Bryntysilio near Llantysilio, that Browning and his sister went for vacation in the s᷑ nmer of 1886.

2. The students of the University of Glasgow wished to nominate Browning for the Rectorship. The present letter is a prompt reply to a note from Sir Theodore dated the same day and delivered in person to Browning's home. "Pray, do not refuse" is the thesis of the note. (*Browning's Letter File*, ed. Armstrong, p. 20. On p. 21 are reproduced the three telegrams sent to Browning urging his acceptance.)

3. This was in or before 1869. (See *Letters to Isa Blagden*, p. 169.) Sir Theodore Martin became Lord Rector of St. Andrews in 1881. (*D.N.B.*)

speak of what you can so well understand,—knowing me to remain ever yours

Affectionately and gratefully

[Huntington]   Robert Browning.

To Mrs. Baker [1]

19, Warwick Crescent, W.
Nov. 19, '84.

Dear Mrs Baker,

The representation [2] about which you enquire takes place next week, and is given by what is called the "Browning Society," for the amusement of its members only—of whom I am not one, nor shall I be present: and, as tickets are only issued to these, I am unable to dispose of one, or should be glad to assist you in the matter.

Believe me, Dear Mrs. Baker,

Yours faithfully

[Boston Browning Society]   Robert Browning.

To Mrs. Charles Skirrow

19, Warwick Crescent, W.
Nov. 23, '84.

Dear Friend,

The only way you ever give me pain is by wanting to give me pleasure on occasions when circumstances render it impossible for me to accept your kindness. On Wednesday, I am engaged all the afternoon, after which I dine out,—which I mention because I might otherwise *crib* a bit from the early end of the afternoon engagement as I hope to do from the other and late end. You know

1. There was a Mrs. Baker of the Florentine days to whom Browning refers in several letters to Isa Blagden. These references are requests to Miss Blagden for information about *anybody* in Florence whom he had known at all. "I don't care," he says, "a brass farthing about the Tassinaris or Mrs. Baker—yet —they are of Florence, and I never see the name without a stir of heart." (*Letters*, ed. Hood, p. 113.) The Mrs. Baker of this letter may be the acquaintance made in Florence.

2. The Browning Society's Fourth Entertainment at the Princes' Hall, Piccadilly, on Friday evening, November 28th, 1884, included the presentation of *In a Balcony* with Alma Murray as Constance, Nora Gerstenberg as the Queen, and Mr. Philip Beck as Norbert. (*Browning Society's Papers* [Appendix to Fourth Report, June 26, 1885], Vol. II.)

how happy I should be to see you anywhere and anyhow if it were in my power.

Ever affectionately yours

[Schiff]   Robt. Browning.

To An Unidentified Correspondent

19, Warwick Crescent, W.
Nov. 26, '84.

Dear Sir,

By the kindness of Mr. Furnivall, I received your gracious poem last evening. All I can say in acknowledgment is that if "Ferishtah" [1] has succeeded in producing such a pupil he is happy indeed—a happiness quite unalloyed by dissatisfaction that the pupil treads so closely on the heels of the Master—who bids him *"I pede fausto"*—or, in the vernacular, "Go a-head," with all his heart. Believe me, Dear Sir,

Very cordially yours

[Huntington]   Robert Browning.

To Mr. and Mrs. Charles Skirrow

19, Warwick Crescent, W.
Jan. 1, '85.[1]

Dearest Friends, I return your affection from my very heart, wishing you a continuance of what you already enjoy—which seems nearly perfect happiness so far as it is obtainable in this world. God bless you both.

[Schiff]   Robert Browning.

To Mrs. Charles Skirrow

19 Warwick Crescent, W.
Apr. 13, '85.

Dear Friend, to my extreme regret, I am already engaged on the 1st. I should have been particularly glad to see our Kosmos—who,

---

1. Since *Ferishtah's Fancies* came out on November 21, its effect on this admirer of Browning did indeed show the pupil treading closely on the heels of the master.

1. During 1885 Browning was in London from January 1 to August 18; Milan on August 18; Pont St. Martin, August 19; Gressoney St. Jean, Val d'Aosta, Italy, from August 20 to about October 1; Venice, from November 23 for the remainder of the year.

I hope, is getting over the effects of a "durance"—in this case, I do consider—"vile" enough.[1] Where I am to dine is not far from your house (Ly. Ducie's, Portman Square)[2] and if I can decently beat an earlyish retreat, I will look in for just a minute to shake hands with him.

Ever affectionately yours
Robert Browning.

[Schiff]

To Mrs. Charles Skirrow

19, Warwick Crescent, W.
Apr. 30, '85.

Dear Friend,

I shall be happy to go to you on the 8th. I much fear I cannot get to you tomorrow evening: if I find it out of my power, please thank Mr. Yates[1] most cordially for his kind message, and say how much I rejoice to hear he is improving in health. I shall, at all events, meet him at the Dinner on the 30th instant.

Ever affectionately yours
Robert Browning.

[Schiff]

To Mr. and Mrs. Charles Skirrow

May 7th, '85.[1]

Dearest Friends,

I *cannot* bring myself to try and do more than say that I thank you with my whole heart. Your friendship is one of the very proudest achievements of the life of

Yours affectionately and gratefully ever
R. Browning.

[Schiff]

1. A reference to Edmund Yates, editor of the *World*, who had just finished serving a sentence for libel against Lord Lonsdale. (See, above, letter of December 4, 1883, n. 5.)
2. Lady Emily Eleanor (Kent) Ducie (d. 1921) was the wife of the fourth Earl of Ducie who in 1885–86 was Minister of Public Instruction of Queensland. (*Burke's Peerage*, p. 853.)
1. Edmund Yates. (See, above, letter of December 4, 1883, n. 5, and letter of April 13, 1885, n. 1.)
1. Since May 7 was Browning's birthday this letter is probably an acknowledgment of a message from the Skirrows.

To Mrs. Charles Skirrow

19 Warwick Crescent, W.
July 1, '85.

Dear Friend, I by no means forget either the 7th or 11th and am yours then as—*nearly* always,—for I have two engagements for next Friday afternoon which I am forced to keep—or I would gladly enjoy taking luncheon with you. I met Mr. Stanley last evening at Millais' party.[1]

Ever lovingly yours

[Schiff]   Robert Browning.

To Mrs. Charles Skirrow

Hôtel Delapierre, Gressoney St. Jean,
Val d'Aosta, Italia.
Aug. 28, '85.

Dear Friend,—of all the complaints which you are least likely to hear from me, I suppose that this which I am about to make is precisely the one: You never asked me to lunch! [1] That is, you promised that we two should have just another talk together before the holiday separation,—and I who counted upon it, did not get it, and—more goose I—made no effort to do so by calling or writing—whereof I suffer the consequence now—for I really wanted to go away with a last flavour of your kindness in my—not *mouth,* as if I meant the lobster-cutlets!—but mind which has taken in and continues to digest so many many pleasures of your procuring this whole season, as of its predecessors. Seriously and sadly, I *did* want to see you once more: but I can think of you at any distance, and I am scribbling just that I may at all events hear from you during my absence. Besides, you know nothing of where I am, I believe:

1. On June 24, 1885, John Everett Millais (1829–96) was asked by Gladstone "to take his place among the baronets of the United Kingdom." (John G. Millais, *Life and Letters of Sir John Everett Millais* [New York, 1899], II, 177.) It is probable that the party alluded to here was in celebration of that honor. "Mr. Stanley" was probably the famous Henry Morton Stanley (1841–1904), explorer, journalist, and author, who "lectured in Germany, England, and America on the commercial possibilities of Central Africa" from 1884 to 1886. (*D.N.B.*) He was the kind of lion whom Mrs. Skirrow would want Browning "to get" for her.

1. See preceding letter, July 1, 1885. Browning's reference here is probably to a time after July 11 when he had seen Mrs. Skirrow.

so this tells you that on the 18th we crossed to Dover,—went on to Bâle and Milan without stopping, and next day reached Ivrea and Pont St. Martin: whence, after an eight-hours' journey,—my sister in a chair borne by six porters (if you please) and myself on a sufficiently good horse,—two mules carrying our luggage—we gained this place which was so much to our hearts the year before last. There is trouble enough in getting to it, but, once arrived, we are in the wildest quietest and most lovely seclusion of my experience: St. Moritz is Cheapside by comparison. We resume our old habits, walk morning and afternoon, and enjoy the perfect air and—almost perfect weather to-match: but the hitherto unbroken season is misty to-day, and it rains in the valley. In the Hôtel are a very few Italians, —good-mannered people,—and how the Hostess can afford us so capital a table,—twice as good as the best at St. Moritz for quality and quantity,—is past guessing. Even these few visitors will soon go their ways, and leave us to stay till the snow drives us Southward —say, in October: when we count upon going to Venice—where Pen will have preceded us,—for he goes to paint there, good boy that he is. Now, dear couple of friends, will you not pay me the owing "lunch," by a "tartine" of a news-letter telling me all your news, and everybody-else's news,—where you are, what you do, whom you see, what you hear,—such as shall satisfy my appetite?— when I say this, how all the figures you have made me intimate with flit between me and Monte Rosa over there!—but it really is about your two selves that I am hungry to know as much as you can afford me: I have a newspaper, and sundry weekly journals. Good Mrs. F. G.[2] has been ill and is better—but the walk seems possible, and I break off. All love to you both,—and I need not say that my Sister's goes with mine. She is already much the better for the change of air.

Ever affectionately yours
Robert Browning.

[Schiff]

To Mrs. Charles Skirrow

Gressoney St. Jean, Val d'Aosta, Italy.
Sept. 10, '85.

I hope, dear Friend, that you got the letter which I sent immediately after arriving here, as soon as—if not before your own kind

2. Mrs. Thomas FitzGerald. For an account of this lady see below, letter of June 23, 1888.

letter reached me. I addressed it to your town-residence, supposing that the servants would send it on to wherever you might be—as you once told me was their practice. Perhaps you may already have left Homburg; but I prefer to think that our own admirable weather extends to where you are, and that you do not already—as I say—turn your steps homeward: Mr. Skirrow surely requires a longer holiday than some three weeks: and if the baths do you evident good you ought to make the most of your opportunity. Of ourselves, I can only say that the old experience of this place is more than confirmed by this new one: I never saw so lovely and quiet a spot,—perhaps, without the extreme beauty, the absolute solitariness would affect us differently. We take our morning walk, and meet some cows and [1] goats with their herdsman, a string of mules, and a peasant or two—for we take the beaten road: but in the afternoon we choose the mountain-side, and not infrequently go for three hours—including the return—without meeting a single person. The weather has been delightful,—sunny with the most bracing air imaginable: to-day, as yesterday,—not one faintest cloud discernible in the universal blue. Then, at the Pension itself, we are *alone*—the two guests! At the beginning, we found a few people, who soon went away; since then, there have been a few arrivals for just a day and a night. The consequence of all this seems to be that we are both of us as well as possible, and we hope to let well alone till the end of the month when we go to Venice,—under circumstances of new interest, for Pen sets out for a short stay there at the close of this week: he will take a studio and paint, having a great desire to try his hand at Venetian subjects as he shall see them for himself—not treated so conventionally as they generally are. He travels with a friend, who likes his company and will make the journey enjoyable: and I anticipate great good from the change of place, and novelty of impression. It is too soon to predict when we shall return to England, but probably at the beginning of December. We are not sure that our friend Mrs. Bronson will not be forced to go to America even before we get to Venice,—but she will do her best to put off the business till the Spring. Having told you so much about the peacefulness of this little human settlement, I ought to mention how thoroughly that may be broken up occasionally. Last January an avalanche destroyed three houses, close to this wherein

1. The word "and" is repeated here.

I write, crushing six people: the only escape was that of a little child, saved by two beams crossing each other above its head. The snow lay, at that time, four *mètres* deep around this Hôtel, blocking it in so completely that two days passed before the news of what had happened a hundred yards off managed to reach the inmates— including the Priest and the Doctor who were imprisoned for some time. Water was only procurable by melting the snow and ice,— provisions were in plenty. The houses thus destroyed had been built so long before, that the poor dwellers in them supposed they would never be more than approached by the mountain accumulations. Then, at this very moment, there is a poor "guide" lying dead at the edge of the Glacier of Monte Rosa, till the officers of justice can suffer a removal of the body. He accompanied two travellers (inhabitants of Gressoney) thus far, felt too unwell to proceed, gave them their "sac" to carry awhile,—and died thereupon—as they found on going back,—after proceeding a little,—to see why he did not follow. I hope and believe that English travellers would not have left the poor fellow so unconcernedly. In a year or two, great changes will take place here: a road, fit for carriages, will be constructed from the higher Gressoney (La Trinité) down to Pont St. Martin, to the great advantage of tourists—not so decidedly to our own. And on the 20th of this month the railway from the latter village to Ivrea will be opened,—our advantage being as certainly great thereby, as we shall go directly by it to Venice—or, if needs be, any other part of Italy. See my paper—how full it is! I think I said that my sister is quite herself again. Be as good as ever and write to me! Give my true love, and hers also, to dear Mr. Skirrow. You must know how any news of you both will be a joy to us: and remember me as ever affectionately yours

                                                          RB
5 p.m.
Since writing my letter, I have been along with S. in company with our Landlady to see the ruins of the houses,—a frightful sight: our guide had never prevailed on herself to bear it since the catastrophe, —her infant child having been, for months before, consigned to the keeping of one of the householders: "that was the little window it used to look out of as I came to see it." The quarry of stones discharged on the buildings, torn down by the mass of snow, was extraordinary,—enough to overwhelm a dozen such constructions:

this was 270 years old, and no avalanche had ever been heard of near it. We climbed about the ruins: "there was the little room, partitioned off from the kitchen, and also the cow-shed": the kitchen is still intact, all the cattle were saved, only the family perished, three, in one house, "along with a neighbour, a girl of 15, who had put on male trousers to get through the snow and see her friends, and was crushed along with them five minutes after." (We saw her sister, by the ruins.) In the next house, two were killed: and, worst of all, in a house at some little distance higher up the same fate overtook a man and his two daughters: in the anxiety to rescue the other sufferers nobody observed what had happened here—and the three were buried in snow without help for 48 hours—when the man was found horribly frost-bitten, and "bitten by his younger daughter in her delirium": she died, the sister survived, and, after prolonged suffering the man also. In the other ruin, I picked up a sort of prayer-book,—covered with lime, but with the characters distinguishable,—and the line my eye fell upon was—in German— "How lovely are thy tabernacles, O Lord,—my soul yearns for thy House!"—well it might. By the way, a woman was pointed out to me, well to do, who had two husbands—each of whom committed suicide: she is open to another offer! I wonder whether this ghastliness will interest you at all: it is in strange contrast to the delicious quietude all round about. Good bye again,—ever yours,
[Schiff]   RB.

To Mr. and Mrs. Charles Skirrow [1]

Palazzo Giustiniani-Recanati, S. Moise.
Nov. 15, '85.

My two dear friends will have supposed, with plenty of reason, that I never got the kind letter some weeks ago. When it came, I was in the middle of an affair, conducted by letters of quite another kind, with people abroad: and as I fancied that every next day might bring me news very interesting to me and likely to be worth telling to the dear friends, I waited and waited—and only two days since did the matter come to a satisfactory conclusion—so, as the Irish

1. This letter has been published in Mrs. Orr, *Life*, pp. 341–343. It is included here to complete the record of available letters of Browning to Mrs. Skirrow.

song has it, "open your eyes and die with surprise" when I inform you that I have purchased the Manzoni Palace here, on the Canal Grande, of its owner, Marchese Montecuccoli, an Austrian and an absentee—hence the delay of communication. I did this purely for Pen—who became at once simply infatuated with the City which won my whole heart long before he was born or thought of. I secure him a perfect domicile, every facility for his painting and sculpture, and a property fairly worth, even here and now, double what I gave for it—such is the virtue in these parts of ready money! I myself shall stick to London—which has been so eminently good and gracious to me—so long as God permits: only, when the inevitable outrage of Time gets the better of my body—(I shall not believe in his reaching my soul and proper self)—there will be a capital retreat provided: and meantime I shall be able to "take mine ease in mine own inn" whenever so minded. There, my dear friends! I trust now to be able to leave very shortly,—the main business cannot be formally concluded before two months at least—through the absence of the Marchese,—who left at once to return to his duties as commander of an Austrian ship: but the necessary engagement to sell and buy at a specified price is made in due legal form, and the papers will be sent to me in London for signature. I hope to get away the week after next at latest,—spite of the weather in England which to-day's letters report as "atrocious,"—and ours, though variable, is in the main very tolerable and sometimes perfect,—for all that, I yearn to be at home in poor Warwick Crescent, which must do its best to make me forget my new abode. I forget you don't know Venice. Well then, the Palazzo Manzoni is situate on the Grand Canal, and is described by Ruskin,—to give no other authority,—as "A perfect and very rich example of Byzantine Renaissance: its warm yellow marbles are magnificent." And again— "An exquisite example (of Byzantine Renaissance) as applied to domestic architecture." So testify the *Stones of Venice*. But we will talk about the place, over a photograph, when I am happy enough to be with you again.[2]

2. The Marchese drew back at the last moment hoping for a better offer. Browning took the matter to the law courts but withdrew from the action when he heard that the walls and the foundations of the palace were unsound. Mrs. Bronson gives the details of why Browning was eventually balked in obtaining Palazzo Manzoni and adds, "Perhaps he had never, in his long life-

Of Venetian gossip there is next to none. We had an admirable Venetian Company,—using the dialect,—at the Goldoni Theatre. The acting of Zago, in his various parts, and Zenon-Palladini, in her especial character of a Venetian piece of volubility and impulsiveness in the shape of a servant, were admirable indeed. The manager, Gallina,[3] is a play-wright of much reputation, and gave us some dozen of his own pieces, mostly good and clever. S. is very well,—much improved in health: we walk sufficiently in this city where walking is accounted impossible by those who never attempt it. Have I tried your good temper? No! You ever wished me well, and I love you both with my whole heart. S's love goes with mine, who [am ever yours].[4]

[Schiff]   Robert Browning.

To Mrs. Charles Skirrow

19, Warwick Crescent, W.
Feb. 19, '86.[1]

Dearest Friend,—I shall not attempt to say how much I wish I were able to dine with you on the 6th.

I am engaged to the Boughtons [2]—kind people as they are,—how I wish—but no matter. As Cleopatra says

"Pity me, Charmian, do not speak to me!"

Ever affectionately yours and
the dear Husband's

[Schiff]   Robert Browning.

---

time, been so thoroughly annoyed by a thwarted project as by the failure of this one." (Katherine de Kay Bronson, "Browning in Venice," *Century Magazine*, LXIII, 572.)

3. Giacento Gallina (1852–97) was born in Venice and wrote and produced plays there during most of his life. Browning's liking for him is perhaps explained by what his biographer says of him: "Gallina fu l'ultimo 'poeta scritturato,' perché seguì sempre le compagnie per le quali scriveva e delle quali spesso era socio equasi sempre direttore." (*Enciclopedia Italiana* [Trèves, 1932], XVI, 327.)

4. The complimentary close and most of the signature have been cut off. The words in brackets are taken from Mrs. Orr's transcription of this letter. (*Life*, p. 343.)

1. During 1886 Browning was in London from January 1 to August 13; in Llangollen, Wales, from August 13 to October 19; in London from October 19 to the end of the year.

2. See letter dated March 3, 1884, n. 1.

To Mrs. Charles Skirrow

19, Warwick Crescent, W.
March 7, '86.

How good your patience with my perverse ways continues to be, dearest Friend! I can go to you on the 16th if you like, and if Miss L.[1] likes! Or indeed, next Tuesday, for the matter of that, or Wednesday or Saturday: *there* is a choice for your catching the poor gudgeon that is

Yours affectionately ever
Robert Browning

You will not only choose, but tell me, will you not?
[Schiff]

To Godfrey Douglas Giles [1]

19, Warwick Crescent, W.
March 25, '86.

My dear Mr. Giles,

I cannot tell you how sorry I am that I have been, fully these five or six weeks, engaged to go to Miss Zimmerman's concert this afternoon—which takes place precisely between 3½-and 6.[2] My sister

1. Unidentified.

1. Major Godfrey Douglas Giles (1857–1941), born in India, spent his early years of maturity in the British Army after training at Sandhurst. He gave up the army for a career in painting and exhibited his first picture at the Royal Academy in 1884. It was probably through Pen that Browning met Giles. Giles was visiting Pen in November, 1889, and on the 24th of that month produced a free-hand sketch of Browning which proved to be the last picture made of the poet during his lifetime. Browning wrote on the picture:

> Here I'm gazing, wide awake,
> Robert Browning, no mistake!

(Wilson, *Browning's Portraits* . . . , pp. 188–190.) Giles's specialty, judging from his exhibits at the Royal Academy, were battle scenes. (See Algernon Graves, *The Royal Academy of Arts; A Complete Dictionary* . . . *1769–1904*, III, 237–238.) The present letter is printed, without annotation or comment, in *Baylor University Browning Interests,* ed. Armstrong, 5th ser. [1932], p. 64. In this same pamphlet is published the "Diary of Miss Evelyn Barclay." Miss Barclay became Mrs. G. D. Giles and was staying at the Palazzo Rezzonico, as was Giles, at the time of Browning's death.

2. Agnes Marie Jacobina Zimmerman (1847–1925), pianist and composer, was something of a prodigy when as a child of nine she began her piano studies at the Royal Academy of Music. At 16 she played Beethoven¹at the Crystal Palace. Grove says that "her name became for many years a household word for purity of interpretation and excellent musicianship." (*Grove's Dictionary of Music*

is laid up with a bad cold,—or she might profit by your kind invitation although I cannot. I am sure you will understand and excuse us.

Ever truly yours

[Baylor]   Robert Browning.

To Mrs. Charles Skirrow

19, Warwick Crescent, W.
Apr. 2, '86.

Dear Friend,

Your "next Thursday" happens to be the day on which I needs must dine with Mr. Murray [1] and go to the Litz-Bache business.[2] I will do my best to look in at 3. o'clock—wishing the visit were earlier.

My Sister discovers—probably—the secret about Miss Hope Glen's account of the advertisement. A cousin of mine, Robert Jardine Browning, of Oxford, Lincoln's Inn, and—Melbourne,—was married there, and the fact duly commemorated in our news-

---

and Musicians, ed. H. C. Colles [3rd ed., London, 1928], V, 784–785.) Her recital was announced in the London *Times,* March 25, 1886, p. 1, col. 3: "Miss Agnes Zimmerman's Recital, Prince's Hall, Piccadilly, this [Thursday] afternoon . . . at 3:30. Beethoven's Grand Sonata, op. 101, Schumann's Fantasie, op. 17 . . . also . . . pieces by Bach, Rameau, Scarlatti, Chopin, Rubinstein, Moszkowski, etc., Tickets 7s., 3s., 1s."

1. John Murray III (1808–92) continued the publishing tradition of his father. The dinner referred to here apparently had nothing to do with the visit of Liszt, for it is not mentioned in the daily accounts of Liszt doings in London. John Murray IV recalls his father's relation with Browning as follows: "My father read little poetry and certainly no Browning, yet Browning was an admired and ever welcome guest; no one was better informed in a wider range of subjects." (John Murray IV, *John Murray III* [London, 1919], p. 37.)

2. Walter Bache (1842–88), pianist, composer, and pupil of Franz Liszt, was host at a "memorable reception at the Grosvenor Gallery on April 8, 1886 in honor of Liszt. (*Grove's Dictionary of Music and Musicians,* ed. H. C. Colles, 3rd. ed., I, 189.) "The *soirée* . . . in honour of the Abbé Liszt was attended by a numerous and distinguished company." Browning's name is not mentioned in the London *Times* report of April 9, p. 9, col. 2. (See letter of April 9, 1886, below.) Liszt had arrived in England for a brief stay but was given such a tumultuous and sustained welcome that he remained a week longer than he had planned. (See London *Times,* April 2, 3, 5, 6, 8, 9, 10, 20, and 21, in which Liszt's engagements are faithfully recorded.) This proved to be his final visit to England, for he died on July 31, 1886. Browning's troubles with the spelling of Liszt continue in the next letter, April 9, 1886.

papers a short time ago: I read the advertisement in the *Times:* the mistake our friend made was in substituting one intermediate name for another.³ Please tell her so—entirely at your convenience —and believe me always

Affectionately yours
Robert Browning

Once again,—how pleasantly spent was last evening, thanks to you! [Schiff]

To Mrs. Charles Skirrow

19, Warwick Crescent, W.
Apr. 9, '86.

Dear Friend, don't think I forgot you, yesterday: I have been unwell, and felt unable to go out as I much wanted to do. There was no getting rid of the Dinner, but I gave up the Listz affair (Listz—isn't it?),¹ which would seem to have been worth assisting at! ² I am much better, to-day, and shall fortunately be able to stay at home. I think it is hardly necessary to assure you of all this,—but I like to lose no occasion of letting you know how much I am ever affectionately

Yours
Robert Browning.

[Schiff]

3. This advertisement appeared in the *Times* on March 13, 1886, p. 1, col. 1: "On 27th January . . . Robert Jardine Browning, M.A. Lincoln College, Oxford, of the Inner Temple and of Sydney, Barrister-at-law to Beatrice Lamonnerie . . ." Robert Jardine Browning collaborated with A. R. Bluett in compiling *A Digest of Australian Cases to Local Government* . . . [Sydney, 1919].

1. The parenthesis was inserted, apparently as Browning struggled with this spelling.

2. See preceding letter, n. 1. Perhaps Browning had read the glowing account in the *Times* for April 9, of Walter Bache's inspired playing of the music of Liszt and of Liszt's own playing. An impression of that evening is best reported by Grove: "I went to Liszt's reception on Thursday and was delighted (1) by his playing, so calm, clear, correct, refined—so entirely unlike the style of the so-called 'Liszt School'—(2) by his face. Directly he sat down he dismissed that very artificial smile, which he always wears, and his face assumed the most beautiful serene look with enormous power and repose in it. It was quite a wonderful night." (Charles L. Graves, *Life of Sir George Grove*, pp. 311–312.)

To Mr. and Mrs. Charles Skirrow

19, Warwick Crescent, W.
Apr. 25, '86.

Dearest Friends, I will joyfully dine with you at Greenwich on May 22d. pursuant to your kind invitation.

How glad I am of the fine weather for both your sakes!

Ever affectionately yours

[Schiff]   Robert Browning.

To Mr. and Mrs. Charles Skirrow

19, Warwick Crescent, W.
May 7, '86.[1]

Dearest Friends, thank you from my heart—I can say nothing better nor more truly whether I live many years longer, or only a few, while they last I shall ever be yours gratefully and

affectionately

[Schiff]   Robert Browning.

To Lady Harcourt [1]

19, Warwick Crescent, W.
May 12, '86.

Dear Lady Harcourt,

I beg to say how sorry I am that an earlier engagement will, in all likelihood, prevent me from obeying your kind invitation this evening, and paying my affectionate respects to your illustrious guest—whom, however, I shall have the gratification of meeting in a day or two, I am promised.[2]

Believe me, Dear Lady Harcourt,

Yours very sincerely

[Library of Congress]   Robert Browning.

1. Browning's birthday.
1. On the back of this folded letter is written in a hand other than Browning's: "Robert Browning," "R. Browning," and the word "Keep." Sir William V. Harcourt (1827–1904), statesman, after the loss of his first wife, married in 1876 Elizabeth Cabot Ives, the widow of T. P. Ives of Rhode Island and the daughter of the American historian, John Lothrop Motley. Sir William described this lady, before his marriage to her, as a "good Liberal," one who he hoped would "do her duty to the Party and its leaders." (A. G. Gardiner, *The Life of Sir William Harcourt* [London, 1923], I, 306.)
2. Many of Lady Harcourt's entertainments were given as part of her "duty

To Miss Violet Paget [1]

19, Warwick Crescent, W.
May 13, '86.

Dear Miss Paget,

I shall never quite believe you have forgiven and forgotten my lapse of memory last year, so long as those strange words—"honoured"—"respectfully"—and the like, come up at intervals in a letter of yours to one whom—if you exact the plain truth—yourself unduly "honour"—and inspire with all conceivable "respect." *"Soyons amis, Cinna."* [2] As it is, the right to make professions of this kind certainly begins with me—whom you greatly obliged by the present of *Baldwin* [3]—which I have waited to thank you for till

---

to the Party and its leaders," as may be seen in Sir Robert Anderson, *Sidelights of the Home Rule Movement* (London, 1906), *passim.* The "illustrious guest" on this occasion has not been identified.

1. Violet Paget (1856–1935), who published all her works under the nom de plume Vernon Lee, was introduced to Browning sometime before November 6, 1882, on which date she wrote to the poet reminding him of "being brought [to him] twice . . . by Mary Robinson." (*Browning's Letter File,* ed. Armstrong, p. 94.) She was the author of over 20 books including novels, essays on art, poetry, and aesthetics, and books of travel. Browning held her in high respect and deliberately courted her good opinion in his letters to her. Then in the poem "Inapprehensiveness" (*Asolando,* 1889) he pays her the tribute of apprehensiveness in the lines:

"No, the book .
Which noticed how the wall-growths wave," said she
"Was not by Ruskin."
I said "Vernon Lee?"

These lines are doubtless based on a memory of Miss Paget's *Baldwin* and its chief character who lived in a "small Italian village" which he had learned to possess much as Browning possessed Asolo. Baldwin, like Browning who said "Oh, fancies that might be, oh, facts that are!" sees "the real, the existing" in its relation to the "purely imaginary."

2. Miss Paget's letter to which this is a reply bears the heading "Florence, Easter Sunday, 1886," and is very formal in tone. (See *Browning's Letter File,* ed. Armstrong, p. 112.) Browning, with all his blandishment, did not succeed in thawing out Miss Paget's stiff manner (p. 129). Browning's failure to bring Miss Paget into the adoring circle of his many women friends may be accounted for by Miss Paget's own character, which she analyzes under the name Baldwin in the book of that name. Baldwin's (Miss Paget's) has been "a life spent in being repelled by the exaggerations of one's friends" (p. 13).

3. Vernon Lee, *Baldwin: being Dialogues on Views and Aspirations* (London, 1886). On the half title of Browning's copy: "Robert Browning from the Author." (Sotheby, *Browning Collections,* item 960, p. 120.) Miss Paget sent this book "because it contains at page 287, some notes of mine upon your Caponsacchi, which I shall feel greatly honoured if you will glance at." (*Brown-*

I could thoroughly read it, as I have just done—with the intention of as thoroughly reading it a second time in a day or two. It is very subtle, very beautiful,—a jewel raying out truth from many facettes. But what I want to say immediately is that I shall certainly be in London for the next two or three months, and count upon your promise to call here. If you kindly apprise me, at any time, that you will do so—say, that you will come to luncheon at 1. o'clock, when I *must* be free of engagements,—you will gratify me indeed: my sister—who reciprocates your regard—will be gratified also: I shall therefore trust in June.

I am truly sorry to hear that Miss Robinson [4] has been out of health, even in Italy: here in England the weather has outdone itself in detestability. Tell her how glad I shall be if she comes back beaming with health and brimful of poetry: I am never demonstrative enough,—it seems on after-thoughts—but I have always taken a great interest in her, and duly valued the sympathy she has given me—or my writings. As for you, I should like, Dear Miss Paget, to set you an example of veracious informality: after all, there is a great deal, if we ponder it, in the simple assurance that I am

Yours truly
Robert Browning.

[Baylor]

To Mrs. Charles Skirrow

19, Warwick Crescent, W.
May 27, '86.

Dearest Friend,—You are always "supplementing" your kindness. Why am I unable to "supplement" my thanks? And what can I say of last week's entertainment but that it was altogether as delightful as its many predecessors?

Ever affectionately yours
Robert Browning.

[Schiff]

ing's Letter File, ed. Armstrong, p. 112.) On p. 285 Baldwin, who is Miss Paget, describes the *Ring and the Book* as "one of the greatest moments of ideal art." The note on Caponsacchi occupies pp. 287–289 and is an explanation of the criticism that Caponsacchi speaks the "most impossible rhetoric."

4. Agnes Mary Frances (Robinson) Duclaux (1857–1944), poetess and critic, had introduced Miss Paget to Browning. (See above, n. 1.) She herself probably met Browning in the late Seventies. Her admiration for the poet is reflected in a study of Browning which she contributed to *Poèmes de Robert Browning*, traduits par Paul Alfassa et Gilbert de Voisins et précédés d'une étude sur sa pensée et sa vie par Mary Duclaux (Paris, 1922). For sketch of Mme. Duclaux's life see London *Times* (April 14, 1944).

To Havelock Ellis [1]

19, Warwick Crescent, W.
June 5, '86.

Dear Sir,

Many thanks for the Selection from Landor's *Conversations:* [2]
I have not yet had time to properly examine them, but the worst
must be better than nearly all the best pieces of writing now in cur-
rency. I rejoice at every fresh attempt to circulate these admirable
works of my old friend.

Believe me, Dear Sir,
Yours very sincerely
[Huntington]   Robert Browning.

To Mrs. Charles Skirrow

19, Warwick Crescent, W.
June 14, '86.

Dearest Friend,

I have great fear that I shall be unable to lunch with you on the
18th,—having an engagement for the afternoon with a friend who
is going away next day. If I can so arrange it—as I will endeavour
to do—I will let you know before Friday: otherwise I cannot now
have the great pleasure of going to you "with no after-prospect of
a dinner"! Another thing,—my poor Sister has had an alarming
return of that inflammatory attack which frightened me so two
years ago: she was intending to go to Paris last Wednesday in
order to see our dear Milsand who is about to leave it—and I was
to go over and fetch her back this present week: when the attack
befell her,—just the evening before,—and has confined her to her
bed ever since, of course. Through the prompt treatment of our

1. Havelock Ellis (1859–1939), editor and psychologist, perhaps did not become acquainted with Browning personally. Though his autobiography contains a half-dozen references to Mrs. Browning, particularly to the influence
upon him and his wife of *Aurora Leigh*, there is only incidental mention of
Robert Browning in its pages.

2. Walter Savage Landor, *Imaginary Conversations*, with an introductory
note by Havelock Ellis (London, 1886). In the introductory note Ellis couples
Landor with Browning as a "great dramátic poet" (p. viii) and again with
Burns, Whitman, and Browning, "substantial men . . . of the same virile
tribe" (p. xxiv). This selection from Landor was the first of numerous volumes
edited by Ellis for the Camelot Series. (Havelock Ellis, *My Life* [Boston, 1939],
pp. 205–206.)

M*

Doctor, the immediate danger is over, and Pen was allowed to go away on Saturday,—but things are still in a very uncomfortable condition, and I hardly dare dispose of my time long beforehand.[1] Of course I have "booked" the day for Richmond,—may I enjoy it!

All love to the Husband, from yours ever affectionately

[Schiff]   Robert Browning

To Mrs. Charles Skirrow

19, Warwick Crescent, W.
June 16, '86.

Dearest Friend,

S. is surprisingly better,—and, excepting the possibility of a relapse, which is never to be lost sight of, I am in no apprehension about her. I shall be delighted to go to you on Friday. Ever affectionately yours

[Schiff]   Robert Browning.

To Felix Moscheles

19, Warwick Crescent, W.
June 23, '86.

My dear Moscheles,

I was obliged to get away furtively yesterday without thanking you and the Exhibitioners for much amusement. I had an engagement close by; on the 2d July I have another at a distance—how is poor flesh and blood to be sufficient for even pleasant requirements like yours? What of the Del Sartian Law of Economy?[1] I will call, as soon as I can, some morning, and settle matters to your kind satisfaction. Ever yours

[Yale]   Robert Browning.

1. This attack of Sarianna's determined Browning not to go abroad for a vacation. Instead, the poet and his sister took their annual holiday in Wales.

1. Reference to the "exhibitioners" may be to those friends of Moscheles who gathered at his studio to "sing and play their best." (Felix Moscheles, *Fragments of an Autobiography*, pp. 339–341.) The reference to "the Del Sartian law of Economy" is a facetious remark concerning Francois Delsarte (1811–71) and his system "of rhythmic exercises in which he coordinated singing, declamation, gymnastics, and dancing." (*Columbia Encyclopedia* [1939], "Delsarte.")

To An Unidentified Correspondent

19, Warwick Crescent, W.
July 9, '86.

Dear Sir,

I can think of no better way than the obvious one of sending the Poems of your friend to a Publisher, and allowing his "Reader" to decide as to the advisability of printing them. I do not believe that the mere recommendation of any friend, however personally intimate with the Publisher himself, would have any other effect than to make him smile—"Yes,—he understands: you are good natured, generous even,—and the 'Reader' will give proper attention to your good word"—that is, the roundabout way would only lead to the straight one. Of course, in the case of some phenomenal genius one had the fortune to discover,—one's opinion, given with the reasons for it, would have its weight: otherwise, none at all: depend on it, I do not speak without experience. Your friend must be stout-hearted and expect little help but from his poetry's own persuasive force. It sounds strange and almost sad to me that I should be imagined of authority in this kind—I who for years and years could not get a line printed except at my own expense—and I began half a century ago and more.

Yours sincerely
Robert Browning.

[Huntington]

To Sir Theodore Martin

19, Warwick Crescent, W.
Aug. 2, '86.

My dear Sir Theodore,

How grateful we both of us are for your goodness and that of Lady Martin there is hardly need to try and adequately tell you —though my Sister will in a measure attempt it. The Doctor agrees with your recommendation of Llangollen; and your kind offer to arrange for us at the Hotel there relieves us altogether of anxiety.[1]

1. The Martins had heard that Browning and his sister were contemplating a vacation in Wales and wrote urging them to visit at their home, Bryntysilio, Llangollen. Sarianna replied that the Martins' letters "decided their wavering resolution." Sir Theodore observed that "a word to the hostess of the Hand Hotel was scarcely needed to secure every attention for the poet and his sister, for she was one of his readers." (Sir Theodore Martin, *Helena Faucit*, p. 388).

Mr. Peel [2] writes this morning to propose that we take a house he mentions in the neighbourhood,—but the independence of Hotel-life is by far more suitable for our moderate requirements. We shall be most pleasantly near you—and, if my Sister's feet have not lost their old cunning, a two-mile walk will be no sort of impediment to our seeing you as often as you permit.

With the kindest of regards to dear Lady Martin, and every acknowledgement of your own efficacious help, believe me ever, Dear Sir Theodore,

Yours most truly

[Huntington]   Robert Browning.

To Lady Martin [1]

Hand Hotel, Llangollen.
Saturday [August 14, 1886] [2]

Dear Lady Martin,

All is going as well with us as your kindness could possibly wish. We are most comfortably installed, and perfectly cared for in every respect. We concluded that the bad weather had prevented your coming for us—and, for our own part, were by no means disinclined to stay at home—as my Sister, in any case, would have been obliged to do: but Mr. Peel came over and carried myself with him, uphill and down dale, so that I saw the performance of the dogs, and had not much to suffer from the rain. Here we are—in fine—as comfortably lodged as we ever expect to be in this world, —and for this, you well know to whom the gratitude should go. I scribble this in haste, and in the dark besides but your goodness will

2. Probably an agent of the Martins who lived in the region. See the letter of August 14 to Lady Martin.

1. Helena Saville (Faucit) Martin (1817–98) took the part of Lucy, Countess of Carlyle, in Browning's *Strafford* in its first presentation by Macready, May 1, 1837. Browning's acquaintance with her, therefore, extended over 50 years. She had played the part of Mildred Tresham in *A Blot in the 'Scutcheon* on February 11, 1843, and of Colombe in *Colombe's Birthday,* on April 25, 1853. Her husband records that "my wife and Browning had been friends in the days of their young enthusiasm, and the renewal of their acquaintance on a footing of easy familiarity was a pleasure to both." (Sir Theodore Martin, *Helena Faucit,* p. 388.)

2. In a letter to the Skirrows, below, dated September 3, Browning mentions "just three weeks' absence from London." That would date the arrival of the poet and his sister as August 13. This letter was doubtless written the next day.

interpret. Whenever we [see]³ you or Sir Theodore,—well, you know what I would say about *that* also.

My sister sends her kindest love to you both: and I am, as of old,

Ever truly yours

[Huntington] Robert Browning.

To Mrs. Charles Skirrow

Hand Hotel,
Llangollen, W. Wales
Aug. 30, '86.

My dear Friend,

It was a true flash of pleasure when your well-known hand-writing startled me among the other letters duly laid on our breakfast-table. You enquire very kindly about my Sister: am I to take for granted that no enquiry needs be made concerning yourself, and that both you and (I suppose) the young Lady are quite well and in full enjoyment of this fine weather? So I will hope,—and go on to say that my Sister is quite well again, in all essential points, and fast recovering her customary strength. We were not prepared for such warm weather,—rather expected the air to be bracing—and indeed when we arrived it was cold enough for a fire: but the last fortnight has been a very different experience. Still, the autumnal weather must come at some time or other, and we mean to wait for it—since it is impossible for any Hotel to be more suited to our wants in every respect than this excellent one,—where we are absolutely as well off as if at home: for instance,—I found, by a paragraph in a newspaper last week, that "Mr. Phelps" ¹ was among the visitors here: on enquiry as to his whereabouts in the neighbourhood, I found that he and his wife had been staying at the Hotel for more than a week. I called at once—and found that he also, having seen the paragraph (in which myself was mentioned) had wondered where *I* could be. He was unluckily summoned next

---

3. The word "see" may be "need."

1. Edward John Phelps (1822–1900), lawyer and diplomat, had the difficult task of succeeding James Russell Lowell as minister to Great Britain in 1885. A graduate of the Yale Law School, he was admitted to the Vermont Bar in 1843. He became Kent Professor of Law at Yale University in 1881. Without training as a diplomat he succeeded, through "tact . . . ability . . . and personal charm," in winning approval from all elements of English society. (*D.A.B.* See letter, below, dated January 10, 1889, n. 2.)

day by a Telegram—as he said "Our people do not like us to be idle." [2] As for the Martins, they are kindness itself—and if I seem to introduce their names abruptly it is because, since writing the last sentence, Sir Theodore presented himself here in person. I told him you had presumed or been certain we should enjoy his company greatly: and he said all you could desire in return. My Sister walks easily for a couple of hours and a half—besides a little enterprise on her own account in the morning—surely that is satisfactory progress during a fortnight's stay. I am pushed out of the paper, and can only add, however unnecessarily that I am as ever —most affectionately yours—R Browning. My sister desires her kindest love to you—and all regards to Miss Proctor. [3]

[Schiff]

To Mr. and Mrs. Charles Skirrow

Hand Hotel, Llangollen, W. Wales.
Sept. 3, '86.

I was really going to write this very day, my two dearest friends, when your welcome letter reaches me. If I did not do so at once, it is because our life here is even more uneventful than at Gressoney —where one could at least talk about glaciers and torrents, and so seem on the edge at least of a possible adventure. With two exceptions, I have not spent an autumn in England for some forty years [1] —while my Sister has been as constantly out of it for thirty—with one season spent in Scotland: so that we might not unreasonably look for novelty in even a stay at Llangollen. But it happens that this Hotel is so quiet and comfortable—and our arrangements for continuing the life we like so completely successful that there is nothing to say but that we are both quite well. To give you a notion of how little we suffer from disturbance,—I noticed—by a

2. Browning perhaps betrays a sign of old age by repeating this episode with Phelps in his next letter to the Skirrows on September 3, below.

3. Possibly Miss Procter is Florence, the only daughter of Bryan Waller Procter (Barry Cornwall), still living at this date. If, however, Miss Procter is the young lady referred to in the letter, she might be a granddaughter of Bryan Waller Procter, and a daughter of Montagu Procter. See Richard Armour, *Barry Cornwall* (New York, 1935), pp. 121–123.

1. Browning may be referring here to the autumn of 1871, which he spent in England and Scotland, and the autumn of 1876, which he spent in England and Arran. Before his final years it was usually his practice to leave London early in August and to return by mid-October.

paragraph in a newspaper last week, that "Mr. Phelps" was at Llangollen: "in the neighbourhood"—I conjectured: but, on enquiry I found he was an inmate of the Hotel, and had been so for a week: on calling, I found further that he also had seen my name in the same piece of news, and was similarly wondering where myself could be. Unluckily he was obliged to leave the next day—having been recalled by a telegram. The Martins have shown us every sort of kindness: I shall see them this afternoon and will duly deliver your message. They are about three miles off, in a charming Villa of their own building, on perhaps the best situation of the whole valley. All this while, I keep you waiting for what you so kindly first of all ask about: S's improvement in health and strength is great and indeed surprising. She walks with me for rarely less than two hours and a half in the afternoon,—having walked a little on her own account earlier in the day. One could hardly wish for a better consequence of just three weeks' absence from London. The weather has been, until to-day, very fine and only too warm —(she would have preferred a more "bracing" air) but things are altered,—there is rain and cold. We went yesterday to Chester,— a town neither of us had seen,—Sir Th[eodore] being our Guide, —and well worth seeing was the fine old picturesque place. How long we shall continue here is uncertain—we cannot be more at our ease anywhere, and I shall be much inclined, if it is possible, to stay to the very edge of winter. Our Venice affair is still in strange uncertainty: it would seem that the adverse party has not put in any answer to our "citation"—and, in England, judgment would go "in default" surely. My lawyer engages to keep me apprised of whatever occurs—and all the authorities—in the shape of intelligent people, with whom I have spoken on the subject, agree that the adversary has no chance,—still it seems inexplicable that, even in a lazy country like Italy, something definite should not be known by this time.[2] Pen will go in person at this month's end to see if he can expedite matters—and it *may* prove proper that I should accompany or follow him,—this causes the uncertainty as to remaining here, as I should much like to do. So much for our

2. In 1885 Browning had attempted to purchase the Palazzo Manzoni in Venice as a gift for his son, but after much litigation he paid his own costs and withdrew upon finding that the foundations of the palace were insecure. See *Letters,* ed. Hood, pp. 241, 250, 252, 372. His son, Robert Barrett Browning, bought the Palazzo Rezzonico in Venice in 1888.

important selves. Need I say at all how glad we are that you once again enjoy Homburg as you say? Only keep the indefatigable Worker from wanting to be too soon again at his toiling and moiling, and both of you will be the better for it. All your news was precious—Salvini, Mrs. B. M.'s "drag[g"],[3] even H. R. H's diversions: [4] I observe that poor Mrs. Brown Potter [5] is out of the running. Is it my fault that I cannot reciprocate intelligence?—only tell you what you know so well that I am ever

most affectionately yours,
Robt. Browning.

My Sister's true love.

[Schiff]

To Mrs. Charles Skirrow

Hand Hotel, Llangollen,
Sept. 6, '86.

Dearest Friend,

I should like you to know by a word from me, rather than incidentally, that I have lost our Milsand: [1] who died on the 4th at his place, Villers la Faye in the Côte d'Or. We heard from him—a letter dated Aug[u]st 28th on his arrival there: he was increasingly

---

3. The edge of the paper has been cut so that the last letter of this word must be guessed at—as either "g" or "y." For Browning's relation to Tommaso Salvini see above, letter of March 3, 1884, n. 2; Mrs. B. M. is Browning's wealthy American friend, Mrs. Bloomfield-Moore.

4. Albert Edward (1841–1910), first son and second child of Queen Victoria and Prince Albert, later (1901) King Edward VII, who was "constant patron of the theatre," but whose "chief amusement from middle life on was horse racing." (D.N.B.)

5. Cora (Urquhart) Potter (1859–1936), born in New Orleans, married J. Brown Potter of New York and then went abroad to exploit her talents as a recitationist. (Who Was Who, 1921–1941.) She published My Recitations in 1886 and, besides including "Hervé Riel," "Ratisbon" ("Incident of the French Camp"), and "Evelyn Hope" in her collection, she dedicated the volume to Browning with these words: "To Robert Browning: Among many pleasures and privileges my recitations have brought me, your friendship is the most valued. With grateful recollection of your encouragement of my efforts, I write your name at the head of this little volume. Cora Urquhart Potter."

1. Joseph Milsand (1817–86), French critic and journalist, whom Browning had known since 1852. The best account of their meeting and friendship may be found in Orr, Life, pp. 173 ff. Browning prefaced his next volume, Parleyings with Certain People of Importance in Their Day with a simple memorial to his friend, and the motto: Absens absentem auditque videtque.

weak in body—his mind remaining the same. I have got the news from Paris, by Telegram, this morning. You liked and were kind to him, both of you.

Ever affectionately yours

[Schiff]   R Browning.

To Sir Theodore and Lady Martin

19, Warwick Crescent, W.
Dec. 5, '86.

Dear Friends,

To my great disappointment I am prevented from doing what I had really set my heart upon, and seeing you once again before you leave us. That affection of the throat which had begun to trouble me a week ago is so increased as to take the ugly name of "Spasmodic Asthma," and I am forbidden to go out on such a day as this: three days imprisonment are a very strange experience to me. I feel happy indeed that you will soon breathe freelier than I can hope to do this many a week: you will not forget your promise —(I cannot write to *one* without thinking of *two*,—it was Lady Martin who promised) that you would let us hear of you by an occasional post-card. But you may well believe our thoughts of you and your kindness will be anything but "occasional." All pleasant chances befall you! ¹ Come safely back, and be sure you will find as you leave us, (*now* I include my Sister!)

Yours affectionately ever

[Huntington]   Robert Browning.

To Sir Theodore Martin

19, Warwick Crescent, W.
Dec. 28, '86

My dear Sir Theodore,

I was indeed startled by your letter "from Paris"—having been congratulating ourselves,—my Sister and I,—on your safe arrival at Cannes before the bitter weather from which we are now suffering could render travelling almost impracticable. The worst,—that

1. The Martins had set out for Cannes at the end of the year where Lady Martin hoped, vainly, to recover from "pains in the chest and throat." (Sir Theodore Martin, *Helena Faucit*, p. 390.) As indicated in the letter below, December 28, 1886, they stopped in Paris before proceeding southward.

middle-passage with its horrors,—you have luckily encountered,—though Lady Martin must have suffered sadly. I wish you well out of the frost and snow which we, of London, are enduring as best we may. Our own particular "best" is of no very good quality. You may remember that on the afternoon when I supposed I had but *that* opportunity of seeing you, I was somewhat indisposed. The ugly thing increased next day, and, in brief, I needed a Doctor—who promised me "Spasmodic Asthma" for this and succeeding winters. A week or two, however,—of much house-keeping and no acceptance of entertainments,—have changed matters for the better: and I feel much as usual. Not so, however, my Sister, who has managed to catch and keep a bad cold and cough. She assures me to-day that she feels better—as I trust is the case. But the habit we both of us have indulged in, of passing the early part of winter abroad, seems to have grown more necessary than we thought—and I shall remember this present experience if we last till another year. Meanwhile we keep ourselves warm with the abundantly pleasurable memories of last Autumn, and your goodness is in every one of them. Perhaps you are well out of the political confusion which is darkening knowledge all round us for the moment. Indeed it is as intelligible to you as to the people here who pass for "men able to render a reason": the prospect is anyhow far from agreeable.[1] Let me go back and, if I may, continue in what is wholly agreeable—the assurance that dear Lady Martin and yourself must intimately know and feel how affectionately and gratefully—as befits good observers of Christmas—we wish you every good gift—my Sister as well as

[Huntington]

Yours truly ever
Robert Browning.

1. On December 23 Lord Randolph Churchill startled the political world by resigning "his post as chancellor of the exchequer and with it the leadership of the house." In the face of "grave fears of an European war," Churchill "was convinced that England ought not to fight [Russia] over Bulgaria and he insisted on a reduction of military expenditures, in order, during this crisis in the near east, to emphasize the pacific policy of the government." (Sidney Low and R. C. Sanders, *The History of England (1837–1901)* [London, 1907], pp. 390–392.) Browning had approved the strong action of the British in Egypt in 1882 and doubtless was not pleased with any weakening of the foreign policy.

To Mrs. Charles Skirrow

19, Warwick Crescent, W.
Jan. 20, '87.[1]

Dearest Friend, I have *no* Proof sheets of the new volume,—nor would be allowed to transmit them, were they in my possession. They are already in America, and will appear simultaneously with the publication here—which takes place in a week; and, being properly paid for, ought not to be forestalled in any way.[2]

Yes, indeed it is long since I have seen you, and very sensible am I of it! I am quite well again, and, could I be sure of seeing you, would soon have a delightful lunch *a quattr' occhi*,[3] as some months ago. I *did* get the flowers, and ought to have grunted at least by way of thankfulness, since even a pig acknowledges the gift of an acorn: but, after all, you know how dearly I love you and ever am, though ungruntingly,

Yours grateful[ly] and affectionately
Robert Browning.

Love to the dear Husband—to be bettered by your presentation. I fear toughness in the fibre of the book [4] and consequent indigestion in the case of the readers—I shall see—and you shall feel!
[Schiff]

To Mrs. Charles Skirrow

19, Warwick Crescent, W.
Jan. 22, '87.

Dearest Friend, I will say—for the *a quattr' occhi*—next Wednes-

1. In 1887 Browning was in London from January 1 to July 23; St. Moritz, including journey thereto, from July 23 to September 12; in Bâle on September 13; in Amiens on September 14; in London on September 15.

2. *Parleyings with Certain People of Importance in Their Day,* which was published in America by Houghton Mifflin and Company with a signed statement by Browning that these were "the authorized publishers for the United States." The *Athenaeum* for January 29 carried the Smith, Elder advertisement announcing the *Parleyings* as "This Day . . . Published."

3. Literally, "at four eyes." Tête-à-tête.

4. The review of the *Parleyings* in the *Athenaeum* (February 19, 1887) reveals a weariness with scolding Browning for his craggy style. The critic labels the volume one more of Browning's contributions to "the poetry of idiosyncrasy" but concludes that, after all, Browning will have "a high place somewhere among the immortals."

day at 1½. unless you forbid, or appoint some other day. Nothing will delight me more.

I want you to amuse the beloved Husband by telling him that my Bills have come in for the Law suit at Venice [1]—from which, as I retired,—all expenses of the adverse party fall on myself: there was really much done, on both sides, consultations, citations and so on—documents in duplicate for the most part. My own advocate had claims on me for previous and subsequent work. Adverse Party's charges 309 f[ran]cs, 55 cent[essime]—or £12.7s.— My Lawyer's ditto—403 f[ran]cs—or £16.2.6. I doubt if litigation is not more costly here!

Ever affectionately his and yours
[Schiff] R Browning

To Mrs. Charles Skirrow

19, Warwick Crescent, W.
Jan. 23, '87.

Dearest Friend—May I anticipate by a day the pleasure you promise me, and go to you on Tuesday instead of Wednesday—always at 1.30. as I said? Unless I hear to the contrary I shall conclude you permit this.

Ever affectionately yours
[Schiff] Robert Browning.

To Miss Violet Paget

19 Warwick Crescent, W.
Jan. 31, '87.

Dear Vernon-Lee-Violet-Paget [1] treats poor R. B. as if he were the Philistine he is not, when she plays at supposing he forgets her existence, and fearing he will detect an impertinence in her kindly taking the trouble to copy out for him a choice and characteristic bit of history,—and moreover bidding *him* not trouble himself to say "thank you"—when the veriest pig does as much for the acorn he grunts over. I do thank you, dear Miss Paget,—as you know I ought and must,—for both the extract and the letter that brings it this morning: and it is pleasant indeed to see your hand-writing,

---

1. The lawsuit over Palazzo Manzoni. (See above, letter of September 3, 1886, and Katherine de Kay Bronson, "Browning in Venice," *Century Magazine*, LXIII, 572–573.)

1. See above, letter of May 13, 1886, and n. 1.

and hear of you, and your friends. Yes, I did have a visit from Mr. Placci,[2] and greatly liked the little I was privileged to get thereby. Yes, my Avison, and very old acquaintance, is the author of an *Essay on Musical expression*, 1752. which was notable in its day; the "March" I talk about was a favorite of my father's, and came into my hand after—oh, no matter how many a *lustrum* since he hummed—or I strummed—its resonancy.[3] But I leave off lest I *tire your good nature*—this is, fugue-fashion, the answer to that sweet subject of my "forgetfulness" and your "impertinence." In sober earnest, I am

Always yours admiringly and lovingly

[Baylor] Robert Browning.

To An Unidentified Correspondent

19 Warwick Crescent, W.
March 9, '87.

Dear Sir,

I beg to return my best thanks for your kind and sympathetic letter, and the interesting poem which accompanies it. When you conjecture that I "must needs love Burns,"—I answer that I have some Scottish blood in my veins,—my Mother's blood, that is to say.

With renewed thanks believe me, Dear Sir,

Yours very sincerely

[Huntington] Robert Browning.[1]

To Godfrey Douglas Giles [1]

19, Warwick Crescent, W.
March 25, '87.

My dear Mr. Giles,

To the great regret of my Sister and myself we fear, and more than fear, that our visit to your Studio will be impossible, this

2. Unidentified.

3. This, of course, is a reference to the "Parleying with Charles Avison." Browning possessed two copies of *An Essay on Musical Expression*, one dated 1752 and the other 1753. (Sotheby, *Browning Collections*, items 360, 361, p. 71.) See also DeVane, *Browning's Parleyings*, pp. 252–283.

1. Below the signature, in another hand, is written "the Poet."

1. This letter is printed without comment in *Baylor University Browning Interests*, ed. Armstrong, 5th ser., p. 64.

afternoon. We fully expected to enjoy the sight of your Pictures,, and Pen—to whom I mentioned our purpose of going to see them, will be disappointed at missing the account he was to receive of their subjects and treatment: but I am kept here by matters I cannot help attending to. We shall of course find your works at the Academy: [2] but would have preferred examining them in your presence. Pray understand and forgive what we would gladly help were it in our power.

Yours truly ever
Robert Browning.

Pen finished and sent in his Salon picture: but is suffering greatly from rheumatism in his right hand,—so that I hardly think he will finish his work for the Grosvenor in time.[3] He left Paris, for a week's change, but returns to-day—not much benefitted, I apprehend, by letter this morning.
[Baylor]

To Lord Mount-Temple [1]

19. Warwick Crescent, W.
April 2, '87.

Dear Lord Mount-Temple,

It has been a great pleasure to find that you still remember me, and I thank you heartily for your kind invitation—unable, as I

2. Giles' picture accepted for exhibition by the Royal Academy in 1887 is called "An Incident at the Battle of Tamaai, Eastern Soudan, March 13, 1884." (Algernon Graves, *The Royal Academy of Arts,* III, 237.) Godfrey Giles' studio was at Maresa Road, 4, Trafalgar Studios. For an account of Giles see above, letter of March 25, 1886, n. 1.

3. The picture here referred to by the poet may be the one by his son, described in Sotheby, *Browning Collections,* item 29, as follows: "*After the Bath,* a nude figure standing, one knee on a couch covered with a tiger skin, R. B. B. 1887."

1. William Cowper, later Cowper-Temple (1811–88), was raised to the peerage as Baron Mount-Temple in 1880. He was active in the debates on education in the Parliament of 1868 to 1874. At the time of this letter he was occupied primarily with philanthropic activities. The principal residence of Lord and Lady Mount-Temple was Broadlands, near Romsey, Hants, an estate of 6,135 acres. A fine picture of Broadlands appears as frontispiece for a curious little book by Edward Clifford, *Broadlands As It Was* (for private circulation only, London, 1890). "No house kept such open doors," observed the author. "Though the wretched were made so welcome, yet the wise and noble were glad to find themselves there" (p. 2).

unfortunately am, to accept it. My Son is in Paris and not expected here for some time,—and my own engagements hinder me from leaving home during the month. I can only repeat my thanks, and, begging you to offer my best regards to Lady Mount-Temple,[2] remain

Yours sincerely ever

[Yale] Robert Browning.

To An Unidentified Correspondent

19, Warwick Crescent, W.

Apr. 23, '87.

Dear Sir,

I at once recognize the book [1] as having belonged to my Father; whose handwriting is everywhere,—in the notes and that rough scribble of an epigram on the cover. The period of Roman History which is the subject of the work was one in which he took great interest, and was thoroughly familiar with,—more especially in its relation to the literature of the time: you may observe that all the notes refer to the famous men,—contemporaries with Virgil and Horace, concerning whom my Father had a life-long purpose of inventing a sort of biographical novel. From the fact that "the Book has been in a private collection since 1849," I can only surmise that, like too many of its companions, it had been lent to a friend with a conscience like that of too many book-borrowers. I am glad it is now in such satisfactory keeping: you will receive it duly on Monday next.

I am, Dear Sir,

Yours very sincerely

Robert Browning

On second thought,—I send the Book at once—with many thanks for the sight of it.

[New York Public Library]

2. Lady Mount-Temple (1822–1901) was one of the three vice-presidents of the London Browning Society when it was first organized in 1881. She was the ninth daughter of Vice-Admiral Richard Delap Tollemache.

1. This letter of Browning was enclosed in a volume, *The History of the Triumvirates*, "trans. by Tho. Otway, lately deceased, 1686." This volume is now in the Berg Collection of the New York Public Library.

To Mr. and Mrs. Charles Skirrow

19, Warwick Crescent, W.
May 8, '87.[1]

Dearest Friends,—add just one piece of kindness more to the accumulation which would otherwise become almost oppressive:— the crowning kindness will be to read in my heart—not take from my mouth—the love and gratitude I have so long gone on increasing that mere words will not help at all to tell you

how affectionately I am ever
Yours while life lasts for

[Schiff]   Robert Browning.

To Felix Moscheles

19, Warwick Crescent, W.
May 26, '87.

My dear Moscheles,

I may just say that I gave the address of Heyermans [1] to two Ladies, on Tuesday evening, who seemed much impressed by what I said about the advantage of getting such an instructor: I also wrote at once to Mrs. Harrison—and hope good will come of it, —as probably will be the case if H. can manage to wait a little.[2]

1. This letter is in answer to a birthday greeting.
1. Jean-Arnould Heyermans (1837–?), Pen's early instructor in painting, recommended to Browning by Moscheles, who wrote that "Browning never tired of expressing his gratitude to me for having found the right man and having put his son in the right place . . . When some years later, Heyermans settled in London, Browning never lost an opportunity of smoothing the artist's path among strangers." (Felix Moscheles, *Fragments of an Autobiography*, pp. 321, 322.) Six months after this letter, however, Browning wrote to Pen that Heyermans "is in a forlorn way." (*Letters*, ed. Hood, p. 285; see also Felix Moscheles, *In Bohemia with Du Maurier*, pp. 25–28, for further description of Heyermans and his relations with Pen.)
2. Mrs. Ethel (Harrison) Harrison became the wife of Frederic Harrison (1831–1923) in 1870 and by him had four sons, for one of whom, perhaps, she was inquiring about lessons in painting. The Harrisons lived near Browning in Westbourne Terrace and were fairly intimate with him. Frederic Harrison had known Browning since 1853 and described him as "the happiest social spirit it has ever been my fortune to meet." (Frederic Harrison, *Autobiographic Memoirs* [London, 1911], II, 106.) Austin Harrison, second son, gives an excellent analysis of his mother and how she controlled the education of her children. (See *Frederic Harrison, Thoughts and Memories* [London, 1926], the chapter on "Boyhood Memories," *passim*.)

The quotation should run thus
> . . . "that bright shape of lucid stone
> Which drew the heart out of Pygmalion"

The whole poem abounds in passages of extraordinary beauty: indeed there is one subject,—quite unmeddled with by anybody, —which you might treat capitally: I will read it to you some day, and hear what you think. *Such* a subject! [3]

Ever yours truly

[Yale]   Robert Browning.

To Mrs. Charles Skirrow

19, Warwick Crescent, W.
May 31, '87.

Dearest Friend,

I did not write about "Werner," [1] but supposed you were certain of my joyful acceptance of your kindness—as indeed I had signified already. I am anticipating great pleasure on Wednesday. Let me be with you at a quarter past 2.,—*not* to Luncheon, which I like to discuss more leisurely than would be possible to-morrow. I *have* received *Gladys* [2]—but the calls on my attention just now are

---

3. The poem is Shelley's *Witch of Atlas* and the lines suggesting a picture are probably these (St. xxxv–xxxvi):

> Then by strange art she kneaded fire and snow
> Together, tempering the repugnant mass
> With liquid love—all things together grow
> Through which the harmony of love can pass:
> And a fair Shape out of her hands did flow,
> A living Image, which did far surpass
> In beauty that bright shape of vital stone
> Which drew the heart out of Pygmalion.
>
> A sexless thing it was, and in its growth
> It seemed to have developed no defect
> Of either sex, yet all the grace of both. . . .

Moscheles does not mention this suggestion from Browning in his reminiscences of the poet.

1. This is possibly a reference to a novel by E. Werner, the nom de plume of Elizabeth Burstenbinder (1839–1918), a very popular German novelist who "schrieb zahlreiche Unterhaltungsromane, die meist zuerst in der 'Gartenlaube' erscheinen." (*Der grosse Brockhaus* [Leipzig, 1935], XX, 242.) Eight of E. Werner's novels were translated into English between 1881 and 1889. (*English Catalogue of Books* [London, 1891], "E. Werner.") But the Skirrows probably became acquainted with the works of this novelist on one of their annual summer trips to Homburg.

2. *Gladys: a frivolous novel*, by Tramio, 3 vols., was first published in Lon-

embarrassing to a terrible degree—and I wanted to read the book
before attempting to write: I will do so as soon as I possibly can.
We are promised the house [3] in a week or two, but I hardly expect
so quick a removal.

I am happy to hear of your renewed health: ah, "the change!"
I have been stationary here, without a single day's release, for
nearly the last eight months.

Ever affectionately yours

[Schiff]   Robert Browning.

To Mrs. Charles Skirrow

[Late June, 1887] [1]

Dearest Friend, I have put down, as briefly as I could, the points
which seem to entitle me to compensation. The dear Husband will
state them as he best knows how,—and I shall be content with
what comes of his most kind and helpful intervention. A person
of my age cannot wait to be turned out by the excavators knock-
ing at his door, and I have not budged till there was a plain
necessity.[2]

Ever affectionately yours

[Schiff]   Robert Browning

---

don in 1882. The author was Gertrude Armitage Smith. (Halkett and Laing,
Dictionary of Anonymous and Pseudonymous English Literature, II, 378.)

3. The house referred to is 29 De Vere Gardens, which became Browning's
residence for the rest of his life. See the following letter.

1. Penciled in the upper right corner in a hand other than Browning's is the
notation "?1887." The letter refers to Browning's removal from 19 Warwick
Crescent to 29 De Vere Gardens. The move was made in June, 1887, probably
on June 24. One may assume that this note was written in late June or early
July, 1887, for the following reason: the note paper used is plain, whereas a
letter to Mrs. Skirrow dated May 31, 1887 is written on stationery embossed with
the address 19, Warwick Crescent, and another letter to Mrs. Skirrow dated
July 22, 1887 is written on stationery embossed with the address 29, De Vere
Gardens. The note on plain paper, therefore, would seem to fit between these
dates. The clause, "I have not budged till there was a plain necessity," implies
that the move to 29 De Vere Gardens has been recently accomplished. (See
also n. 2, below.)

2. According to the lease entered into on June 24, 1862, Browning could
not relinquish 19 Warwick Crescent without giving such notice, at least six
months in advance, as would cause the lease to expire on the month and day
of commencing the tenancy; i.e., on June 24. Browning was apparently unaware of this provision and gave notice too late to fulfill the requirements in
time to be released before June 24, 1888. Consequently William Buddle, the

To Mr. and Mrs. Charles Skirrow

29, De Vere Gardens, W.[1]

July 22, '87.

Sad, sad it is and strange too that all at once I should seem to be at a distance from my two dearest of friends: it shall not be so, next year or next Autumn, if I can control events. But I have been really out of my usual health, besides being teazed with matters requiring my attending to,[2]—and believe that the best remedy is to at once go away from all the bother, and get renovated by St. Mori[t]z—whither my Sister and myself go to-morrow,—the Sister being, in Yankee language, more "wilted" than I. You shall hear from me, depend on it,—depend also on my not forgetting for a moment all your goodness to ever

Yours truly and affectionately

Robert Browning.

We count upon returning at the end of September—not meaning to go to Italy this year but return and try to get snug in our new house—which you will come and see, will you not?

Once again, your loving

RB

Address

Villa Berry,

St. Mori[t]z.

[Schiff]

owner, sent a "Statement of Amounts due from R. Browning, Esq. on or before the expiration of his tenancy of No. 19, Warwick Crescent." The sum billed was £202–18–9. It is probable that Mr. Skirrow secured a compromise, for on September 27, 1887, Buddle accepted from Browning £100 "in full payment . . . of all demands to this date." (See *Browning's Letter File*, ed. Armstrong, pp. 114–115.)

1. Browning and his sister moved into their new home in June. According to Mrs. Orr 19 Warwick Crescent "had faults of construction and situation which the lapse of time rendered only more conspicuous; the Regent's Canal Bill had also doomed it to demolition." (*Life*, p. 375. See also pp. 376 ff. for a good description of 29 De Vere Gardens.)

2. One of these matters was doubtless the relinquishing of 19 Warwick Crescent. (See above, letter of late June, 1887.)

To Sir Theodore and Lady Martin

St. Moritz,
Sept. 6, '87.

Dear Friends, we have been waiting here for some event to happen,—something worth writing about,—and the days glide by, we are in the seventh week of our sojourn, yet unless I inform you that the weather is splendid, I am at a loss for news—even this last matter of the fine weather has appeared in the Newspapers. Still, it was so delightful for us to hear that you, both of you, were well and in complete enjoyment of your beautiful Bryntysilio that we hope you will like to hear that ourselves are thoroughly the better for this divine air. We think of staying a week longer— but it would be too hard to leave all this beauty should the sky continue as blue as it now glorifies everything. All love to you both.
[Huntington]   R and S. Browning.

To Mr. and Mrs. Charles Skirrow

29, De Vere Gardens, W.
Sept. 30, '87.

Dearest Friends,

The news, in the main, is quite true. While we were at St. Moritz, Pen announced to me his intention, with my leave and good will, of marrying Fanny Coddington,—an American lady, he and ourselves had known fifteen years ago, when her parents, our friends, resided in London—people we respected altogether. Pen had actually "proposed" to her fourteen years ago,—when she was a girl —five years younger than the "proposer." She was brought up in England, and, on the death of her Mother, kept her Father's house in New York, till his own death, in the February of last year: she was returning to England for the sake of a younger sister's health, —which was expected to benefit by a visit to St. Moritz,—when Pen and his early love met by mere accident at a country house, last July—and at once the smouldering fire was set flaring,—with the result of a fresh proposal and cordial acceptance. Now, it so happens, of all the young persons of my acquaintance, I could

1. The persons addressed in this letter are identified by the references to Bryntysilio, the Martins' home near Llangollen, Wales, near which Browning and Sarianna had spent the vacation of 1886.

not pick out a single one so fitted,—if I can judge at all,—to make Pen, with his many peculiarities, the best of wives—she is deficient in no one quality requisite for doing so—and you will readily believe I am somewhat critical and perhaps exacting in such a case. They are simply devoted to each other, and on what would seem to be rational grounds enough. She is a fine handsome generous creature—and honest and good—every inch of her. They will be married next Tuesday at Hawkwell, near Pembury, Tunbridge Wells, from the house of a relative, Mrs. Schlesinger,—and thence start for Folkestone, with a view to spending a month at Venice. On their return, they sail to New York at the beginning of November, where the Lady needs to settle her affairs,—and we expect them in London again early in the New Year,—after which—themselves must arrange for their eventual life together. I may tell you that the lady's means are ample,—and indeed would render Pen quite independent of my contribution, if I could allow *that*—as you may be sure, I do not. This will in no way interfere with his sedulous prosecution of his Art—which the Lady is as anxious to further as he can possibly be. I and my Sister leave town to-morrow for our friends' house at Hawkwell,—where we stay over the ceremony, and return next day. You may well believe it is a great relief to me that Pen should make so satisfactory a conclusion of his comfortless foreign life,—beneficial to his Art, I dare say, but not conducive to his health and peace,—a life, too, which, in the nature of things, could not be prolonged indefinitely. He is here— and sends both of you his truest love and gratitude for your never-failing kindness to him—to us all: a lucky fellow I account him. I scribble this, fast as fingers can fly,—having to tax them still further or I would tell you of our poor friend Mrs. F. G.[1] whom I saw yesterday. She is recovering from the carriage accident which might have been serious indeed. I shall be hungry and thirsty to see you,—and it will be soon, I trust. Meantime, and ever remember me as affectionately yours

Robert Browning

My Sister is absolutely of the same mind with me as to the advantages of the match: She sends—however needlessly—her best love. [Schiff]

1. For an account of Mrs. Thomas FitzGerald, the friend here referred to, see below, Letter of June 23, 1888, n. 1.

To Mr. and Mrs. Charles Skirrow

29, De Vere Gardens, W.
Oct. 5, '87.

Dearest Friends,—we are *just* returned from Hawkwell Place, Pembury, where the wedding was accomplished yesterday, under the most pleasant circumstances conceivable: the little "Old Church,"—A.D. 11—, —was decked out with the prettiest of autumn flowers,—and, as nobody had been invited but the few relatives of the Bride,—we saw none but really sympathetic faces, some fifteen or eighteen in all—but the neighbours seemed to share in our satisfaction. Our Hosts, the Schlesingers, (Fanny's Cousins by the wife's side,) were full of care and hospitable kindness, and had taken all the trouble on themselves: after the Breakfast, Pen and his wife set off for Dover, and to-day go on to Milan and Venice, —whence, at the end of the month, they return here,—to proceed to New York, where the lady must settle her affairs with a view to residing in—Europe, certainly,—London,—if Heaven so please. She is altogether a dear and admirable person,—the fittest companion for Pen conceivable—at least by my Sister and myself— my Sister having always been a mother-and-a-half to the fortunate fellow. If I did not apprise you earlier of this great event in our little household, it was simply because I never dreamed of such a thing a few weeks ago. It is an attachment, however, of fifteen years' standing,—with the more likelihood, therefore, of being durable. Both parties have decided happiness-on-the-brain at present,—and I do trust and believe that it will subside into chronic mutual contentment and esteem. I should mention, that Fanny was very apprehensive of the report of her engagement reaching the ears of her American friends through the newspapers first of all —with the usual embellishments and mistakings—hence the start which I was forced to allow her own explanatory letters. All this anybody may know. There were two American reporters at the Church yesterday,—and sundry other "representatives" of our own Press: but all information was with[h]eld—which will probably give the greater scope to fancy. I write in all haste—but in all affection, too, for my dearest Friends—whose I am ever

R. Browning

There has been profuse sympathy from both sides of the Atlantic. [Schiff]

To Miss Emily Henrietta Hickey

29, De Vere Gardens, W.
Oct. 25, '87.

Dear Miss Hickey,

Thank you exceedingly for the *Strafford* [1]—which I had fancied might contain more important corrections than proves to be the case. I will return the copy to you—fortunately in person, since you promise myself and my Sister that great pleasure—which I have been waiting to speak about till I could get the notice which has just come—of the arrival here of my Son and his wife who leave Venice to-morrow and will be with us on Saturday for a few days before they sail for America. I fear there would be little chance of my enjoying your company as it deserves, did you visit us while they are in possession—with friends of their own to see. What may I expect of your kindness therefore? Will you take luncheon here tomorrow or on Thursday or Friday—at 1. oclock—or will you prefer letting the busy next week pass, and coming *any* day in the week after—or indeed on the Saturday of next week? I trust to your goodness to understand that I want only two things—your company,—and the least possible inconvenience to yourself in bestowing it on us: please let me be satisfied on both points by a word, and believe me ever, Dear Miss Hickey,

Yours most truly
Robert Browning.

My Sister is not in the house while I write, but she is as anxious to see you as I am, of course.
[Yale]

To Mrs. Charles Skirrow

29, De Vere Gardens, W.
Nov. 3, '87.

Dearest Friend, I shall be indeed delighted to go to you, if you will let me, next Tuesday, at 1 o'clock: I will talk myself out, and tell you all the news. The Couple arrived from Venice on Saturday last, and leave to-morrow for Liverpool and New York. They stayed with us,—but—I will tell you how happily all things are going on and likely to go.

1. Presumably Browning had not kept a list of the changes he had made in Miss Hickey's edition of *Strafford* (1884), and had borrowed her copy for comparison in preparation for the 1888 edition of his collected works.

Pen sends his kind love to you and to the dear Master. I myself am far from well, and hitherto have refused every invitation to go out—but *you* are irresistible.

All love to you both from
Yours ever lovingly

[Schiff]   Robert Browning

To Felix Moscheles

29, De Vere Gardens, W.
Nov. 14, '87.

My dear Moscheles,

Each of your translations is good—especial[ly] numbers 2. and 3. (There is a little ambiguity about our use of the word "Musician" which generally designates a practitioner merely) The quite literal translation would seem to be "In recognition of his signal services to the Art of Music." [1]

I was far from being sorry to find you were "out"—and presumably enjoying yourself: I shall soon look in again, depend on it— and believe me ever

Affectionately yours

[Yale]   Robert Browning.

To Mrs. Charles Skirrow

29, De Vere Gardens, W.
Nov. 25, '87.

Dearest Friend,

I did indeed receive—and was grieved for the reason of—your intimation that the Dinner was not to take place. Any sorrow of yours—of Mr. Skirrow's—will always be sure of my sympathy. And as I know that you and he know this perfectly, I did not write,— it seeming superfluous to do so.

We heard last evening of the safe arrival and perfect condition

1. Moscheles writes: "Unvarying kindness too he [Browning] showed me when, as he puts it, I 'entrusted him with a piece of business.' Such a piece was my preface to the Mendelssohn Letters. In this he made six or eight corrections, suggestions he insisted on calling them, when he brought the papers back himself that he might explain verbally why he had substituted a word here and added another there." (*Fragments of an Autobiography*, pp. 343–344.) Moscheles' book which Browning helped him with was called *Letters of Felix Mendelssohn to Ignaz and Charlotte Moscheles;* translated from the originals in his possession and edited by Felix Moscheles (London, 1888).

of our couple—and more news may [be] expected shortly. With all love to Mr. Skirrow and yourself,

I am ever affectionately yours,

[Schiff]

R.B.

TO FELIX MOSCHELES

29, De Vere Gardens, W.
Nov. 30, '87.

My dear Moscheles,

Pray forgive my delay in doing the little piece of business with which you entrusted me: an unexpected claim on my mornings interfered with it, till just now. Will this answer your purpose any way?

> Hail to the man who upward strives
>   Ever in happy unconcern:
> Whom neither praise nor blame contrives
>   From his own nature's path to turn.
>
> On and still on, the journey went,
>   Yet has he kept us all in view—
> Working in Age with Youth's intent,
>   In living—fresh, in loving—true.[1]

Were my version but as true to the original as your Father's life was to his noble ideal, it would be good indeed [2]— As it is, accept the best of

Yours truly ever

[Yale]

Robert Browning.

TO MISS EMILY HENRIETTA HICKEY

19. Warwick Crescent, W.
Dec. 17, '87. [1883] [1]

Dear Miss Hickey,

Tell Professor Gardiner by all means—with the same entreaty for a discretion in the use of the fact. He will understand that I

---

1. Browning drew a line to indicate that "praise" and "blame" in the third line should be transposed. The verses are a free translation of Horace, *Sermones* I, 2, 11.

2. The father of Felix Moscheles was Ignaz Moscheles (1794–1870), a fine pianist ("the greatest executant of his age") and the teacher of Mendelssohn.

1. This letter, on Warwick Crescent stationery, is plainly dated in Browning's own hand, but it is obviously misdated. He had moved to De Vere Gar-

had no notion of scribbling anything but as a rough piece of work which F. might fill up, file away, and make his own: he had no time to do as much in that way as both he and I expected.[2]

I go into the Country this afternoon and return to Warwick Crescent at the end of the week: I should have been delighted to see you: perhaps it may not be too late: I will write when I am fairly back.

Ever yours truly

[Yale]   R Browning.

To Mrs. Charles Skirrow

29, De Vere Gardens, W.

Jan. 24, '88.[1]

Dearest Friend,

You would have heard from me long before this, had I not been suddenly attacked by my old spasmodic cough complicated with rheumatism—a quite new experience. I was forced to keep the house for ten days, and am now only allowed to take the air on such occasions as just this pleasant Tuesday furnishes. I am forced to give up all old—and refuse all new temptations in the shape of dinner-parties. Do understand that if I fear to go to your Luncheon next week, it is solely because I know that I should only enjoy

dens in June, 1887, and he mentions Warwick Crescent in the letter itself. The envelope preserved with the letter is postmarked December 17, 1883. The letter fits into the sequence of letters about her edition of *Strafford*. The date is confirmed by a comparison with the letter to Mrs. Frank Hill, also written on December 17, 1883.

2. Professor Samuel R. Gardiner (1829–1902) of Oxford, authority on English history of the 17th century, wrote a critical preface to Miss Hickey's edition of *Strafford* (1884). He had little respect for Browning's play as history: "Not merely are there frequent minor inaccuracies, but the very roots of the situation are untrue to fact."

The envelope bears the notations, probably by Miss Hickey, "About Mr. Forster's *Strafford*" "leave to tell Professor Gardiner." Furnivall's statement that Browning and not Forster was the author of the prose life of Strafford has not been generally accepted, but this lends some support to Furnivall's contention. See above, letter of June 5, 1854, and DeVane, *Browning Handbook*, pp. 58–62.

1. In 1888 Browning was in London from January 1 to June 18; in Oxford from June 18 to June 24; in London from June 24 to August 13; at Primiero, Austria, soon after August 13 until mid-September; in Venice with Mrs. Bronson until mid-December; and in London for the rest of the year.

myself too well with you, and properly suffer in consequence. By continuing prudent, I hope to get back the power of being happy with you and the beloved Master as so often has been the case. Very sorry I am to hear that your own ailment has returned—for but a little while, I trust. Sarianna continues perfectly well; but we are very anxious about the Couple in America,—poor Fannie being in a condition. that prevents us from too much confidence at present.[2]

I am not aware of any "New Edition" of my wife's poems being announced: my own works are going to be republished in monthly volumes,—in a cheaper form,—but with no alterations except of the most trifling nature.[3] There has been issued a little shilling volume of *Selections* from E.B.B's poetry—but merely to attempt to neutralize the rascality of the pirates who reprint from the earlier works,—errors and all,—of which the copyright is expired. Of course, if you would like *that,* it shall be yours with all my heart.

Give my true love to the Husband and believe me ever affectionately yours

[Schiff]   Robert Browning

To Mrs. Charles Skirrow

29, De Vere Gardens, W.

Feb. 8, '88.

My dearest Friend, how very good you are! To be sure, you always have been so, but it continues to strike me as a novel experience. I ought to have told you that I am happily quite well again. I was confined to the house for ten days, and expected a longer confinement, but my illness left me all at once—and, though I take precautions, I find myself so much as usual, that I am beginning to go about, socially, in a moderate degree—dined from home yesterday for the first time: so that whenever you are inclined to concede me *"a quattr' occhi"* I will go to you most gladly—prefer-

2. Browning had received a cablegram from the United States the night before (January 23) and letters the morning of January 24 from Pen telling him of Fannie's miscarriage. (See *Letters,* ed. Hood, p. 284.)

3. Smith, Elder and Co. issued a cheaply bound edition of *The Poetical Works of Robert Browning* in 16 vols. in 1888. *Pauline* is the only poem which Browning revised extensively, a fact which he acknowledged in the preface. Apparently, too, the revision of *Pauline* was done on an impulse after the proofs of Vol. I were in his hands. (See Orr, *Life,* p. 380.)

ably, however, on any other day than a Monday or Thursday, though even then I might manage, if required to do so.

The Couple have taken their passage for Liverpool by a boat which leaves on the 10th March: poor Fannie has been seriously ill, through a continuance of the sickness provoked by the voyage in October, and the consequence has been a disappointment: Pen has naturally felt greatly alarmed—but he kept us aware things grew better,—by a telegram,—and his letter, received last Monday, was thoroughly re-assuring. You should chat with S., if but for a few minutes some day, and she would tell more than comports with my ignorance on the subject. Do you see into what a scrape poor Furnivall's incontinence of tongue (in the witness-box!) has brought him? [1] So can a man be really in the right, as to feeling, and the wrong, as to the expression of it. I was myself annoyed at the man—applying to Ly. Martin for money, in virtue of her friendship for me—at the pretended instigation of Dr. Furnivall! He was naturally angry, but played into the fellow's hands by folly enough. All love to you and the beloved Husband from your

affectionate

[Schiff]
Robert Browning.

1. The case was *Outram* vs. *Furnivall* for libel. The charge is summarized as follows: "Mr. L. S. Outram, an actor, was in 1886 engaged under the auspices of the Browning Society to produce Roberts [*sic*] Browning's play of *Strafford*. Miss Alma Murray was to act in the play. Admission to the performance was to be free, and the plaintiff was to get £60 and whatever sum could be raised by subscription. On the 23rd of October the defendant, who is Chairman of the Committee for the Browning Society, issued a circular headed 'Warning from Dr. Furnivall. Mr. L. S. Outram's appeal for a subscription to himself for playing Strafford.' This circular contained the remark that the defendant considered the issue without his sanction to his name being appended to it, 'as a scandalous attempt to get money from the members of the Browning Society under cover of his name.' The defendant also wrote to Miss Alma Murray a letter, which had the result of causing her to decline to act at a benefit of the plaintiff's at which she had promised to do." Furnivall, on the witness stand, said, among other things: "I cannot say I feel any regret for what I did in this matter. At first I thought it a moral and legal attempt to hoodwink the members of the Society. After taking legal advice, I think it now a moral wrong only." This "incontinence of tongue" brought from the presiding judge the statement that "the defendant by his conduct in the box has turned a mere friction into a serious matter." At the close of the judge's charge, "the jury at once found a verdict for the plaintiff—damages £100, for which his Lordship gave judgment with costs." (London *Times*, February 3, 1888, p. 13, col. 4.) Browning wrote two letters to Dr. Furnivall expressing in one the opinion the verdict was "a grotesque perversion of equity" and assuring Furnivall in the

To Mrs. Charles Skirrow

29, De Vcre Gardens, W.
March 13, '88.

Dearest Friend, I shall be happy to lunch with you on the 21st.

The Couple you so kindly enquire about left New York on Saturday for Liverpool—where they may be hoped to arrive at the end of this or the beginning of next week: we had letters yesterday containing the last accounts which were very satisfactory as to the wife's regained health.

Yes, poor Mrs. Procter is gone—after much suffering, which made her anxious to have release from it.[1] I had known her for fifty years at least.

With all love to you both
Yours affectionately ever
Robert Browning.

[Schiff]

To Mr. and Mrs. Charles Skirrow

29, De Vere Gardens, W.
May 7, '88.

How long ago it is since I first tried to thank my two dearest friends for their kindness in remembering my Birthday! I ought to have improved enormously in the art of returning them thanks, —for no year has gone by without giving me an opportunity of doing justice to the gratitude I feel,—and yet, now that there is yet another occasion of showing what I can do—what profit is in the experience which tries in vain to express itself? All I shall say is—I love you both from my heart of hearts and am ever most

Gratefully and affectionately your
Robert Browning.

[Schiff]

---

second that "everybody I have seen takes the right view of the subject." (*Letters,* ed. Hood, p. 287.)

1. Anne (Skeppers) Procter (1799–1888), the wife of Bryan Waller Procter (Barry Cornwall), was one of Browning's oldest friends. To her home the poet went almost every Sunday afternoon during all the years following the death of Mrs. Browning. Mrs. Procter's Sunday afternoons were a London version of Madame Mohl's Paris salon where all persons of rank in literature or art found a congenial atmosphere for an exchange of chitchat. Mrs. Procter, whose letters are fairly scarce, referred to the poet as "our dear old friend Mr. Browning" in a letter to Emma Lazarus in 1883. (*Letters to Emma Lazarus,* ed. Ralph L. Rusk, p. 53.)

To [MRS. THOMAS FITZGERALD (?)] [1]

Balliol College, Oxford
June 23, '88.[2]

Dear Friend, I had thought to leave this place for London earlier, —and, in that case, write from home where news may await me. Perhaps it will be better to say my extremely little say at once. We had a disastrous beginning of the week,—a rainy cold Wednesday, which spoilt the festivities, and a stormy next day, which prevented all walking. Yesterday was fine however—and the dinner to Ld. Lansdowne went off exceedingly well.[3] To-day is perversely fine—and but that I am engaged in the evening [4] I should accept the kind Master's invitation to stay longer: [5] but I leave at 4. p.m. It has been pleasant to meet many old friends—besides the love I have for Oxford generally—perhaps all the more that I am an adopted child, and not an heir with his natural rights to sit at the dais, and be welcomed as a Fellow—so my chance was last night.

1. There is no direct evidence that this letter was written to Mrs. FitzGerald. Circumstantial evidence, however, is fairly strong. For one thing, Browning on other occasions had detailed his Oxford doings to her. (See particularly letter of March 10, 1877 in Orr, *Life*, pp. 295–297.) For another thing, Mrs. FitzGerald was probably in Paris (See *Letters*, ed. Hood, p. 292), out of touch with Browning, and, therefore, a more likely recipient of such a newsy letter than, say, Mrs. Skirrow who might qualify as the recipient in all respects except that she was in London and likely to see Browning immediately upon his return. Finally, Browning calls his correspondent "learned lady," a phrase which perhaps eliminates Mrs. Skirrow. Mrs. Orr, one other possibility, had returned to London in May in a bad state of health (p. 293). Browning in this letter does not mention the state of health of his correspondent, nor, once again, would he have written news to someone whom he could soon see in London. Of the few women Browning addressed as "Dear Friend" and declared himself as "ever affectionately," Mrs. FitzGerald in this instance appears to be the best choice.

2. The date as written by Browning is June 23, but the Balliol dinner to which he refers occurred on June 23, and Browning refers to this banquet as "last evening." (The dinner was reported in the London *Times* on June 25, 1888, p. 12, col. 1.)

3. The Balliol College dinner in honor of the Marquis of Lansdowne (1845–1927) who was pausing in England after concluding his term as Governor-General of Canada (1883–88) and before beginning his term as Viceroy of India in November, 1888.

4. Possibly the engagement was with W. G. Kingsland. (See *Letters*, ed. Hood, p. 294.)

5. Benjamin Jowett was the Master of Balliol, with whom Browning regularly stayed on his trips to Oxford.

Pen's portrait is certainly good, as a likeness and a picture too. The artists generally decline to give the gown in its truthful aspect,—Millais refused to attempt it: Pen of course would refuse to try anything else: the fact is there,—and if my nose had been thrice as long as it is, would he be justified in making it more symmetrical than he found it? [6] We had a little music in Hall—the fine Organ being the Master's gift: the room is excellently adapted for music.

All the same there is a soft sadness about this place,—such a perpetual remembrance is it of the fleeting state of mortal things. The Master said, last evening, in his speech—that already, since the last College dinner of the sort, he had to think of ten eminent members of the College whose places know them no longer.[7] Even the three-years' stay of the undergraduates, the departure of the old and arrival of the new, in turn to become the old soon enough,—this is melancholy in some respects. "Well, we can smile and say —'my all was not laid here!' " Now, who wrote *that?*—learned lady and my dear friend whose I remain ever

Affectionately

[Mr. Richard L. Purdy]   Robert Browning.

To Mr. C. Butler [1]

June 25, '88.

Dear Mr. Butler,

Pray excuse the delay in replying to your kind note—caused as it has been by my absence from Town.[2] With respect to the

6. This is Pen Browning's 1882 oil portrait of Browning in academic gown, holding in his hand the Old Yellow Book. It was presented to Balliol in 1885 and hung the following year. (See Wilson, *Browning's Portraits* . . . , pp. 129–132.)

7. Among the losses mentioned by Jowett was the recent death of Matthew Arnold. (London *Times*, June 25, 1888, p. 12, col. 1.)

1. The present letter is a reply to a request that Browning fill one of two vacancies "to complete the 40 members" of the Roxburghe Club, whose object "was to perpetuate among Book Lovers and Collectors the memory of that eminent Bibliophile, the Duke of Roxburghe." Each member paid five guineas yearly subscription and at "sometime that suits him, prints some work for distribution among the members." (The whole of Butler's letter, dated June 22, 1888, is printed in *Browning's Letter File*, ed. Armstrong, p. 127.)

2. Browning had spent several days, probably from June 18 to June 24, at Oxford (*Letters*, ed. Hood, p. 294) where he attended the Balliol College dinner in honor of the Marquis of Lansdowne and heard tribute paid to Matthew Arnold who had recently died. (London *Times*, June 25, 1888, p. 12, col. 1.)

invitation it contains, I am sincerely gratified as well as flattered by such a proposal. I have long been acquainted with the objects and character of the Roxburghe Club,[3] and often admired the works issued under its protection,—but I am but a humble producer of works myself, and can only pretend to sympathize from the outside,—so to speak: the inner circle is for more fortune-favoured lovers of books than any writer of them is now-a-days likely to become. I must (as a bibliophile) remain contentedly amused at the fact that a little affair of my own, published more than half a century ago at my own expense,—and absolute loss of every penny,—then selling (were there buyers) at some three shillings and six pence, now is hardly procurable for £25. and has already been reprinted in *facsimile* as a curiosity! [4] Pray accept my best thanks for your kind intervention and believe me

Yours very sincerely

[Huntington]   Robert Browning.

To Mrs. Charles Skirrow

29, De Vere Gardens, W.
June 28, '88.

Dearest Friend,—how much I wish that the Benefit to which you invite me did really take place on the 9th (as your note informs me) and not on the 7th—as I learn from the newspaper! For I could have enjoyed your company, together with Miss Terry's acting, on Monday—whereas I have been engaged these five weeks or more to a dinner on the Saturday preceding.[1] It is always so: I have six invitations to dine to-morrow,—and am engaged, by right of priority, to the least pressing of all. Be assured that the neighbourhood to Sussex Gardens is the one thing I regret—the old easy way of walking in—your earliest of visitors—to the enter-

3. The Roxburghe Club was founded, probably at St. Albans' Tavern in 1812, by a group of bibliophiles who had witnessed the auction of Lord Roxburghe's books and had been stirred to bibliophilic frenzy by the duel between the Marquis of Blandford and Earl Spencer over possession of a Valdarfer *Boccaccio*. (*Encyclopaedia Brittanica*, 11th ed., IV, 223.)

4. This is a reference to *Pauline*, which, with Browning's permission, T. J. Wise reprinted in facsimile for members of the Browning Society late in 1886. (See *Letters*, ed. Hood, pp. 248, 253, 256.)

1. The London *Times*, July 7, 1888, carried the following advertisement: "Lyceum—Last night of the Season. Benefit of Miss Ellen Terry. Tonight *The Amber Heart* at 8:15 and *Robert Macaire*, Mr. Henry Irving."

tainment I always met there. Still, there is no insuperable difficulty
in reaching you, and every time the beloved hand beckons it will
bring you the old friend unless he finds himself hindered as now
—alas!

All love to the Husband and to you from

Yours ever affectionately

[Schiff] Robert Browning.

To Mrs. Charles Skirrow

Alb[erg]o Gilli, Primiero, Tirolo, Austria
Sept. 5, '88.

Dearest Friend, I gladly enclose the "due sighs" your friend is
good enough to desire. We leave this place—from which I think
that my Sister and myself have derived more good than we remember obtaining elsewhere—this day week, and our address will be
at "Palazzo Giustiniani-Recanati, S. Moise, Venezia"—the house
adjoining that of our kind hostess Mrs. Bronson. The weather has
continued propitious until last Saturday when we were visited by
a thunderstorm and torrents of the much-to-be-desired rain. The
latter lasted till next day's noon, and since then the old sun and
air are a settled delight. Pen went to Venice, two days ago, on a
summons to complete his purchase of the house: he returns, however, this evening or to-morrow, in order to finish a picture which
promises well at present. I need not say how happy I am that Homburg does you and the dear Master its accustomed good. Pray
enjoy it, both of you, as long as possible. We made an excursion,
yesterday, to a place a thousand feet higher up the mountain,—
St. Martino di Castrozza,—an old monastery turned into an Hotel,
surrounded by wonderful mountains,—no sort of village,—even a
hut,—in the neighbourhood: and I found a number of people I
know,—Sir James Paget [1] and his family among them: the whole
place is admirably beautiful, and the mountain range above and
around sublime.

My people were delighted with your messages to each and all
of them: they bid me return their best love. You see how I scribble,

---

1. Sir James Paget (1814–99) became serjeant-surgeon to Queen Victoria in
1877. Browning had known the Pagets as early as 1870, before Queen Victoria
had knighted Paget in 1871. (See letter to Sarianna Browning, April 15, 1870
n. 5.)

N*

—but forgive the hurry for the sake of the desire to lose no time in communicating with you. I need not say, should we have left, any [2] letter arriving subsequently would be forwarded at once—the innkeeper and his family being thoroughly trust-worthy and anxious to please us—who, the main of us, are no longer strangers. So,—all good go to you, dearest two friends, from yours

Affectionately ever
Robert Browning.

I happen to have the "Proofs" of Vol. VII of my new edition,—so have been able to transcribe what I could not remember.[3]
[Schiff]

To the Reverend Frank Wakely Gunsaulus [1]

29, De Vere Gardens, W.
Dec. 19, '88.

Dear Sir,

On returning to England after some little absence, I find your Book and a very gratifying letter. Nothing can interest me more than, or so much as, any testimony like yours to the success of my endeavours to be of what use I can during this short day of a lifetime.[2] I will read your work with great interest the moment I am at liberty to do so—but I could not delay for a moment assuring you of the gratitude with which I am

Dear Sir, Cordially yours
Robert Browning

The Rev. Frank Gunsaulus
[Ohio Wesleyan University]

2. This word appears as "and" in the manuscript.
3. This was the edition in 16 vols. of *The Poetical Works of Robert Browning* which Smith, Elder, and Co. issued in 1888.

1. Frank Wakely Gunsaulus (1856–1921), Congregational clergyman, was from 1887 to 1899 pastor of the Plymouth Congregational Church in Chicago. He was a man of broad interests with a reputation as a powerful speaker. (*D.A.B.*) It was he who gave Moscheles' portrait of Browning to the library at Ohio Wesleyan.

2. The book was probably *The Higher Ministries of Recent English Poetry* which considered "the literary phases of the religious problem" as revealed in Arnold, Tennyson, and Browning. It is possible that Gunsaulus sent to Browning a copy of the lecture on Browning's poetry which he delivered before the Chicago Theological Seminary. The lecture itself was apparently not published until 1907. (*D.A.B.*) Browning's gratitude was based upon Gunsaulus'

To Mr. and Mrs. Charles Skirrow

29, De Vere Gardens, W.
Christmas Day, '88.

Dear and kind friends, I am back, you may know, but how glad I am to feel myself again within the warmth of your love you hardly know. I got,—weeks ago when at Venice,—an invitation to take luncheon with you,—it reached me on the very day appointed for that festivity: I believe I ought to have written to say so, but, after my usual foolish fashion, I said to myself—"She will certainly understand." Did you? I had a wonderful three months at Venice after a month at beautiful Primiero: and the weather was uninterruptedly fine as fine could be. I never enjoyed Venice—the place—so much: I cared to see nothing but to be on the lagune, —landing, as I did every day, at Lido for a long walk on the sand. Then, the doings of my couple, Pen and his wife, were always calling on me for notice. The latter has again had a disappointment: indeed the uncertain state of her health is all that seems to stand between them and much happiness. My last news is favourable, I am glad to say. You know Pen has bought the huge Rezzonico Palace,—one of the best in Venice,—and he finds it not a bit too big, but is occupied all day long in superintending a *posse* of workmen who fit the rooms into comfortable inhabitedness. But you owe *me* a luncheon *here,* and when you return you must come and be talked to death to about painted ceilings, marble statues and the like. It is an excellent purchase,—and surprises everybody now that it has been effected: for the mere adornments might be sold tomorrow for the price of the palazzo itself. You know how unwell I was at the end of my stay here,—Venice cured me speedily —but I am far from reconciled yet to the fog and impure air one breathes—or coughs at. I find poor Mrs. F-G. is in town: I have not seen her. I do not doubt you have heard a shocking account of my silence during the time I was away: but she found such fault with what she called my "scolding her," that I thought a little stopping in our intercourse would have a soothing effect. I shall call on her soon.

---

conclusion, stated as follows: "I know of no discovery for which he will not prepare the soul—I know of no experience for which his lines will not equip the minds of modern men." He calls Browning the "poet of reverence . . . deeper than Arnold . . . richer and stronger in endowment than Tennyson."

Dear friends,—I am—I repeat—delighted to be within reach of you—bodily reach, for the mind goes far, and mine often and often went back to the "quattr' occhi" and other delights. Bless you both! S. sends her truest love with that of

Yours affectionately ever

[Schiff] ·   RB.

To Walter Hamilton [1]

29, De Vere Gardens, W.
Dec. 28, '88.

Sir,

In reply to your request for leave to publish two of my poems along with "Parodies" upon them,—I am obliged to say that I dis-approve of every kind of "Parody" so much that I must beg to be excused from giving any such permission. My Publisher will be desired to enforce compliance with my wish, if necessity should arise.[2]

Believe me, Sir,
Yours obediently

Walter Hamilton, Esq.   Robert Browning.
[Huntington]

1. Walter Hamilton (1844–99), a fellow of the Royal Geographical and Royal Historical Societies, began in 1884 the publication of a series of volumes of parodies on the work of English and American authors. The annual volumes were successful and provide now a useful reference guide to "nearly every Parody of literary merit, or importance." (*Parodies of the Works of English and American Authors,* ed. Walter Hamilton [London, 1889], Vol. VI, preface.)
2. Browning had not always been averse to parodies. In a letter to Mrs. Mark Pattison (March 15, 1872) he wrote of "a funny parody . . . of my things—four parodies of them indeed—which might amuse you." (The letter to Mrs. Pattison, unpublished, is in the British Museum. The four parodies include "Angelo Orders His Dinner," which is a parody on "The Bishop Orders His Tomb," and "On the Track" with the opening lines:
        Where the crags are close, and the railway-curve
        Begins to swerve,
which is a parody on "Love Among the Ruins." See "Diversions of the Echo Club," *Atlantic Monthly* [January, 1872], pp. 76–84.) Browning's distaste for parodies was perhaps created by some knowledge of Hamilton's collections of parodies, five volumes of which had already appeared. In Vol. V Mrs. Browning's "The Cry of the Children" is parodied by a half-dozen poems. Probably more offensive to Browning was the inclusion of a tasteless little poem called "The Spirit of Mrs. Browning to Her Husband." Furthermore, Hamilton in his biographical note on Mrs. Browning—a note which seems gratuitously sarcastic in tone—accepts the date and place of Mrs. Browning's birth as set forth by J. H. Ingram and rejects Browning's published statement that Ingram was

To Lady Martin

29, De Vere Gardens, W.

Jan. 10, '89.[1]

Dear Lady Martin,

I think you will understand with what reluctance and regret I have to say that your—as always—kindest of invitations finds me unable to accept it. I return to this dismal weather after four months' absence,—three months of which were passed in Venice, —bright sun and blue sky to the very last: indeed there were only two days on which rain fell: and the contrast has begun by affecting me so strongly that I somewhat rashly determined to keep at home every evening till this month should end. Many of the temptations to break this rule were easily withstood, but of late certain others show me I ought to have been less precipitate and more courageous—and here comes your letter which "almost persuades me to be a"—rule-breaker! And but for the many cases in which I have given the reason for declining similar pieces of kindness, I assuredly would do so. I have been forced, of course, to promise attendance at the Farewell Dinner to be given at the Mansion House.[2]

---

wrong. (See *Parodies of the Works of English and American Authors* [1888], V, 228–229.) Finally, after this display of what Browning must have regarded as impudence, Hamilton further tempted Browning's wrath by declaring Mrs. Browning's poetry to be "wordy, intricate, and obscure." Hamilton, for his part, was ruffled by Browning's curt refusal to allow a reprint of his poems. Said he: "A courteously worded letter was sent to Mr. Browning. . . . Mr. Browning's reply . . . refused permission to quote a few extracts from his shorter poems, adding in somewhat ungracious language, that his publisher would be instructed to see that his wishes were complied with. Perhaps the world does not greatly care whether Mr. Browning approves of Parody, or does not. . . . Byron or Scott could . . . enjoy a merry jest, even at their own expense, but let no dog bark when the great Sir Oracle opens his lips, and no daring humourist venture to travesty the poems of Mr. Robert Browning!" (*Parodies of the Works of English and American Authors* [1889], VI, 46.) Then Hamilton printed parodies of "How They Brought the Good News," "The Pied Piper," "Wanting Is—What," and numerous others, including one of the parodies from the *Atlantic Monthly*, "Angelo Orders His Dinner."

1. In 1889 Browning was in London, with occasional journeys to Cambridge and Oxford in June, from the beginning of the year until about August 29; he arrived at Asolo, Italy, at the beginning of September and stayed with Mrs. Bronson there until November 1, when he went to pay a visit to his son in Venice, at his home, the Palazzo Rezzonico.

2. On January 24 the lord mayor of London gave, at the Mansion House, a

My Sister does not suffer to the same degree as myself, but she also finds it safest to bide her time and share my solitariness—so she desires me to say,—with true thanks for an affection she cannot overvalue. My goings in and out in the day time are by no means interfered with by a rule which applies to the evening only; and I shall trust to see you and see Sir Theodore very shortly,—indeed, if you permit, very often.

We both of us reciprocate most heartily your New Year's wishes: and, with all best regards to both of you, I am ever,

Dear Lady Martin
Affectionately yours

[Huntington]   Robert Browning.

To Mrs. Charles Skirrow

29, De Vere Gardens, W.
Jan. 16, '89.

Yes, dearest Friend, I shall be delighted to go to you on the 23d. I suffered so much from the change you speak of—that I refuse all invitations to leave home of an evening till this black January shall be at an end—the Phelps dinner excepted of course.[1]

All love to Mr. Skirrow from his and yours affectionately ever
[Schiff]   Robert Browning.

To Mrs. Charles Skirrow

29, De Vere Gardens, W.
March 4, '89.

Dearest Friend,

You know how gladly I would go to you, were it in my power, as—unluckily—it will not be on the 11th—I being engaged early in the afternoon of that day. On the other hand,—let me make up for my loss of pleasure by seeing *you* here, according to your prom-

---

banquet in honor of Edward John Phelps, American minister to Great Britain. (See above, letter dated August 30, 1886, n. 1.) "A more representative company has seldom, if ever, sat down to dinner in the Egyptian-hall of the Mansion House . . . the names of the distinguished persons present were read by the toast-master." "Mr. Robert Browning" appears on this list as one of the "highest representatives of . . . literature." (London *Times*, January 25, 1889, p. 10, col. 1.) Phelps sailed for New York on January 31.

1. The dinner took place on January 24, 1889. See letter of January 10, 1889, above, n. 2.

ise, to luncheon—say the next day, Tuesday 12th. It will immensely delight S. and myself. With all love to your Husband—ever yours
[Schiff]   R Browning.

To Robert Wiedemann Barrett Browning [1]

29, De Vere Gardens, W.
March 6, '89.

Dearest Pen, We were exceedingly glad to get your letter and that of Fannie this morning; we were uneasy about her health, as she wrote with an increasing headache, and spoke of the coldness of the rooms. It is indeed a piece of the Layards' [2] usual kindness, —or something over,—that they help you in this emergency. Here the cold continues to be severe; the sun shines at this minute, however: but I have felt the effects of it in various ways: the comfort of our house being warm is great in proportion: I have never needed a fire in my bedroom. I trust that when the apartment gets used to occupancy it will get tolerable. When you and F. speak of the church being accommodated in the drawing room—do you mean the 1st floor room—which F. says is "warm"? That has been

1. Robert Wiedemann Barrett Browning, called "Pennini" and "Peni" in his earlier years and later "Pen," was born in Florence on March 9, 1849. References to him are constant in the Browning letters after that date and in all biographies of the poets. As a child he was educated at home, and after Mrs. Browning's death mainly by tutors. To Browning's great regret he failed to pass the examination for entrance to Balliol, but matriculated at Christ Church, Oxford, on January 15, 1869. He cultivated a passion for rowing and hunting, and failed to take a degree. In 1873, encouraged by Millais, he determined to become a painter, and studied under Heyermans in Antwerp and Rodin in Paris. He exhibited his enormous pictures and statues in London and Paris, especially in the Eighties, but was only moderately successful as an artist. In 1887 he married Miss Fannie Coddington, of a wealthy American family, and established himself in Venice in 1889 as the owner of the Palazzo Rezzonico, where his father died in 1889. After this event he lived until 1912 in Venice, Asolo, and London, but did little more with painting and sculpture worth preserving. The marriage of Pen and Fannie Browning was without issue.

2. Sir Austin Henry Layard (1817–94), politician and excavator of Nineveh, during the latter part of his life wrote much on art, including in 1887 a revision of Kugler's *Handbook of Painting*. (*D.N.B.*) Pen's association with the Layards in Venice may be explained by this mutual interest in painting. Pen's "emergency" was doubtless the problem of repairing and redecorating the Palazzo Rezzonico, which, wrote Browning in late December, 1888, "Pen is doing his best to make as comfortable as it is magnificent." (*Letters*, ed. Hood, p. 300.)

lived in, certainly. Well, I sent last night the paper from Leighton, which you will fill up and return: there was another, which I did not enclose, containing a resolution of the Council to decline, for the works they send, any competition for the medals and honours; about which, silence on your part was to imply consent: I think it a wise determination, and likely to avoid quarrelings.[3] With respect to the pillars, we wish, as you know, [to] let all that stand over: when you are here the matter can be discussed: as for "curtains," they are not wanted at all—the rooms being quite warm enough, and needing more light rather than the exclusion of what there is: it is a pity that my first notion was not adopted—to take down the walls entirely: but Smith, with his English ideas of "snugness" overruled me. The two marbles will be very effective in the long passage, each fronting each: the sizes are just suitable, and in simple black frames they would fill a couple of blank spaces, each opposite each: I shall be glad if you will buy them for as much under the money asked as Rietti will take; see that they are safely packed, and sent at once. I also should like another brass lantern "fanale," like those of Mrs. Bronson; one of which she offered me, and I refused; a very good one, I saw at the shop opposite the Post Office, —gone now, probably: I want it to match with the one I have, which is on the stair-case, above the two which I bought of Rietti, —these, with the large one opposite, are much admired by everybody.[4] All this, quite at your leisure, and so as not to interfere with your own operations which I know must give you trouble enough. I dined with Boughton on Sunday, and met, among others, Sargent —who expressed his astonishment at your possessing the whole Rezzonico. "What, *all* of it?" He then said that he had lived in the room above—paid 10 f[ran]cs a month for it. I told him I knew that, and had seen his autograph and scratch of a drawing on the wall,—which you intended to keep uneffaced from its place, —whereat he seemed pleased. He is painting Ellen Terry as Ly

3. Sir Frederic Leighton (1830–96) was president of the Royal Academy of Art and a long-time friend of Browning. He contributed a design for Mrs. Browning's poem "The Great God Pan," and like his sister, Mrs. Sutherland Orr, was in numerous ways attached to the poet and his family. (There is a further reference to Leighton and Pen's picture in *Letters*, ed. Hood, p. 305.) Leighton became one of the vice-presidents of the Browning Society in 1881.
4. These details of house arrangement and decoration refer to 29 De Vere Gardens. The "Smith with . . . English ideas of 'snugness' " may be George Murray Smith, Browning's publisher and friend.

Macbeth.[5] Leighton was very kind about the Paris business,—said he had seen all the works and could judge of them. S. sent to Fannie a copy of the very handsome note from the Grosvenor. I considered about it,—being pretty sure, from various indications, that there would be a real desire on the part of L. and the others to receive any work you might send: and had there been another picture,—as I hoped at one time would be the case,—I should have sent at least one to the Academy: but you have been so long unrepresented in London that it is important to put your single work well in evidence,—and, with so many competitors at the Academy, we could not expect such a place as is promised at the Grosvenor; accordingly I have written to Coults [6] and to thank him and accept his offer: when you give me the dimensions of the picture, I will write again. The work will be *seen*, at all events: and if it meets with approval, you can all the better next year contribute to the other establishment. *Take care to be in readiness.* I saw Natorp two days ago,—he is still at work on that bust I found nearly as finished as it now is, nearly three months ago,—he preferring to work without a model, and adding and undoing by [*sic.*] all the time: at last,—I found him wisely letting a "ghost" do it for him,—in any presence: so, it will get completed easily enough.[7] He is also painting a three-quarters life-size portrait of Mrs. Rathbone,[8]—always a good conception, I think, but between *that* and

5. John Singer Sargent (1856–1925), portrait painter, was born at Florence while the Brownings were in residence there. In March, 1889 he had just returned from America to London, where he was to exhibit three portraits at the Royal Academy: those of George Henschel, Mrs. George Gribble, and Henry Irving. (Graves, the *Royal Academy of Arts: A Complete Dictionary . . . 1769–1904* [1906], VII, 25.) The picture of "Miss Terry as Lady Macbeth" was finished in 1889 and now hangs in the Tate Gallery. (*D.N.B.*, "Sargent.")
6. Pen had last exhibited at the Royal Academy in 1884. Coults was in charge of the Grosvenor Gallery.
7. Gustav Natorp (1836–?), sculptor, studied under A. Legros and Rodin. Possibly his acquaintance with Pen was brought about through Rodin who was also Pen's teacher in sculpturing. (A meager sketch of Natorp may be found in *Allgemeines Lexikon der bildenden Künstler* [1931], XXV, 355.) In 1888 Natorp had exhibited at the Royal Academy a "low relief, bronze" of Browning for which the poet sat "day after day." The result Browning found "highly satisfactory." Then in 1889 Natorp exhibited a bronze statuette called "Byblis," which is possibly the work to which Browning refers here. (See Graves, *The Royal Academy of Arts*, [1931], V, 343; also *Letters*, ed. Hood, p. 285.)
8. Perhaps the second wife of William Rathbone (1819–1902), Liverpool merchant and philanthropist who, on the death of his first wife, married Emily Acheson, his cousin, in 1862.

execution—a great gap. I also have seen Moscheles—who is about a large figure-picture.[9] I dined last night at Ly [Thurston's ?]—met Locker,[10] who spoke doubtfully of Tennyson's condition.[11] I refuse as many invitations as I can, but am delighted to think I shall meet (in all likelihood) the Layards at Mrs. Drummond's [12] next Saturday—and, on the 14th, at Mrs. M. Burr's [13]—if I can get away from a house close by in time—as I shall endeavour to do. I dine the day before with Ly Airlie, to meet Ly Dufferin,[14] there being always some particular reason for breaking my rule of staying at home. I shall say no more, but give the pen to S. Give dearest Fannie my whole love, bid her take all possible care of herself for all our sakes, and none more than mine. Bless you, Dear Boy:—
I am ever affectionately yours,
[New York Public Library]   R B.

9. "The Isle's Enchantment," for which Browning provided five lines of poetry. (See Letters, ed. Hood, letter of March 30, 1889, and n. 89:6–1.)

10. Frederick Locker (1821–95), later Locker-Lampson, author of excellent light verse, had been for many years a friend of Browning and a figure of consequence in London society.

11. Tennyson's serious illness had begun in late 1888. In January, 1889, Browning wrote a letter of sympathy. By the end of February Tennyson had improved but it was April 17 before he was declared "perfectly recovered." (Hallam Tennyson Alfred Lord Tennyson, A Memoir, II, 351–354.)

12. Mrs. Drummond was the widow of Thomas Drummond (1797–1840), who as Under Secretary of State for Ireland was from 1835 to the time of his death "practically Governor" of Ireland. (D.N.B.; see also, Sir A. Henry Layard: Autobiography and Letters [London, 1903], II, 228, for relation of the Layards to Mrs. Drummond.)

13. Mrs. Margaretta (Scobell) Burr, artist, married Higford Burr (1811–85) in 1835. (Allgemeines Lexikon der bildenden Künstler [1931], V, 271.) Mrs. Burr traveled far on sketching expeditions and in 1841 published Sketches in Spain, The Holy Land, Egypt, Turkey, and Greece. (Allibone's Dictionary of Authors [Philadelphia, 1859], I, 303.) On later tours she and her husband traveled with the Layards. (See Sir A. Henry Layard: Autobiography and Letters, II, 209, and passim.)

14. Hariot Georgina Hamilton (ca. 1844–1936) married the first marquess of Dufferin in 1862. The marquess was the only son of Helen, Lady Dufferin, a poetess, and for him Browning wrote the sonnet "Helen's Tower" in honor of her. Hariot, Lady Dufferin, published Our Vice-Royal Life in India in 1889. Lady Airlie's dinner was doubtless given in honor of Lord and Lady Dufferin on their return to London. (For biographical data see Burke's Peerage, p. 860; Who Was Who, 1929–1940; also Songs, Poems, and Verses by Helen, Lady Dufferin, ed. with a memoir . . . by the Marquess of Dufferin and Ava [2d ed. London, 1894], pp. 103–104. Browning's "Helen's Tower" appears on the page before the table of contents.)

To Mrs. Frank Harrison Hill [1]

March 9, '89.

Dear Mrs. Hill,

I have at once been to the Club,[2] and added my name to the many which cover the card of Mr. Hill; I will do my best to be present and vote on Monday,—but if any accident hinders me, I cannot believe it will in any way affect the result—so numerous and efficacious are the vouchers for his eligibility.

Ever affectionately yours

[Huntington]   Robert Browning.

To Mrs. Charles Skirrow

[March, 1889?] [1]

Ah, dear dear Friend, I much fear I can do neither thing that you desire so kindly. On the 16th I and my Sister dine with Mrs. Drummond:[2] but it is near your house, and I will look in, if I get away in time—as I shall try hard to do. To-morrow I have an engagement at two o'clock. What can I do? Surely you know what I *would* do, if I could.

I send a couple of American Papers. You know the only reason I do not call is because you are always out (I *hope*) at the time when I *can* call.

Ever affectionately yours

[Schiff]   Robert Browning.

1. Mrs. Frank Harrison Hill was the wife of the editor of the London *Daily News* who in 1884 had sent to Browning for approval a paragraph concerning the first performance of *A Blot in the 'Scutcheon*. Browning thought this action "kind and considerate" and wrote in reply to Hill his well-known account of the circumstances surrounding the presentation of the *Blot*. (See Orr, *Life*, pp. 110–116.)

2. The Athenaeum Club, to which Frank Harrison Hill was elected to membership in 1889. (Francis C. Waugh, *Members of the Athenaeum Club*, p. 70.)

1. The evidence for dating this letter is meager. Browning mentions an engagement to dine with Mrs. Drummond "on the 16th." In a letter of March 6, 1889, he says that he is to dine with Mrs. Drummond "next Saturday." This would be March 9. If Browning is using the word "next" loosely, then he might mean the second Saturday, which would be March 16.

2. See above, letter of March 6, 1889, n. 12.

To Mrs. Charles Skirrow

29, De Vere Gardens, W.
March 23, '89.

Dearest Friend,

If I possibly can, I will gladly go to you on the 8th.

But when do you come and redeem your promise to me? Mrs. Orr wants me particularly to invite her on the same day,—you would like that? [1] Any day *but* a Monday—*your* day, unfortunately for me whose Mondays are engaged. All love to the dear Husband from his and yours ever affectionately

[Schiff]   Robert Browning.

To Sir Theodore Martin

29, De Vere Gardens, W.
Apr. 1, '89.

Dear Sir Theodore,

If by any happy chance you should pass by our street, I venture to tell you that my Son's portrait will be on view here during the week.[1] I well know what your engagements are: but cannot help taking any occasion that may be of saying how much your presence delights us. With all regards to Lady Martin, believe me, Dear Sir Theodore,

Ever truly yours

[Huntington]   Robert Browning

1. One must assume that these two long-time friends and admirers of Browning, Mrs. Skirrow and Mrs. Orr, are to meet now for the first time. Mrs. Orr very likely obtained from Mrs. Skirrow the letters of Browning to Mrs. Skirrow which are used in Mrs. Orr's *Life of Browning*. Yet, Mrs. Orr does not identify or describe Mrs. Skirrow by so much as a phrase, a fact which may lead one to believe that the acquaintanceship between Mrs. Orr and Mrs. Skirrow was extremely casual.

1. This is Pen's oil portrait of his father. Browning was well pleased with it and wrote special notes to others to come see it. (See R. C. Lehmann, *Memories of Half a Century*, p. 125.) The portrait was exhibited at the Grosvenor Gallery and also in Paris and New York. The original now hangs in the Browning Library, Baylor University, Waco, Texas. (Wilson, *Browning's Portraits*, pp. 181–183.)

To An Unidentified Correspondent

Apr. 25, '89.

Dear Sir,

You do me far too great honour by supposing that the addition of my signature to a copy of the works of Burns will be of a moment's interest as prefacing the glory and beauty which follow. However, it is for me to acquiesce and not demur at so unexpected a distinction, and I shall be happy to do as you so kindly desire.

> Believe me, Dear Sir,
> Yours very sincerely
> Robert Browning.

[Huntington]

To Felix Moscheles

29, De Vere Gardens, W.
May 8, '89.

Dear Moscheles,

As I have said I would do, I have been thinking of an illustration for your picture—such as I suppose its subject to be, from what I saw of it.[1] The witch would well enough represent Myrthyr sister of Dalica,—in Landor's poem of "Gebir,"—as engaged in concocting a poison for Gebir. The description is somewhat long,—but here are a few of the salient points in it. The witch speaks:

> Therefore the death of Gebir is resolved.
> Precious my arts! I could without remorse
> Kill—though I hold thee dearer than the day—
> E'en thee thyself, to exercise my arts!
>
> . . . . .
>
> Away she hastened with it to her home,
> And sprinkling thrice fresh sulphur on the hearth,
> Took up a spindle with malignant smile,
> And pointed to a woof, nor spake a word.
>
> . . . . .
>
> But Myrthyr seized with naked sinewy arm
> The grey cerastes,† writhing from her grasp

1. Browning spent the afternoon of his birthday, May 7, in Moscheles' studio where he watched his friend paint a London street urchin. (See Felix Moscheles, *Fragments of an Autobiography*, pp. 347–348.)

And twisted off his horn, nor feared to squeeze
The viscous poison from his glowing gums.

. . . . .

"Take this" she cried—"and Gebir is no more!"

† Cerastes is a horned serpent: but she also uses
"The blue urchin that with clammy fin
Holds down the ship." [2]

There is a picturesque account of the ruined City whereby is the "lonely house" in which the operation takes place: but the whole poem is wild and fascinating in the highest degree—and unillustrated, so far as I know, up to the present time. I fancy this passage might suit you—but I hardly am sure enough of what you exactly intend to paint. Some day when you are at work—not too far advanced—I will bring the poem and see if it meets your requirements: perhaps on Friday.

Ever truly yours

[Yale]   RB.

To Mr. and Mrs. Charles Skirrow

29, De Vere Gardens, W.
May 8, '89.[1]

Dearest Friends,—you know I can say nothing while I must feel everything that is grateful and loving. I have felt on this occasion —but it is of no use: I leave it to your generous hearts to understand what is in mine.

Bless you both—prays ever
Your affectionate

[Schiff]   Robert Browning.

2. *Gebir*, Bk. V, ll. 192, 194–196, 211–214, 228–231, 243, 235–236, as printed in *The Complete Works of Landor*, ed. Stephen Wheeler [London, 1933], I, 37–39. This edition records variant readings, and it is interesting to see how close Browning, who had not looked into *Gebir* "for many years," could come to the exact wording of the poem. (See letter of May 9, below.) He did recall "naked sinewy arm" for "bare bold-sinew'd arm." Except for that and the shortening of "the tossing vessel" to "the ship," he made only the error of misspelling the name Merthyr.

1. This note is in answer to a birthday remembrance from the Skirrows.

To Felix Moscheles

29, De Vere Gardens, W.
May 9, '89.

My dear Moscheles,—On looking again into Landor's poem,—a thing I have not done for many years,—I see that Merthyr and Dalica are both *crones,* not nearly the coevals of Charoba, the girlish queen; so that the illustration was a mistake. Besides, I like your own notion much better in every way,—the idea being more original, as you express it, than the old Canidia-type of witch-hood.[1] I fancy there are descriptions,—if I can catch and keep certain misty remembrances in my head,—which would suit your picture, if you care to have them: but keep to your own way.

An original way of treating an incantation-scene would be to suppose a half-initiated witch who, proceeding as instructed by an aged proficient in the business,—recoils frightened at her own success from the phantom she has evoked,—her terror contrasting with the authoritative composure of the experienced and imperturbable hag beside or behind her.

I scribble this, in case I should be unable to look in to-morrow afternoon—as I will if I can, however: always enjoying, as I do, the sight of creation by another process than that of the head— with only pen and paper to help. How expeditiously the brush works! Hurriedly, but—

Ever yours—
[Yale]   R Browning.

To Mrs. Charles Skirrow

May 30, '89.

Oh yes—dearest Friend—I will joyfully go to your Luncheon and drink the health of the Emancipated One with all my heart.[1] All happiness to you both from

Yours ever affectionately
[Schiff]   Robert Browning.

1. Canidia was a courtesan, beloved by Horace; but when she deserted him he revenged himself by holding her up to contempt as an old sorceress. See Horace, *Epodes* V (*The Witches' Orgy*) and XVII (*Recantation to Canidia's Reply*).
1. Probably a reference to Mr. Skirrow's retirement from his position as Master in Chancery.

To the Reverend J. D. Williams [1]

29. De Vere Gardens, W.
June 1, '89.

Dear Mr. Williams, I am pretty sure to get away from Cambridge early enough on Monday,—but I feel unable to manage the visit to Bottisham: [2] the return to Town, though just seeming to allow of my getting home and going out again, would tire the flesh and even more considerably the spirit. And when I go to Bottisham I hope to enjoy it without any drawback: you will understand this.

The little book [3] wants looking into and shall have it. I don't remember any De or Du Belley, except the versifying Cardinal of that name, who wrote so much which Spenser translated: I remember some on the vicissitudes of fortune: how an elephant in all the glory of his strength, "with all his bells and bosses," tumbled down —slain, I think. [4] I will try and find out what I can.

1. Browning apparently first became acquainted with the Reverend J. D. Williams in 1880 when he was rector at Ragleigh, Essex. (See next note.) Four letters to Williams appear in *Letters,* ed. Hood. All are antiquarian or scholarly, much in the vein of the present letter.

2. In a letter of November 1, 1880, J. D. Williams announced to Browning: "I have been, by the grace of the Masters and Seniors, Vicar Elect of Bottisham midway between Cambridge and Newmarket." (*Browning's Letter File,* ed. Armstrong, p. 85.)

3. At the end of Browning's letter the following note, signed "J. D. W.," is appended: "The bagatelle referred to is 'Elisa, ovvero l'Innocenza Colpevole' (Eliza, or the Guilty Innocence), translated from the French of the 'Vescovo di Belley' (Bp. of Belley), by the 'Conte Onofrio Beirlacquer'—which sounds very like 'Earl Humphrey Drinkwater'—some three centuries ago. Fancy our old friend 'Duke Humphrey,' and the 'Earl of Drinkwater,' exchanging hospitalities, or contriving to give an 'At Home.' How intensely jolly it would be!"

4. Browning had in mind Spenser's "Visions of Bellay," a translation of Du Bellay's *Antiquitez.* Spenser, however, wrote an original set of sonnets, similar in kind to the "Visions of Bellay," entitled "Visions of the Worlds Vanitie." (See H. S. V. Jones, *A Spenser Handbook* [New York, 1937], p. 118.) It is in "Visions of the Worlds Vanitie" (St. viii) that the anecdote of the elephant occurs, a portion of which we quote:

> Soone after this I saw an Elephant,
> Adorn'd with bells and bosses gorgeouslie, . . .
> And shortly gan all other beasts to scorne,
> Till that a little Ant, a silly worme,
> Into his nosthrils creeping, so him pained,
> That casting downe his towres, he did deforme
> Both borrowed pride, and native beautie stained.
> Let therefore nought that great is, therein glorie,
> Sith so small thing his happiness may varie.

You very well know what pleasure your visit and that of your Daughter gave us: we hope for more when you can be generous enough. I speak for my Sister,—whose best regards go with mine.

Ever truly yours

[Yale]   Robert Browning.

To Robert Wiedemann Barrett Browning

29, De Vere Gardens, W.
June 19, '89.

Dearest Pen,—delighted as I was to get your two letters, it seemed as if I should do better by waiting till you were arrived at Paris, before writing in reply. I find you are to be there to-night, and this will tell you, however unnecessarily, how glad I shall be to hear news of you from your old quarters. How things have changed since you were established there, two years ago! And, I do believe, for the better—in every respect. You are bound to justify in some degree your good fortune by showing that an artist is not spoiled by becoming happy in every way. The visit you and Fannie paid us— short as we found it—was an invaluable experience: but I ought to try and put down some sort of trifle by way of news. First, in answer to your kind enquiries; I am quite well again, having soon got over my cold, which was troublesome enough just when I should have otherwise enjoyed Cambridge entirely. I found many friends there, and all manner of civility and hospitality: a beautiful place, too, and in most perfect condition. I was photographed several times by Mrs. Myers, Dolly Tennant's sister,[1] (your photographs and those of Fannie are capital: I have ordered a quantity to give away)— On returning, I excused myself from several engagements, and "lay by" for a week in order to get well. I went (on a second invitation) to Herkomer's performance,—very clever in all but the higher qualities without which cleverness does little or no good. The

---

1. Eveleen Tennant, youngest daughter of Charles Tennant of Cadoxton, Glamorganshire, in 1880 married Frederick William Henry Myers (1843–1901), poet and essayist. In 1881 they took up permanent abode in Lechthampton House, Cambridge. Dorothy (Dolly) Tennant, one of her older sisters, in 1890 married the African explorer Sir Henry Morton Stanley. (Burke's *Landed Gentry*, p. 2218, and *D.N.B.*) Mrs. Myers' photographs of Browning are reproduced in Wilson, *Browning's Portraits*, pp. 179–181. This letter suggests that the statement (p. 179) that these photographs were "taken from life in August, 1889" should probably be corrected to read "in June, 1889."

scenery, dresses, grouping, dumbshow—unexceptionable: the music piquant and Wagner-like: the poetry execrable, and the whole purpose of the piece so commonplace that I felt bored to extinction, and got away by a train even earlier than the special one.[2] I have since dined with Sir H. Thompson (the Layards there,—she appearing for the first time, and seemingly quite recovered.)[3] I had a pleasant dinner at Miss [Garwood's?],[4] an invitation to Ly B. Coutts' Fête (which I avoided),[5] and to Ld Albemarle's reception yesterday, Waterloo Day,—the 74th anniversary,—he being 90,—and in fine health;[6] I dined with J. Duke Coleridge[7]—could not go to a great affair at Tadema's.[8] To-day,—I have five engagements of one

2. Hubert von Herkomer (1849–1904) was a man of great versatility as his listing in *Allgemeines Lexikon der bildenden Künstler* (1923), XVI, 474, indicates: "Maler, Graphiker, Holzschnitzer, Kunstsgewerber, Bildhauer, Emailleur, Musiker, Komponist, Dramatiker, und Kunstschriftsteller." Eight pictures of his were being exhibited at the Royal Academy in 1889 (Algernon Graves, *The Royal Academy of Arts* [1906], IV, 84), while he was presenting at the Herkomer Theatre, Bushey, Herts, his "pictorial-music-play, entitled *An Idyl*." (See London *Times*, June 10, 1889, p. 1, col. 3, for advertisement of Herkomer's play.) The reviewer for the *Times* described *An Idyl* as "an outstanding exhibition of cleverness, if not of actual genius," equipped with "very pretty words by Mr. Joseph Bennett" and accompanied by music which showed the "strong influence of Wagner." The "management of the lights and of the clouds . . ." showed "simply inconceivable ingenuity." (London *Times*, June 5, 1889, p. 10, col. 2.)

3. Sir Henry Thompson (1820–1904), surgeon, had artistic talent and, under the tutelage of Alma-Tadema, produced paintings which were exhibited at the Royal Academy between 1865 and 1885. "As a host he was famous for his 'octaves,' which were dinners of eight courses for eight people at eight o'clock. . . . The company was always as carefully selected as the food, and for a quarter of a century the most famous persons in the world of art, letters, science, politics, diplomacy and fashion met at his table in Wimpole Street." (*D.N.B.*)

4. Unidentified.

5. Angela Georgina, Baroness Burdett-Coutts (1814–1906), philanthropist, "in 1889 . . . opened a pleasure ground which had been made out of the old St. Pancras cemetery, and she erected there a memorial sundial, with a record of famous persons buried there." (*D.N.B.*) Apparently it was the fete in connection with this opening that Browning avoided.

6. George Thomas Keppel, sixth Earl of Albemarle (1799–1891), at the age of 16 was present at the Battle of Waterloo with the 14th Foot Regiment. (*D.N.B.*).

7. John Duke Coleridge (1820–94) was Lord Chief Justice of England from 1880 till his death. He was also the first Baron Coleridge. See also above, letters of January 29, 1872, and March 15, 26, 31, 1873.

8. Sir Lawrence Alma-Tadema (1836–1912) was born in Holland but took up his abode in London where he was treated as a citizen of the country. He was

or another kind. On the 25th I go to Oxford; Commemoration next day,—and stay over for the Balliol "Gaudy"-dinner to the Provost and Fellows of Eton, on July 1.[9] I shall try and get a quick dose of air and country,—and by this time I know the ways of Balliol so well that I can manage to steal out and come in when I please. By this visit, I escape dinners every day in London, and the wedding of Farrar's daughter [10]—which otherwise I should have liked to attend in spite of the trouble and fatigue. On coming back, the most notable of my dinners will be at Ld Rosebery's "to meet the Shah" [11] —men only. Millais, by the way, invited me to meet the P. Louise and Ld Lorne [12] on the Gaudy Day: he never asks me, as I should

a prolific painter with credit for 408 pictures during his career. "Few people of importance," states his biographer, "living in or visiting London failed to find their way to [his] fine house in St. John's Wood." (D.N.B.)

9. Browning's final visit to Oxford was doubtless busy and pleasant, for Commemoration was "signalized by somewhat more than the average coruscation of balls and concerts . . . [and] the weather [was] unintermittingly perfect." (London Times, June 27, p. 10, col. 5.) "Gaudy: the annual dinner of the Fellows of a college, in memory of founders and benefactors. From gaudeamus. Oxford University." (The Slang Dictionary [London, 1913], p. 174.)

10. Frederick William Farrar (1831–1903) had for many years counted Browning one of his "eminent friends" and "seldom preached a sermon without quoting from him." Browning for his part "was particularly cordial" because he credited Farrar's American lectures on his poetry with having "promoted the sale of his writings" in the United States. (R. A. Farrar, The Life of Frederic William Farrar [New York, 1904], pp. 177, 287–288.) Farrar's fourth daughter, Sybil, was married to the Reverend E. Sidney Savage on June 25 in a ceremony performed by the Archbishop of Canterbury. (London Times, June 26, 1889, p. 1, col. 1.)

11. Archibald Philip Primrose, fifth Earl of Rosebery (1847–1929), apparently first met Browning at a dinner given by G. W. E. Russell and records his impression of the poet as "very agreeable." (The Marquess of Crewe, Lord Rosebery [London, 1931], p. 280.) The Shah was making one of his frequent politico-social progresses to Berlin, Brussels, London. (See London Times, June 6, 1889, p. 5, col. 1. The Times covered every move of the Shah after his arrival in London.) The dinner took place on July 5, and Browning's colloquy with the Shah is recorded in a letter to Miss Alma Lehmann. (Letters, ed. Hood, pp. 309–310.) The dinner with the list of distinguished guests, including Gladstone, the Prince of Wales, Millais, and the Shah's retinue, is reported in the London Times of July 6, 1889, p. 7, col. 4.)

12. Princess Louise Caroline Alberta was the fourth daughter of Queen Victoria and Prince Albert. She married the Marquis of Lorne, later the ninth Duke of Argyll (1845–1914), in 1871. From 1878 to 1883 the Marquis was Governor General of Canada. He writes of Browning as "a man loving society, and often seen at assemblies," and he recalls meeting him, not for the first time apparently, at the opening of the Grosvenor Gallery in 1876. (See the Duke

like him to do, to look in when he is by himself. I miss also the
R. A. soirée which I should attend out of compliment to Leighton.[13]
There, you have a list of my doings actual and intended. I saw Smith
yesterday,—he spoke rapturously of Fannie. I never heard of anything more fortunate, in its way, than her and your meetings with
that dear Marie [14] on board the ship at Southampton: how happy
you must, all of you, have been up to this present. I never heard
of Bremen being so pleasant a place—it must be, from your description; an old town with young surroundings is just what I
should choose for an abode. Natorp [15] knows it, and corroborates
your praise. He left a week ago,—I forget for what "cure-place,"—
to get rid of the gout which clings to him apparently: on his return for a brief space, he starts for California to see his brother—
and stays there till the autumn. Smith will bring out, later in the
year, the edition of dearest Ba's works [16]—in six volumes like mine;
these last come to an end in July—and it is not considered expedient, in a bookseller's point of view, to print anything new of my
own till about November. I hear, to my great relief, that Tennyson
is much better—so people tell me who have seen him.[17] Lowell is
here, but I have not met him.[18] I was invited to meet Boulanger at

---

of Argyll, *Passages from the Past* [New York, 1908], I, 55–57.) John Everett
Millais met Lord Lorne in 1865 and painted his portrait for the Canadian
Art Gallery in 1884. The Princess Louise called on Millais during his last illness. (John G. Millais, *The Life and Letters of Sir John Everett Millais*, I,
386; II, 165, 335.)

13. Frederic Leighton was president of the Royal Academy of Art at this
time. Leighton, afterward Lord Leighton, had been on intimate terms with
Browning since the poet and his wife lived in Rome in 1854. For the close
association of the painter and the poet see Griffin and Minchin, *Life*, pp. 193,
194, 207, 224, 234, 245, 246, 285, 300.

14. Probably Marie Coddington, the sister of Pen's wife.

15. Gustav Natorp, who was a native of Germany. (See above, letter of
March 6, 1889, n. 6.)

16. This edition of Mrs. Browning's works contains Browning's prefatory
note, dated December 10, 1887, repeating his correction of the errors in John
Ingram's *Elizabeth Barrett Browning*. Smith, Elder and Co. announced his
new edition as "uniform with the recently published edition of Mrs. Robert
Browning's Works." It was to be completed in October. (*Athenaeum*, October
5, 1889.)

17. See letter of March 6, 1889, above, n. 11.

18. James Russell Lowell was in London until August, but it is doubtful
that Browning saw him. (*Letters of J. R. Lowell*, ed. C. E. Norton [New York,
1894], II, 374.)

dinner to-day but declined.[19] I am very anxious to hear what you think of the Exhibition: what pictures and sculpture strike you—but what is there you can profitably tell me that will not interest me? There are few things I am more grateful to Fannie for than her inestimable punctuality in writing—we are kept aware of what we most want to know. S. communicates to me what she pleases—and I rejoice most heartily that dear Marie is so much better, and, I trust, in a fair way of getting altogether well. It is a great temptation—little as I now like travelling—to think of possibly finding myself with you all some day. Did S. mention that I heard from Mrs. Bronson, at Asolo,—which she found altogether lovely,—and which, after returning to Venice, as she was going to do at once, she hoped to revisit with Edith for a two-month's stay? I think that an injudicious step, as I told her: it is insufferably hot there, in spite of its hilly situation, and Mrs. B. wants a more bracing air. Well, dearest, I am at the end of the paper, not of my inclination to go on gossiping. Give my true love to Fannie and to Marie: S. helps me there, but it cannot be given too often. Our weather is very fine,—the leaves and grass wonderfully luxuriant, and I make much use of the gardens. Bless you, Dear Pen,—

Ever yours affectionately

[New York Public Library]   Robert Browning

To Thomas Hutchinson [1]

July 6, '89.

Dear Sir, I beg to return you my best thanks for the Magazine which you have so obligingly sent me, and which contains an article of much interest to us all.

Yours very sincerely

[Yale]   Robert Browning.

19. George Ernest Jean Marie Boulanger (1837–91), French general, had escaped from France to Brussels, then London, after a warrant for his arrest had been issued on the charge of menacing the parliamentary republic. *In absentia* he was found guilty of treason. (*Encyclopaedia Brittanica*, 14th ed., "Boulanger.") Browning would not have wished to give comfort to an enemy of free government.

1. Thomas Hutchinson printed a series of small volumes, in limited editions, between 1887 and 1890. The editions ranged from 130 to 300 copies and were "elegantly printed . . . on hand-made paper." (See advertisement at the end of Thomas Hutchinson, *Ballades and Other Rhymes of a Country Bookworm*

To Mrs. Charles Skirrow

29, De Vere Gardens, W.
July 20th, '89.

Dearest Friend,

For a wonder, I am engaged to lunch next Wednesday—and cannot escape, having caused a deal of letter-writing and invitation by refusals of one kind or another. I shall hope still to see both of you before you leave and—I suppose—I leave: meanwhile and ever, bless both of you!

Yours affectionately ever

[Schiff]   Robert Browning.

To C. W. Deschamps

29, De Vere Gardens, W.
July 25, '89.

Dear Mr. Deschamps,

I received yesterday a note kindly addressed to my Son requesting him to inform you if he wished to sell his picture "By the River," [1] and, if he did so, at what price. The letter was at once forwarded to Paris, where I supposed him to be resident; but, by a letter just received, I find he is at Milan and, in a day or two will be at Venice. Your letter will be forwarded to him in due course: but should you wish to communicate with him directly, have the kindness to direct to him at Venice—"R. B. B. Palazzo Rezzonico."

Believe me, Dear Mr. Deschamps,

Yours very truly

[Yale]   Robert Browning.

To Mrs. Howe [1]

29 De Vere Gardens, W.
Aug. 8, '89

Dear Mrs. Howe,

Indeed I shall not "hate you" for recalling yourself to me, however unnecessarily: I am likely to "hate" nothing but the long

---

[London, 1888].) This note is on a post card, addressed to Thomas Hutchinson, Esq., Pegswood, Morpeth.

1. Possibly this is "Riverside, Dinant," item 21 of Sotheby, *Browning Collections*, p. 8.

1. Possibly the wife of William Henry Howe (1846–1929), landscape and

distance which separates us. Yet it puts a light, a real star, in the dark places of the world I shall never see, to know that there lives and burns there a dear friend such as you so soon grew to me.

Your letter came with a word or two added to the else bare address,—and the magic word on the stamp "Asolo." I may—it is possible—go there and have the delight of again finding myself near the beloved woman whom we both know so well.[2]

I will enclose the poor autographs—what a present! Give my kind regards, and those of my sister, to Mr. Howe. My sister is quite well, and wishes to be remembered to you emphatically. And you—remember me always as yours affectionately

[Boston Athenaeum]   Robert Browning

To Mrs. Charles Skirrow

Asolo, Veneto, Italia.
Oct. 15, '89.

Dearest Friend,—surely I wrote to you just before leaving London; acquainted you with the place to which I was bound, and trusted to find an answer on arrival there: I think I cannot be mistaken about this—but—who can say?[1] We have been here some six weeks and, except that the weather was not exempt from the universal plague of rain, nothing could surpass the beauty of what fine days were really conceded us. As for the place itself, it remains what I first conceived it to be—the most beautiful spot I ever was privileged to see. It is seldom that one's impressions of half-a-century ago, are confirmed by present experience but so it is: and Pen who visited us here the other day, and is a thoroughly "travelled" fellow declared himself altogether fascinated by its romantic character and general loveliness. Then—such a view over the whole Lombard plain,—not a site in view, or *approximate* view at least, without its story. Autumn is now painting all the abundance of verdure,— figs, pomegranates, ches[t]nuts, and vines, and I don't know what

cattle painter, who married Julia May Clark in 1876. Howe studied at Düsseldorf and Paris during the Eighties and took a first class medal at the Paris Exhibition in 1889. The Howes returned to America to live in Bronxville, New York.

2. Mrs. Arthur Bronson, Browning's American friend, who had bought a house in Asolo and entertained the poet and his sister in the last autumn of his life.

1. See note to Mrs. Skirrow of July 20, 1889.

else,—all in a wonderful confusion,—and now glowing with all the colours of the rainbow. Some weeks back, the little town was glorified by the visit of a decent theatrical troop who played in a theatre inside the old palace of Queen Catherine Cornaro—utilized also as a prison in which I am informed are at present full five if not six malefactors guilty of stealing grapes and the like enormities. Well, the troop played for a fortnight together exceedingly well—high tragedy and low comedy: and the stage-box which I occupied cost 16 francs. The theatre had been out of use for six years, for we are out of the way and only a baiting-place for a company pushing on to Venice. In fine, we shall stay here probably for a week or more, —and then proceed to Pen, at the Rezzonico: a month there, and then homewards! [2] My Sister,—I should have begun by saying,— is quite well: we take long walks—and longer drives about the delightful neighbourhood.

This morning, I despatched to Smith the MS. of my new volume, —some thirty poems long and short,—some few written here, all revised and copied.[3] There was an advertisement which mentioned "The" Poem or "A" Poem—I don't know how the mistake occurred.[4] It was said too to be "in the Press"—really being in my portfolio till a couple of hours ago.

It was very kind of you to get them to send Mr. Archer's letter,[5]—

2. Mrs. Orr printed portions of this letter, from the words "Then—such a view" to "and then homewards," and the final paragraph. (*Life*, pp. 289–290.)

3. *Asolando*. (See *Letters*, ed. Hood, pp. 320–321.) The title for the volume was first announced by Smith, Elder, and Co. in an advertisement appearing in the *Athenaeum* for November 30, 1889.

4. "Smith, Elder and Co.'s Publications . . . a new poem by Mr. Browning is in the press and will be issued in the course of the autumn." (*Athenaeum*, September 21, 1889.) This advertisement was changed to "new Poems" on October 26, and the phrase "in the press" was dropped.

5. William Archer (1856–1924), dramatist, critic, and biographer, wrote to Browning in 1888 asking that the poet comment upon passages from Macready's diary in which Browning's name appeared. Browning complied in a letter of June 29, 1888. (*Letters*, ed. Hood, pp. 295–298.) In a letter thanking Browning for this service Archer promised to submit proofs of "the passages embodying" Browning's note. (*Browning's Letter File*, ed. Armstrong, p. 128.) On September 28, 1889, therefore, Archer submitted the promised proofs (p. 132). Archer's volume on *William Charles Macready* appeared in 1890, and the preface (p. vi) thanks "the late Mr. Robert Browning for some very valuable notes as to his relations with Macready." Archer quotes Browning's estimate of the actor in the last paragraph of his book and then comments: "Macready in a nutshell!"

the answer to which he might otherwise have long waited for: he behaved considerately about a simple matter enough.

I am glad indeed that the Portrait is in hand. I need not say how happy I was to be allowed to append my name to those of the other friends, and contribute my *obolus at once;* which I mention because, just before I left England, I got a printed invitation to do what I had already done: I conclude the matter was soon set right, but, if my name is really left out, I should be vexed indeed: it is unlikely however.[6]

I delight in finding that the beloved Husband and precious friend manages to do without the old yoke about his neck, and enjoys himself as never anybody had a better right to do. I continue to congratulate him on his emancipation [7] and ourselves on a more frequent enjoyment of his company in consequence. Give him my true love: take mine, dearest friend,—and my sister's love to you both goes with it. Ever affectionately yours

[Schiff]   Robert Browning.

The last letter of this volume was written while Browning was visiting Mrs. Arthur Bronson in Asolo on October 15, 1889. After that date very few letters were written. On November 1 Browning reached Venice to be with his son at the Palazzo Rezzonico. Here he corrected the proofs of his last volume, *Asolando,* and took his customary walks on the Lido. Late in the month he caught a cold which developed into bronchial trouble. Symptoms of heart failure followed. On December 12 *Asolando* was published in London, and word of its favorable reception was telegraphed to the poet. At ten o'clock on that same evening he died. On the last day of the year he was buried in the Poets' Corner of Westminster Abbey.

6. Perhaps the friends of Charles Skirrow had subscribed to a fund for the purpose of having his portrait painted.

7. "Mr. Skirrow had just resigned his post as Master in Chancery." (Orr, *Life,* p. 390, n. 1.)

APPENDICES

A. Undated Letters

The 15 notes printed here are all to Mrs. Charles Skirrow and are either undated or incompletely dated. Whereas it has been possible to advance a fairly reasonable conjecture as to the dates of all the other undated letters of this collection, both the internal and the external evidence of the following notes is too meager for a fair supposition. We print these notes for the sake of completing the group of letters from Browning to Mrs. Skirrow.

The notes, with one exception, are arranged according to the numbers which appear in the upper right corner of the holographs. The exception is one note sent from De Vere Gardens, which is placed after the notes sent from 19 Warwick Crescent. It will be understood, of course, that all letters from 19 Warwick Crescent precede July, 1887, and all from De Vere Gardens come after June, 1887. There is little virtue in this arrangement according to numbers, for the numbering has proved almost useless in ordering the chronology of this correspondence. Nevertheless, as Browning told the democratic Kate Field when she ridiculed the English system of social precedence at dinner parties, there has to be some way of getting to the table and of being seated once there. The English system, he observed, was one way of accomplishing this. Printing these notes according to numbers, however unreliable, is one way of ordering them.

The penciled number and notation of conjectural date on each letter is added below it.

To Mrs. Charles Skirrow

Dear Friend,
Expect me on Wednesday, as you so kindly desire. I shall be delighted to see you and your Husband both, and would say more but that I have somebody with me at this moment.

Ever affy. yours
[Schiff—#26—Ap.–June, 1881(?)] Robert Browning.

To Mrs. Charles Skirrow

Monday M[ornin]g.
Dear Friend, I got your telegram very late last evening, or you should have been answered and thanked before. Thursday the 22. I *believe* I

am disengaged: should it be a Philharmonic Night unhappily, I am engaged even then. I write at once, but will ascertain the facts to-day.

Ever affy yours

[Schiff—#27—Ap.–June, '81.]   RB.

To Mrs. Charles Skirrow

Saturday M[ornin]g.
Dear Friend, do forgive me if I found myself quite unable to get to you last evening, as I had every desire to do. I enjoyed (spite of the fatigue I brought with me) the last dinner too much not to want a renewal of my pleasure; but I could not do as I so gladly would have done.

Ever,—(with best Christmas love to you and your Husband)—

Affectionately yours

[Schiff—#28—Ap.–June, 1881]   Robert Browning

To Mrs. Charles Skirrow

Dear Friend,

How very much I should like what I assuredly shall not get: for I am going to dine at Dr. Chambers's on Wednesday.—What can I do but greatly grieve, and as greatly thank you?

Ever affy yours

[Schiff—#31—Ap.–June, 1881(?)]   RB.

To Mrs. Charles Skirrow

Friday.
My dear Friend,

I am thoroughly done up with a cold and cough that make it impossible for me to leave the house for some days. I had (most unwillingly) to excuse myself last evening from an engagement, which I know tried the patience of the friend with whom I made it: I am just about to release myself from a still more pressing engagement (marriage-day and birthday combined celebration!) for to-morrow—and a third, of less importance, on Monday must be broken also. Do forgive me, if I care very much for you, and a little for myself, in keeping my noisiness and other nuisances to myself for a few days more,—if Syrup of Squills please!— I want to see you very much, and will go to Leicester Terrace the first day, at 2. oclock, I can properly do so.[1]

Ever affectionately yours
Robert Browning.

Somebody came and, of course, caught up and carried off your book the other day: I will get another and bring it.

[Schiff—#32—Ap.–June, '81(?)]

To Mrs. Charles Skirrow

19, Warwick Crescent, W.
Saturday

Dear Friend, I cannot employ the last minute I have at disposal, before leaving for Cambridge and the Greek Play, better than by thanking you heartily for the delicious pie (as I am sure it will prove) which you have so generously bestowed on me. As for our talk—be certain I enjoyed it altogether, and am quite ready for a repetition of the same. S. promises to certify as to the character of the pie,—due justice to it being first done. She returns your love to the full. Give mine to the dear Husband, and believe me ever

Affectionately yours
Robert Browning.

[Schiff—#76—Ap., '86(?)]

To Mrs. Charles Skirrow

19, Warwick Crescent, W.
Saturday M[ornin]g

Dearest Friend,—cn Wednesday at a punctual 3—do let it be so! I have to dine out, perhaps go to a party, in any case so tire myself that your love will spare me, I know. The spirit is so willing, and the flesh so weak!

Ever affectionately yours
Robert Browning.

[Schiff—#79—May, '86(?)]

To Mrs. Charles Skirrow

19, Warwick Crescent, W.

There, dearest friend! If you can mediate with Mrs. B.B. I am sure you will: it is altogether out of my province—unless I found myself side by side with the Manageress at your table, as not so very long ago—where goodnature and sympathy seem to settle down naturally. They did abound, last evening, anyhow: I greatly enjoyed myself,—no wonder!

Ever affectionately yours and the other dear one's
Robert Browning.

[Schiff—#89—May, '87(?)]

To Mrs. Charles Skirrow

19, Warwick Crescent, W.

Yes, dear Friend,—I can,—and joyfully *will* go to you next Friday. I have never forgotten your invitation "a quattr' occhi," but am really slaughtered almost by this cold weather: it still must be, I hope and believe. Meanwhile,—all love and thanks "a *tea,* O Cara!" and every affectionate wish from

Yours ever
R.B.

[Schiff—#92—'87(?)]

To Mrs. Charles Skirrow

19, Warwick Crescent, W.
Dearest Friend, I am most anxious to know how the Husband is this
morning. I was not aware of what had happened till some time after.
No need to say how earnestly I hope there was only a passing faintness.
Pray send word down to my Sister, who will carry this note,—a more
precise word than she would get from the servant. How the pleasant din-
ner was spoiled by this sad ending! but I will trust for good news—
Affectionately ever

Yours
[Schiff—#93—'87(?)]   R. Browning

To Mrs. Charles Skirrow

Tuesday M[ornin]g.
Dear Friend, your goodness and that of your Husband is like you—
I can say no more. Certainly, I shall enjoy it immensely. I think it will
be simply wise, after such enjoyment, to keep quiet next day. I am
consumed with heat and visiting—and should like Saturday Night to
end the season for

Yours affectionately and gratefully ever
[Schiff—#114]   RB.

To Mrs. Charles Skirrow

19, W[arwick] C[rescent] Dec. 14.
Dear Friend, I am engaged particularly on Tuesday afternoon, the worse
luck mine! Thank you heartily for caring to have me.
  Mr. Yates sent me a book out of which I made an extract and sent it
in a closed envelope to the Lady,—with a word of explanation,—and
she sent the same, unopened of course, to Wiesbaden where her father
lives. There was no difficulty about the procedure, you see.[1]
  And,—you feel, don't you?—that I am ever affectionately yours
[Schiff—#115]   RBrowning—in *such* haste!

To Mrs. Charles Skirrow

19, W. C. Saturday.
Dear Friend, you know how happy it always makes me to find myself at
your most pleasant of boards—but next Tuesday I am engaged unfortunately, and can only be as sorry as you could *not* desire. My Sister

---

1. The "Mr. Yates" is probably Edmund Yates, editor of the *World* and
author of 20 novels. He wrote to Browning in 1884 as a "friend of thirty years'
standing." (*Browning's Letter File*, ed. Armstrong, p. 98.)

thanks you warmly, and unites her regrets with mine. I am just going
to Oxford—till Monday only— All my love to Mr. Skirrow from yours
affectionately ever
[Schiff—#116]   Robert Browning

To Mrs. Charles Skirrow

Tuesday M[ornin]g.

Dear Friend,
    My sister was in some misapprehension about the time when she ought
to answer your letter and invitation. She is out, at this moment: but I
take it upon myself to say she will be delighted to accompany me to-
morrow evening: should I be exceeding my rights in taking the word
out of her mouth, she will correct me the moment she returns: otherwise, expect her, and

Yours affectionately ever

[Schiff—#117]   RB.

To Mrs. Charles Skirrow

Dear Friend, Louis acted quite properly—for, supposing your friend had
really something of importance to say, my entrance would have been
just as embarrassing to *me* as to you: besides, I can call *any* morning—
in fact, it was on my mind that I had been prevented from doing so by
unforeseen calls on my time. As for the Dinner, I am sorry to be forced
to forego what would have been a great pleasure—being engaged already. "Better luck next time!" and best love to you this and every other
time from

Yours affectionately,

[Schiff—#118]   Robert Browning.

To Mrs. Charles Skirrow

29, De Vere Gardens, W.
Alas, dearest Friend, I have mislaid the letter, and cannot be certain of
the day for the dinner! Will you indulge me with a word on a card?
    Good, good, and thrice good of you to like and care to repeat the
luncheon: *we* will keep you to your promise, depend on it—and on the
love of

Yours ever
Robert Browning

Would that the dear Husband could come too!
[Schiff—#99—Nov.–Dec., 1887(?)]

B. Receipt for Money Received from Chapman and Hall

193, Piccadilly, London, W.
Jany. 29, 1864.

Received of Messrs Chapman Hall the sum of Two Hundred and twenty-two pounds for value as per annexed statement.[1]

Robert Browning

Robert Browning, Esq.
In account with Chapman & Hall
By Royalty for the sixth Edition
of E. B. Browning's *Poems* 3 vols
      one thousand copies   210–0–0
By Royalty for the sixth Ed
of *Aurora Leigh* 750 copies
By ½ share of a/c to Decr.
31/63   7–0–0
By ½ share of the remaining
stock of *Men & Women. Christmas
day & Easter Eve* [sic] &c as on
hand Dec. 31/63   15–0–0

                                      232.0.0
By cash overpaid   10 –

                                  £222.0.0

[Morgan]

1. This statement is apparently the only surviving account of the earnings of the Brownings' books while they were still being published by Chapman and Hall. Dated from the executive offices of the publisher, it is a handwritten receipt made out by Chapman or someone in his office, and signed by Browning. Since the sixth edition of Mrs. Browning's *Poems* did not appear until 1864, it is clear that Chapman in this account is paying the royalty in advance. The first three volumes of the four-volume sixth edition were reprinted from the fifth edition (1862) of the *Poems,* which in turn was a reprint of the fourth edition (1856). The fourth volume of the sixth edition contained *Aurora Leigh,* which by coincidence was here being reprinted for the sixth time. The printing was so arranged as to make the *Poems* or *Aurora Leigh* available separately.

The receipt confirms the continuing popularity of Elizabeth Barrett Browning's poetry two and a half years after her death. Browning's poor showing in this account—a total of £22 in payment for small stock remainders—is misleading. The sale of his *Collected Poems* of 1863 was for him substantial, and the sale of the volume of *Selections* chosen by Procter and Forster was excellent. These sales are not reflected in the present account, which consequently gives us no information concerning his current popularity. For the tremendous rise in Browning's income from his own books in the last four years of his life, and as a contrast to his meager earnings of the earlier years, see Roma A. King, *Robert Browning's Finances from His Own Account Book,* pp. 16–24.

C. Why Browning Severed Relations with Chapman and Hall

It has been said that Browning broke with Edward Chapman, his publisher, because of difficulties existing between Isabella Blagden and Chapman.[1] It has been said, too, that Browning left Chapman and Hall and went to Smith and Elder because he had "formed a personal friendship with Mr. George Murray Smith, who practically was the firm, and this put business dealings on a pleasant footing." [2] That Browning was influenced to hasten the break because of his sympathy with the plight of Miss Blagden is true. That a developing friendship with Mr. Smith made a shift to his firm a pleasant prospect is also true. There were, however, other contributing causes, all personal. It is the purpose of this appendix to examine Isa Blagden's complaints as they affected Browning and to indicate other causes which influenced his decision to leave Chapman and Hall.

On June 20, 1866 Browning wrote a letter to Chapman which has been lost, or perhaps, because of its contents, destroyed. The tone and something of the text of this letter are revealed in two letters to Isa Blagden. The first of these, dated June 20, reads in part as follows: "I returned to London last night—the 19th—I could not write then.[3] I have at once gone on with business this morning, and begun by writing to Chapman. I am profoundly discontented with him, and shall dissolve our connection,—on my own account, not yours only." [4] The second letter, dated August 7, refers again to the missing Chapman letter of June 20: "Tell me about your book,[5] your arrangements with the Publisher,—and whether you have heard anything from Chapman: I told you I had written a letter to him that morning—which I had in my pocket, on the chance that you might say something admitting of excuse for him,—for I hate quarrelling with the poor fellow,—but I could not make matters better, so the letter was posted in the evening,—a decisive one. I don't believe he meant worse than delay—but that is a vile thing, and the carelessness also that he cannot deny." [6]

Browning omits reference to two other letters of his to Chapman, both of them published in this volume for the first time.[7] Since the first of

---

1. *Letters*, ed. Hood, p. 352, n. 66:8–2.
2. Griffin and Minchin, *Life*, p. 239.
3. From June 13 to 19 Browning was in Paris, called there by the mortal illness of his father. After the funeral he returned to London and plunged immediately into the unpleasant business with Chapman.
4. *Letters*, ed. Hood, p. 99.
5. A novel called *Nora and Archibald Lee*, published the next year, 1867.
6. *Letters*, ed. Hood, p. 101. This letter indicates that Browning had meantime seen Miss Blagden in London.
7. The holographs of these, as well as of almost all other letters to Chapman, are in the J. P. Morgan Library.

these, dated June 26, 1866, provides further information concerning the "decisive" letter of June 20 and also important additional details affecting the break with Chapman, I quote it here in full.

19, Warwick Crescent,
Upper Westbourne Terrace, W.
June 26, '66.

My dear Chapman,

I was prevented by various circumstances from calling yesterday, and do not know whether I can get to you to-day: so I write. I am sure I felt as much pain, as you possibly could, in taking such a step as, at first, seemed incumbent on me: and I felt as real a pleasure when your explanation proved sufficient. As for the agreement, I will sign it, of course—though it leaves matters pretty much where it finds them: for I have never complained that you did not make me a sufficient allowance on the copies printed,—nor that the payments were not made precisely at the proper time, for I never doubted but you would be ready to do so if I took the trouble to ask you; still less did I ever blame you for not giving me an exact account of copies on hand,—on the contrary you have always proposed to examine the books and report progress,—the less necessary a thing, because, once paid for an edition, I have no further money-interest in the copies on hand. Of course, absolute punctuality is best for us both; still, I repeat, my supposed grievance did not lie *there*—but in what I thought the fact that a publication from which we were entitled to expect considerable results had proved a comparative failure, and it did strike me that my trees of this sort would gain by changing the soil. I desire no better than that you show me I was wrong. You must do me justice to say, I neither show suspiciousness nor inordinate expectation of gain,—nor do I ever pretend to teach you on matters which you cannot but understand better than myself. But really my income may be seriously affected by affairs in Italy, and I ought to care a little about what most of my fellows of the pen care abundantly for.

I don't see anything to remark on—except the obligation, in case we part company, to buy *steel plates*—are they not paid for out of the first expenditure?—*Ex. gr.* £25 in the case of the *Selections*. It seems to me that the *stereotyping* which is *not* so charged for (I believe)—is a different thing: am I right or wrong?

I shall wait for the account—the exact sum due to me—before I pay in the cheque: and *that* I shall be glad to have at once.

I return the letters,—which quite satisfy me as to what may be your unforeseen liabilities: for the future, I am warned.

You see, poor Miss Blagden has been too well justified in her complaints; and it is a worse case apparently than I or she supposed,—

though *you* are happily out of it. I sent her your letter at once. If you tell me, when you write, that the agreement is drawn up, I will go and sign it on any day you appoint.

> Very truly yours ever
> Robert Browning.

One may now piece together the sequence of communications between Browning and Chapman. On the evening of June 20 Browning announced his decision to change publishers and doubtless listed the grievances which led to his decision. Chapman must have received this letter on the 21st. He must immediately have prepared his defenses which included answers to all Browning's charges, along, perhaps, with an admission of carelessness and unintentional delay in settling accounts. He enclosed with his letter certain other letters intended to convince Browning that he had been liable to expenditures about which the poet was unaware but which served to explain returns less than the poet had expected. This letter, sent to Browning perhaps on June 22, requested a conference at the publishing house offices. It is probable that Browning refused this invitation not because of "various circumstances" but because he wished to retain the advantage of forcing Chapman to set down his counterclaims in writing.

The second sentence of the letter of June 26 poses the question of what Browning meant by the "step" it had "seemed incumbent" upon him to take. It is obvious that this step was not simply a parting with Chapman. If Chapman's explanation had been sufficient to make Browning change his mind on this point there would have been no occasion for the phrase, used late in the letter, "in case we part company," nor for the suggestion that Chapman show cause why Browning should not go with his "trees" to other "soil." The step was apparently something more drastic than a simple leave-taking. It may have been a demand for an audit of Chapman's books; it may have been the threat of some legal process. Whatever it was, Chapman acted quickly and effectively to placate Browning.

The remainder of paragraph one of this letter of June 26 is a curious disclaimer of various possible complaints against Chapman and the acknowledgment of only one grievance. Yet, it is probable that Chapman, in preparing his reply to Browning's letter of June 20, had consulted his file of correspondence with the poet over the past 15 years. There he would have found more than 40 letters from Browning,[8] many of which *did* complain of delays in rendering accounts and in sending remittances. It is true that Browning had not blamed Chapman for any failure to give him "an exact account of copies on hand." His disgust

8. These letters are all to be found in the present volume.

was great, however, when, upon sending for a copy of his collected works from Chapman, "came the avowal, all were gone." Browning concludes that he "is well rid of such a publisher." [9]

The publication which had proved "a comparative failure" was probably *Dramatis Personae* (1864), a volume which achieved, for the first time in Browning's career, a genuine second edition. When one considers that Browning had been a practicing poet for some 30 years it is natural surely that he should be impatient with a half-success, enough so to call it a "comparative failure." Yet, in 1866, Browning had nothing new to offer the public and had, therefore, no pressing need to seek another publisher. Apparently his purpose was to close accounts with Chapman so that he could feel free to offer *The Ring and the Book,* now in mid-process of composition, to the highest bidder.

Since Isabella Blagden's relations with Chapman accentuated Browning's displeasure with the publisher and perhaps hastened his decision to part with him, it will be necessary to trace something of Miss Blagden's career as a novelist and her experience with publishers. Her first novel, *Agnes Tremorne,* had been published in 1861 by Smith and Elder. Doubtless she thought to gain an advantage by a shift to Chapman and Hall, the long-time publishers for her best friends, the Brownings. Apparently Browning saw no reason at that time to dissuade her. In 1863, therefore, Chapman and Hall brought out *The Cost of a Secret* and the trouble began at once. Miss Blagden was paid less than she thought fair. She blamed Chapman. Browning, on her behalf, talked to Chapman and reported the conversation as follows: "Chapman tells me the sale is very good: you will get better and better prices for your books. He said it was wholly thro' a mistake of yours that *he* did not publish it and pay you that price—he waited for some reason or other, and *you would* not wait: but then, he tells more than I vouch for." [10] This at first is a puzzling statement, for how could Chapman publish the book (the name of his firm is on the title page) and yet say that it was Miss Blagden's fault that *"he* did not publish it"? The answer apparently is that Bradbury and Evans, printers for Chapman and Hall, paid for the book, printed it, and simply used Chapman and Hall as distributors. This answer gains validity as one traces further the Blagden-Browning-Chapman relationship.

As early as the fall of 1864 Miss Blagden sent to Chapman another three-volume novel, *The Woman I Loved and the Woman Who Loved Me.* The novel was accepted but not paid for. Publication was delayed until the summer of 1865 and payment much longer. Browning, well aware of Chapman's forgetfulness, was willing to attribute the delay to carelessness. "Chapman's carelessness," he wrote to Miss Blagden on March 19, 1866, "is quite natural in that matter [the delayed payment]:

9. *Letters to Isa Blagden,* ed. Armstrong, p. 152, letter dated December 30, 1867.

10. *Letters,* ed. Hood, p. 74, letter dated January 19, 1863.

I have suffered nearly as much as I can from his peculiarities." [11] He goes on to relate that when he heard of the death of Mrs. Chapman—"pretty, cheerful, good"—his feeling toward Chapman was well on its way to complete softening, only to be chilled through the shock of seeing how lightly Chapman took his loss,—"the man 'under his thunder-split tree, playing Pan's pipes.'" He concedes, however, that Chapman is honest enough though "a scatter brain creature, forgets, makes excuses, and worse; but the *worst* he is not." Doubtless Browning spoke to Chapman, for the following month Miss Blagden received her money.[12]

This payment cleared Chapman's books of the amount owed for *The Woman I Loved and the Woman Who Loved Me*, but the complication involving payment for *The Cost of a Secret* remained three years after its publication. Again Browning took a hand and succeeded, after sifting the conflicting stories of Bradbury and Evans versus Chapman and Hall, in obtaining payment. His faith, however, in Chapman's honesty was shaken, for, as he admits, his investigation involved "serious considerations concerning the character of a person I have to trust." [13] Incidentally, this statement may indicate that Browning had not yet (July 13, 1866) formally broken with Chapman. On the other hand it may simply mean that he must trust Chapman for the final liquidation of his account.

The situation with respect to *The Cost of a Secret* may be briefly summarized. Chapman had told Browning in 1863 that his firm had paid Bradbury and Evans £75 for the rights to this novel. As a consequence, he contended, it was the responsibility of Bradbury and Evans to settle with Miss Blagden on the basis of whatever their agreement was. Chapman, in other words, disclaimed any direct business agreement with Miss Blagden. Bradbury and Evans declared, however, that Chapman had not paid the £75 until 1866. Browning concludes that "one or the other statement must be false, and till I know that C.'s is true, I refrain from seeing him." He is willing, nevertheless, to give Chapman "the benefit of the doubt" and reminds Miss Blagden that "whoever told the lie, would be apt enough to make the subsequent excuse. . . . You and I would 'snub' anybody for telling anybody else we had been owing, and promising to pay, and breaking our word for three years together, if it were altogether a mistake." [14]

By August 7, after an interchange of letters with Chapman, Browning had decided, as I have shown, that the publisher meant no "worse than delay." Perhaps with this assurance in mind, Miss Blagden sent her next novel, *Nora and Archibald Lee*, to Chapman. It was published in March, 1867. Browning apparently thought that the book was to appear in February, for on the 19th of that month he wrote as follows

11. *Letters to Isa Blagden*, ed. Armstrong, p. 129.
12. *Ibid.*, p. 132, letter dated April 19, 1866.
13. *Ibid.*, p. 134, letter dated July 13, 1866.
14. *Ibid.*

to Miss Blagden: "I have not seen Chapman since he saw you—can't help it, but distrust the man, without dislike of the poor, goodnatured fellow otherwise. I suppose he won't send me the book, but I can get to read it." [15] After the book was published, Browning repeats that he never sees Chapman "and there is no wonder he don't send it or lend it." [16] In April Browning still has not seen the novel. "If," he exclaims, "I could put up with my pride and ask Chapman to send it! But that would be too bad, poor fellow. Let me say no more." [17] In this same letter Browning says that he wants to get done with his poem (The Ring and the Book) and that booksellers are making "pretty offers for it." It is apparent from this that the rift between Browning and Chapman was now well known in publishing circles.

On July 19, 1867, Browning, after mentioning Robert Lytton's discontentment with Chapman, adds: "I need not say, it is a matter in which I have not the remotest interest. I have not seen Chapman since that Finis on business [probably July, 1866]: I am sorry for him, but my mind is made up." [18] On November 19 he reaffirms this stand: "I part from Chapman pursuant to my resolution taken when you were last in England [July, 1866, when Miss Blagden arranged with Chapman for the publication of Nora and Archibald Lee],[19] and go to Smith and Elder, who bring out a new Edition presently." [20]

It was for Smith and Elder's use that Browning wanted a copy of his collected works. As mentioned above, Chapman had sold the last copy, the final annoyance which drew Browning's exclamation of relief to be "well rid of such a publisher."

Miss Blagden, however, was not yet through with Chapman. She had another book, The Crown of Life, ready for publication. She faced a dilemma because Browning, her champion, had parted with her publisher, leaving her as a possible scapegoat of Chapman's displeasure. In a letter of January 19, 1868, Browning candidly summarizes his services to Miss Blagden. For one thing, through his interference Chapman had eventually paid for The Cost of a Secret; then, in spite of the alleged failure of The Woman I Loved and the Woman Who Loved Me, he had accepted and paid for Nora and Archibald Lee. Why, Browning asks, had Chapman performed these services? The answer is succinct: "as a bribe to me." Furthermore, Browning implies, if Chapman is willing to take Miss Blagden's latest book, he is still offering a bribe to the poet, himself. One must interpret this to mean that Browning saw himself now as a real asset in the eyes of Chapman or, one surmises, any pub-

15. Letters, ed. Hood, p. 110.
16. Ibid., p. 112, letter dated March 21, 1867.
17. Letters to Isa Blagden, ed. Armstrong, p. 139, letter dated April 23, 1867.
18. Letters, ed. Hood, p. 115.
19. See ibid., p. 103, for reference to this bargaining between Miss Blagden and Chapman.
20. Letters to Isa Blagden, ed. Armstrong, p. 151.

lisher. Also, it is apparent that even at this late date Browning conceived of Chapman's trying to win him back. His final advice to Miss Blagden is to "Try the whole of the publishers in turn, and be sure that the worst one be no worse than a man who don't put your book on his list." [21]

What effort Miss Blagden expended in finding a new publisher, or looking for one, is not known. By February, however, she is able to tell Browning of one offer, from Chapman! Browning was gratified but issued a warning, certainly superfluous by now: "Mind, never trust C.'s mere word and promise, nor believe his report, the habit of loose statement is inveterate and incurable. I myself would on no account have another business transaction which could not be settled 'over the counter.'" [22] After a final anecdote relating an unpleasant experience of Procter's with Chapman Browning closes fittingly with these valedictory words: "Enough of him."

These words end the references to Chapman in presently available letters of Browning. In attempting to set down the decisive reason which made Browning leave Chapman one should not be misled by the admittedly complicating misadventures of Browning's friends with the publisher. Even Browning's friendship with Miss Blagden could not blind him to the fact that she was no shining asset to the publisher's list. Lytton and Procter could take care of themselves. Chapman's tardiness in sending accounts—a tardiness which provoked the writing of more than half of Browning's letters to him—was irritating. The habit of loose statement and general carelessness in money matters doubtlessly pained the honorable and meticulous poet. Nevertheless, none of these things, taken separately or together, would have caused the rupture. The truth seems to be that Browning, long weary of absolute failure, had tasted his first popular success with the publication in 1864 of *Dramatis Personae*. The way for this volume had been prepared by the publication the year before of his *Collected Works* and, more significantly, by a book of *Selections* prepared by Forster and Procter and published in 1863. All these books sold well, well indeed for Browning, but the poet realized little. *Christmas-Eve and Easter-Day* and even *Men and Women* had given him no basis for pressing demands upon any publisher. The *Selections,* on the other hand, opened many English eyes. *Dramatis Personae* kept them open for longer by far than usual, but they began to close after the second edition. Who was responsible? Not the poet. Not the critics this time. Who then? A fairly indifferent publisher, a niggardly publisher at that; a publisher who gave him only £120 for three volumes of his collected poems, £50 less than he was to give for a three-volume novel by Isa Blagden! Browning wanted more money and felt, correctly, that another publisher would give it to him.

21. *Ibid.,* pp. 152–154.
22. *Ibid.,* p. 156, letter dated February 19, 1868.

Smith and Elder gave him "exactly five times as much for an edition" as Chapman had given him.[23] Since this is a direct reference to the edition of his *Works* of 1868 and since Chapman had paid £120 for a similar edition, Smith and Elder must have paid Browning £600, surely an appreciable increase.

Browning's side of this story is fully documented. As in his own dramatic monologues, one must read into the lines of the speaker the character not only of the monologist but also of the silent person or persons referred to in the monologue. Browning's own testimony when given proper perspective tends to clear Chapman of all but carelessness and to make his behavior toward the poet as a commercial asset seem reasonable. The charge Browning made that Chapman attempted to bribe him through the publishing of Isa Blagden's novels is probably true. On the other hand, it is probably just as true that for ten years and more Chapman had bribed Mrs. Browning to remain with him by retaining her profitless husband on his list. When one considers that after 13 years Chapman had some of the first edition of *Christmas-Eve and Easter-Day* remaining and that after eight years he had copies of the first edition of *Men and Women* on hand, it is fair to assume that only the multiplied editions of Mrs. Browning's various volumes of poems kept Chapman in comparative good humor with Browning. After Mrs. Browning died Chapman would have been optimistic indeed to consider Browning as a possible successor to her in popularity. Even after the *Selections* and *Dramatis Personae* Chapman did not immediately see that Browning was destined to break through the hardened crust of unpopularity. He was still thinking in terms of Mrs. Browning, as is significantly indicated in a letter of June 27, 1866, published in this volume, in which the chief subject is gaining an American market for Mrs. Browning's works. Possibly the worst that should be said of Chapman is that he lacked confidence in Browning's ability to achieve a popularity sufficient to justify large advance royalties on the product of his pen.

Kenneth Leslie Knickerbocker

23. *Ibid.,* p. 152.

INDEX